CW00742974

THE BIRDS OF GHANA

An annotated check-list

by

L. G. GRIMES, Ph.D.

B.O.U. Check-list No. 9

British Ornithologists' Union, 1987
c/o Zoological Society, Regent's Park, London NW1 4RY, UK

© British Ornithologists' Union 1987

ISBN 0 907446 08 6

Printed in Great Britain by Henry Ling Ltd., at the Dorset Press, Dorchester, Dorset

DEDICATED

to

those that have gone before,
an encouragement to those that follow

"What is the use of going to the Gold Coast? So and so have already been there"
"True, but people who make such remarks little know the vast country and its tremendous difficulties. Our little effort, embracing two winters' work of less than six months all told, does not touch the fringe of the subject. There are creatures, perhaps, that will only be seen once in a generation, if at all, by a white man. After one hundred years' incessant hard work a naturalist might say he knows the birds of the Gold Coast, and to do that he would have to have the longevity, health, and hide of a pachyderm, with the combined eyes of a Hawk and an Owl and the agility of an ape. As no one is likely to have these requirements, we must go plodding along, each doing his little bit for generations to come and adding facts to our store of knowledge."

W. P. LOWE
Ibis 1937: Ser. 14(1): 347

CONTENTS

6

Tables

Table 1. The 7 major forest types in Ghana distinguished by Hall & Swaine (1976, 1981) and some of their characteristics.

Table 2. The decrease of the unreserved forest during the decade 1970–1980 and the corresponding increase in degraded forest in Ghana.

Table 3. List of forest reserves which are now wildlife reserves. Data from Hall & Swaine (1981).

Table 4. The area and locations of the National Parks (N.P.P.), Game Production Reserves (G.P.R.) and Wildlife Sanctuaries (W.S.) that have been established in Ghana. See Fig. 5 for their approximate positions. Data partly taken from Hall & Swaine (1981).

Table 5. The breeding data for Ghanaian Non-Passerine birds.

Table 6. The breeding data for Ghanaian Passerine birds.

Table 7. Status categories of Ghanaian birds.

Table 8. Summary of species totals and numbers of migrants for different ecological and taxonomic groups in Ghana.

Table 9. Species totals of Palaearctic migrants to Ghana analysed according to habitat.

Table 10. Faithfulness of 5 Palaearctic species of birds ringed in Ghana to their wintering areas.

Table 11. The numerical differences between the avifaunas of Ghana and Nigeria according to habitat.

Figures

Figure 1. The administrative regions of Ghana and the main towns. UR: Upper Region, which has been subdivided recently into the Upper Western Region (Capital Wa) and the Upper Eastern Region (Capital Bolgatanga); NR: Northern Region; BAR: Brong Ahafo Region; AR: Ashanti Region; ER: Eastern Region; VR: Volta Region; CR: Central Region; WR: Western Region; GAR: Greater Accra Region.

Figure 2. The position of Ghana within West Africa and the location (shaded) of the Upper and Lower Guinea forest blocks.

Figure 3. The main geo-morphological regions of Ghana: (1) the Accra–Ho–Keta Plains; (2) PreCambrian rocks and the forest region; (3) the Palaeozoic sediments forming the Voltaian basin; (4) & (5) the area of crystalline rocks to the north and west of the Voltaian basin.

Figure 4. The topography of Ghana.

Figure 5. The main rivers of Ghana and the approximate locations of the game reserves within Ghana. The numbering sequence follows that in Table 4.

Figure 6. The mean monthly rainfall (cm) in the south of Ghana showing the double peak in the rainfall at Accra (70 years of records) and Kumasi (50 years of records). Below each month are the mean number of rain days.

Figure 7. The mean monthly rainfall (cm) in the north of Ghana showing the single peak in the rainfall at Tamale (49 years of records) and Navrongo (30 years of records). Below each month are the mean number of rain days.

Figure 8. The mean monthly maximum (B) and minimum (C) temperatures (Centigrade) and the highest monthly maximum (A) and the lowest minimum (D) temperatures at 4 locations within Ghana.

Figure 9. The relative humidity (expressed as a percentage) at selected stations in the humid zone (Accra and Kumasi) and the dry zone (Tamale and Navrongo). The data used are the mean of values measured at 3 hourly intervals beginning midnight.

Figure 10. The forest/savanna boundary (—·—·—) and the main vegetation zones identified by Swaine *et al.* (1976) and Hall & Swaine (1976): (1) Wet evergreen; (2) Moist evergreen; (3) Moist semi-deciduous; (4) Dry semi-deciduous; (5) Southern marginal; (6) Southeast outliers; (7) Upland evergreen.

Figure 11. The towns of the Accra Plains and the Akwapim hills.

Figure 12. The percentage of all breeding records expressed in months for the coastal region (a,b,c), and for the northern savanna (d) and the forest region (e).

EDITOR'S FOREWORD

This is the third check-list in the BOU series to cover part of W. Africa, the other two being for The Gambia and Nigeria. The former is what might be termed a riverine enclave with some 490 bird species, while Nigeria is the largest non-desert African country north of the Equator, at least in the western half of the continent, with over 830 species. Ghana, previously the Gold Coast until independence, is half as large as Nigeria and separated from it by the Dahomey Gap in the Guinea forests, as well as extending less far north and then not into true desert.

Ghana, like its neighbouring states, has its own political and financial problems, so that expatriates become an increasing rarity, and regrettably Ghanaians have only recently begun tentatively to replace them in the observation and analysis of the avifauna, though those that have give promise of good progress. The present is, therefore, an excellent time to provide a base line from which to assess in the future the bird-life of an attractive country with over 720 species, of which the breeding data for the residents and others are minimal and for whose migrant birds little information is available.

Dr Llewellyn Grimes combines his personal experience in Ghana (1960–1975) with a detailed coverage of the literature to provide what is hoped will be recognised as a comprehensive review on which future workers, especially Ghanaians, may confidently base their ornithological research.

James Monk

PREFACE

Bannerman (1930: 359) expressed the hope to publish in his final 8th volume (1951) a list of references covering published papers on the avifauna of The Gambia, Sierra Leone, Ghana and Nigeria, the countries covered in his work. This was not done and a special effort, therefore, has been made to include in the *References* of this check-list all published papers on the avifauna of Ghana up until mid 1987. I have not listed citations for type specimens as they are available in the standard works. Not all the papers listed are referred to in the text, but all have been read and their relevance ascertained.

Much time has been spent in delving into the *History of Ghanaian Ornithology,* enlarging the account in Bannerman (1931) and bringing it up-to-date. This has been fascinating and has led me down some interesting and unexpected paths. The early workers such as Pel, Ussher, Aubinn, Nagtglas and others mentioned in the text have won my admiration, particularly after I had handled some of their specimens at Leiden and Tring, and it would have been good to have known them. They accomplished much in conditions far more difficult than today and I hope the brief historical account reflects this and, thereby, duly acknowledges their pioneering work.

Within the last decade, weather satellites have shed new light on the structure of the inter-tropical convergence zone. These details are included in the section on *Climate* together with descriptions of the various weather systems that control the rainfall within Ghana.

The detailed study in the 1970s of Ghanaian *Forest Vegetation* by Hall & Swaine (1976, 1981) has enabled them to describe 7 forest types and these are detailed in the section on vegetation together with new information on the forest/savanna boundary obtained from the Earth Resources Technology Satellite. The inevitable destruction of the tropical forest within Ghana is also highlighted.

In the chapter on *Biological Seasons* I have referred to the work of Gibbs & Leston (1970), who studied numerical fluctuations in insect populations (mainly ants) in cocoa farms at Tafo, Ghana. They point out that the customary division of a tropical year into a dry and wet season is too simple when attempting to account for the observed fluctuations in abundance of the insects studied. They proposed 6 seasons and named them:—

    (1) The dry and sunny season
    (2) The first wet sunny season
    (3) The first wet dull season
    (4) The dry dull season
    (5) The second wet dull season
  and (6) the second wet sunny season

Whether or not these divisions are applicable to the breeding seasons of forest birds will require careful and painstaking investigation, and this may be possible in the future.

In the chapter on *Breeding,* no proof of breeding has been admitted for records of males in breeding dress or with enlarged gonads, nor of adults involved in nest building. This section purposely follows the format in Elgood (1982) so that a comparison with Nigerian data may be made. For a similar reason the section on *Migration* has been developed along the lines of Elgood *et al.* (1973).

The most unsatisfying parts of the check-list to write have been the individual *species accounts.* Because of the large number of species (721), each account has had to be short and concise. Although I am confident of the occurrence of the species listed, the exact distribution, abundance, status and preferred habitat are unknown for the majority, for there are vast areas of Ghana which have never been explored ornithologically, and in several cases our knowledge is still only based on collected specimens. There has, therefore, been the inevitable extrapolation of data and I have found this an unsatisfying task, though none the less necessary. When describing *abundance,* the following five categories are used: abundant, common, not uncommon, uncommon and rare. These are subjective terms and the accuracy of usage depends on several factors, such as the length of time an observer has spent in a particular area, the observer's expertise and the time of day, to mention a few. This is particularly the case with forest species and it is easy to envisage the difficulties of quantifying abundance, the chosen allocation depending very much on the observer's audio/visual skill. Again the allocation of abundance given to a species will not apply throughout its range because of the variation in the quality of the habitat. A judgement, therefore, has had to be made taking into consideration the statements of various observers with differing capabilities and in different habitats. Although others may disagree with a status assigned to a given species, it is hoped that any error will not affect the usefulness of the check-list too unduly. The definitions of the abundance terms follows closely those used by Gore (1981) and are as follows:

Abundant	invariably encountered without much effort in large numbers in their preferred habitat
Common	invariably encountered singly or in small numbers in their preferred habitat
Not uncommon	often, but not invariably, met within their preferred habitat
Uncommon	infrequent and sporadic in preferred habitat
Rare	rarely seen, often implying less than 10 or so records

If this publication successfully acts as a launch pad for others in Ghana, it will have fulfilled its purpose. Although an amount of information is available, it is still relatively small and the lack of breeding data and details of migratory movements are but examples of what awaits discovery. This should encourage, therefore, any future workers, and possible avenues of research are discussed in the text. The words of W. P. Lowe written 50 years ago are still appropriate today: "we must go on plodding along, each doing his little bit for generations to come". I had the privilege of plodding for 15 years and eventually felt ornithologically confident in certain habitats and locations where I had worked for long periods. I believe Lowe was, therefore, correct in suggesting that after "one hundred years' incessant hard work a naturalist might say he knows the birds of Ghana".

3 St Nicholas Court
Warwick CV34 4JD
U.K.

LLEWELLYN GRIMES
March 1987

INTRODUCTION

POLITICAL HISTORY

Ghana first became known through Portuguese navigators who discovered gold at Shama, near Elmina, in 1471. They built a chain of forts along the coastline and these served as trading posts. Subsequently, and partially through the development of the slave trade, other western European countries took an interest and the trading posts often changed hands. By 1750 only those at Cape Coast (British), Elmina (Dutch) and Christianburg (Danish) remained. In 1821 the British Government assumed control of the English settlements and by February 1872 had purchased the last remaining Dutch settlement at Elmina.

Although the Gold Coast was declared a colony on 24 July 1874, the boundaries were only finally defined in 1906. The northern areas (the Northern Territories) came under British rule in 1897, and the Ashanti Kingdom became part of the Gold Coast in 1901 after the fall of Kumasi in 1900. In 1914 the German colony of Togoland was occupied by the British and French, and in 1922 was divided into 2 zones by the League of Nations. The zone adjacent to the Gold Coast was administrated by the British and in 1956 the people, who lived there, elected to join the Gold Coast, which attained independence and became Ghana a year later on 6 March 1957. As a member of the Commonwealth, Ghana became a Republic on 1 July 1960. Civilian rule has been terminated 3 times by military coups, the last one occurring on New Year's Eve 1981/1982 and ending the Third Republic. At the time of publication Ghana remains under military rule.   (Fig. 1.)

THE HISTORY OF ORNITHOLOGICAL WORK IN GHANA

The earliest records of the birds of Ghana are those of W. Bosman, a Dutchman, who worked for the Dutch East India Company and spent 14 years at Axim and Elmina. Some of the sketches in his account of his stay (Bosman 1705) are of well known African birds such as the Crowned Crane, Guinea-fowl, Turaco and Grey Parrot. In the 18th Century, P. E. Isert, a gifted German doctor, botanist and traveller, worked for the Dutch Guinea Company at Accra (1783–1787) and then at Akropong in Akwapim (1788–1789), where he died. He wrote an account of his stay at Accra (Isert 1788), which became a best seller, and he collected several species of birds including the Violet Plantain-eater *Musophaga violacea* and Red Bishop *Euplectes orix*.

Interest in the avifauna of West Africa was rekindled by collections sent to Museums in Holland, Germany and England in the 1840s. Louis Fraser, the naturalist to the ill-fated Niger Expedition of 1841, spent a few days in late March 1842 at Accra and collected 45 species, 5 of which were named by him (Fraser 1843a,b,c,d). C. A. Gordon, a medical officer to troops of the 57th Regiment stationed at Accra and Cape Coast, described 30 species that were collected between June and November 1847 (Gordon 1849), and is remembered in a subspecies of the swallow *Hirundo semirufa*.

Gustav Hartlaub's interest in West African birds was stimulated through a collection of 31 species which he received while at the Hamburg Museum from Carl Weiss, who mainly collected at Elmina, but also at Winneba, Anamobu and Accra (Hartlaub 1848, 1850). Hartlaub then worked through the species sent to the State Museum of Natural History (SMNH) at Leiden by H. S. Pel (see Appendix 5). Pel, a member of the Museum's staff, was a gifted person and very desirous of collecting in Africa. His hopes were fulfilled through the influence of C. J. Temminck, the Director of the Museum, and Pel found himself a commander of the Dutch fort at Elmina (1840–1841). He then occupied similar positions at Sekondi (1841–1842) and Butri (Boutry) (1842–1843). Later, as Governor of the Dutch possessions, he

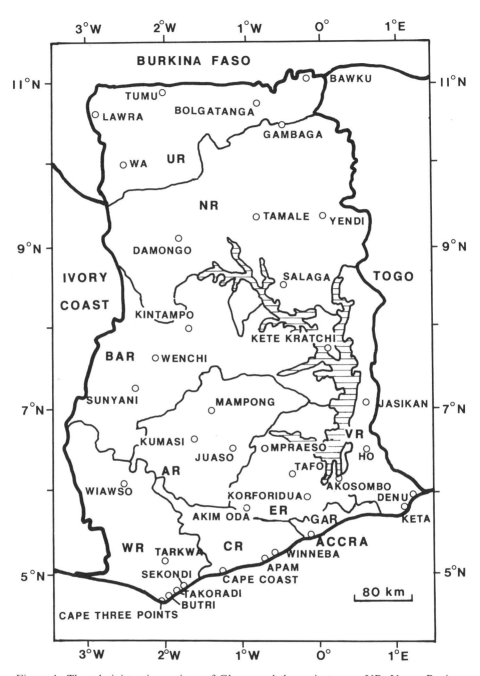

Figure 1. The administrative regions of Ghana and the main towns. UR: Upper Region, which has been subdivided recently into the Upper Western Region (Capital Wa) and the Upper Eastern Region (Capital Bolgatanga); NR: Northern Region; BAR: Brong Ahafo Region; AR: Ashanti Region; ER: Eastern Region; VR: Volta Region; CR: Central Region; WR: Western Region; GAR: Greater Accra Region.

resided at Accra (1844–1845), Elmina (1845–1847), Butri (1847–1850) and finally at Elmina (1851–1855). When he returned to the Netherlands to claim a pension, he created a problem, for there was no precedent; no one had previously returned alive to claim one (G. F. Mees). He made valuable collections of both vertebrate and invertebrate material, and is remembered in an owl (*Scotopelia peli*) and a barbet (*Gymnobucco peli*). His bird species were collected between Accra and Cape Three Points, but mainly at Butri (Butre or Boutry, 4°50′N, 1°56′W) and nearby Dabocrom, which Pel considered his best collecting site (see Holthuis 1968 for further details).

Andreas Riis, one of the first group of Basel missionaries to Ghana, established a lasting work at Akropong in Akwapim where he stayed from 1835 to c. 1850. His collection of 92 species was studied by Hartlaub, who followed it by a review of what was known of West African birds and, in particular, those of Ghana (Hartlaub 1853, 1854, 1855a,b, 1857, 1858), and he is remembered in a hornbill *Tockus hartlaubi.*

Several small collections were received by R. B. Sharpe at the British Museum (Nat. Hist.) (BMNH) and described by him (Sharpe 1869a,b, 1870a,b, 1871a,b). E. T. Higgins, a medical doctor, sent 4 collections from Cape Coast, B. Hinde and H. Whitely, a professional collector, sent one each labelled "interior of Fantee country", the British Governor H. T. Ussher and Captain J. W. Haynes of the 2nd West Indian Regiment, both sent 2 each, and A. Swanzy sent another. Haynes is remembered in a subspecies of the babbler *Phyllanthus atripennis.* Swanzy, of Sevenoaks, Kent, was a successful businessman whose family had long-standing links with Cape Coast. He equipped several scientific expeditions into the interior of Ghana while living there, and was well respected by the people. He is remembered in a subspecies of the cisticola *Cisticola cantans.*

Another competent Dutch naturalist was Lt Col C. J. M. Nagtglas who, after some years service in the Gold Coast, was made Governor in 1858. He sent zoological material in spirits to SMNH in 1858, and further collections of bird skins in April 1860, December 1861 and November 1862, together with many insects, snakes and mammals (Gijzen 1938: 136–138; Mees 1986: 157). The bird skins (Appendix 5) were examined by R. B. Sharpe. Nagtglas retired from service, as did Pel, but was recalled in May 1869 as Royal Commissioner and Governor of the Dutch possessions (Claridge 1964). At about the same time, Finsch (1869), who is remembered in a thrush subspecies *Stizorhina fraseri finschi,* gave details of skins collected by S. M. Sintenis at Elmina and Accra, and a new species of *Smithornis* was described by Gray (1864) from a skin received from Mr Gould, a dealer, which had originated in Ghana.

Further papers (Sharpe 1872a,b; Sharpe & Ussher 1872; Ussher 1874) resulted from collections by Ussher and S. Thomas David Aubinn, a Ghanaian, who also obtained skins for others (E. T. Higgins, Governor Nagtglas and H. F. Blissett, a Deputy Commissary at Cape Coast). Ussher was made acting Administrator in February 1867, Administrator in July 1867, Governor in June 1879, and died in office at Accra on 1 December 1880. Ussher's paper (1874) was a major contribution and it added a number of forest birds to the Ghana list; he is remembered in an owl (*Scotopelia ussheri*), a spinetail (*Chaetura ussheri*), a flycatcher (*Artomyias ussheri*) and 3 subspecies (*Indicator minor ussheri, Tchagra australis ussheri* and *Pholidornis rushiae ussheri*). Aubinn often obtained skins for Ussher in "Denkera" or "from Denkera". This almost certainly refers to the area inland from the coast, bordering the Ivory Coast and stretching as far north as Wiawso, through which the river Tano flows. Similarly, Wassaw, another name on skins collected by him and others in the 19th century, refers to the district centred around Tarkwa (= Takwa) (Claridge 1964). In this same period (1865–1882), 3 Württemberg (Basel) missionaries sent collections to Stuttgart Museum; Mr Leimenstoll collected at Elmina and Cape

Coast, Mr Mohr at Begoro, and Mr Werner at Abetifi. Anton Reichenow and Dr Wilhelm Lühder visited Accra, Abokobi and Aburi in August 1872. During their stay of 2 months, during which Dr Lühder died, they identified 100 birds and made a collection of 150 skins (Reichenow 1872; Reichenow & Lühder 1873). A further review of West African birds followed (Reichenow 1874, 1875). Reichenow is remembered in a subspecies of *Trochocercus nitens*.

G. E. Shelley and T. E. Buckley arrived at Cape Coast on 12 January 1872 with the express purpose of studying Ghanaian birds. They collected at Cape Coast, Accra, Abokobi and Aburi during February and March, and recorded details of the vegetation and bird life seen on their journey (Shelley & Buckley 1872). On his return to London, Shelley produced several papers based on his collection and those of Ussher and Aubinn (Shelley 1873, 1874a,b, 1875, 1879, 1884) and is remembered in an owl (*Bubo shelleyi*). Buckley is remembered in a subspecies of *Francolinus albogularis* and of *Mirafra rufocinnamomea*. Further papers by Sharpe (1873a,b) were based on collections already listed above together with the additional ones of H. F. Blissett, who is remembered in a flycatcher (*Platysteira blissetti*), G. Lagden, and A. Moloney, an Acting British Governor. Sharpe further described (Sharpe 1877, 1882, 1884, 1892) 4 additional skins collected by Aubinn, Ussher, Lagden, who is remembered in a shrike *Malaconotus lagdeni,* and Moloney, who is remembered in a subspecies of the babbler *Trichastoma fulvescens*; and later too described the collections made by Col H. P. Northcott, the Commissioner of the Northern Territories, at Gambaga (Sharpe 1899). Sharpe is remembered in a subspecies of *Caprimulgus tristigma* and *Pogoniulus bilineatus* and in the species *Apalis sharpii*. At about the same time Captain W. Giffard also collected at Gambaga and in Burkino Faso between February and December (Hartert 1899a,b) and is remembered in a subspecies of *Cossypha albicapilla*.

Just prior to 1882, R. Burton and Captain V. L. Cameron visited western Ghana from late January to late March (Burton) and late April (Cameron) respectively. They surveyed the gold mines along the Ancobra river and collected butterflies, plants and birds. The birds were skinned by their cook Dawson who "was an excellent stuffer of birds and beasts" and were later identified at the BMNH by R. B. Sharpe. Burton makes the interesting comment "that [their] collection found its way to the BMNH after the usual extensive plunder, probably at a certain port, where it is said professional collectors keep custom house men in pay" (Burton & Cameron 1883). The 35 skins that reached the BMNH covered about 22 species (Appendix 2 in Burton & Cameron 1883). In addition, some skins collected by Dr F. Roth were sent to Lord Rothschild's collection at Tring.

During these years Reichenow (1891, 1892, 1897, 1902) published data on birds of German Togoland. This had become a German protectorate in 1885 and the Volta and Dako rivers formed part of its western border with British Gold Coast. In 1922, after the First World War, the protectorate was divided into 2 parts. The western part, a north–south strip containing towns such as Bawku, Yendi, Kete Kratchi and Ho, came under British control and eventually elected to become part of Ghana. The eastern part became present day Togoland. Contrary to what is stated in Cheke & Walsh (1980) only the 1897 and 1902 papers (the latter not listed by them) refer to what constitutes present day Ghana geographically. In the first 2 papers (1891, 1892), Reichenow describes 133 species collected by Dr Büttner near the German military post of Bismarckburg (8°12'N, 00°41'E) which was situated on a prominent hill, 770 m high, in the Adélé area of Togoland (Douaud 1956), and lists the localities in British Gold Coast where the same species had been collected earlier. In the 1897 paper, in which the number of species for German Togoland was raised to 279, Reichenow describes collections made by E. Baumann, who is remembered in a bulbul *Phyllastrephus baumanni,* Lieutenant Klose and Count Zech at Kete Kratchi, the new site of the German military post after Bismarckburg had been abandoned in December 1894, and at Akrose (both these last 2 in Ghana), and at Misshöhe (6°57′N, 0°35′E) in Togoland. The 1902 paper contains information on birds collected by G. Thierry, Dr Rigler and F. Schröder, mainly near the Togoland towns of Sansanne Mangu (10°18′N, 0°28′E) and Sokode (8°59′N, 1°08′E), and those collected by Mr Kurz in coastal areas. The only information on Ghanaian birds collected by G. Thierry and Dr Rigler was from Yendi, Kete Kratchi and Oti. The number of species for German Togoland then stood at 355.

Captain Boyd Alexander landed at Cape Coast on 1 June 1900 and was attached to the Kumasi Relief-Column. After the fall of Kumasi, Alexander went northwards to Gambaga, the capital of the northern territories, and discovered 2 breeding colonies of the Wood Ibis *Ibis ibis,* one at Daboya and one at Gambaga. Throughout this time, he and his Portuguese skinner, José Lopez, collected nearly 1100 skins of both forest and savanna species, many of which were new to Ghana and one (*Muscicapa gambagae*) new to science (Alexander, 1901a,b).

For the next 2 decades only the occasional skin from Ghana reached BMNH (see Bannerman 1922, 1923), but then a major series was received from A. W. J. Pomeroy, who had been appointed medical entomologist in 1925 and collected in the Yeji district and later in the northern region of Ghana. Although the paper by Millet-Horsin (1923) is cited by Cheke & Walsh (1980) as being relevant to present day Ghana, his records were all made near Anecho (6°10′N, 1°30′E), which is on the coast on the eastern edge of Lake Togo.

During a magnetic survey of the west coast of Africa, Willoughby P. Lowe was invited to join the survey ship and make skin collections wherever and whenever possible. Rough weather only allowed him 7 days (22–27 December 1910, 1 March 1911) collecting at Sekondi and 16 at Axim (12–28 February 1911) (see Bannerman 1912a,b; Sclater 1924). Some 23 years later, Lowe was back in Ghana and, together with Miss F. Waldron, made a major collection of skins of forest and savanna birds between December 1933 and late February 1934. A year later they repeated their effort (Lowe 1937; see also Bannerman 1934, 1935a,b,c,d,e, 1939) and, in addition, collected avian blood samples. Miss Waldron is remembered in a subspecies of *Anthoscopus flavifrons.* Many birds previously collected by Aubinn were rediscovered, and their distributions were much better known as a result of these visits of Lowe's. Details of the vegetation at each collecting station were given and a noteworthy addition was photographs of the forest at Mampong, Ashanti and the savanna at Lawra. The majority of Lowe's skins are in BMNH, but some are in the Royal Natural History Museum at Stockholm.

Just prior to these visits of Lowe, Admiral H. Lynes and J. Vincent visited Ghana (11–26 May 1931) to study the cisticolas (Lynes 1932; Lynes & Sclater 1934). Using local transport they visited Accra, Kumasi and Salaga and Gambaga in the north. At Salaga and Gambaga, they rediscovered, as they had hoped, the Rufous Cisticola *Cisticola rufa* and the Red-pate Cisticola *Cisticola ruficeps* and described a new race of the Red-pate Cisticola. In addition, and unexpectedly, a race of the Black-backed Cisticola *Cisticola eximia* was found in the dry coastal strip at Winneba. The main paper (1934) contained descriptions of vegetation and a photograph of the savanna at Salaga.

During these early decades, when the priority was to collect skins, no less than 132 species and subspecies were described and named from skins collected in Ghana, the last subspecies *Eremomela badiceps fontiensis* being named by Macdonald (1940) from a skin collected at Prahsu by Boyd Alexander in 1900 (see Appendix 8).

From the mid 1930s until 1960 knowledge of Ghanaian birds increased substantially as a result of field data carefully collected by resident ornithologists, many of whom were in Government service of one kind or another. A noteworthy contribution was that of Holman (1947) who spent a period of 20 years in Ghana, being resident for many months at a time at Keta, Kumasi, Oda, Takoradi and Tamale. Data collected by A. Allnut, W. J. Birkle, G. S. Cansdale, J. D. Clarke, D. Cooper, R. E. Crabbe, K. M. Guichard, M. T. Horwood, M. H. Hughes, P. I. Lake, J. R. Marshall, C. M. Morrison, K. O'Carrol, A. W. Pomeroy, A. C. Russell, J. B. Shaw, J. Symonds and J. M. Winterbottom were included in D. A. Bannerman's 8 volume work on West African birds (Bannerman 1930–1951). Of these individuals special mention must be made of C. M. Morrison, who spent 12 years (1938–1950) as a missionary training Ghanaian teachers at Akropong, Akwapim and M. T. Horwood, a Conservator of Forests, who spent 19 years (1938–1957) in Ghana. He stayed at Akim Oda, Bekwai, Cape Coast, Dunkwa, Ho, Korforidua, Mpraeso, Wiawso, Sekondi, Sunyani, and Tamale, often trekking for long periods in the forests. Both made copious notes on Ghanaian birds and have made them available for this check-list.

During the Second World War, T. A. Cockburn was asked to investigate the presence of yellow fever antibodies in bird sera at Sa, some 48 km north of Wa in northern Ghana. His bird skins (200) and slides were lost through 'enemy action', but some of his findings were published (Cockburn 1946). Morrison (1947, 1952) of Akropong, Russell (1949) of Accra, and Gass (1954, 1957, 1963), who stayed for 5 years mainly at Kete Krachi and Accra, published some of their observations, and A. C. Russell produced in the mid 1950s a stencilled list of 627 Ghanaian birds, basing his work on Bannerman's volumes. In October 1942, Dr J. Chapin, of Congo fame, made a brief visit (4 days) to Juaso and Agogo with W. B. Collins, a Conservator of Forests. D. W. Lamm, an American career diplomat, chose Ghana as one of his postings and travelled extensively within Ghana. He trained a Ghanaian skinner, and his collection (made between February 1955 and April 1957) is now at the Smithsonian Institution (see Appendix 5). Lamm published a breeding study of the Pied Crow *Corvus alba* (Lamm 1958), some feeding rates for the Grey-headed Sparrow *Passer griseus* (Lamm 1959), and with M. T. Horwood added 11 new species to the Ghana list (Lamm & Horwood 1958). Contrary to what is stated in Cheke & Walsh (1980), the publications of J. Douaud over this period do not add any new information on Ghanaian birds, and only contain passing reference to already known data.

After Ghana became independent on 6 March 1957, many expatriates, some interested in ornithology, went to teach in schools and colleges and were resident at different locations for a number of years. After 1960 expatriates were only granted overseas leave every 2 years and this was a blessing in disguise for ornithologists. Significant contributions to local avifauna were made by Sutton at Denu and later at Tumu (Sutton 1965a,b, 1970), by Grimes (1972a) at Legon, by MacDonald (1977a, 1978a,c, 1979b) at Cape Coast. F. Walsh, at Bolgatanga (data to be published), made monthly censuses of birds of prey between Tamale and Bolgatanga in 1971–72 and at least twice weekly made counts of waders at Vea reservoir, near Bolgatanga, between early July 1972 and early February 1973.

Several ornithologists visited Ghana for shorter periods, a few months to a year, in the 1960s and 1970s. Of these, the wet season visits to the Mole Game Reserve by student groups from Oxford (one visit in 1968 — Hancock 1968) and Aberdeen (5 visits from 1974–1978) proved particularly valuable. Reports on the Aberdeen expeditions were produced and much of the data formed the basis of honours theses of several of the students (see Appendix 6). Publications have appeared mainly in the *Bulletin of the Nigerian Ornithological Society* (now *Malimbus*) and the *Bulletin of the British Ornithologists' Club*. In addition, a number of long term breeding studies were carried out, the vocalisations of some species were studied, and wader and tern migrations followed using radar (see, particularly, references under both Grimes and MacDonald).

J. P. Jones was the first to use mist nets in Ghana (Sharland & Harris 1959) and 74 birds from 25 species, both Palaearctic and Afrotropical, were ringed. Only one bird was recaught subsequently, a Sudan Brown Babbler *Turdoides plebejus,* recaught alive 18 months later some 11 km northwest of its release point at Achimota (Sharland & Harris 1961). Some passerines were ringed by R. G. Donald at Tafo in 1962 and 1963, but little apparently came of this venture (Sharland 1963, 1964). Mist nets were used in the late 1960s and early 1970s to colour ring breeding populations of the Yellow-billed Shrike *Corvinella corvina* (Grimes 1979a, 1980) and H. Houston attempted to ring waders at the saltpans west of Accra. The only major ringing study of Palaearctic birds has been that of Mary Lockwood at Tafo within the forest region. She mainly worked at a swallow roost, but ringed 22 Palaearctic species and a total of 8212 birds between 1973 and 1978 (see Appendices 1 and 2).

Many Palaearctic terns (see Appendix 3) have been trapped along the shore line of Ghana since the Dutch-ringed Sandwich Tern *Sterna sandvicensis* was the first to be caught near Denu on 23 November 1911 (data from the Euring Data Bank, Arnhem, Holland — see also Yates 1937). More than 75% of all recoveries in West Africa of British ringed Roseate Terns *Sterna dougalli* are from Ghana and the number caught between 1967 and 1975 was double that for the previous decade (Dunn 1981). An increase in capture rate of all terns off Ghana occurred in the same period and Dunn & Mead (1982) have shown that the capture rate is greatest when the sardine (*Sardinella* spp.) catches by local fishermen are high. Although this high capture rate has caused no little concern in conservation circles, a good deal of useful information on tern migration has resulted (see Langham 1971). In addition, a joint project involving the Ghana Game and Wildlife Department and the RSPB and the ICBP was sanctioned by the Ghana Government in June 1985 and started in November of the same year. The aim was to survey the numbers of coastal birds (particularly terns) in Ghana, encourage conservation at a local level and train technical staff of the Game and Wildlife Department. The first census by E. Dunn, R. Broad and A. Grieve was in November and December 1985 and the second by I. Hepburn, A. J. M. Smith and B. Scott in January and February 1986 (Hepburn 1986). Both were very successful and achieved their goals and, in addition, added 7 new vagrant species to the Ghana list. An RSPB Film Unit consisting of T. Broad, C. H. Gomersall, G. Horder, I. McCarthy and C. Watson also visited Ghana in October 1986.

In recent years, the internal parasites found in some Ghanaian birds have been studied in some detail — see publications of Barus, Hodasi, Ukoli and Wink & Bennett.

From the foregoing, it is apparent that the knowledge of Ghanaian birds is based mainly on the activities of European expatriates, usually on short term contracts. None has been a professional employed by the Ghana Government or earlier Colonial administration. As a result there has been neither planned long term research, nor a national collection built up with the backing of a University or National Museum. The skin collections at Legon and at the Mole Game Reserve are small, both in numbers and species, and are not representative of the country as a whole (see Appendix 5). The small collection at the Department of Biological Sciences at Kumasi University contains some interesting forest species, but the details of this collection are uncertain at the time of writing (October 1985).

The current political and economic situation in Ghana, with its many pressing social problems, mitigates the pursuit of ornithology and there may well be a prolonged period of stagnation in the immediate future. Fortunately, however, there are now several Ghanaians employed by the Game and Wildlife Department who

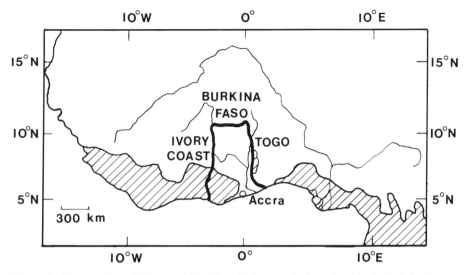

Figure 2. The position of Ghana within West Africa and the location (shaded) of the Upper and Lower Guinea forest blocks.

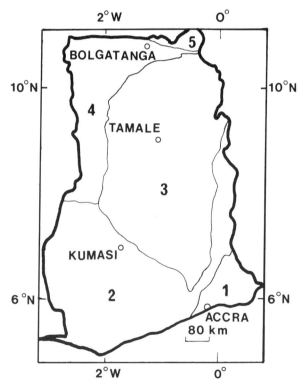

Figure 3. The main geo-morphological regions of Ghana: (1) the Accra–Ho–Keta Plains; (2) PreCambrian rocks and the forest region; (3) the Palaeozoic sediments forming the Voltaian basin; (4) & (5) the area of crystalline rocks to the north and west of the Voltaian basin.

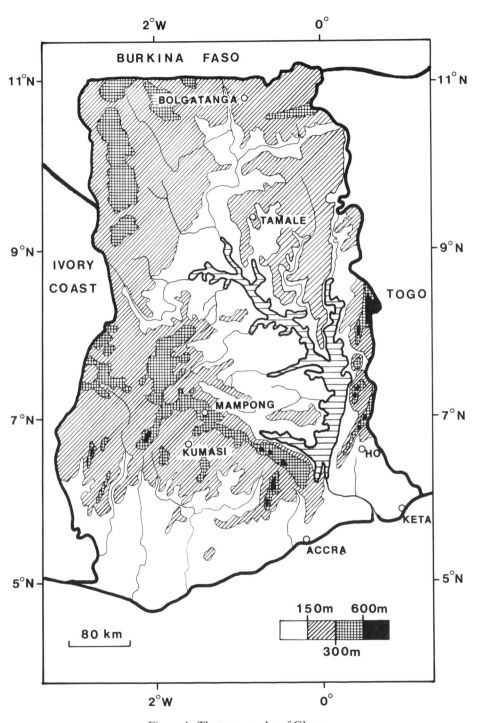

Figure 4. The topography of Ghana.

are taking an active interest in ornithology. Among these known to me are Emmanuel Agemfra, Yaa Ntiamoa-Baidu, Ali Nuoh, and David Daramani who has begun work on queleas and other potential bird pests at the various irrigation projects in the north and on the Accra Plains; at least 3 of them took a leading part in the 1985–1986 RSPB/ICBP project. There must be a modern day Aubinn equivalent among these or others who could carry on what he began over 100 years ago. It is to them that I hope this checklist will be most beneficial and act as a stimulus for their future work.

GEOLOGY AND TOPOGRAPHY

Ghana is roughly rectangular in shape and lies between latitudes 4°44′ and 11°11′N and longitudes 1°12′E and 3°15′W. It is bordered by Togo on the east, Burkina Faso (Haute Volta) on the north, Cote d'Ivoire on the west and by the Gulf of Guinea on the south (Fig. 2). Ghana's coastline runs approximately WSW — ENE for most of its length (c. 550 km); west of Cape Three Points it runs approximately ESE — WNW.

Nearly half the surface of Ghana (total area c. 242,000 km^2) is composed of PreCambrian metamorphic and igneous rocks, and most of the remainder is a platform of Palaeozoic sediments believed to be resting on the older rocks. About one third of the country is at an altitude of less than 150 m and about one half at 150–300 m (Figs 3 and 4).

The Palaeozoic sediments make up c. 115,000 km^2 of the *Voltaian basin* (Fig. 3) which extends northwards on the eastern side of the central part of the country, and consists of uniform, gently dipping sandstones, shales and mudstones. The rim of the basin on the north and south consists of a high plateau, which has impressive outward facing scarps. Its southern edge for most of its length lies between 610 and 670 m, but rises to 840 m close to Mpraeso (Fig. 4). The rim runs northwest from south of Korforidua, through Mpraeso and Mampong (Ashanti), to Wenchi. It then turns northwards and eventually eastwards, becoming a prominent landmark again between Gambaga and Nakpanduri where the height of the rim ranges from 460 to 520 m. The eastern edge of the basin is formed by a narrow zone of high hills (460 m upwards to 600–920 m), consisting of older rocks of the Togo and Buem formation (late PreCambrian), which run north–south along the Togo border. Further south the hills run southwest to form the Akwapim hills (See Fig. 11) which reach the sea just west of Accra. Within the basin the land elevation is 120 to 150 m.

PreCambrian rocks (c. 74,000 km^2) lie south and west of the Voltaian basin, reaching as far north as Wenchi, and form the main area in which tropical forest of one kind or another is found (Fig. 3). It contains many small ranges of hills which are aligned along a NE — SW axis, generally at right angles to the southern scarp of the Voltaian basin. These ridges consist mostly of Upper Birrimian greenstone and some, such as the Atewa range near Kibi, are more than 500 m high, flat topped, often capped with bauxite, and have soils rich in clay. In addition, large areas of granite occur and there are some smooth-topped granite inselbergs, a notable one near Nsawam being 490 m high. Towards the southwest, there are many small but steep hills, often more or less surrounded by fresh water swamps (Fig. 4).

The coast from Accra to Axim is rocky and marine terraces occur. West of Axim the rocks are covered by a sandbar, which is continually being eroded and reformed through a long-shore drift from west to east; a number of elongated lagoons occur behind it. In the extreme southwest of the country is a belt of tertiary deposits.

PreCambrian crystalline rocks (in area c. 42,000 km^2) lie north and west of the Voltaian basin (Fig. 3). This region is gently undulating and its topography resembles the Voltaian basin, but more extensive ranges of hills occur and there are granite inselbergs, notably near Navrongo (Fig. 4).

The Accra–Ho–Keta Plains (Fig. 3) occupy the southeast corner of the country and cover c. 11,000 km². They are underlain by the oldest of the PreCambrian series (dahomeyan) and are flanked on the west and north by the Akwapim and Togo hills, on the south by the coast, and on the east by the Togo border. The plains rarely rise to above 75 m, but there are several high inselbergs consisting of either basic gneiss or granite, Adaklu, the highest (c. 600 m), lying just south of Ho. On the western section of the plains the Shai hills and Krobo hill are prominent features. Ghana's southeast corner and the broad delta of the Volta river, which effectively divides the plains in two, consist of relatively young rocks of Pleistocene to Recent age (see Figs 10, 11).

DRAINAGE OF THE COUNTRY

Drainage of the country is dominated by the Volta system (Fig. 5), which occupies the Voltaian basin and since early in 1966 includes the 8480 km² Volta Lake, which has a length of 400 km and a shore line of c. 4800 km. In the rains an additional area of c. 1000 km² is flooded. The dam wall is situated at Akosombo and from there the Volta river flows southwards through a gap in the Akwapim/Togo range of hills, and enters the sea at Ada just west of Keta (see Fig. 11). Most of the other major rivers, including the Pra, Ankobra and Tano, flow from the southern edge of the Voltaian basin to the sea. Southeast of Kumasi is lake Bosumtwi, believed to be of volcanic origin with an area of c. 100 km², the highest hills in its rim rising to 520 m and its bottom estimated to be just above sea level; its water level is rising at about 0·3 m per year.

On the Accra Plains, west of the Volta river, a low watershed running east–west divides the small streams flowing north into the Volta from those much larger ones flowing to the sea. Most of the well defined south-flowing steams receive their water from the Akwapim hills and near the coast these streams broaden into lagoons. East of the Volta the small tributory rivers flow into the Volta, apart that is from the Todzie, which flows into the Avu lagoon (Fig. 5). Of the major lagoons, those of Songaw and Angew (the western inland arm of the Volta river just north of Ada — see Fig. 11), and the one near Keta at the Ghana/Togo border are saline, but those further inland are fresh for the greater part of the year and are supplied by water from the Todzie (Fig. 5) (Beattie & Willis 1962; Brash 1962).

CLIMATE, RAINFALL, TEMPERATURE AND WIND

The climate of West Africa, and Ghana in particular, is mainly controlled by the movement of the inter-tropical convergence zone (ITCZ), currently termed the Intertropical Confluence (ITC) (Barry & Chorley 1982), which effectively moves in phase, with a lag of 1–2 months, with the apparent movement of the sun. The position of the ITCZ within Ghana in February is c. 5°N and in August lies north at 17–21°N. The zone, which is essentially the atmosphere's equator, is formed by the movement or convergence of 2 air masses, one the northeast trades of the northern hemisphere and the other the southeast trades of the southern hemisphere, into the equatorial belt. The inflowing air escapes by rising and weather satellites have shown the presence of a number of isolated but extensive cloud systems, often 100–1000 km across, distributed along the axis of the ITCZ. Within each cloud system, very large numbers of individual cumulus clouds, 1–10 km in diameter and reaching as high as 12 km, occur and several of these make up a convective cell (10–100 km in diameter). Within a convective cell, which drifts slowly and erratically, but often towards the west, there are frequent showers and thunderstorms.

This picture of the ITCZ is modified in West Africa by a belt of moist westerly

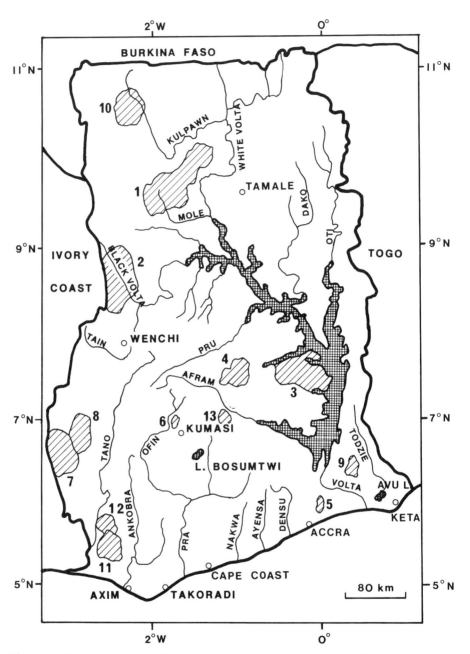

Figure 5. The main rivers of Ghana and the approximate locations of the game reserves within Ghana. The numbering sequence follows that in Table 3.

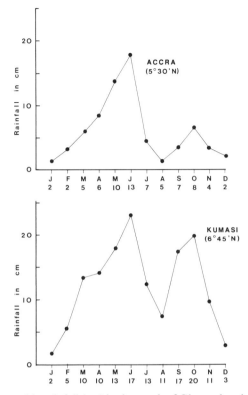

Figure 6. The mean monthly rainfall (cm) in the south of Ghana showing the double peak in the rainfall at Accra (70 years of records) and Kumasi (50 years of records). Below each month are the mean number of rain days.

winds (the southwestern monsoon) which persists throughout the year but is more extensive and well marked in the summer (May–September) when thermal heating over the African continent assists the northern displacement of the equatorial trough. These westerlies are not simply trade winds whose direction has changed in crossing the equator but are partly global and partly regional in origin (Barry & Chorley 1982: 133). The moist westerlies form a wedge of 2–3 km thickness, whose apex penetrates at ground level as far north as the southern Sahara by August and September. The monsoon brings cloud and showers and retreats southwards with the ITCZ to coastal areas for the remaining months of the year and occasionally (in January) further south over the Gulf of Guinea. A further complication in West Africa to the structure of the ITCZ arises during the period November to March when a dry northeasterly current (the harmattan), analogous to the trade wind, blows off the desert and over-rides the moist westerlies (see later). Because of these modifications to the ITCZ, sharp temperature and moisture gradients can occur and give to the ITCZ characteristics that are associated with weather fronts of higher latitudes (Barry & Chorley 1982; Hare 1982).

As a result of the structure and movement of the ITCZ, areas of Ghana south of a line joining Kintampo to Ho have 2 rainy seasons each year. Inland, south of this line, the 2 rainfall peaks, the one in May and June and the other in October, are equally heavy, but rain falls all the year around. Nearer the coast the October maximum is much smaller than that in May and June. Little rain falls in coastal

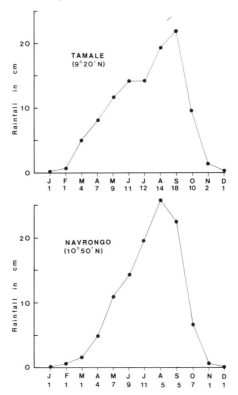

Figure 7. The mean monthly rainfall (cm) in the north of Ghana showing the single peak in the rainfall at Tamale (49 years of records) and Navrongo (30 years of records). Below each month are the mean number of rain days.

areas in July, August and September because of an inversion layer, although the skies are overcast (Fig. 6).

Areas to the north of the line through Kintampo have only one wet season (Fig. 7). In the southern part of this northern zone, the rain falls between March and October in approximately equal amounts each month; whereas in the northern part, north of a line joining Wa and Salaga, the monthly totals rise slowly from March, level off in June and July, and build up to a maximum in August and September, thereafter decreasing rapidly (Walker 1962). The ensuing long dry season of 5–6 months is characterised by cloudless skies, but the intensity of radiation is reduced by the dust-laden air associated with the harmattan.

Another regular and characteristic weather pattern in West Africa is the line squall, which occurs most frequently between November and March, and is produced when the low-level moist westerlies are over-run by the dry harmattan. The disturbance originates within the upper air stream, the cloud and rain developing in the underlying moist air. The line squall is characterised by a narrow line of thunderstorm cells, orientated north–south, which may extend over several hundred kilometres and travel westwards at c. 50 km/hr, beginning in Nigeria. The approach of a line squall is unforgettable. There is first an uncanny calm as the edge of the disturbance, made visible by a dust column and bank of cumulus reaching at least 10 km high, approaches steadily from the east with increasing noise. On the other side of the dust column high gusty winds and heavy rainfall occur with a temporary lowering of the air temperature, and there are some awesome lightning displays. The

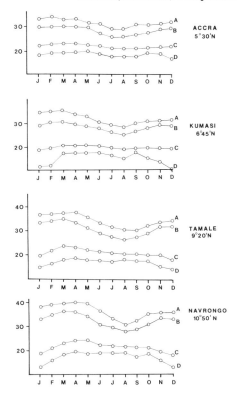

Figure 8. The mean monthly maximum (B) and minimum (C) temperatures (Centigrade) and the highest monthly maximum (A) and the lowest minimum (D) temperatures at 4 locations within Ghana.

width of the squall is only some 50 km, so that rain falls for only 1–2 hrs. The percentage contribution of rain from squalls to the annual rainfall depends mainly on the latitude, the larger percentage occurring at higher latitudes. Thus in 1955 the rainfall from line squalls contributed only 30% of the annual rainfall at Axim on the coast, but as much as 90% of the rainfall at Navrongo in northern Ghana (Trewartha 1962; Barry & Chorley 1982). At Accra on the coast, rain from line squalls is significant in March and April. When 5, 10 or 15 day rainfall means are used to obtain an annual rainfall profile, rather than monthly means, an additional secondary peak in March and April is apparent just before the main peak in May and June (Trewartha 1962: 102).

The average annual rainfall over the greater part of the country, ranging from 100–180 cm, is typical of tropical lands. The greatest rainfall occurs in the southwest of the country (216 cm) where the coastline runs approximately at right angles to the prevailing winds from the southwest, and the least falls on the Accra Plains (76 cm or less at Accra). Rainfall in coastal areas from Takoradi eastwards to Togo and Dahomey is much less than elsewhere in West Africa. This dry belt, defined approximately by the 100 cm (40 inch) isohyet, runs parallel to the coast and is c. 30 km wide in Ghana but swings inland some 160 km or so in eastern Togo and Dahomey. Surrounding this region there are steep rainfall gradients reaching 1·6 cm per km between Takoradi and Axim. The probable causes for this dry region are (1) the wind direction is essentially parallel to the coastline and (2) cold upwelling water occurs off Accra and eastwards to Togoland during July, August and September

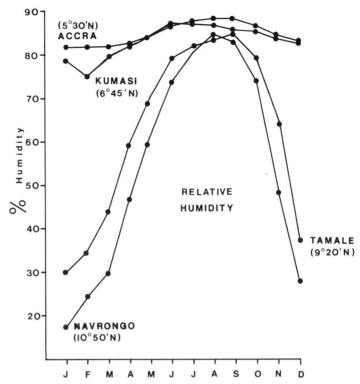

Figure 9. The relative humidity (expressed as a percentage) at selected stations in the humid zone (Accra and Kumasi) and the dry zone (Tamale and Navrongo). The data used are the mean of values measured at 3 hourly intervals beginning midnight.

(Trewartha 1962). Annual rainfall is highly variable and the range considerable, e.g. Accra (28–119 cm), Axim (119–330 cm), Kumasi (102–190 cm) and Tamale (81–157 cm). Falling rain is rarely prolonged over any part of the country and on average lasts 2–3 hours. In the dry season, rain is likely to fall during less than 10 hrs in a month and during only 30–40 hrs per month in the wet season.

Because the movements of the ITCZ are not regular, the times of onset and duration of the dry and rainy seasons vary considerably from year to year. In addition, the local weather is affected by the local topography; any modification of the local climate by the Volta dam has still be be quantified.

In summary, in the north there is one rainy period (March–September, maximum August/September) ending abruptly and followed by 5–6 months rainless dry season. In the south there are 2 rainy seasons, May/June and October, though rain falls in all months.

Annual mean temperature (average of the mean maximum and mean minimum temperature) varies little, after altitude effects have been allowed for, between coastal areas (26°C) and northern areas (29°C); the range in the annual mean temperature is equally small, only about 3°C in the south, and about 5°C in the north. The mean daily range of temperature is approximately double the annual range. Average maximum temperatures are highest in March over the entire country except for an area between Akuse, Ho and Tafo where temperatures are highest in February. The annual mean maximum temperature in the north is 34°C and in the south on the coast is 29°C. Average minimum temperatures usually occur in January except for the coastal areas, where it is coldest in August, and the extreme north where the coldest month is December. The range in the average monthly minimum temperature is only 1·4°C in the south and 5·7°C in the north (Fig. 8).

No quantitative data are available on dew precipitation, but ground temperatures fall to the dew point throughout most of the year. The higher altitudes of ranges in the forest region and along the southern ridge of the Voltaian basin are shrouded in mist during most nights of the year and for much of the day as well between May and October (Walker 1962; Fig. 9). The importance of dew precipitation to the soil and vegetation was recognised by Thompson (1910) and he considered that it had appreciably delayed the degradation of the soil on the Akwapim hills and its vegetation.

Wind speeds average less than 8 km/hr inland and range from 8 to 16 km/hr on the coast. The coastal winds reach their highest speeds in the afternoon.

THE VEGETATION ZONES

The Forest zone (c. 82,300 km^2)

The forest zone boundary with the savanna vegetation has recently been mapped using a ground survey, correlated with infra-red photographs taken from the Earth Resources Technology Satellite (ERTS-1) (Swaine *et al*. 1976). For much of its length the boundary follows the line of the upper Voltaian hills on the southern side of the Voltaian basin (Fig. 10), and its boundary appears to be determined by a combination of geology, elevation and mean annual rainfall. Swaine *et al*. distinguished 2 types of forest/savanna boundary: one in which forest persists both on hilltops and along streams, separated by savanna, typically found near Wenchi; and the other in which the forest is only found along the streams flowing through

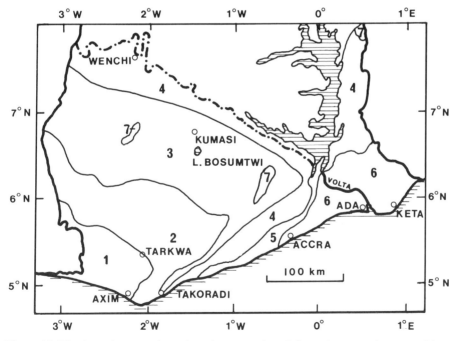

Figure 10. The forest/savanna boundary (—·—·—) and the main vegetation zones identified by Swaine *et al*. (1976) and Hall & Swaine (1976): (1) Wet evergreen; (2) Moist evergreen; (3) Moist semi-deciduous; (4) Dry semi-deciduous; (5) Southern marginal; (6) Southeast outliers; (7) Upland evergreen.

Table 1. The 7 major forest types in Ghana distinguished by Hall & Swaine (1976, 1981), and some of their characteristics

Type	Percentage deciduousness[b]	Mean number of tree species per 625 m² plot	Mean height (m) of tallest tree in or near plot	Mean annual rainfall (cm)	Area[c] Sq Km	% of total forest area
Wet Evergreen	19	138	32	175	6570	8·1
Moist Evergreen	22	120	43	150–175	17770	21·9
Upland Evergreen	6	113	40	150–200	292	0·3
Moist Semideciduous[a]	35	105	49	125–175	32890	40·4
Dry Semideciduous[a]	60	75	36	125–150	21440	26·4
Southern Marginal	48	47	28	100–125	2360	2·9
Southeast Outliers	—	25	15	100	20	0·03
					Total 81342	100·03

[a] Hall & Swaine (1976) subdivide each of the Semideciduous zones into 2 types. The data quoted here represents the mean and total range of their data
[b] See text for definition of this index
[c] Data based on Table 8.1 in Hall & Swaine (1981)

savanna, typically so on Voltaian sediments. Any difference in the avifauna of these 2 boundary types has not been investigated.

Only about 19,442 km² (24%) of the forest zone is under forest (the data are for 1975), none of which can be considered primary, and of this about 16,800 km² (86%) is in reserves. In contrast, in 1955 the estimates were 36·8% under forest and 53% of this in reserves. The present forest canopy is uneven, ranging from 10 to 40 m above the ground with emergents reaching 60 m. Some of the canopy trees are deciduous, but the understorey vegetation is evergreen; woody climbers are always present.

Seven major forest types have been identified in Ghana by Hall & Swaine (1976, 1981) (Table 1 and Fig. 10). Five of these are widely distributed in West Africa, but the other 2 are not found outside Ghana, one being the 'southern marginal', which is coastal from near Takoradi to Accra and on to Akosombo, and the other, the 'south-east outliers', found on the inselbergs and hills on the Accra Plains and on the eastern side of the Volta. Previous workers (e.g. Taylor 1960) have combined these last 2 types and named them 'coastal or scrub zone'. The vegetation on the inselbergs and hills on the Accra Plains are greatly influenced by the southwest monsoon, tree savanna occurring on the west and southwest slopes and semi-deciduous forest on their eastern slopes (Jeník & Hall 1966).

The limits of the forest types of Hall & Swaine (Fig. 10) are based on some 285 plots within the closed canopy forest, which forms 24% of the total forest zone. They used environmental, physiognomic and geographical considerations to define their forest types. The terms *wet, moist,* and *dry* refer to mean annual rainfall. Deciduousness has been traditionally used to characterise forest types and was retained by Hall & Swaine, though they found it difficult to quantify their data due to the smallness of their plots. Forests, in which the trees are all deciduous or all evergreen, probably do not occur in West Africa (Hall & Swaine). Of the 59 deciduous species that occur in Ghanaian forests, 34 are able to reach heights greater than 30 m (megaphanerophytes). The number of megaphanerophyte species present in a forest type expressed as a percentage of the total (34) present in Ghanaian forests was the index of deciduousness chosen by them (Table 1). The degree of deciduousness decreases from the drier to the wetter forest types, but the boundary between *evergreen* and *semideciduous* is not sharp. Perhaps the most interesting forest type identified was 'upland evergreen', which they considered might be classified as submontane and which only occurred on isolated, often mist-covered hills above 500 m. It contained few deciduous trees, many epiphytes found elsewhere on mountains in Africa, the tree fern *Alsophila* (= *Cyathea*) *manniana* and brambles (*Rubus* spp.). Other montane vegetation species are found on the Djebobo Massif northeast of Kete Kratchi. The vegetation on these hills and those extending southwards towards Amedzofe is greatly affected by the harmattan and annual fires, some hills (e.g. Mt Game near Amedzofe) having grass summits. On the summit of Djebobo mountain (876 m), where in 1959 J. B. Hall found montane plants (*Hypoestes triflora, Haumaniastrum alboviride,* and *Senecio lelyi*), Jeník & Hall (1966) recorded an unusually high total diurnal evaporation (62 ml) in late December. This exceeds values recorded in deserts and is the joint product of the harmattan which blows throughout the night and morning, low humidity and high daytime temperatures. A study, using mist nets, of the avifauna of this type has yet to be carried out.

The remainder (76%) of the forest zone is degraded through cultivation, mainly of cocoa, and through timber extraction and use of timber for fuel, the latter use being vastly greater in volume than the commercial crop (Foggie & Piasecki 1962). Crops (other than cocoa) are usually grown in cleared forest and are planted or sown in April with the coming of the rains. In the first year, plantain *Musa paradisiaca,* cocoyam *Xanthosoma sagittifolium,* corn *Zea mays,* garden eggs *Solanum melongena,*

Table 2. The decrease of the unreserved forest during the decade 1970–1980 and the corresponding increase in degraded forest in Ghana

| | Area* in km² of the forest zone given to | | |
	Reserved forest	Unreserved forest	Degraded forest
1970	15571	5786	60902
1971	15571	5399	61289
1972	16788	3745	61726
1973	16788	3443	62028
1974	16788	3054	62417
1975	16788	2654	62817
1976	16788	2274	63197
1977	16788	1674	63797
1978	16788	1674	63797
1979	16788	1419	64052
1980	16788	1069	64402

*The total area of the forest zone, 82,259 km² differs only slightly from that, 81,342 km², estimated by Hall & Swaine (1981).

okra *Hibiscus esculentus,* pepper *Capsicum annuum* and occasionally yam (*Dioscrorea* spp.) are grown. In subsequent years only plantain and cocoyam continue to yield fruit until the 4th or 5th year. By then the nutrients in the soils are greatly diminished and only cassava *Manihot esculenta* can be grown. The forest farms are then abandoned and left fallow. The resultant vegetation depends on the length of the fallow period, and this in turn depends on the demand for and availability of land and food. Frequent cultivation results in a shrub vegetation with many climbers and with only the scattered shade trees remaining of the original forest.

The economic crop of cocoa takes up most of the forest zone degraded by farming. This is grown under shade from emergents and upper canopy trees. During initial growth there is little disturbance to the ground vegetation, but this is eventually shaded out by the cocoa canopy (6 m high) and thereafter annually cleared by the farmers. During its development, therefore, the cocoa canopy receives insect fauna from both ground vegetation and the upper canopy. Although cocoa is an effective monoculture, its insect fauna is, nevertheless, rich and similar to the surrounding forest (Gibbs & Leston 1970; Bigger 1976). The shade trees are essential for a healthy and lasting cocoa crop, and their absence can have a disastrous effect on the local vegetation. Cocoa was introduced to a very large area of forest north of Korforidua (the Bisa area) in 1903 by farmers from Krobo on the Accra Plains. They had little experience of forest farming and by 1920 had deforested the whole area, leaving no shade trees. The first notable effect of this deforestation was seen in 1925/1926 when the cocoa trees, which are evergreen when healthy, shed their leaves, the net result being the development of a scrub layer about 5 m high and the failure of the cocoa crop (Taylor 1960). It has been estimated that a farm becomes a secondary forest after some 75–100 undisturbed years, and indistinguishable from primary forest in 250 years (Lane 1962; Hopkins 1974).

Data (Table 2) supplied by Mr Friar of the Department of Forests, Accra, for the period 1970–1980, indicate that unreserved forests were being lost to timber exploitation and agriculture at an average rate of c. 470 km² per year. If this depletion rate is maintained, unreserved forests would have ceased to exist by about 1983. The export of timber taken from reserved forests reflects this depletion of unreserved forests. In 1958 it was 13% of the total and 78% in 1975. Hall & Swaine (1981) conclude that "very little of forest as we know it today is likely to survive beyond the next century".

The Ankasa Game Production reserve, rain forest in southwest Ghana. Photo J. B. Hall.

Moist semi-deciduous forest at the Agricultural Research Station at Kade. Photo Dr. M. D. Swaine.

Cultivation within the secondary forest. *Celtis milbraedii* with crown off the photograph and another beyond. Lower storey on left of centre contains *Musanga cecropioides* and *Raphia vinifera*. Photo Prof. C. J. Taylor.

Secondary forest developing in a gap in the Tewa Forest Reserve. Young *Musanga cecropioides* in foreground, *Terminalia superba* in centre. Photo G. Vanderstichelen.

The lowland forest, forest edge near Korforidua with *Musanga cecropioides* appearing on top left and right edges of photograph, *Triplochiton scleroxylon* in centre and *Celtis* spp. on right. Photo L. G. Grimes.

The Mpraeso escarpment, near Nkawaw with *Elaeis guineensis*. Photo L. G. Grimes.

Riverain forest along the Afram river in the Guinea Savanna zone. On riverside *Feretia canthiodes*, *Mimosa pigra*, *Vit chrysocarpa* and other vegetation. Photo C. J. Taylor.

The escarpment of the Volta Basin near Gambaga during the wet season. *Balanites aegyptiaca* in foreground and *Loph lanceolata* on right. Background mainly *Daniella oliveri*, *Combretum* and *Terminalia* spp. Photo Prof. C. J. Taylor.

mpeded drainage in savanna woodland south of Tamale. *Combretum* and *Terminalia* spp. with *Mitragyna inermis* in 'ight foreground. Photo Prof. C. J. Taylor.

lills to the north of Tumu with some *Acacia dudgeoni* in middle distance and savanna grassland. Photo Prof. C. J. Taylor.

Bawku hills with *Combretum* spp. and annual grasses. Photo Dr. M. D. Swaine, Nov 1986.

Parkland east of Bolgatanga, Nov 1976. Some *Daniella oliveri* and annual grasses. Photo Dr. M. D. Swaine.

oking south over the shrub savanna of the Accra Plains near the University Experimental Farm at Nungua. The
egetation is fire controlled and locally described as 'peppercorn tree savanna'. December. Photo G. B. Reynolds.

oking northwest across the western edge of the Accra plains to the Akwapim hills from the University of Ghana,
gon. July. Photo L. G. Grimes.

Looking eastwards across the Accra Plains from the foot of the Akwapim hills with the Shai Hills in the far distance. Jul_
Photo L. G. Grimes.

Ningo hill on the Accra Plains from Shai hills with *Combretum* and *Terminalia* spp. Photo Dr. M. D. Swaine.

The Guinea Savanna Woodland (area c. 146,000 km^2)

This covers the whole of Ghana north of the forest zone except for the northeast corner, where Sudan savanna woodland occurs. In 1975 the Guinea Savanna Woodland was estimated to contain c. 8800 km^2 (6% of total area) and c. 84,000 km^2 (57% of total area) of reserved and unreserved woodlands respectively. The annual depletion rate of the unreserved woodland was then c. 1000 km^2. The Guinea savanna woodland has a low human population due to the poor soils, and consequently the vegetation, although secondary as a result of grazing and cultivation, is less actively degraded.

Hopkins (1974) divides the Guinea savanna zone into 4 types, each of which is met in turn in Ghana as one moves northwards. In *savanna woodland* there is a mixture of trees and shrub species which form a light canopy, often less than 15 m high. In *tree savanna* the trees and shrubs reach similar heights to those in savanna woodland but are well scattered and pure communities of one species of tree often exist. In *shrub savanna* there are no trees and in *grass savanna* there are neither trees nor shrubs. The last 3 are often considered degraded forms of the first. Riverain or fringing forest occur along water courses in the north, but the vegetation differs from that found in the riverain forests further south; *Acacia polyacantha* and *Khaya senegalensis* (Mahogany) are typical of the northern riverain forest and *Antiaris africana, Bombax buonopozense* (Kapok) and *Chlorophora excelsa* typical of those along the forest/savanna boundary. The results of a preliminary study of the savanna in Ghana may be found in Hall & Jeník (1968).

In the Guinea Savanna the grass layer appears to be continuous, but tussock grasses are characteristic and some reach 4 m high in the wet season. Annual burning of the grass occurs (between December and April) and the trees are fire resistant. Because of the more intense heat produced by fires at the end of the dry season, controlled early burning (beginning of the dry season) is used in forest reserves to protect trees against accidental fires later in the dry season. After the fires, but before the rains, trees come into new leaf and some flower, and fresh grass appears. The foliage density increases with the rains and the grasses flower and seed. In the dry season the soil is baked hard and the early rains run off the surface and most is lost to the soil (Lane 1962).

The Sudan Zone (area c. 2700 km^2)

This occurs only in the northeast corner of Ghana. The annual rainfall (50–100 cm) is confined to a 7-month period (March to September), although most falls in August and September. In uncultivated or ungrazed areas the vegetation consists of open grassland with scattered deciduous trees, some of which are broadleaved and found in the Guinea Savanna zone, others being fine-leaved Acacias. Human population is, however, usually quite dense, with a pattern of family units rather than villages, resulting in a more settled agriculture, and in vegetation which is highly modified through over cultivation and grazing by cattle and goats. The only common trees are the economic ones such as the Boabab *Adansonia digitata,* the Sheabutter tree *Butyrospermum paradoxum* and *Acacia* species. The grasses produce a less complete cover and are shorter than in the Guinea Savanna zone, fires as a result being less severe (Taylor 1960; Baker 1962).

The Southern Marginal or Coastal Thicket Zone (area c. 2360 km^2)

This extends as a triangular strip (about 160 km long) whose apex is just east of Takoradi and whose base, some 30 km or so wide, lies just west of Accra and along the base of the Akwapim hills to Akosombo. None of this zone is covered by forest except for a few forest reserves and sacred groves, a notable one, Amoawa Hill, lying between Winneba and Mankesim. Similar vegetation occurs on localised hills within

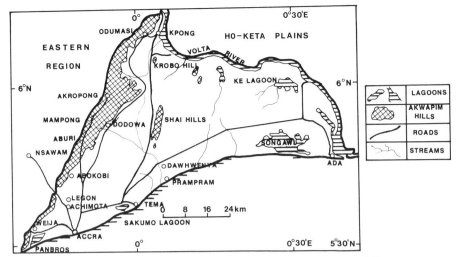

Figure 11. The towns of the Accra Plains and the Akwapim hills.

the forest zone with high rainfall (Hall & Swaine 1981). The vegetation consists of dense scrub tangle (average height 4–5 m) with little grass and some scattered taller forest trees. It is possible that forest existed over much of the area before it was destroyed by centuries of farming and firewood extraction.

The Accra–Ho–Keta Plains (area c. 11,000 km^2)

The Accra Plains (area c. 4000 km^2) stretch from Accra eastwards to the Volta river and northwards to the Akwapim hills (Fig. 11). Today they are basically grassland with a variable development of thicket and scrub and scattered trees. There is a similar tract of land surrounding Winneba some 50 km west of Accra and this extends westwards towards Apam. Although there are many similarities between the avifauna of these 2 areas there are notable differences, the most obvious being the absence of the Long-tailed Shrike *Corvinella corvina* from the Winneba Plains. The avifauna of the Winneba plains is not as well known as that of the Accra Plains for a meaningful comparison to be made, but it would make an interesting study. About 30% of the Accra Plains is covered with short tussocky grass (basal coverage never greater than 25% and height rarely exceeding 80 cm) in which thickets and tree clumps, which occupy the sites of old termite mounds, are sparsely scattered, the characteristic trees being *Fagara xanthoxyloides* and *Elaeophorbia drupifera*. The whole area is very heavily grazed and swept annually by fire. Extensive thickets occur inland along the base of the Akwapim hills, but since the 1960s they have been greatly reduced through farming and security requirements (Lawson & Jeník 1967).

There is much evidence to suggest that forest once grew out onto the plains along the base of the Akwapim hills. In 1786, P. E. Isert found the Akwapim hills covered in "majestic trees and inpenetrable bush" with "trees of unbelievable circumference" reaching 4·6 m in diameter. A hundred years later little had changed, Shelley & Buckley (1872) found the bush at Abokobi, which is on the plains, so dense that they were unable to obtain birds and collected instead 50 species of butterflies in one morning. Recently, in an important study on the mammalian fauna of the plains, Booth (1959) concluded that the savanna species represented a recent invasion onto the plains rather than a relic group and suggested that the vegetation had been vastly different from the present. Lawson & Jeník (1967) studied the micro-climate within one of the tree clumps found on the Accra Plains and their data support the suggestion that thicket or even woodland would cover the plains in the absence of fires. Fairly heavy forest certainly occurred until the 1920s within 14 km of Accra on both the Dodowa and Nsawam roads (Miles 1955). In the annual report (1923/1924) of the Department of Forests, a reserve in existing forest near Dodowa (180 km²) and another near Odumasi–Krobo (130 km²) were proposed, but were prevented through local politics from being established. In 1945 C. M. Morrison recorded the Grey Hornbill *Tockus nasutus* for the first time at Akropong, and wondered whether this was due to the cutting down of the forest on the ridge. In contrast, both Riis and Reichenow in the 1850s and 1870s recorded the forest trogon *Apaloderma narina* there. Today the whole area is essentially bare of large trees. There are, however, local fetish groves (c. 1–2 ha) used for indigenous ceremonies, which are protected from fire and felling activities. A notable one lies just northeast of Kwabenya and another at Dodowa. They appear as small islands of relic forest surrounded by grassland and support the view that past vegetation was forest. The most positive evidence, however, for the previous existence of forest is the presence of old nests of the Yellow-headed Rockfowl *Picathartes gymnocephalus* (discovered by D. W. Lamm, M. T. Horwood and G. B. Reynolds) in a gully at the foot of the hills near the Accra to Aburi road; these were still visible in 1975.

On isolated inselbergs, mainly on the Accra Plains and near Dodowa, is found the *south-east outlier* forest-type of Hall & Swaine (1972, 1981). It contains relatively few species, maximum 40, some of which are not known elsewhere in West Africa. Most of it is protected but the main threat to its survival is the demand for firewood.

The Ho–Keta Plains, c. 7000 km², lie east of the Volta river and stretch south from Ho to the coastline, and eastwards to the Ghana/Togo border. The vegetation of this zone is similar to the Guinea Savanna woodland.

The Coastline

Waves pound the coast of Ghana continuously. Between Cape Three Points and Accra, there is a succession of bays, in which the rocks have been readily eroded and sand has been deposited, and headlands, of no significant height, have been formed from harder rocks. On either side of this stretch of coastline, the land is much flatter near the sea, and lagoons tend to form when river mouths are 'ponded' up (Boateng 1959) by the surf and currents. The lagoons near the mouth of the river Volta are particularly large and are part of its delta (Boateng 1959).

Bordering the coastline, more extensively near the mouths of rivers, is saline vegetation with mangroves and bare salt flats. The lagoons at the mouths of rivers east of Cape Coast, except for those of the Densu and Volta, are only open to the sea after periods of heavy rain. As a result their salt content fluctuates considerably between the dry and wet seasons. In saline conditions the tree *Laguncularia racemosa* and the Red Mangrove *Rhizophora racemosa* grow, while on the landward side of a lagoon the Black Mangrove *Avicennia nitida* is found. Large areas around lagoons are covered with the reed *Cyperus articulatus* and reed mace *Typha australis,* and along the shore line are coconut groves (*Cocos nucifera*).

Man-made or man-induced habitats

Mention has been made of the extensive shore line of the Volta Dam lake and the area of land exposed between its wet and dry season water levels. The potential of the habitat for *Acrocephalus* species and other Palaearctic migrants should be high judging from data collected at smaller dams in the north and south of Ghana (Walsh & Grimes 1981), but as yet the lake has few Anatidae (Roux & Jarry 1984). The Bui Dam, situated just northeast of Wenchi, should also provide similar habitat. In addition, there are innumerable small irrigation dams and small reservoirs throughout both the forest and savanna areas, and there are relatively large irrigation developments, mainly for rice growing, at Dawhenya on the Accra Plains, at Vea near Bolgatanga, and at Tono just north of Navrongo, both these latter in the north. The Tono irrigation lake provides permanent open water of several square miles and the irrigated area extends some 25 km down stream from the lake. All-the-year-round cropping is now possible and a new habitat for the area has resulted (R. Passmore). Sewage farms, such as the one at Kumasi, are also an attractive bird habitat. During years when extensive rain falls (e.g. 1968) in the Volta basin, the flood gates of the Volta dam remain open for several weeks in September and October. The resulting flow of water and turbulence is quite impressive, and spray fills the valley. During this period, hundreds of terns (mainly Black Tern *Sterna nigra*) surface feed over the turbulent water at the base of the dam wall. Only the occasional tern is seen there when the overflow gates are closed.

The granite used in the building of Tema harbour in the late 1950s and early 1960s came from the Shai Hills on the Accra Plains (Fig. 11). Two quarries were opened, in 1954 and 1955, and were abandoned after completion of the harbour in 1968. The largest, Mampong quarry, just south of the main block of hills, now has 3 breeding species, 2 of which were apparently not present in the 1950s. Lamm & Horwood (1958) recorded the Rock-loving Cisticola *Cisticola aberrans,* but did not see 2 other more conspicuous species now present, namely the Mottled Swift *Apus aequatorialis* and the White-crowned Robin-Chat *Cossypha albicapilla*. The break-waters of Tema harbour have been utilized as roosting sites for terns, in particular the Roseate Tern *Sterna dougallii,* which was located there in numbers by A. J. M. Smith and N. P. E. Langham in February and March 1970.

A "saltwater lake" some 10 km west of Accra was an important site for water birds in C. A. Gordon's day (1849). A small salt industry (Panbros) there, where salt is produced by evaporating sea water, was greatly expanded in the early 1960s. Large areas of lagoons on the eastern side of the Densu river were converted into saltpans, each c. 0·25 ha, and the numbers of herons, waders and terns that gather there are quite impressive (Grimes 1969b, 1972a, 1974b, 1977b); they were not there in such numbers during the 1950s (D. W. Lamm). Other salt pans, not as large as at Accra, occur between Cape Coast and Elmina, at Apam and at several small sites along the coast east of Accra; larger pans occur at Songaw lagoon (Fig. 11).

The electrification of southern Ghana, during the development of the Volta hydro-electric project, required numerous high pylons. These were constructed during 1963 and 1964 and stretch along the coastal areas to Cape Coast and on to Takoradi and have provided excellent nest sites, in areas devoid of large trees, for the Red-necked Buzzard *Buteo auguralis,* the Black Kite *Milvus migrans* and the Pied Crow *Corvus alba*. Crows were first noticed using pylons in 1964. In June 1969 at least 31 of the pylons visible from the road between Accra and Cape Coast were used by crows and this had increased to 52 in June 1970. Use of pylons on the Accra Plains has not been so rapid although they were among the first to be built; 15 were used as nest sites in 1970 and 13 in 1971.

Road works throughout the country have included bridges and culverts and these have provided nest sites for swifts and swallows. Telegraph poles and the associated wires provide foraging perches for rollers and kingfishers, especially in treeless tracts, and the poles for resting perches for birds of prey. Earthroads are used frequently by nocturnal species, such as nightjars, for foraging.

Important man-induced habitats have resulted from the development of old residential areas in the major towns and cities, such as in Accra and Kumasi, from the lay-out of the University campuses at Legon, Kumasi and Cape Coast together with their botanical gardens, and from the several golf courses that have been created within the forest zone, mainly at centres of the diamond, gold and timber industries. These maintained parklands provide a variety of habitats from close cropped grassy

Table 3. List of forest reserves which are now wildlife reserves. Data from Hall & Swaine (1981)

Reserve	Location	Area km^2	Date of establishment
Tonton	6°00′N 2°05′W	146·3	1936
Totua Shelterbelt	5°55′N 2°23′W	63·5	1941
Upper Wasaw	6°07′N 2°13′W	100·8	1925
Volta River	6°11′N 0°01′E	50·5	1928
Wawahi	5°40′N 1°06′W	138·9	1929
Worobong Kwahu	6°31′N 0°33′W	55·2	1930
Worobong North	6°37′N 0°26′W	13·2	1927
Worobong South	6°28′N 0°28′W	106·2	1929
Yaya	7°27′N 2°08′W	51·2	1930
Yenku	5°24′N 0°43′W	21·2	1937
Yogaga	6°11′N 0°03′E	0·8	1957
Yongwa	6°13′N 0°03′E	7·8	1957
Yoyo	5°55′N 2°48′W	235·7	1932

Table 4. The area and locations of the National Parks (N.P.), Game Production Reserves (G.P.R.) and Wildlife Sanctuaries (W.S.) that have been established in Ghana. See Fig. 5 for their approximate positions. Data partly taken from Hall & Swaine (1981)

Name	Year of establishment	Area km^2	Location
1. Mole N.P.	1971	486·4	9°15′N 01°50′W
2. Bui N.P.	1971	204·9	8°30′N 02°20′W
3. Digya N.P.	1971	307·2	7°30′N 00°15′W
4. Kogyae Strict Nature Reserve	1971	30·7	7°20′N 01°10′W
5. Shai Hills G.P.R.	1971	54·4	6°00′N 00°00′
6. Owabi W.S.	1971	14·5	6°44′N 01°42′W
7. Bia N.P.	1974	77·7	6°20′N 03°00′W
8. Bia G.P.R.	1974	227·9	6°29′N 03°06′W
9. Kalakpa Falls G.P.R.	1975	32·0	6°25′N 00°25′E
10. Gbele G.P.R.	1975	38·4	10°20′N 02°10′W
11. Nini-Suhien N.P.	1976	174·5	5°20′N 02°30′W
12. Ankasa G.P.R.	1976	348·7	5°30′N 02°30′W
13. Bomfobiri W.S.	1976	50·0	6°57′N 01°10′W

areas, hedgerows, roads lined with flowering trees to areas of closed canopy, together with a variety of building structures. A visitor to the administrative capital Accra would not suspect that in 1909 the city was almost devoid of trees (Miles 1955). Neem and Cassia trees became established only in 1921 after the availability of piped water. Today, the older residential areas are well wooded and the avifauna enriched since the days of Winterbottom (1933).

The above influences may rightly be considered as providing positive contributions to the avifauna and making it more accessible to an observer. Man's influence, however, has not always been positive; the destruction of the forests and their replacement by crops is a notable example, although there are some 200 forest reserves, 13 of which are wildlife reserves (Table 3). Nevertheless, forest clearings left to fallow form a forest-edge type habitat which has its own distinctive avifauna. Lowe (1937: 349) noted that cocoa plantations "seldom held anything of interest", the major reason being that they are effectively managed monocultures. Although their avifauna is noticeably less rich than that of the surrounding forest, specific comparisons have not been made. The probable major contributing factor to the difference is the twice yearly spraying of the cocoa crop with gamma BHC — a chlorinated hydrocarbon. This insecticide is applied in June and July and again in November and December, and on each occasion the crop receives two sprays at 28 day intervals (Wood 1975). As a result the insect fauna, although potentially as rich as that of the surrounding forest (see earlier), is not available as a food source.

Finally mention must be made of the strenuous efforts made by the Department of Game and Wild Life to establish a variety of game reserves within Ghana (Table 4, Fig. 5). Further reserves in the Western, Brong Ahafo and Ashanti Regions are planned, together with a Marine National Park. Such praiseworthy activities are fraught with difficulties and frustrations, and receive little immediate thanks in return; in 1974, the Bia National Park, for example, covered an area of 305 km^2, but within 3 years was reduced to only c. 80 km^2 (Hall & Swaine 1981).

BIOLOGICAL SEASONS IN FOREST AND SAVANNA

Within tropical Africa it is generally agreed that the breeding seasons of birds are governed by food supply and that this acts both as a proximate and ultimate factor (Maclean 1976; Sinclair 1978; see Earlé 1981 for recent savanna data). It is also usual to assume that rainfall is the main factor controlling food supply, and the traditional approach when discussing biological seasons within the tropics, in particular those of birds, is to divide the year into dry and wet seasons, according to the rainfall and humidity.

Recent studies on insect phenology in Ghana, however, have indicated that this approach is far too simple, at least for the forest region. Gibbs & Leston (1970) studied insect population in cocoa plantations within the forest region at Tafo, and analysed the data on the forest trees of Ghana given in Taylor (1960). They identified 6 seasons that were characterised by both biological and physical events:

(1) A *dry sunny season* between late November and mid-February, which includes the harmattan period, during which fruit production is at a maximum and fruit-feeding and seed-feeding insects are abundant.

(2) The *first wet sunny season* between late February and late May when sunshine is rather less than in the *dry sunny season* but radiation at ground level more intense due to the absence of harmattan dust. In this period there is maximum leaf production and leaf-feeding insects and their predators are abundant. Maximum breakdown of leaf litter occurs and litter-feeding and fungus-feeding insects are abundant.

(3) *The first wet dull season* in June and July during which leaf-feeders and their predators decline in numbers but timber-boring insects are abundant.

(4) *The dry dull season* in August in which cloud cover is at a maximum. Biologically it is similar to the wet dull season.

(5) *The second wet dull season* in late August to mid-October when insects that feed on cocoa pods are now in abundance and timber-boring insects are still available as a food source.

(6) *The second wet sunny period* in late October to mid-November when leaf production reaches a sub-maximum and there is a corresponding increase in insect leaf-feeders and their predators.

Most deciduous species of the forest zone do not begin to shed their leaves until they are sexually mature, and this also applies to those individuals growing outside the microclimate of the forest. The complexity of the situation is well illustrated by the Silk Cotton *Ceiba pentandra,* which, although not indigenous, is of ancient origin and is now a typical emergent tree, especially near settlements. At varying times between October and March, individual Silk Cotton trees lose all their leaves. Those that are not going to flower and fruit grow fresh leaves after only a short bare period, whereas in sexually mature trees leaves only appear much later and after the fruiting period. Additional to this, some individual trees may show both conditions simultaneously (Taylor 1960). Some other deciduous trees in Ghana are known to shed their leaves and renew them 3–4 times a year, others twice a year, in the March–April and the late September–November periods. Using the data in Taylor (1960), Gibbs & Leston (1970) found that between 35 and 42 species were bare of leaves in each of the drier months December–February. They concluded that in a semi-deciduous forest a large proportion of tree species, whether deciduous or not, have a major flushing period, when new shoots and young leaves fully expand in quick succession, in *the first wet sunny season* (late February to late May). A second flush in *the second wet sunny season* (late October to mid-November) appears to vary in importance from one area of the forest to the next.

Although some fruiting trees were present throughout the year, the number of species fruiting at any time increased approximately linearly from 15 out of 158 in June to 80 out of 158 in the following March, and then rapidly decreased to the previous June level (Gibbs & Leston 1970). The periods of flowering and fruiting vary with the tree species and are usually annual events. Some, however, flower and fruit twice a year (e.g. *Combretodendron africanum*); others flower and fruit errati-cally (e.g. *Triphochiton scleroxylon*), and yet others have semi-continuous flowering and fruiting throughout the year, although the latter are not canopy species. A high degree of synchronization of flowering over a wide area within the forest zone does occur in some species (e.g. *Oxyanthus pallidus, O. formosus*) (Taylor 1960; Hall & Swaine 1981).

Gibbs & Leston (1970) found that insects, which depend for food on fruit and leaves, have maximum numbers in the 3 sunny seasons, their abundance responding directly to the seasonal changes in their food supply. Seasonal change occurred in populations of most insect species examined and in every month some species were in a period of major increase. Insect population curves were often bimodal, with peaks in the first and second wet sunny periods. Bigger (1976) also worked at Tafo and found oscillations in the insect populations were regular and, in addition, that the amplitude of the cycle was comparable to that found in temperate insect populations. In the equatorial forests of Sarawak, Fogden (1972) found a clear correlation between rainfall, leaf production and insect abundance.

In the Guinea Savanna woodland, leaf shedding is the norm during the dry season, and following the annual fires there is a flush of new leaves before the main rains. Some trees are, however, evergreen (e.g. Mahogany *Khaya senegalensis*) and others (e.g. *Acacia albida*) shed their leaves in the wet season and have leaves throughout the dry season. In most indigenous trees and shrubs, flowering occurs in well defined periods. Some flower in the first half of the dry season and seeds are produced in time for the early rains. The majority, however, flower in the second half of the dry season and at the beginning of the rains (Taylor 1960; Pettet 1977). In the coastal savanna areas that have a double peaked rainfall pattern, such as on the Accra Plains and eastwards to Dahomey, the situation is more complex. Yanney-Ewusie (1968) studied 100 tree species from 26 families over a period of 3 years, mainly at the University campus at Legon, and found that flowering and fruiting took place once a year in 48 species, twice a year in 44 species, 3 times a year in 6 species, 4 times a year in *Terminalia catappa* and throughout the year in the shrub *Lawsoni inernis*. East of Legon on the Accra Plains, Rose Innes & Mabey (1964) found that the timing and amount of flowering and fruiting depended on the severity of the dry season and that, in general, they occurred twice a year in *Antiaris africana* and *Millettia thonningii,* but not in every year.

The insect populations, excluding ants and termites, in savanna woodland near Lamto (6°13′N, 5°02′W) studied by Gillon & Gillon (1967), were greatly reduced during the dry season and reached a minimum just before the bush fires in January and February. Their biomass and numbers increased rapidly during the rains and reached a peak value at times which varied from one group to another. Fluctuations in insect populations in savanna south of Nairobi, Kenya, which has a 2 peaked rainfall pattern similar to coastal areas of central and eastern Ghana, have been detected by Owen (1969). The major increase was in the biomass rather than numbers and coincided with the main rains, followed by a smaller peak in the shorter rains.

Sinclair's (1978) work in the Acacia woodland of the Serengeti (2°S, 34°E) is of relevant interest. He found 2 peaks in insect abundance which could be correlated with a 2-peaked rainfall pattern. However, unlike the broad leaved species which have fresh growth before the rains, the acacias do not have a flush and the build up in insect numbers coinciding with the first rains was due to wind borne insects brought in on the leading edge of the ITCZ. In contrast to this, the flush of new leaves in broad-leaved species leads to an increase in insect abundance before the rains which is reflected in an earlier start to the beeeding season for birds than in acacia wood-land (Reynolds 1968; Sinclair 1978). Broad-leaved species predominate in northern Ghana, apart from the extreme northeast where acacia species are more abundant. The work in east Africa suggests that insectivorous birds should begin breeding before the rains. The movement of the ITCZ is a regular feature of West Africa and presumably wind borne insects are present; but their importance to the feeding and breeding ecology of birds has not been studied apart from their importance to migrating raptors (Thiollay 1978).

BREEDING DATA

The breeding data used have been extracted mainly from the literature. Each breeding record was assigned to the month in which it was established that egg-laying began. This proved not too difficult for those records involving either eggs or females with well formed eggs in their oviducts; but there was the inevitable uncertainty for records involving parental care. No use has been made of records involving males with either enlarged testes or in breeding dress, nor of records involving nest building.

Nearly all the data have been gathered by observers as opportunity arose, and were not collected systematically. Of the 263 non-passerine species suspected of breeding in Ghana (Table 5), breeding information is available for 54% (141), and for 62% (172) of the 278 passerine species (Table 6). Much of the information consists only of single records or of data collected in different years and from widely spaced areas within Ghana, and consequently is of limited usefulness. The picture that emerges is that of the breeding activity in particular habitats rather than the breeding habits of any individual species.

All the available breeding data from the coastal region have been divided into sections for insectivorous birds (Fig. 12a), which include all Ploceidae and Estrildinae that feed their young on insects or their larvae, for raptors and scavengers (Fig. 12b), and for the wetland and ground nesting birds (Fig. 12c). The data for the northern savanna (Fig. 12d) and the forest region (Fig. 12e) are insufficient to warrant division into 3 groups.

Individual species whose breeding activities have been studied in Ghana include wetland species (Bowen et al. 1962; Grimes 1972a; Macdonald 1977a), Black Kite Milvus migrans (Macdonald 1980d), Shikra Accipiter badius (B. Schmidt in Grimes 1972a), Kakelaar Phoeniculus purpureus (Grimes 1975b), Yellow-billed Shrike Corvinella corvina (Grimes 1979a,b, 1980), Fiscal Shrike Lanius collaris (Macdonald 1980b), Heuglin's Masked Weaver Ploceus heuglini (Grimes 1973b), Red-headed Quelea Quelea erythropus (Grimes 1977c), combassous and their estrildine hosts (Macdonald 1980a). All these studies were carried out in southern Ghana which has a markedly contrasting wet and dry season. Of particular interest were the studies of

Table 5. The breeding data for Ghanaian Non-Passerine birds

Family	Total spp.	Breeding data (B + B?)	B	Dry	Breeding season Wet	Protracted	?
Podicipedidae	1	1	1	—	—	1	—
Pelecanidae	2	1	—	—	—	—	—
Phalacrocoracidae	2	1	1	—	1	—	—
Anhingidae	1	1	1	—	1	—	—
Ardeidae	18	15	12	1	11	—	—
Scopidae	1	1	—	—	—	—	—
Ciconiidae	8	4	3	3	—	—	—
Threskiornithidae	6	4	—	—	—	—	—
Anatidae	16	6	4	1	3	—	—
Accipitridae	45	31	18	13	—	4	1
Falconidae	9	6	4	3	—	—	1
Phasianidae	11	9	5	4	—	1	—
Turnicidae	3	2	1	1	—	—	—
Rallidae	12	10	8	—	6	2	—
Heliornithidae	1	1	—	—	—	—	—
Otidae	4	2	1	1	—	—	—
Jacanidae	1	1	1	—	1	—	—
Rostratulidae	1	1	—	—	—	—	—
Recurvirostridae	2	1	1	—	1	—	—
Burhinidae	3	2	—	—	—	—	—
Glareolidae	7	5	3	1	1	—	1
Charadriidae	15	8	4	—	4	—	—
Laridae	22	1	1	—	1	—	—
Rhynchopidae	1	1	—	—	—	—	—
Pteroclididae	1	1	1	1	—	—	—
Columbidae	17	15	8	3	2	2	1
Psittacidae	7	7	3	—	4	—	—
Musophagidae	5	5	1	—	—	1	—
Cuculidae	19	16	9	—	6	2	1
Tytonidae	1	1	1	1	—	—	—
Strigidae	14	14	4	4	—	—	—
Caprimulgidae	9	6	2	1	—	—	1
Apodidae	12	9	4	—	2	—	2
Coliidae	1	1	—	—	—	—	—
Trogonidae	1	1	—	—	—	—	—
Alcedinidae	12	12	7	2	4	1	—
Meropidae	11	7	5	4	1	—	—
Coraciidae	6	4	2	1	1	—	—
Upupidae	1	1	—	—	—	—	—
Phoeniculidae	4	4	2	—	1	1	—
Bucerotidae	12	12	8	6	—	1	1
Capitonidae	13	13	9	6	—	3	—
Indicatoridae	7	7	2	1	1	—	—
Picidae	13	12	4	4	—	—	—
Totals	**358**	**263**	**141**	**62**	**51**	**19**	**9**

Not included in the total species are 44 species from 11 families which have no breeding representative in Ghana

B Breeding proven

B? Breeding not proven

(B + B?) Total number of species suspected of breeding

? Breeding season uncertain

the 2 shrikes and the Kakelaar, which were found to have extended breeding seasons covering both the wet and dry periods. The only months in which eggs were not laid by both shrikes were those during which moult in the population was at a maximum. One group of Kakelaars nested successfully at Legon on 3 separate occasions in

Table 6. The breeding data for Ghanaian Passerine birds

Family	Total spp.	Breeding data (B + B?)	B	Dry	Breeding season Wet	Protracted	?
Eurylaimidae	2	2	—	—	—	—	—
Pittidae	1	1	—	—	—	—	—
Alaudidae	5	5	2	1	1	—	—
Hirundinidae	18	15	13	1	5	4	3
Motacillidae	9	4	3	—	2	1	—
Campephagidae	5	5	2	1	—	—	1
Pycnonotidae	24	24	12	1	1	5	5
Laniidae	21	18	12	1	4	6	1
Muscicapidae							
Turdinae	22	14	9	2	1	1	5
Timaliinae	8	8	3	1	—	2	—
Picathartinae	1	1	1	—	1	—	—
Sylviinae	46	33	27	1	8	9	9
Muscicapinae	18	15	6	—	3	2	1
Platysteirinae	8	8	5	1	1	2	1
Monarchinae	8	8	4	—	1	1	2
Remizidae	2	2	1	1	—	—	—
Paridae	2	2	2	—	—	2	—
Certhiidae	1	1	1	1	—	—	—
Nectariniidae	23	22	11	1	4	5	1
Zosteropidae	1	1	1	—	—	1	—
Emberizidae	3	3	2	1	1	—	—
Fringillidae	3	3	1	—	—	1	—
Estrildidae	28	27	15	3	7	4	1
Ploceidae							
Bubalornithinae	1	1	1	—	—	—	1
Passerinae	4	4	4	1	1	1	1
Ploceinae	28	25	21	3	13	4	1
Viduinae	7	7	2	—	2	—	—
Sturnidae	12	11	5	—	3	1	1
Oriolidae	3	3	2	—	—	—	2
Dicruridae	3	3	2	1	—	1	—
Corvidae	2	2	2	—	2	—	—
Totals	**319**	**278**	**172**	**22**	**61**	**53**	**36**

B Breeding proven
B? Breeding not proven
(B + B?) Total number of species suspected of breeding
? Breeding season uncertain

1972 — January to March, May to July and September to November. Comparably, the breeding season at Legon of the Splendid Sunbird *Nectarinia coccinigaster* population lasts throughout the year and consecutive broods have been found in the same nest.

The only forest species that has been studied in any detail in Ghana is the Yellow-headed Rockfowl *Picathartes gymnocephalus* and then only at one breeding colony (Grimes 1964; Grimes & Darko 1968). Although birds were not individually marked, the evidence suggested that it has 2 distinct breeding seasons in a year, one from March to May and the second from September to November, which is in marked contrast to the protracted breeding season which is usually assumed to be the norm for equatorial forest species (and see Fig. 12e). In Gabon, for example, Brosset (1971a, 1981a) found that the Green-tailed Bristle-bill *Bleda eximia* had a protracted breeding season, though, in contrast, the sympatric Yellow-whiskered

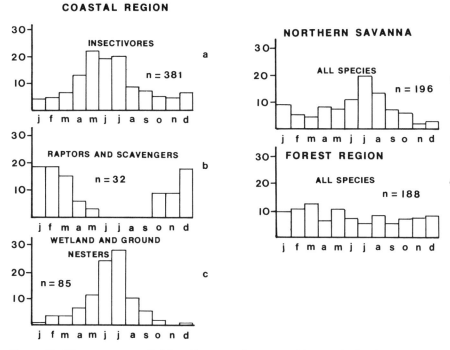

Figure 12. The percentage of all breeding records expressed in months for the coastal region (a,b,c), and for the northern savanna (d) and the forest region (e).

Bulbul *Andropadus latirostris* had only a short single breeding season (Brosset 1981b).

The results of the analysis for the coastal and northern savanna regions (Fig. 12) contain no surprises and are similar to those for other tropical areas which have climatic and vegetational zones similar to Ghana's. Thus insectivorous birds breed throughout the year, but have a peak laying period just prior to and during the main wet season when the biomass and numbers of potential prey increase rapidly and reach a maximum (see previous section). The extended breeding seasons of the Kakelaar and the 2 shrikes imply that food availability is not a critical factor for them and this is undoubtedly helped by the wide variety of prey they take, at least in the case of the shrikes. In all of these species parental care is prolonged (7 or 8 weeks or more) and it is of interest that elsewhere in the tropics, such as in Sarawak (Fogden 1972: 322) and in the Serengeti (Sinclair 1978: 494), when this has been found to occur, it has been interpreted to mean that food was short. The long breeding season of the Splendid Sunbird is not surprising as flowering shrubs and trees are present in varying degrees throughout the year at Legon (Yanney-Ewusie 1968). However, in contrast to this, the sympatric Copper Sunbird *Nectarinia cuprea* has a restricted breeding season during the main rains, after which the males moult into a non-breeding dress. Raptors and scavengers breed during the dry season, often towards its end, and some Black Kite and Shikra are double brooded at Legon and Cape Coast and have large nestlings in late May (B. Schmidt *in* Grimes 1972a; Macdonald 1977b). Similar data have been obtained by Thiollay (1976) in the savanna of the Ivory Coast. He found that the dry season breeding preference by raptors coincided with an increase in numbers and accessibility of their major prey species. Fledglings were present from February to mid June during which there was a peak in food and the growth of grasses was incomplete. The wetland and ground nesting species breed mainly after the main rains, with a peak laying period, at least in the coastal area, in late June, July and early August. The vegetation then is rich and would provide cover and nesting material whenever necessary.

Unfortunately the data for the forest region (Fig. 12e) are inadequate to make any meaningful comparison with the 6 biological/physical seasons of Gibbs & Leston (1970), which should always be taken into account in any future breeding study of a forest species despite the extreme difficulty of the task. The apparent biannual breeding of the rockfowl is of interest, since the first breeding period (March to May) coincides with the *first wet sunny period* of Gibbs & Leston, in which litter-feeding insects are abundant, and the second (September to November) overlaps the *second wet dull* and the *second wet sunny period,* the latter being in many ways biologically similar to the *first wet sunny period.* Thiollay (1971) also found apparent biannual breeding in 2 forest species in the Ivory Coast: the Fire-bellied Woodpecker *Mesopicos pyrrhogaster* nested in the period February–April and again in October and November, and the White-browed Forest Flycatcher *Fraseria cinerascens* in January and February and again from May to August. Closer analysis shows that the present data indicate that insectivorous forest birds nest in each month of the year and this is not unexpected, Gibbs & Leston having shown that in every month some of the insect species they studied were in a period of major increase. There is a slight hint that breeding activity is least at the height of the main rains, during the *wet dull season,* when leaf-feeding insects and their predators decline in numbers, but this is possibly an artifact of the available data. Until the breeding seasons of individual species are studied and their diets known, one may only speculate on the implications of the 6 seasons described by Gibbs & Leston in relation to forest species.

MIGRATION

The area of West Africa south of the Saharan desert acts effectively as an island for land birds; on its north, at c. 17°N latitude, is the desert and on its south, at c. 5°N, is the Atlantic Ocean. Most of Ghana's land mass lies just west of the Greenwich meridian, approximately midway along the Guinea coastline, and stretches northwards from the coast to latitude 10°N.

The migratory status of the birds occurring in Ghana has been deduced from data collected systematically and regularly at certain localities using mist nets or censuses or both (Grimes 1972a, Accra; Greig-Smith 1977a, Mole; Macdonald 1977a, 1978a, 1979a, Cape Coast; Walsh & Grimes 1981, Bolgatanga and Accra). Other data have been collected as opportunities arose for observers to stay for shorter periods at different locations. Statements may be made confidently for Palaearctic species which spend the northern winter in Ghana (apart from those few with Afrotropical populations) and also for those Afrotropical species that are either transequatorial migrants or migrants within the northern tropics, both of which are absent from Ghana during a part of the year. However, difficulties of interpretation of the data remain and these have been usefully raised and discussed by Greig-Smith (1978b) and Taylor & Macdonald (1979b). A census study at Mole provided Greig-Smith with sufficient data for a seasonal analysis of 82 of the 269 Afrotropical species that have been recorded there. The numbers herein are different from his but agree with the list of species he gives. He identified 6 groupings for the 82 species:

- (A) Resident species (46), with no obvious change in abundance or frequency of occurrence throughout the year.
- (B) Species wholly migrant (5), present at Mole only in the dry season: *Pterocles quandricinctus, Coracius abyssinica, Anthreptes platura, Emberiza tahapisi, Oriolus auratus.*

(C) Species wholly migrant (2), present in the wet season only: *Dendrocygna viduata, Eurystomus glaucurus.*

(D) Partial migrants (9), which augment resident populations of the same species in the dry season: *Scopus umbretta, Milvus migrans, Streptopelia vinacea, Tockus nasutus, Emberiza cabanisi, Passer griseus, Petronia dentata, Lamprotornis chalybeus, L. purpureus.*

(E) Partial migrants (12) which augment resident populations of the same species in the wet season: *Bostrychia hagedash, Numida meleagris, Mirafra rufocinnamomea, Campephaga phoenicea, Prionops plumata, Laniarius barbarus, Malaconotus sulfureopectus, Turdus pelios, Nectarinia cuprea, Terpsiphone viridis, Estrilda melpoda, Ploceus cucullatus.*

(F) Passage migrants (8) only recorded for brief periods but at the same time each year: *Ardeola ibis, Buteo auguralis, Merops albicollis, M. nubicus, Coracias cyanogaster, C. naevia, Cinnyricinclus leucogaster, Corvus alba.*

Although some of these placements have been questioned (Macdonald 1978d; Taylor & Macdonald 1978a), they usefully summarize the likely groupings into which savanna species may be placed. However, in savannas at other latitudes, the allotted grouping of many of the species would be different from that at Mole, since many of the 82 species listed are known to make north–south movements to and from their breeding ground in West Africa. Thus on the Accra Plains, for example, *Buteo augularis* and *Merops albicollis,* and most *Milvus migrans,* would be placed in grouping B (wholly migrant) rather than F (on passage) and D (partial migrant) respectively, while *Corvus alba* would be in grouping A (resident) rather than F. In addition, yearly changes in some species' migratory status may occur at one locality if the habitat quality varies sufficiently from one year to the next due to local changes in weather pattern. Differences in migratory status also may arise when climatic differences occur at different localities along the same latitude, as for instance in the coastal region between Accra and Cape Coast, which is some 160 km west of Accra; when Macdonald (1977a, 1978a, 1979a, 1980a) compared his data from Cape Coast with that of Grimes' (1972a) at Accra, differences in migratory status in *Sterna albifrons, Eurystomus gularis, Cinnyricinclus leucogaster* and *Estrilda troglodytes* were found.

Systematically collected data are available for Nigeria (see Elgood *et al.* 1973; Elgood 1982) and Ivory Coast (see publications of Thiollay) and these have been used for comparison and supplementation (where necessary) of the Ghana data. This is considered justifiable as the climate and vegetational zones of all 3 countries are essentially parallel to the same latitudes and there are no topographical barriers to any north–south movements. There are, however, fewer vegetational zones in Ghana than in Nigeria as a result of Ghana's smaller latitudinal range.

The migratory status of Ghanaian birds has been listed in Appendix 4 for each family and according to their preferred habitat following the format of Elgood *et al* (1973). An attempt has been made to distinguish between those species that are found in a wide variety of habitats (eurytopic) and those that are not (stenotopic), and Afrotropical migrants are separated from the Palaearctic (extra-African) species. These data are summarised in Tables 7 and 8. The families with Palaearctic representatives and the number of species in each are given in Table 9. The difference between the total of Palaearctic migrants to Ghana (132) in Table 9 and that under Non-breeding birds (117) in Table 7 arises because those species (15) from the Palaearctic which have Afrotropical populations are omitted from the latter table.

Of the stenotopic species, the lowland forest dwellers are not expected to migrate. One (*Pitta angolensis*) of the 205 (in Table 8) may indeed be doubtful, as there is no circumstantial evidence for long distance migration for this species in West Africa as there is in East Africa (Moreau 1966: 234). It has been collected outside the forest

Table 7. Status categories of Ghanaian birds

	Non-Passerines	Passerines
Breeding birds		
Resident	210	237
Moving within Ghana*	36	31
Afrotropical visitor	14	10
Subtotal	*260*	*278*
Uncertain status	3	4
Non-breeding birds		
Palaearctic**	86	31
Afrotropical	21	2
Subtotal	*107*	*33*
Vagrants		
Holarctic	1	0
Nearctic	3	0
Antarctic	2	0
Afrotropical	26	4
Subtotal	*32*	*4*
Total	**402 Non-passerines**	**319 Passerines**

*Including species which have resident populations
**Excluding those with Afrotropical representatives

region near Achimota but so have 2 other forest species — a francolin, *Francolinus lathami,* near to Legon (30 April 1966), and a bulbul, *Bleda canicapilla,* which flew into a lecture room of the University of Ghana (21 October 1966) at Legon. There had been no unusual weather disturbance that might have accounted for the last 2 records and significantly all 3 species have been located outside the forest in Nigeria (Elgood 1982). The other lowland forest migrant in Table 8 refers to *Merops malimbicus* (see Appendix 4, Section D) which occurs in numbers within the Ghana forests during its non-breeding season. Movements of frugivorous species within the forest region due to local food shortages and abundances elsewhere in the forest are well known. Thiollay (1970) has recently found the forest/savanna boundary at Lamto (Ivory Coast) an important resource area for them and recorded an influx between July and September of Bucerotidae, Psittacidae, Columbidae, Capitonidae, Musophagidae and Sturninae species, marked increases in numbers occurring for *Bycanistes fistulator, Psittacus erithacus* and *Treron australis.*

In contrast to the forest species, about one third (22) out of a total of 71 stenotopic savanna species migrate. Many more savanna species are eurytopic than stenotopic, having wide habitat tolerances and living in habitats whose quality varies considerably between the wet and dry seasons; they are, therefore, potentially migrant species, but surprisingly from the present data, only one quarter (77) of 309 such species are suspected of migrating (Table 8).

Of the 164 aquatic species (A in Table 8) recorded in Ghana, 92 (56%) are Afrotropical species, of which 33 migrate; of these 92, 12 are marine, but only 4 of them (*Sula bassana, Larus cirrhocephalus, Sterna balaenarium* and *Sterna maxima*) are known to migrate. The other 72 aquatic species (44%) migrate into Africa, mainly ducks (Anatidae), waders (Charadriidae, Scolopacidae) and terns (Sterninae). Radar studies at Accra and visual observations at the saltpans just west of Accra, have revealed that many, probably all, of the Charadriidae and Scolopacidae cross the Saharan desert directly in a NE direction, and probably retrace the same routes in autumn (Grimes 1974b). The radar also detected large easterly movements of

Table 8. Summary of species totals and numbers of migrants for different ecological and taxonomic groups in Ghana

	Total number of species in Ghana (a)	Extra-African species	% of (a)	African species (b)	Marine	Lowland forest	Lowland savanna stenotopic	Lowland savanna eurytopic	Total Intra-African migrants	% of (b)	% of (a)
Non-Passerines											
A: Aquatics	164	72	44%	92	12(4=33%)	10	37(20=55%)	33(9=27%)	33	36%	20%
B: Predators	70	11	16%	59		18	7	34(14=41%)	14	24%	20%
C: Ground birds	25	1	4%	24		4	1	19(10=53%)	10	41%	40%
D: Others	143	9	6%	134		52(1=2%)	6(2=33%)	76(24=32%)	27	20%	19%
Sub-total	*402*	*93*	*23%*	*309*		*84(1=1%)*	*51(22=44%)*	*162(57=35%)*	*84*	*27%*	*21%*
E: Passerines	319	31	10%	288		121(1=0.8%)	20	147(20=14%)	21	7.3%	7%
Total	**721**	**124***	**17%**	**597**	**12(4=33%)**	**205(2=0.9%)**	**71(22=31%)**	**309(77=25%)**	**105**	**17·5%**	**14·5%**
Total as a % of (b)		20·5%			2%	34%	12%	52%			

The number in brackets represents the number of migrants (and is included in each total) and its percentage of each category
*This total includes one Holarctic, three Nearctic and two Antarctic species and does not include species which have Afrotropical representatives

terns in autumn during the day and night along the inshore waters, movements which are absent in spring, suggesting that the return flight to breeding grounds takes place further off-shore beyond the range of the radar (Grimes 1977b). Two southern Atlantic Ocean birds, *Procellaria gravis* and *Oceanites oceanicus* have been collected along the Ghana shoreline, the last mentioned being regularly recorded in autumn by M. Horwood off Takoradi. The transatlantic species *Sterna fuscata* is a regular visitor from Bush Key, off southern Florida, to the off-shore waters and coastline of Ghana (see Appendix 3).

Of the remaining 238 non-passerine birds (B, C, D in Table 8), 21 are migrants from the Palaearctic and 51 migrate within Africa (Table 8). The data confirm the finding of Elgood *et al.* (1973) that a larger percentage of African species of ground birds (41%) migrate than do predators (24%) (Table 8). Thiollay's study of the movements of birds of prey, mainly in Ivory Coast but also in Ghana and Burkina Faso (Upper Volta) (Thiollay 1977, 1978), has shown that predator migration timings are closely related with the seasonal movements of the inter-tropical convergence zone (ITCZ), and he found that the numbers of birds involved were positively correlated with the abundance of grasshoppers.

The data for passerines show that few Afrotropical species migrate (21 out of 288), but this is probably an underestimate as their migration is difficult to detect. As forest species (42% of the total) are not expected to migrate, a more realistic proportion to consider would be 20 out of 167 savanna passerines (c. 12%). Not included in this total of migrating species are those many species which make shorter journeys to areas where there is a temporary abundance of food, resulting in an increase in numbers, while the food lasts, of a resident population of the same species. Such movements may be either irregular or sometimes regular in direction and timing, as Thiollay (1970) found at Lamto, Ivory Coast. After the annual burning of ground vegetation in late January, grass seeds of the previous year become accessible to granivores, and Thiollay noted a temporary influx from the north of both *Estrilda melpoda* and *Euplectes macrourus,* the increase in the latter being the more notable. The remaining migrant passerines (31) come from the Palaearctic.

Some 42 Palaearctic species ringed abroad have been found in Ghana (Appendix 3, in which the data for several tern species (*Sterna*) are so numerous that most of the details cannot be included). The data have been obtained mostly from the Euring Data Bank at Arnhem, The Netherlands, and the rest abstracted from literature not covered by the Data Bank. Great circle distances, their directions, and the time intervals between captures are given. The great circle directions taken by species that migrate over land to Ghana all lie between 9°E of S and 29°W of S (clock directions 171°–209°), but over threequarters (93) of these lie between S and 15°W of S (180°–195°). Six non-passerines recorded have journeyed to and from the Palaearctic for at least 10 years, and one of these (*Pernis apivorus*) for at least 18 years. Of the passerines, a Willow Warbler *Phylloscopus trochilus* has made the double journey at least 5 times, and a Swallow *Hirundo rustica* at least 4 times. Only one bird ringed in South Africa has been recorded in Ghana, a Turnstone *Arenaria interpres* caught near Kumasi, but many more waders from further south probably pass through Ghana than this single record suggests. Visual observations in early morning of European Swallows *Hirundo rustica,* which winter in Ghana, flying northwards near the coast at Accra in late March and early April are thought to have involved birds whose journey had originated further south (see Moreau 1972: 124).

The only ringing study in Ghana of any significance has been that of Mary Lockwood at Tafo, in the forest region (1973–1978). She ringed 8212 birds of 21 species, the bulk being *Hirundo rustica* (84%) and *Motacilla flava* wagtails (10%) (Appendix 1). Individuals of 8 species have been retrapped at Tafo in subsequent

Table 9. Species totals of Palaearctic migrants to Ghana analysed by habitat

	Total number of species, including those with Afrotropical representatives	Marine	Lagoons and wetlands	Forest	Savanna	Aerial
Non-Passerines						
Procellariidae	1	1	—	—	—	—
Hydrobatidae	2	2	—	—	—	—
Pelecanidae	1	—	1	—	—	—
Ardeidae	6	—	6	—	—	—
Ciconiidae	2	—	2	—	—	—
Threskiornithidae	1	—	1	—	—	—
Anatidae	8	—	8	—	—	—
Pandionidae	1	—	1	—	—	—
Accipitridae	9	—	—	—	9	—
Falconidae	5	—	—	—	5	—
Phasianidae	1	—	—	—	1	—
Rallidae	1	—	—	—	1	—
Haematopodidae	1	—	1	—	—	—
Recurvirostridae	2	—	2	—	—	—
Glareolidae	1	—	1	—	—	—
Charadriidae	5	—	5	—	—	—
Scolopacidae	24	—	24	—	—	—
Stercorariidae	3	3	—	—	—	—
Laridae	14	11	3	—	—	—
Columbidae	1	—	—	—	1	—
Cuculidae	2	—	—	—	2	—
Strigidae	1	—	—	—	1	—
Caprimulgidae	1	—	—	—	1	—
Apodidae	3	—	—	—	—	3
Meropidae	1	—	—	—	1	—
Coraciidae	1	—	—	—	1	—
Upupidae	1	—	—	—	1	—
Picidae	1	—	—	—	1	—
Sub-total	*100*	*17*	*55*	*0*	*25*	*3*
Passerines						
Hirundinidae	3	—	—	—	—	3
Motacillidae	5	—	2	—	3	—
Laniidae	1	—	—	—	1	—
Muscicapidae: Turdinae	7	—	1	1	5	—
Sylviinae	13	—	4	2	7	—
Muscicapinae	3	—	—	—	3	—
Sub-total	*32*	*0*	*7*	*3*	*19*	*3*
Totals	**132**	**17**	**62**	**3**	**44**	**6**

Species with both Palaearctic and Afrotropical populations are *Pelecanus onocrotalus, Ixobrychus minutus, Nycticorax nycticorax, Ardea cinerea, A. ralloides, Egretta garzetta, Milvus migrans, Falco peregrinus, F. tinnunculus, Himantopus himantopus, Sterna albifrons, Clamator glandarius, Otus scops, Upupa epops, Hirundo rustica*

years, and individuals of 7 of these species have been trapped more than once in the same winter season. Of those birds retrapped within the same winter, all but 2 were recaught only once, the longest interval, of 144 days (10 October 1976–3 March 1977), being recorded for a Swallow. One Swallow was retrapped twice and another 3 times. Many individual birds retrapped in subsequent years were caught in the winter following their initial capture, but 18 (Table 10) were retrapped 2 or more years after being ringed. One Swallow made 6 return journeys from Tafo to the

Table 10. Faithfulness of 5 Palaearctic species of birds ringed in Ghana to their wintering area

Species	Number of return journeys to and from the Palaearctic				
	2	3	4	5	6
Tringa hypoleucos	6	1	1	1	—
Tringa ochropus	1	—	1	—	—
Hirundo rustica	4	—	—	—	1
Motacilla flava	—	1	—	—	—
Saxicola rubetra	1	—	—	—	—
Totals	12	2	2	1	1

Palaearctic. Only 18 Swallows (0·2% of the total number of Swallows ringed) have been found abroad (Appendix 2) — Algeria (2), Morocco (5), Spain (2), France (6), Germany (2), Belgium (1) — the percentage return comparing well with data from Nigeria (Elgood 1982). The great circle directions all lie between 10°E of N and 13°W of N (clock directions 10°–0°–347°). One Swallow ringed at Tafo travelled 3014 km to Morocco, where it was caught 18 days after being ringed. During her studies Mary Lockwood trapped 13 *Hirundo rustica* ringed in Belgium (7), France (5) and Spain (1), one *Motacilla flava* ringed in Germany, and one *Acrocephalus arundinaceus* ringed in Austria (Appendix 3).

Of the 3 recognised intra-African transequatorial migrants that have occurred in Ghana, the movements of Abdim's Stork *Ciconia abdimis* are the easiest to detect. There are no Ghanaian breeding records and most sightings are in the north between April and May, with only stragglers seen in January both in the north and on the coast near Cape Coast (Macdonald 1979a). Of the other 2 species, one is not recent and the other requires confirmation. The plover *Vanellus superciliosus* was collected in eastern Ghana in the last century but is unrecorded since; and there is one sighting only of the nightjar *Caprimulgus vexillarius,* at Accra, by M. J. Field in early February 1933 (Bannerman 1933: 174) which is a relatively early migration date. The statement in Bannerman (1953: 615) that the species is recorded from the savannas of Ghana may well be true but requires confirmation. The Open-bill *Anastomus lamelligerus* populations in West Africa have usually been thought to migrate to south of the equator to breed, but the populations in southern Ghana are apparently present all year, although non-breeding; they are recorded in each month of the year in wetlands west of Accra and there are coastal movements, but these are thought only to be local.

The north–south migrations of several Afrotropical species take place throughout West Africa (Elgood *et al.* 1973; Thiollay 1977, 1978) and several, such as *Ibis ibis, Milvus migrans, Buteo auguralis, Caprimulgus climacurus, C. longipennis, Halcyon leucocephala, Tockus nasutus,* move southwards into Ghana to breed and then return northwards after breeding. Others, such as *Elanus riocourii, Batastur rufipennis, Coracias abyssinica, Merops albicollis,* and some populations of *Bubulcus ibis,* breed in areas north of Ghana and spend the non-breeding season in Ghana. There are other species, conspicuous in the field, that undergo migrations to, as yet, unknown destinations. The bulk of the records of the cuckoo *Cuculus canorus gularis* occur from January to July, its breeding season. A small but definite easterly movement across the Accra Plains was recorded in mid June on one occasion, but little else is known. The period during which the Lesser Moorhen *Gallinula angulata* occurs in Ghana is even shorter than that of the cuckoo — June to September, during which time it breeds — and a similar pattern occurs in Nigeria, where Elgood (1982) thought it might migrate to southern latitudes. The Banded Martin *Riparia cincta* has only been recorded in coastal areas of Ghana between November and May (Macdonald 1979a); in contrast, in northern Nigeria it occurs almost exclusively in the other half of the year, between early May and November, although there are some coastal records in February and March (Elgood 1982). Elgood suggested that the northern populations probably migrate to breeding areas south of the equator, but the Ghana data indicate that the species' movements are not so clear cut and need further study. The comings and goings, to and from one locality, of small but conspicuous passerines, such as *Hirundo abyssinica* and *Cinnyricinclus leucogaster*, are only too apparent, but the lack of precise data makes the interpretation of their movements at present impossible.

DIFFERENCES BETWEEN THE AVIFAUNAS OF GHANA AND NIGERIA
Numerically the avifauna of Ghana is about 18% less in species than that of Nigeria (using the lists in Elgood 1982) (Table 11), mainly because of the wider range of vegetation zones that occur in Nigeria, some of which (e.g. montane forest and savanna, and Sahel savanna) are absent altogether from Ghana.

Table 11. The numerical differences between the avifaunas of Ghana and Nigeria according to habitat

Habitat	Number of species in Nigeria but not in Ghana			Number of species in Ghana but not in Nigeria		
	Non-Passerines	Passerines	Total	Non-Passerines	Passerines	Total
Lowland forest/forest edge	6	14	20	14	18	32
Lowland savanna	6	9	15	4	0	4
Marine	7	0	7	8	0	8
Montane forest/forest edge	5	35	40	0	0	0
Montane savanna/stream	4	11	15	0	0	0
Northern, Sudan Guinea and Sahel zone	34	42	76	0	0	0
Totals	**62**	**111**	**173**	**26**	**18**	**44**
Residents	35	89	124	16	18	34
Palaearctic migrants	14	21	35	2	0	2
Intra-African migrants	6	1	7	0	0	0
Vagrants	7	0	7	8	0	8
Totals	**62**	**111**	**173**	**26**	**18**	**44**

Although 32 forest species found in Ghana do not occur in Nigeria, they are found further eastwards; similarly 16 Nigerian species do not occur in Ghana but are found west of Ghana. When these species are eliminated from the bird lists, together with those species, both forest and savanna, that form superspecies or species-groups (Hall & Moreau 1970; Snow 1978), there is little difference between the respective forest and savanna avifaunas. This suggests that the dry Dahomey Gap, where savanna reaches the coastline and separates the Ghana forest from that of Nigeria, is, therefore, relatively recent in geologic times and has not acted as a barrier to bird dispersion (see Moreau 1966: 163). However, it has acted as an effective barrier to tree dispersal, and Ghana has about 18 endemic forest species (Hall & Swaine 1981: 34).

The forest bird species that have not yet spread further west than Nigeria are *Tauraco leucolophus*, a widespread species, *Apalis rufogularis*, a species of forest edge or secondary growth, and the 2 malimbe, *Malimbus erythrogaster* and *M. ibadanensis*. Of the savanna lowland species, only 3 have not yet penetrated west of

Nigeria; these are *Sarathrura bohmi,* and the dry reed-bed warblers *Bradypterus baboecola* and *Chloropeta natalensis.* Apart from the forest babbler *Trichastoma rufescens,* which some consider closely related to some Nigerian babblers, there are no forest or savanna species in Ghana which do not have close relatives either within or east of Nigeria.

FUTURE LINES OF STUDY FOR ORNITHOLOGY IN GHANA

The following suggestions mainly arise out of the previous work that has been carried out in Ghana, and are not intended to be exhaustive. Any future work will depend very much both on the opportunities that arise at any given time and on the interests of the individual.

The majority of observers in Ghana, and elsewhere in the tropics, would probably affirm that the avifauna of crop plantations, such as cocoa and oil palm, is poorer than that of the surrounding forest. This affirmation has never been quantified and a comparative study of the 2 avifaunas would be of great value to conservationists not only in Ghana. So would similar studies of the avifauna (a) of the 2 types of forest/savanna boundaries described earlier, (b) of the Accra and Winneba Plains, and (c) of the sub-montane forest areas and their surrounding forests.

The dearth of breeding data speaks for itself, and any systematically collected breeding data will add valuably to present knowledge. Long term breeding studies of individual species, preferably with colour marked individuals, are rewarding both in the data they produce and because they may well incidentally reveal new aspects, for example unrecognized cases of cooperative breeding behaviour other than are known at present (Grimes 1976). At Legon there are 4 species that breed cooperatively (2 babblers, the Kakelaar and the Yellow-billed Shrike) and only one (the shrike) has been studied in any detail (Grimes 1980). A comparison of their breeding behaviour and ecology would be difficult but very worthwhile. Studies involving colour ringed birds can provide data unobtainable in other ways, e.g. to establish the presence or absence of (a) biannual breeding by individuals within a population, and (b) overlapping moulting and breeding periods, breeding strategies which have only recently gained the attention of ornithologists in Africa (see Craig 1983; Wilkinson 1983). To quote another aspect, in Gabon, Brosset (1982) found that the Yellow-whiskered Greenbul *Andropadus latirostris* forms leks whenever its population density is high and is monogamous when it is low. In the Gabon forests near Makokou (0°24'N, 12°00'E), where leks occurred, the Yellow-whiskered Greenbul most interestingly outnumbered the closely allied Little Greenbul *A. virens*; but in other areas *virens* outnumbered *latirostris*. The latter situation occurs in Ghana; Brosset postulates that leks might be found in *virens* under a similar demographic balance.

Radar studies of tern movements have shown that in winter the Black Tern *Sterna nigra* is maritime, spending daylight hours at sea far from land, many, however, returning at and after dusk to roosts at saltpans and lagoons; but, as well, flocks of Black Terns have been located at sea during the night, though how long they remain and what is their final destination are not known. In stark contrast, *S. nigra* breeds in fresh water marshes and the marked differences in its summer ecological requirements with those in winter would make an interesting study.

The attractiveness of saltpans to many species of herons and waders has often been remarked upon, but the difference in the ecology of these species, and the food chains that are present have not been unravelled.

The accidental discovery, in East Africa, that night migrants during misty nights are attracted to brightly illuminated white-washed walls of buildings caused much excitement. Certain localities in Ghana have similar illuminated surfaces, and although night-time migrants have not been reported by the local people, neither have they been looked for by ornithologists. On the Akwapim hills, the President's Palace is illuminated at night for security reasons and frequently shrouded in mist. At Abetifi, a high point on the southern scarp of the Voltaian basin, the buildings of the Ramsayer centre of the Presbyterian Church are frequently illuminated, as are those of the Teacher Training College at Amedzofe, the highest point in Ghana on its border with Togo. At Legon, the university tower stands high above the campus and is illuminated as a safeguard for incoming air traffic to Accra; nights during which it is in mist are fewer than those at the other 3 locations but they do occur.

Detailed movements in Ghana are known only for a few Afrotropical species. So far, no attempt has been made to coordinate a country-wide census using biological departments in schools. Although there would be difficulties, such a census is feasible for species that are readily visible and easily identified without the use of field-glasses and might well be administered through the Game and Wild Life Department. The most obvious choice of species is the Black Kite *Milvus migrans*, whose movements are probably closely related to the movements of the ITCZ, themselves clear cut and regular in West Africa (Brown 1970: 200; Thiollay 1978). Equally, the movements of the Striped Swallow *Hirundo abyssinica* and the Amethyst Starling *Cinnyricinclus leucogaster*, both of which appear to have both regular and irregular movements in different localities, might well be tackled in this way.

ACKNOWLEDGEMENTS

The gestation period for this check-list has been long, and over the years many have provided help of one kind or another at the right time and given words of encouragement. Ellis Owen and Jeffrey Marshall helped in translating German and French papers. Malcolm Fry introduced me to the word processor just when the systematic list began to take shape. Gilbert Vanderstichelen, Dr M. Swaine, Norman Little, G. B. Reynolds and Professor C. J. Taylor CBE, ED provided a selection of photographs and/or negatives of habitat from which I was free to select. Prof Taylor also viewed these and identified for me the main plant and tree species that occurred on each. Help with museum skins was given generously by A. Brossett (France), P. R. Colston (British Museum, Tring) and G. F. Mees (Leiden), who also drew my attention to publications on H. S. Pel and C. J. M. Nagtglas. The list of bird skins at Legon and Mole were kindly sent by Barry Hughes and Dr P. Greig-Smith respectively. For copies of the diary kept by Dr J. Chapin whilst in Ghana and the list of skins collected by D. W. Lamm, I am grateful respectively to Mary LeCroy of the American Museum of Natural History and Dr G. E. Watson of the Smithsonian Institution. While gathering ringing data I have received help from R. Hudson and C. Mead (both of the BTO, Tring), G. Jarry (France), T. Oatley (South Africa), and from Roland Staav (Sweden), who updated data that I had gathered on Swedish birds. I am indebted to all who have corresponded with me, often more than once, and given freely of their unpublished data. Their names appear in the appropriate places in the text and are as follows:— Dr J. Callow, Dr Leo Cole, R. J. Dowsett, Dr E. Dunn, M. D. I. Gass, Dr P. Greig-Smith, E. Hall, I. Hepburn, M. F. Hodges Jr, M. Horwood, Dr D. James, D. W. Lamm, M. Lockwood, Dr M. MacDonald, the late Rev C. M. Morrison, P. J. Olney, R. G. Passmore, Drs R. B. Payne, L. L. Short and D. W. Snow, J. Stewart, and Drs I. Taylor, J. M. Thiollay and F. W. Walsh, J. Wallace, N. Wood and B. Woodell. In addition, I would like to thank Dr E. Dunn for help in checking references.

It gives me satisfaction that the preliminary chapters on the history of Ornithology in Ghana and its vegetation were read by D. W. Lamm and M. Horwood, 'old coasters' who have contributed much to our knowledge of Ghanaian and African birds in general. My wife, Jean, has had to put up with the sight and inconvenience of beds and table tops covered with books and papers throughout, but she is a true helpmeet.

Finally, my greatest debt is to Dr James Monk, the general Editor of the series of Check-lists. His ability to ask the right questions, make constructive and critical comment, remove ambiguities in the written word and at the same time encourage, has always impressed me and has been invaluable.

SYSTEMATIC LIST

Following the earlier check-lists on Gambian Birds (Gore 1981) and on Nigerian Birds (Elgood 1982), the families and subfamilies used in the Systematic List follow Morony *et al.* (1975), except Accipitridae (q.v.), where, in the absence of such subfamilies and tribes in Morony *et al.,* those of other workers have been used. Within these taxa, genera and species are in alphabetic sequence.

For the sake of conformity and ease of comparison with earlier check-lists, the scientific names used are those of White (1960–1965), with Bannerman's names (1930–51) in brackets where these differ. The only exception is for species within Viduinae, where those proposed by Payne (1982, 1985) together with his English names are used. White's subspecies are given when applicable. The other English names are those used by Mackworth-Praed & Grant (1970 & 1973, Vol I and Vol II), each being preceded by a number (e.g. I.99, II.500) which allows easy identification in Mackworth-Praed & Grant (MP&G) of the species being described. For some species alternative English names appear in parenthesis; these are either used in Bannerman (1953) or Serle *et al.* (1977), or else thought more appropriate for the West African form.

The status of each species is abbreviated as follows:—

RB	Resident breeder
R(B)	Resident, but breeding unproved
PM	Palaearctic migrant
Afm	Migrates within Ghana
AfM/B	Migrates to and from Ghana to breed in Ghana
AfM/NB	Migrates to and from Ghana to spend the non-breeding season in Ghana
V	Vagrant
?	Indicates a doubt over the *status immediately preceding the question mark,* but not of occurrence

If more than one category is applicable, the more important is stated first. Where there is uncertainty about the occurrence of a species, it is placed in square brackets, is unnumbered and reasons for the uncertainty given.

Each species account contains information on abundance, status, habitat and distribution within Ghana (for place names see figures and the gazetteer), and, whenever applicable, details of any known migration to and from Ghana and within Ghana. The 5 categories of abundance adopted are abundant, common, not uncommon, uncommon and rare (see page 10 for a discussion of the difficulties of their definitions and their subjective nature). It has been difficult to state concisely the habitat information, particularly for those species found in a wide variety of habitats (eurytopic species), but the following broad divisions are used:— forest, savanna, aquatic and marine.

Details are given of the genera used by MP&G when they differ from those used by either White or Bannerman. In addition, the 2 subspecies of *Cuculus canorus* (*C. c. canorus* and *C. c. gularis*) are treated separately as they are easily distinguished by their voices, and also the 2 subspecies of *Egretta garzetta* (*E.g. garzetta* and *E.g. gularis*), one of which (*garzetta*) occurs both in the Palaearctic and Afrotropical Regions.

Recoveries of ringed birds are included in the species accounts, but fuller details appear in Appendices 1, 2 and 3).

For the benefit of future workers, the published source of any data is given in the text as well as the full name of the various workers whose data has been used. The willingness and generosity of these workers (see Acknowledgements) in making their data available is gratefully acknowledged.

NON-PASSERINES

PODICIPEDIDAE

1.   PODICEPS(= POLIOCEPHALUS) RUFICOLLIS
      (I.3)   Little Grebe or Dabchick   RB
Resident (*P. r. capensis*) but locally distributed where there is any fresh still water, both natural and man-made, occasionally on lagoons and within the forest zone. Sedentary at Accra, regular at fish farm in the Subri River Forest Reserve, 1981–1983 (M. F. Hodges, Jr), but occasional Kade, Apr (Sutton 1965b) and 3 Tafo, 20 Jan 1986 (R. E. Scott), although none recorded Tafo in 1970s (M. Lockwood). Occurs only during the rainy season at Tumu (Sutton 1970), at Tamale only Feb–Mar (E. Hall); no other records in north.
      Breeding. All months at Accra, where up to 3 broods have been raised annually on a flooded quarry at the centre of the city (Grimes 1972a, L.G.G.). Has nested Takoradi, no date (Snow 1978).

PROCELLARIIDAE

2.   PROCELLARIA (=ARDENNA) GRAVIS
      (I.13)   Southern Greater Shearwater   V
Coastal vagrant. One record: a male collected by Pel on the beach near Boutry (Butri) sometime between March 1842 and March 1843 (G. F. Mees). Listed by Hartlaub (1855a,b) and subsequently by Bouet (1955), but not by Bannerman (1930). West African seas (Serle *et al.* 1977).

3.   PROCELLARIA PUFFINUS
      (I.15)   Manx Shearwater   V, PM
Coastal vagrant. One record: one ringed in the U.K. was picked up near Half Assini 61 days after release (Appendix 3).

HYDROBATIDAE

4.   HYDROBATES (=CYMOCHOREA) CASTRO
      (I.5)   Madeira Petrel   V
Coastal vagrant, probably more numerous than data suggest. One certain record: numerous on 24 Oct 1979 in off shore waters south of Tema (E. Dunn, A. J. M. Smith).

5.   HYDROBATES (=CYMOCHOREA) LEUCORHOA
      (I.6)   Leach's Petrel   V
Coastal vagrant (*H. l. leucorhoa*), probably overlooked. Only one record: one presented to BMNH by Roland Ward in 1899 and labelled 'Ashanti' (P. Colston).

Bannerman (1930) states that it "has occurred off the Gold Coast". Winter visitor Cape Verde Islands and West African seas (Serle *et al.* 1977).

6.   HYDROBATES PELAGICUS
(I.4)   Storm Petrel   V

Coastal vagrant, but no recent sightings. Ussher (1874) obtained specimens (BMNH) and was brought birds caught by children along the sea shore at Cape Coast. One was lured at night onto a ship of a Danish expedition (23 Jan 1946) while off the coast of Ghana, though birds were not seen during the day (Bannerman 1930, 1951).

7.   OCEANITES OCEANICUS
(I.7)   Wilson's Petrel   V

Coastal vagrant to West African seas (Serle *et al.* 1977), migrant from the Antarctic. Ussher (1874) was brought one caught by children along the sea shore at Cape Coast (BMNH). 2–6 off Takoradi harbour throughout Sep 1954 (M. Horwood).

PHAETHONTIDAE

8.   PHAETHON LEPTURUS
(I.19)   White-tailed Tropic Bird   V

Off-shore vagrant (*P. l. ascensionis*). One sighting 24 Oct 1979, c. 25–30 km south of Tema (E. Dunn, A. J. M. Smith). Breeds on islands off São Thomé and probably Fernando Po (Bannerman 1953).

PELECANIDAE

9.   PELECANUS ONOCROTALUS
(I.31)   White Pelican   AfM/NB, PM?

All records, dates coinciding with the dry season (northern winter), are from coastal regions of southeast Ghana, presumably Afrotropical in origin. Holman (1947) recorded up to 400 at Keta lagoon, M. Horwood 50–100 in 1957, Sutton (1965a) up to 300, and R. E. Scott c. 470 more recently. Occasionally recorded at Panbros saltpans. An African population breeds in Nigeria at Wase Rock (9°04′N, 9°56′E) in the dry season (Elgood 1982). White kept the species monotypic.

10.   PELECANUS RUFESCENS
(I.32)   Pink-backed (or Grey) Pelican   R?(B)

Uncommon, presumed resident, 4–10 occurring sporadically during both wet and dry season months on lagoons just west of Accra (saltpans) eastwards to Keta (Holman 1947). No records for inland Ghana, although the Volta lake would now provide suitable habitat. Bannerman (1953) states that it breeds "north of latitude 12°N in the Northern Territories of the Gold Coast", but this must be an error since the northern border of Ghana lies at 11°N.

Breeding. Unrecorded. In Nigeria, formerly in many northern towns, Sep–Mar (Elgood 1982).

SULIDAE

11.   SULA (= MORUS) BASSANA
(I.24)   Cape Gannet   V

Coastal vagrant. Young birds from breeding colonies in South Africa (*S. b. capensis*) occur in Ghanaian off-shore waters Jun–Aug. Recorded off Nungua and Labadi beaches east of Accra (A. C. Russell), and observed off Prampram (W. N. L. Goldie-Scot, Broekhuysen *et al.* 1961). Recorded at sea off Accra late Jul 1939 by Good (1952–1953). It is presumed that no records are of the northern (nominate) race.

12.   SULA LEUCOGASTER
(I.20)   Brown Booby   V

Coastal vagrant. The only record is an immature female (*S. l. leucogaster*) collected by Pel (SMNH) at Sekondi, Aug 1843 (G. F. Mees). Overlooked by both Bannerman (1930–51) and Bouet (1955/61).

PHALACROCORACIDAE

13.   PHALACROCORAX AFRICANUS
(I.26)   Long-tailed Cormorant or Reed Duiker   RB

Resident (*P. a. africanus*) and common at saltpans and lagoons along the coast and on inland freshwater lakes and rivers in the savanna areas, occasional in similar habitat within the forest zone (M. F. Hodges, Jr). Subject to local movements related to water levels. More numerous in the wet season at Cape Coast (Macdonald 1979a); recorded regularly at Tamale and Tono dam only Feb–Apr with stragglers Aug–Oct (E. Hall, R. Passmore).

Breeding. In southern Ghana Jun–Jul in mixed colonies with herons and darters at saltpans, Nungua and Weija. Clutch size at Nungua 2–8, mean 3·8 (Bowen *et al.* 1962).

14.   PHALACROCORAX CARBO (= LUCIDUS)
(II.25)   African Cormorant   AfM?/NB

Uncommon (*P. c. lucidus*), only recorded at Tono dam in the far north, Feb–May and Aug and Oct, max c. 20 in Feb (R. Passmore). No other records except a possible singleton at Panbros Salt Pans, 6 Mar 1965 (J. D. Thomas, L.G.G.).

ANHINGIDAE

15.   ANHINGA RUFA
(I.28)   Snake Bird or Darter   RB

Uncommon resident (*A. r. rufa*), likely to occur on any large fresh water reservoir, particularly in savanna areas; occasional Vea dam (F. Walsh). Recorded on reservoirs south of the forest belt at Sekondi (M. Horwood) and Brimsu near Cape Coast (M. Macdonald) but not at Tafo within the forest region (M. Lockwood).

Breeding. In mixed colonies of herons at Weija and Nungua, mid June to November; double brooded (Bowen *et al.* 1962).

ARDEIDAE

Botaurinae

16. BOTAURUS STELLARIS
    (I.52)   Bittern   V, PM
Rare Palaearctic migrant, only one certain record: one shot, skin at Mole Game
Park, late Oct or early Nov 1971 at Mole, and labelled *Ardea purpurea,* but identified
as *B. s. stellaris* by F. Walsh (wing 300 mm, tarsus c. 100 mm, bill (tip to feathers)
68 mm). A possible sighting on 1 Nov at Elmina (D. James).

17. IXOBRYCHUS MINUTUS
    (I.50)   Little Bittern   RB, Afm/B, PM?
Resident (*I. m. payesii*) in some areas such as the mangrove swamps and reed beds
west of Accra, and at Mole (Greig-Smith 1976a), but elsewhere mainly a wet season
visitor. A large influx of breeding birds occurs at the coastal belt at Cape Coast,
Accra and Denu late Apr to Jul (Holman 1947, Sutton 1965b, Macdonald 1977a).
Very occasional at Vea dam, 1 May 1971, 3 Aug 1977 (F. Walsh), and Tono dam,
Feb, May and Aug (R. Passmore). No records from within the forest zone (M.
Horwood, M. Lockwood). Some records for Accra and Mole in dry season and one
(3 Mar) at Cape Coast may involve Palaearctic birds (*L. m. minutus*) as it has
occurred in northern Nigeria (Elgood 1982).
Breeding. C/3–5, Jun–Sep at Weija and Keta lagoon (Holman 1947); probably
breeds at Cape Coast (Macdonald 1977a, 1979b).

18. IXOBRYCHUS (=ARDEIRALLUS) STURMII
    (I.51)   Dwarf Bittern   RB, Afm?
Uncommon but widespread resident throughout the savanna zone, in swamps,
marshes and seasonal wetlands. In coastal areas, Denu (Holman 1947, Sutton
1965b), Legon (Grimes 1972a) and Cape Coast, recorded only in the wet season
except for one at Nakwa (11 Feb) (Macdonald 1979a) and another at Akropong,
Akwapim (C. M. Morrison) in Feb. Northern records are mainly in the wet season:
one near Walewale, Jun (E. Hall); 3 at Mole, Jul–Sep (Harvey *et al.*); recorded twice
at Tumu, 20 Oct, 15 Jan (Sutton 1970).
Breeding. Eggs: C/4, 17 Jul at Denu (Holman 1947). Fledgling: Akropong in
Akwapim, 12 Feb (C. M. Morrison). Juveniles: Cape Coast, Jul (Macdonald
1979b).

Ardeinae

Tigriornithini

19. TIGRIORNIS LEUCOLOPHUS
    (I.49)   White-crested Bittern (Tiger Bittern)   R(B)
Uncommon resident along streams within forest region. Collected by Pel
(SMNH) near Boutry and by M. Horwood in Bimpong Forest Reserve north
of Cape Coast (skin not preserved). Sight records from Atewa Forest Reserve
(G. Vanderstichelen).
Breeding. Unrecorded. In Nigeria, an immature, 17 Sep (Elgood 1982).

Nycticoracini

20.   NYCTICORAX LEUCONOTUS
(I.48)   White-backed Night Heron   R(B)

Resident, probably widespread but uncommon in wetlands within the forest and along riverine woodlands; the few records are probably due to its nocturnal and solitary habits. Collected by Pel at Boutry (SMNH), and by Ussher (1874) at Winneba. Found regularly along the lower stretches of the Volta river, but only rarely at Yeji (A. W. J. Pomeroy *in* Bannerman 1930) and once at Navrongo (Sutton 1970), which is far to the north of its expected range.

Breeding. Unrecorded. In Nigeria, Sep–Oct (Elgood 1982).

21.   NYCTICORAX NYCTICORAX
(I.47)   Night Heron   RB, PM?

Local resident (*N. n. nycticorax*), numbers probably augmented by Palaearctic birds in the dry season, but there are no ringing records to confirm this. Recorded at Keta and in coastal wetlands west to Cape Coast. Roosts have been recorded near Cape Coast (J. Hall, Macdonald 1977a), one sited in a fettish grove (J. Hall), and at Legon (Botanical gardens). Recorded every month at Weija, max 250, Jan (M. D. I. Gass). Occasionally occurs within the forest zone (Tafo — M. Lockwood). Few records from the north: Tumu, 23 Feb; Navrongo, 28 Jun (Sutton 1970); Mole, 23–26 Mar, Oct (Greig-Smith 1976a); Vea dam, 1–4, 5 Aug–15 Oct, 6 on 8 Jan, 1 on 31 Jan (F. Walsh); Tono dam, Feb–May, Aug and Oct (R. Passmore).

Breeding. A colony, c. 40 pairs, with egrets, at Weija, Jul–Aug, 1966 and 1972, but not annually.

Ardeini

22.   ARDEA CINEREA
(I.33)   Grey Heron   PM, RB

Common Palaearctic migrant (*A. c. cinerea*), mainly mid Sep to early Mar, in all types of coastal and inland wetlands and at irrigation dams throughout. At Vea dam present mid Jul to mid Feb, peak of 14 on 27 Sep (F. Walsh). Some birds are recorded in every month at Accra and Cape Coast and may belong to the resident population of West Africa.

Birds ringed in Yugoslavia (1) and France (1) recovered at Apam and Anloga respectively.

Breeding. One record, a nest with adults present just south of Yeji, no date (F. Walsh).

23.   ARDEA (=TYPHON) GOLIATH
(I.35)   Goliath Heron   R(B)

Uncommon resident, in mangroves and wetlands bordering rivers in the coastal strip from Cape Coast eastwards to Weija, and along the larger rivers in the north. Records for Weija reservoir and Panbros saltpans are of single birds, Oct–Apr. Several recorded singly along the Volta river in the north (Holman 1947); at Mole, 23–26 Mar, 25 Aug; Sugu, 12 Jan, and Bui, 3 Apr (F. Walsh). Recorded at Cape Coast (J. Hall) but not observed there by M. Macdonald 1975–78.

Breeding. Unrecorded. In Portuguese Guinea, Aug (MP&G).

24.   ARDEA MELANOCEPHALA
(I.34)   Black-headed Heron   Afm/B

Uncommon dry season visitor to the coastal region, from Cape Coast eastwards to Accra and Keta, birds remaining until the beginning of the rains (Mar/Apr). Occasionally recorded from clearings within the forest zone: Kumasi (Holman 1947), Korforidua, Mar only (M. Lockwood). Resident and much more common in the northern savannas (F. Walsh, R. Passmore), numbers at Tamale reservoir building up as the breeding season approaches, max 65 on 12 Mar (Holman 1947).

Breeding. Jun–Aug; colonies at Hamale (Aug 1974), Pong Tamale (19 nests 23 Jun 1977) and at Yendi, with well grown chicks 4 Aug 1977 (F. Walsh). A colony at Pong Tamale in 1940's (Holman 1947).

25.   ARDEA (=PYRRHERODIA) PURPUREA
(I.36)   Purple Heron   PM, R?(B)

Not uncommon Palaearctic migrant (*A. p. purpurea*) along shores of fresh water lakes, lagoons, and in reed beds of rivers and wetlands throughout. Mostly Oct–Jun but some (probably immatures) remain throughout the year at Vea dam (F. Walsh), at Panbros saltpans and at Tafo (M. Lockwood). At Mole, Greig-Smith (1976a) thought that representatives of both Palaearctic and African populations occurred.

Birds ringed in Holland (7), France (2) have been recovered in forest and savanna areas.

Breeding. The nearest breeding colony is in Senegal. Adult carrying stick, May (Macdonald 1979b).

26.   ARDEOLA (=BUBULCUS) IBIS
(I.42)   Cattle Egret or Buff-backed Heron   Afm/B, RB

Common dry season visitor (*A. i. ibis*) throughout, often associated with cattle and habitation. Main arrival Oct at both Tamale and Vea dam (F. Walsh), in the north, and at Accra on the coast, and by Nov at Tafo; earliest date 20 Sep at Vea dam and occurs Aug at Tono dam (R. Passmore). Most leave by May, but a resident population is well established near Accra.

Breeding. No records from the north; first recorded breeding near Accra in 1960 (Bowen *et al.* 1962) and regularly since during wet season, late May to Jul, at Panbros saltpans (Grimes 1972a). No breeding records during mid 1950's (D. Lamm, M. Horwood).

27.   ARDEOLA RALLOIDES
(I.43)   Squacco Heron   PM, RB

Locally common throughout the north, mainly as Palaearctic migrant Oct–May; at Tamale reservoir up to 20 birds early Oct to early May (E. Hall). However at Vea dam present mid June to mid Feb (F. Walsh) and Tono dam, Aug–May (R. Passmore). More numerous in coastal wetlands and lagoon edges, occasionally found at reservoirs and sewage farms within the forest zone (Kumasi, Tafo). At Cape Coast, Weija, and at Panbros saltpans, there are resident populations; considered by Macdonald (1977a) more numerous at Cape Coast in the wet season, when Palaearctic birds would not be present.

Breeding. Since c. 1970, has bred regularly, Jul, in mangroves near the Panbros saltpans in mixed colonies of *Ardeola ibis* and *Egretta garzetta*. Has nested Cape Coast, 17 Jun (D. James) and possibly at Keta in wet season (Holman 1947).

28.   BUTORIDES STRIATUS
(I.45)   Green-backed Heron   RB

Common resident (*B. s. atricapillus*) in coastal wetlands, saltpans and edges of reservoirs, but also occasionally away from water, e.g. Shai Hills. Occasional within forest clearings (Tafo, Kumasi sewage farm). In the north less numerous, but well distributed as scattered individuals in suitable wetland habitat (E. Hall, F. Walsh, R. Passmore).

Breeding. Jul–Sep at Accra (Grimes 1972a) and probably Cape Coast (Macdonald 1977a). A male with large testes collected at Mole, July (Greig-Smith 1977b).

29.   EGRETTA (=CASMERODIUS) ALBA
(I.37)   Great White Egret   RB

Common resident (*E. a. melanorhynchos*) in the south at lagoons, freshwater reservoirs, streams and wetlands, and in similar habitat within the forest zone (Tafo, Kumasi sewage farm, fish farm within Subri River Forest Reserve): abundant at the Panbros saltpans and Weija. Much less common, mainly sporadic in the north; occurs Tono dam, Feb and Mar (R. Passmore), recorded once at Tumu, 19 May (Sutton 1970), singly at Tamale reservoir, Mar, Oct and Dec only (E. Hall) but regularly 1–5 mid Jul to mid Feb at Vea dam (F. Walsh). Numbers at Cape Coast are fewer Aug–Apr (Macdonald 1977a).

Breeding. 50–60 pairs present 1967 and 1968 at Weija, Jul–Aug in mixed colony of herons. Birds have black bills when breeding and yellow when non-breeding; black-billed birds present, Mar, at Cape Coast (Macdonald 1977a), but no evidence of breeding.

30.   EGRETTA (=MELANOPHOYX) ARDESIACA
(I.39)   Black Heron   RB, Afm/B?

Not uncommon resident in south at lagoons, Panbros saltpans and open water (Weija). Recorded each month at the Panbros saltpans, usually 30–40, max c. 100, Apr–Jun (Grimes 1967). Absent Aug–Jan, at Iture, Cape Coast (Macdonald 1977a). Recorded once at Keta, 31 Oct (Holman 1947), but not at Denu (Sutton 1965b). Few records from the north: a single in Feb, and 2 in Mar, at Tamale reservoir (E. Hall); R. E. Crabbe recorded it at Kete Kratchi; single, 28 Nov 1985, at Tono (J. Stewart).

Breeding. 3 nests with eggs, one C/3, 15 Aug 1966, in mangroves along Densu river (Grimes 1967); nests with eggs and young, 8 Jul 1977, Accra (Macdonald 1979b).

31.   EGRETTA GARZETTA GARZETTA
(I.40)   Little Egret   RB, PM

Not uncommon resident at lagoons, saltpans and reservoirs along the coast; present at reservoirs within the forest zone (Tafo, Kumasi, Kade, Subri River Forest Reserve) and at irrigation dams in the north. An influx of Palaearctic birds begins in late Jul in the north (6 on 22 Jul at Vea dam — F. Walsh) and is apparent at the coast in Oct. Migrating flocks leave Panbros saltpans in Mar, initial flight direction NNE (Grimes 1974b). Most Palaearctic birds leave by early Apr.

Breeding. Jun–Aug with other herons in mangroves near Panbros west of Accra, and Weija (Grimes 1972a).

One ringed in the Ukraine was recovered at Elmina.

32.   EGRETTA (=DEMIGRETTA) GARZETTA GULARIS
(I.41)   West African Reef-Heron   RB

Common resident in mangrove swamps, saltpans and lagoons along the coast, also on rocky and sandy beaches (Cape Coast and further west). Occasional along larger rivers near the coast and inland, sporadic at fish farm within Subri River Forest Reserve (M. F. Hodges, Jr), single Tafo, 29 Jan 1978, Vea dam 6 times 22 Jul to 31 Aug 1972, and at Pwalugu on White Volta, 18 Apr 1977 (Walsh 1987).

Breeding. Jun–Aug in mixed heronries at saltpans west of Accra (Grimes 1972a); several nests with chicks Cape Coast, July (Macdonald 1979b), one nest (C/5) in mixed colony of *Phalacrocorax africanus, Ardeola ibis* and *Ahinga rufa* at Nungua (Bowen *et al.* 1962).

33.   EGRETTA (= MESOPHOYX) INTERMEDIA
(I.38)   Yellow-billed Egret   AfM/NB
Locally not uncommon passage migrant (*E. i. brachyrhyncha*), in wetlands bordering lagoons, saltpans and freshwater dams in south, some possibly remaining all year, with isolated records inland at Tafo (M. Lockwood) and Mole, Jul–Aug, Nov (Greig-Smith 1976a), but more regular Vea dam, Aug–Jan (F. Walsh) and Tono dam, Dec, Feb–Apr and Aug (R. Passmore). First located at Nungua (N. Gardiner *in* Thomas 1966) and at Panbros saltpans (13 Feb) (M. Edmunds *in* Grimes 1972a), but otherwise overlooked until Macdonald (1978e) distinguished it from *E. alba*. Present all months in drier coastal belt; at Cape Coast largest counts (mean c. 30) occur May and Jul; breeding colours develop late Mar to mid June. Macdonald (1978e) suggests the possibility of a westerly movement, May–Jul, through southern Ghana from further east, and that it "may represent one stage in a circular migration within West Africa taking birds on a circuit of 2 or more colonies (e.g. Mali and Lake Chad) . . . allowing 2 or more breeding cycles to be compressed into one year".

SCOPIDAE

34.   SCOPUS UMBRETTA
(I.53)   Hammerkop   R(B)
Common resident (*S. u. umbretta*) north of the forest belt, but locally distributed, often along edges of main rivers. Frequent at Tumu (Sutton 1970) at Mole and further north (F. Walsh, R. Passmore); in the past, occurred at Kete Kratchi (Reichenow 1897). Only one coastal record, west of Accra (Reichenow & Lühder 1873), presumably *S. u. minor*.

Breeding. Unrecorded, although empty nest and display flight, Mole, Jul and Aug (Harvey & Harrison 1970). In Nigeria, *minor* in Dec, *umbretta* mainly Mar–Jun (Elgood 1982).

CICONIIDAE

Mycteriini

35.   ANASTOMUS LAMELLIGERUS
(I.59)   Open-bill   AfM/NB
Formally regarded as a transequatorial migrant (*A. l. lamelligerus*), but is present all year at wetlands near Weija, max numbers (c. 300) recorded in dry season, Dec–Feb. Small flocks (c. 10–15) are seen at Nungua sporadically throughout the dry season and at Abokobi. Recorded at Takoradi, 3 Apr (Holman 1947), not yet at Cape Coast; also at Tafo reservoir, Mar and Aug (M. Lockwood). In north, records are fewer, mainly Nov–May, but also Jun and Sep (F. Walsh).

36.   IBIS IBIS
(I.62)   Wood-Ibis   AfM/B
A dry season breeding visitor, Nov–May, to northern savanna areas, much less common in south, only occurring in dry areas east of Accra. Recorded Mar and Oct near Tema (D. Lamm) and in small numbers at Keta (Holman 1947), although not recorded there by Sutton in 1960s. Nest sites colonised in Nov and abandoned late Feb. Migration northwards from Ghana begins Mar and ends by mid May.

Breeding. Eggs/young, Dec–Feb. Well established colonies, in Silk Cotton *Ceiba pentandra* trees, 15–40 nests, recorded at Daboya and Gambaga (Alexander 1902), Kombungu (Holman 1947), Bimbilla (M. D. I. Gass) and Tuluwe (M. Horwood). The colony at Daboya still existed in 1946 (M. Horwood) having in 1944 contained 51 nests (Cockburn & Findlay 1945). A nest site used in 1968 in a village near the eastern boundary of Mole Game Park reported to Harvey & Harrison (1970) may have been that of *Leptoptilos crumeniferus*.

Ciconiini

37.   CICONIA (= SPHENORYNCHUS) ABDIMII
(I.58)   White-bellied or Abdim's Stork   AfM/NB

Locally not uncommon transequatorial migrant in the northern savanna, on passage (Mar to mid Jul) to breeding sites further north. Up to 50 present at Tamale reservoir, Apr–May (Holman 1947), regular at Vea dam until mid Jul (F. Walsh), at Tumu in May only (Sutton 1970). Two records only in the south: 2 stragglers at Nakwa, 13 Jan (M. Macdonald) and a juv near Accra, 30 Nov (G. Vanderstichelen). No evidence of major southward return through Ghana.

38.   CICONIA CICONIA
(I.55)   White Stork   PM

A not uncommon Palaearctic migrant (*C. c. ciconia*) in flocks of 10–20, occasionally reaching 90 (F. Walsh), in wetlands and rice farms throughout the north, south to Golokwati (M. Horwood) in the Volta Region, Dec–Mar. Single, 5 Aug 1977, on dried rice field 25 miles north of Tamale (F. Walsh). Occasionally reaches Keta.

Birds ringed in Germany (2), Spain (2) and Algeria (1) have been recorded in Ghana.

39.   CICONIA (= DISSOURA) EPISCOPUS
(I. 57)   Woolly-necked or Bishop Stork   Afm/(B)

Uncommon African passage migrant (*C. e. microscelis*), mainly mid Oct to early Jun, throughout the north, south to Kete Kratchi; occurrence sporadic, usually 2–3 on the wing. Only 3 records from south: 14 daily at Sekondi reservoir, Apr (Holman 1947); 7 at Brimsu reservoir, Cape Coast, 16 May (Macdonald 1977a); one at Esiama, 29 Nov 1985 (E. Dunn, R. Broad, A. Grieve).

Breeding. Unrecorded. Breeds Jan and Feb in Sierra Leone (Bannerman 1953).

40.   CICONIA NIGRA
(I.56)   Black Stork   V, PM

Rare Palaearctic migrant, only 2 records. One collected by Pel at Boutry prior to Feb 1843. The skin is no longer extant but the validity of the record listed in Hartlaub (1857) is confirmed by archives in SMNH (G. F. Mees). The other record is of a pair in low flight along the White Volta near the junction of the Kulpawn river, 4 Feb 1987 (F. Walsh).

Leptoptilini

41.   EPHIPPIORHYNCHUS SENEGALENSIS
(I.60)   Saddle-bill or Jabiru   AfM/B

Rare, mainly dry season breeding visitor, only to wetlands in the north. Records are sporadic: a pair at Pong Tamale, 1937 (Holman 1947), single birds at Mole, 25 Mar, between Tumu and Navrongo, 19 Jan (Lowe 1937), and near road bridge over the Black Volta, 2 Jan (D. James) and 23 Feb (F. Walsh). Two records from the south: Count Zech collected it at Kete Kratchi (Reichenow 1897); 9 on the wing at Keta, 24 Jan (Holman 1947).

Breeding. C/3 Mole Game Reserve, nest in canopy of *Ceiba pentandra* tree, 22 and 29 Oct 1986 (D. McLaughlin, J. Henderickx, F. Walsh); the second definite record for West Africa (see MP&G). Ivory Coast: 3 well grown chicks on 4 Dec 1975 at 8°56'N, 3°54'W was the first West Africa record; the nest was also in a *Ceiba pentandra* (Walsh 1977).

42.   LEPTOPTILOS CRUMENIFERUS
(I.61)   Marabou   AfM/B

Uncommon breeding migrant to northern Ghana in dry season, mainly Oct–Apr, locally distributed often near towns or villages. In south once recorded, at Abokobi, sometime during Aug–Sep by Reichenow & Lühder (1873) (noted by Bouet 1955, but overlooked by Bannerman 1930, 1951).

Breeding. Young in nests, Mar, in a long-standing colony at Mole Game Park (L.G.G. & M. Edmunds). Also a colony of 5 nests, some containing eggs, 22 Oct 1986 at 9°28'N, 1°50'W, were thought to be this species. Nests and birds were located from a helicopter and the description by J. Henderickx and D. McLaughlin fitted Marabou description (F. Walsh).

THRESKIORNITHIDAE

Threskiornithinae

43.   BOSTRYCHIA (=HAGEDASHIA) HAGEDASH
(I.65)   Hadada   R(B)

Not uncommon resident (*B. h. brevirostris*), along wooded streams throughout the north, south to Kete Kratchi; flocks (c. 15) frequently recorded at Mole, but only one record at Tumu, 4 Mar (Sutton 1970). Within the forest, frequent along major rivers Ancobra, Bia, Offin, Pra and Tana (M. Horwood); also at Tarkwa, 12 Aug (Sutton 1970) and Cape Coast (J. Hall).

Breeding. Unrecorded. Breeds in Nigeria, Apr–Jun (Elgood 1982).

44.   BOSTRYCHIA (=LAMPRIBIS) OLIVACEA
(I.67)   Green Ibis   R?(B)

Very rare (*B. o. olivacea*), confined to lowland forest, sympatric with *B. rara*: only one (uncertain) sighting, of 3 small noisy birds along the road from Kade to Akropong, Akwapim (Holman 1947). Widely distributed within the West African forest and should occur in Ghana, where it may possibly be resident.

Breeding. Unrecorded from West African mainland; breeding condition, Jan, in Principe (MP&G).

45.   BOSTRYCHIA (=LAMPRIBIS) RARA
(I.66)   Spotted-breasted Ibis   R(B)

Rare, only 2 records, but probably a widespread resident in lowland forest wherever there are swamps. Collected by Ussher at Denkere (present day location uncertain), 5 Nov (Rothschild *et al.* 1897), and at Mampong, Ashanti, 25 Feb (Lowe 1937).

Breeding. Unrecorded from West Africa.

46.   PLEGADIS FALCINELLUS
(I.68)   Glossy Ibis   PM

Not uncommon Palaearctic migrant (*P. f. falcinellus*) to wetlands at Weija and the Panbros saltpans, early Aug to early Jun, usually 2–4 but up to 15 occasionally. Elsewhere few records, all singletons: Iture, just west of Cape Coast, 5 Dec (Macdonald 1977a); Tamale, 8 Nov (E. Hall); Vea dam, 12–16 Nov and 18 Dec (F. Walsh), but 9 on 6 Oct 1984 (J. Stewart). Possibly overlooked. Has bred in Mali (MP&G) and early and late records may involve birds from an African population.

47.   THRESKIORNIS AETHIOPICA
(I.63)   Sacred Ibis   Afm/(B)

Uncommon in wetlands (*T. a. aethiopica*), 2–5 together, but occurrence is sporadic at any one location: Panbros saltpans, Feb–Sep; Mole, Jul–Sep; Tamale, Feb–Mar (Holman 1947), but not recorded there by E. Hall in late 1970s and early 1980s; one Vea dam early Jan (F. Walsh); Tono dam, 5 on 22 May 1985 and 2 on 9 Mar 1986 (J. Stewart).

Breeding. Unrecorded. The colony of unoccupied nests at Mole shown to Harvey & Harrison (1970) and ascribed tentatively by them to *T. aethiopica* belongs to *Leptoptilos crumeniferus*. In Nigeria, breeds Jun and Jul (Sokoto), Jan (Malamfatori) (Elgood 1982).

Plataleinae

48.   PLATALEA ALBA
(I. 70)   African Spoonbill   V

Rare vagrant: singletons Panbros saltpans, Jun (H. Houston), 8 Jul (L.G.G.), and 2 Oct (N. Wood); south of Yapei, 24 Oct (N. Wood); and 3 at Sakumo Lagoon, 3 Oct 1986 (RSPB Film Unit).

PHOENICOPTERIDAE

[PHOENICOPTERUS (= PHOENICONAIS) MINOR
(I.72)   Lesser Flamingo

Vagrant; no records since last century. Ussher mentions in a letter (Sharpe 1870b) seeing a small pink and black flamingo with pelicans and waders on the lower regions of the Volta river.]

ANATIDAE

Anserinae

Dendrocygnini

49.   DENDROCYGNA BICOLOR (= FULVA)
(I.94)   Fulvous Tree-Duck   V, AfM?/B

Rare vagrant to wetlands and marshes. Only one record: at Keta up to 7 seen Jul 1942, but absent in 1943 (Holman 1947) and during 1960s and 1970s (Sutton 1965b, 1970). No records from the north, possibly overlooked.

Breeding. Nest and egg fragments, 26 Jul, found by Holman (1947) at Keta, accepted by Bannerman (1951).

50.   DENDROCYGNA VIDUATA
       (I.93)   White-faced Tree-Duck (Whistling Teal)   RB, Afm
Locally common resident in wetlands throughout, except forested areas. Apparently less common in the north than in Holman's days (c. 1925–1945). Subject to much local movement, possibly migratory, but data are confusing; night movements very apparent in coastal areas Oct–Nov. Numbers fluctuate considerably during a year at any one location and from one year to the next: Mole, common Jul–Aug 1968 (Harvey & Harrison 1970), but rare Jul 1976 (D. J. Fleming); Tumu, only 3 records 1968/1969, 10 Nov, 14 Feb, 24 Jun (Sutton 1970); Tamale reservoir in 1980s Aug–Mar only (E. Hall). Recorded each month in coastal wetlands east of Takoradi, numbers reaching max, c. 100 at Accra, Apr, just before the main rains. Absent from Cape Coast and Nakwa in Oct, min counts Oct–Dec (Macdonald 1977b), at which period in most years is commoner at Accra (L.G.G.); in contrast, only 4 at Weija, 13 Oct 1979, but c. 500, 5 Nov 1979, at Songaw lagoon east of Ada (E. Dunn, A. J. M. Smith).
    Breeding. Eggs, in south May–Jun, in north Jul–Aug; C/9, 5 Jul, Cape Coast (Macdonald 1979b). Juv in Oct, Cape Coast, Nov at Mole, half grown young (20 with 2 adults) 19 Dec, between Navrongo and Bawku (M. Horwood).

Anatinae

Tadornini

51.   ALOPOCHEN AEGYPTIACA
       (I.97)   Egyptian Goose   V
Vagrant, only 2 records: Mole, 2 on 3 occasions, early Aug (Genelly 1968), but not recorded there subsequently; one, 2 Jan 1971, near Black Volta road bridge (D. James).

52.   TADORNA TADORNA
       (Not in MP&G)   Shelduck   V, PM
Vagrant from the Palaearctic. 2 records in 1986: 2 at Weija, 8 Jan and 10 Jan, and 2 at Sakumo lagoon to the west of Tema (R. E. Scott, I. Hepburn, A. Smith, D. Daramani, A. Nuoh). Occurs Morocco and Senegal; the singleton recorded at Port Elizabeth and Cape Recife in South Africa (Blake 1975) is considered a bird escaped from a waterfowl collection (Clancey 1976).

Cairinini

53.   NETTAPUS AURITUS
       (I.95)   Pigmy Goose   RB
Not uncommon resident on fresh water lakes with permanent surface vegetation; mainly absent from within the forest region but 4 at Amansuri lake in the south west (E. Dunn). Occurrence often sporadic and dependent on water level and vegetation cover. In the north: Yapei, occasional Jun–Feb (F. Walsh); Tumu, max 6, 10 Nov and May–Jun (Sutton 1970); Tamale, c. 4 in Feb only (E. Hall); Tono dam, 2–3 usually together, Nov–Apr (R. Passmore). In the south resident at Cape Coast (Macdonald 1979a), but on the Accra Plains, most records Mar–Apr, absent at height of wet season due to excessive flooding of irrigation dams.
    Breeding. Prospecting old trees Mole, late Aug (Harvey & Harrison 1970); an immature Weija, 26 Jan (N. Wood).

54.   PLECTROPTERUS GAMBENSIS
(I.98)   Spur-winged Goose   R(B)

Not uncommon resident, widespread in permanent wetlands in the north, where Holman (1947) found it common throughout his travels. At Mole considered resident (Greig-Smith 1976a) but Taylor & Macdonald (1978a) thought it emigrated in the dry season. Regular at Tono dam (R. Passmore, J. Stewart), but elsewhere records are sporadic. In the north: Tamale, Mar only (E. Hall); Tumu, 2 on 16 Jan; Navrongo, 2 on 28 Jun (Sutton 1970). In the south: Denu, 3 on 31 May (Sutton 1970); Panbros saltpans, May 1967, 27 Mar 1974 (L.G.G.); Nungua, 24 May 1977; Nakwa, 2 on 8 May 1977 (M. Macdonald).

Breeding. Unrecorded. Aug–Nov in northern Nigeria (Elgood 1982).

55.   PTERONETTA HARTLAUBII
(I.92)   Hartlaub's Duck   RB

Resident and not uncommon along the major southern rivers of Ancobra, Bia, Prah, Offin and Tano (M. Horwood) and at reservoirs within the forest region (e.g. Kade, Tafo). Occasional at lagoons: Cape Coast, 20 Feb, 20 Mar; Nakwa, 7 on 26 Oct (E. Dunn, A. J. M. Smith).

Breeding. Pair display, 31 May, young seen later in year, at Opintin Gallery Forest (N. Wood). Nested Subri River Forest Reserve, no date (M. F. Hodges, Jr).

56.   SARKIDIORNIS MELANOTA
(I.96)   Knob-billed Goose   R(B)

Uncommon, presumed resident (*S. m. melanota*), on reservoirs and wetlands in the northern savanna. Records are sporadic: Tamale, 1♀, 2y present for a few days 27 Oct 1938, and isolated records May and Aug (E. Hall); Mole, Jan (Maze 1971); Vea dam, Dec, Jan, Aug and Nov (F. Walsh); occasional Tono dam, Aug–Oct, Mar–May (R. Passmore). Collected Lungbunga, 9 Dec 1951 (Appendix 5). Pel seems likely to have forwarded a skin to SMNH (listed by Hartlaub 1857), but it is no longer possible to verify this nor to identify the locality (G. F. Mees).

Breeding. Unrecorded. Senegal, Aug and Sep; Nigeria, Aug (MP&G).

Anatini

57.   ANAS (=DAFILA) ACUTA
(I.91)   Pintail   PM

A not uncommon Palaearctic migrant (*A. a. acuta*), mainly Dec–Feb, to wetlands and reservoirs in northern savanna, occasionally reaching coastal areas. At Vea dam records are sporadic, max c. 100, Dec (F. Walsh). Coastal records: Teshie, east of Accra, c. 6, Dec 1948 (M. Horwood); Nakwa, c. 7, 18 Dec 1977 (M. Macdonald); Keta lagoon, 12–16, 20 Jun 1943 (Holman 1947) — a very late date; a singleton, 15 Nov 1985 and 31 Jan 1986 (R. Broad, E. Dunn, R. E. Scott).

A bird ringed in U.K. recovered at Half Assini.

58.   ANAS CAPENSIS
(I.88)   Cape Wigeon   V

Vagrant, only 2 records: singles in wetlands at Weija, 11 Dec 1975 (Macdonald & Taylor 1976) and Iture, near Cape Coast, 8 Mar 1976 (M. Macdonald).

59.   ANAS (= SPATULA) CLYPEATA
      (I.79)   Shoveler   PM
   Uncommon Palaearctic migrant, Nov–Mar, to fresh water lakes in northern
savanna and south to Yeji (A. W. J. Pomeroy *in* Bannerman 1930). Only one record
for Vea dam 5 (1♂, 4♀), 7 Jan 1973 (F. Walsh). No recent records.

60.   ANAS CRECCA
      (I.85)   Teal   PM
   Previously not uncommon Palaearctic migrant (*A. c. crecca*) to the Keta lagoon
(F. C. Holman *in* Bannerman 1951: 65) in dry season, Dec–Mar. Surprisingly this
data is not in Holman (1947). Only one recent record; a singleton Nungua, 31 Dec
1969 (M. Edmunds *in* Grimes 1972a). No records from the north, possibly
overlooked.

61.   ANAS PENELOPE
      (I.84)   Wigeon   V, PM
   Vagrant from the Palaearctic, only recorded at Vea dam near Bolgatanga; 1♂, 8
Dec 1972 and 1♀, 9 Dec 1972 (F. Walsh).

62.   ANAS QUERQUEDULA
      (I.86)   Garganey   PM
   A common Palaearctic migrant, mainly late Aug to Mar, to fresh water lakes and
wetlands north of the forest region and south later to lagoons at Accra and eastwards to Keta as drier conditions develop in the north. Occasional at Kumasi
sewage farm (F. Walsh). Numbers at Vea dam build up from late Aug to c. 1600 in
Feb (F. Walsh, Roux & Jarry 1984) and reach c. 1000 in late Jan at Keta (Holman
1947); at Tamale c. 50, Feb–Mar 1974 (E. Hall). Occasional Accra Plains: Panbros
saltpans, 6 Mar 1963, 26 May 1973; Akuse, east of Shai Hills, c. 6, 17 Mar 1974
(N. Wood); Sakumo lagoon, near Tema, 88, 10 Jan, and 75, 31 1986 (R. E. Scott,
I. Hepburn, A. Smith, D. Daramani, A. Nuoh). No ringing recoveries.

Aythyini

63.   AYTHYA (= NYROCA) FERINA
      (I.76)   Pochard   V, PM
   Vagrant from the Palaearctic, one record: a female on Sakumo lagoon west of
Tema, 10 and 14 Jan 1986 (R. Scott, I. Hepburn, A. Smith, D. Daramani, A. Nuoh).
Not uncommon in wetlands in the far north of Nigeria, but only twice recorded in
southern Nigeria (Elgood 1982).

64.   AYTHYA (= NYROCA) NYROCA
      (I.75)   White-eyed Pochard (or Ferruginous Duck)   PM
   Rare Palaearctic migrant, only 2 records: sewage works at Kumasi, 7–11 Dec 1966
(Moorhouse 1968); Tamale reservoir, Feb–Mar 1974 (E. Hall).

PANDIONIDAE

65.   PANDION HALIAETUS
      (I. 172)   Osprey   PM
   Common Palaearctic migrant (*P. h. haliaetus*), mainly late Sep to mid May, single
birds being likely to turn up at any large lake, lagoon or river throughout. Recorded
Tafo, Dec–Feb 1975, Nov–Dec 1977 (M. Lockwood); Cape Coast, mid Dec to early

Jun (Macdonald 1978c); fish farm in Subri River Forest Reserve, Mar only (M. F. Hodges, Jr).

Birds ringed in Sweden (20) recovered from widely separated localities within Ghana.

ACCIPITRIDAE

Aegypinae

66. GYPOHIERAX ANGOLENSIS
    (I.148)   Palm-nut Vulture   RB
Common resident in coastal region, widespread but local in forest zone (e.g. Tafo, Kumasi, Lake Bosumtwi), and gallery forest, reaching Mole, Kete Kratchi and Yendi. On Accra Plains occasional throughout the year at Abokobi and Shai Hills, mainly in wet season, May–Jul.
Breeding. Flying young at Tafo, Mar–May (M. Lockwood). Immatures: Mole, 8 Aug (Harvey & Harrison 1970); Muni lagoon, near Winneba, 7 and 9 Oct (RSPB Film Unit).

67. GYPS BENGALENSIS (= PSEUDOGYPS AFRICANUS)
    (I.102)   White-backed Vulture   R(B)
Resident (*G. b. africanus*), not uncommon, and widespread throughout except in forest and the adjacent coastal region. Commonest vulture at Mole, Dec–Jan (Sutton 1970). Records at Shai Hills on Accra Plains always associated with a carcase — 28 Oct 1956 (Lamm & Horwood 1958), c. 30 on 3 Oct 1973, c. 20 in Nov 1973 (K. Rice, G. Vanderstichelen).
Breeding. Unrecorded. Jan–Mar, N. Nigeria (Elgood 1982).

68. GYPS RUPPELLII
    (I. 101)   Rüppell's Griffon   V
Vagrant (*G. r. ruppellii*). Snow (1978: 66) accepted the first record, an uncertain sighting by Sutton (1970) at Mole, 11 Jan, although excluded by Greig-Smith (1976a). Another sighting, Jan or Feb 1986, within forest zone (I. Hepburn).

69. NEOPHRON (= NECROSYRTES) MONACHUS
    (I.106)   Hooded Vulture   RB
Abundant resident near towns and villages throughout the savanna and forest zones except the wet evergreen forest in southwest.
Breeding. Nest site often in *Ceiba pentandra*; eggs, Oct–Jan; large young in nest as late as Apr at Accra and Akropong, Akwapim (Grimes 1972a, C. M. Morrison, Macdonald 1979b).

70. NEOPHRON PERCNOPTERUS
    (I.105)   Egyptian Vulture   V
Vagrant (*N. p. percnopterus*). Snow (1978: 68) accepted the sighting of an adult by Harvey & Harrison (1970), but it was omitted by Greig-Smith (1976a). No other records.

71. TRIGONOCEPS OCCIPITALIS
    (I.104)   White-headed Vulture   RB
Not uncommon resident in northern savanna from Bole (W. P. Lowe, G. Cansdale *in* Bannerman 1951: 82) and Tumu (Sutton 1970) in the northwest,

eastwards and south to River Basso (8°30'N, 0°20'E) on the Togo border (M. Horwood).

Breeding. Mole, 2 immatures, Aug (Harvey & Harrison 1970).

Accipitrinae

Circini

Following White (1970), *Circaetus gallicus,* a Palaearctic migrant, and *C. beaudouini,* an African resident, are both given specific rank. Elgood (1982) also follows this arrangement but the 2 are treated as subspecific by Brown (1970) and Snow (1978) and others. They are virtually alike in the field, and most observers tend to attribute dry season (winter) records to migrant *gallicus* and wet season (summer) records to resident *beaudouini.*

72. CIRCAETUS BEAUDOUINI
(I. 143)   Beaudouin's Harrier-Eagle   V

Status uncertain because indistinguishable in the field from *C. gallicus.* Identified with certainty, Aug, a pair on several dates at Mole (Harvey & Harrison 1970). No other records. See *Circaetus gallicus.*

73. CIRCAETUS CINERASCENS
(I.144)   Banded Harrier-Eagle   R(B)

Uncommon resident in northern savanna south to Yeji and Kete Kratchi (G. Thierry *in* Reichenow 1902). Recorded Kulnaba, near Navrongo, 28 Jun; Tumu, 23/24 Sep (Sutton 1970); Mole, occasionally in wet season (Greig-Smith 1976a) and a probable breeding pair, 27–29 Mar (Thiollay 1977); a singleton, Kintampo/Tamale road, 17 Jul (Thiollay 1977).

Breeding. Unrecorded in West Africa.

74. CIRCAETUS CINEREUS
(I.141)   Brown Harrier-Eagle   R(B)

Uncommon resident in northern wooded savanna: a singleton Tumu, 24 Nov (Sutton 1970); a ♀ collected by Giffard at Gambaga, 14 Jan 1899 (Hartert 1899a); Mole, several records. Twice recorded on the Accra Plains, 8 and 14 Feb 1973 (L.G.G., F. Walsh, G. Vanderstichelen), probably overlooked.

Breeding. Unrecorded in West Africa.

75. CIRCAETUS GALLICUS
(I.140)   Short-toed Eagle   PM

Uncommon Palaearctic migrant, Oct–Mar, to northern savanna woodland, south to coastal belt east of Cape Coast. No sightings from within the forest zone. Confusion with *C. beaudouini* makes data uncertain. Mole, Mar 1969 (M. Edmunds, L.G.G.); Accra Plains, 18 Mar, 11 Oct (Gass 1954); Cape Coast, 17 Dec 1975 (M. Macdonald). Early sighting, 24 Sep, on Accra Plains by M. Edmunds (Grimes 1972a) might well refer to *beaudouini.*

76. CIRCUS AERUGINOSUS
(I.170)   Marsh Harrier   PM

Uncommon Palaearctic migrant (*C. a. aeruginosus*), Oct–Apr, to wetlands and margins of lakes in northern savanna and also lagoons at Accra and eastwards to Keta. Not recorded from Cape Coast (M. Macdonald). In the north: Bawku, Nov–Dec (M. Horwood); Tamale reservoir, Feb–Mar (E. Hall); occurs Tono dam, Oct–Apr (R. Passmore). In the south, Keta, singles or pairs, Feb–Mar (Sutton 1965b);

Weija and saltpans, west of Accra, Dec to early Apr (Grimes 1972a), but one Sakumo lagoon, near Tema, 14 Oct 1986 (RSPB Film Unit).

77.   CIRCUS MACROURUS
(I.169)   Pale Harrier   PM
Common Palaearctic migrant, Nov–Mar, mainly in drier less wooded savanna in north, and south to Ho, but also in the dry coastal belt from Takoradi (M. Horwood) eastwards to Cape Coast (Buckley & Shelley 1872), Winneba, 13 Jan (M. Macdonald) and Accra Plains (Gass 1957; Grimes 1972a). In the north regular; up to 6, at savanna fires (M. Horwood) and at rice paddies (F. Walsh). Occasional in forest clearings (F. C. Holman *in* Bannerman 1951) but not at Tafo (M. Lockwood).

78.   CIRCUS PYGARGUS
(I.168)   Montagu's Harrier   PM
Not uncommon Palaearctic migrant, Dec–Mar, to northern savanna, particularly at rice paddies, where they are as common as *C. macrourus,* ratio 6 : 8 respectively (Walsh & Grimes 1981). Three records in south: Sakumo lagoon west of Tema, 2♂♂ 10 Jan 1982; Volta mouth, 2♂♂ 19 Jan 1986; Shai Hills, 1♀, 3 Jan 1986 (E. Dunn, R. E. Scott).

79.   DRYOTRIORCHIS SPECTABILIS
(I.139)   Serpent-Eagle   R(B)
Rare resident (*D. s. spectabilis*) in forest region. Collected Akwapim area (Riis *in* Bouet 1955), Prahsu, Mar (B. Alexander), Bibiani, 4 Jul, Sefwi district (M. Horwood) and "fantee area" (received by G. E. Shelley, *in* Bannerman 1930). Recent sightings: north of Cape Coast (D. James); near Bibiani (M. Horwood).
Breeding. Unrecorded in West Africa.

80.   POLYBOROIDES RADIATUS (= GYMNOGENYS TYPICUS)
(I.171)   Harrier-Hawk   RB
Common resident (*P. r. pectoralis*), within forest, widespread but less common in more wooded areas of northern savanna, and south to Kete Kratchi and Ho. Occasional on the Accra Plains; Weija (D. Lamm) and Shai Hills, 24 Feb, 19 Jun, 11 Nov (L.G.G.).
Breeding. Nest building: within forest region, Aug (Holman 1947); Akwapim, Nov (nest used Apr) (C. M. Morrison). Nestling: Mampong, Ashanti, 21 Feb (Lowe 1937). Fledgling: Akropong, Akwapim, 21 Jan (C. M. Morrison). Flying young: Tafo, Aug (M. Lockwood).

81.   TERATHOPIUS ECAUDATUS
(I. 146)   Bateleur   RB
Common resident, in ones or two's throughout the northern savanna, occasional within forest clearings, e.g. Goaso and Mampong, Ashanti (Lowe 1937). Sporadic, Feb–Nov, on the Accra Plains and in Volta region.
Breeding. Juveniles at Mole, Dec (R. W. W. Sutton).

Accipitrini

82.   ACCIPITER BADIUS
(I.160)   Shikra   RB, Afm/B
Locally common resident (*A. b. sphenurus*) in the more wooded areas of the Accra Plains. and at Cape Coast (2 pairs only, M. Macdonald); mainly seasonal in northern savanna and in larger forest clearings. In the north, Oct to early Jul, Tumu (Sutton 1970), Tamale (J. Callow) and Wenchi (Russell 1949a). Within the forest at Kumasi, Nov–Mar (dry season) (Holman 1947).

Breeding. At least 10 pairs nested at Legon, near Accra, in 1972. Eggs: C/3, mid Dec to mid Mar; one female raised 2 broods. Old nests occasionally used by *Otus leucotus* (Grimes 1972a). Nestlings: Cape Coast, Feb–Mar (Macdonald 1979b).

83.   ACCIPITER ERYTHROPUS (= MINULLUS)
      (I.156)   Western Little Sparrow-Hawk   R(B)
Uncommon resident (*A. e. erythropus*) within forest region. Skins collected Boutry (Pel), Mampong (2) in Ashanti, Feb (Lowe 1937) and Axim (Bannerman 1930). Recent sightings; Jukwa, Jul (M. Macdonald), Tafo (M. Lockwood) and Akropong in Akwapim (C. M. Morrison).
Breeding. Unrecorded in West Africa (MP&G).

84.   ACCIPITER MELANOLEUCUS
      (I.159)   Great Sparrow-Hawk   R(B)
Uncommon resident (*A. m. temminckii*) in both lowland forest and gallery forest reaching as far north as Kete Kratchi (R. E. Crabbe) and Mole (Harvey & Harrison 1970, although omitted by Greig-Smith 1976a); probably overlooked. Recent sightings: May–Jun, Akropong in Akwapim (C. M. Morrison). Skins collected in last century at Cape Coast (E. T. Higgins), Akwapim (A. Riis), Boutry (Pel) and Kete Kratchi, Mar (Zech).
Breeding. Unrecorded. Breeds southern Nigeria, Jan–Feb, Aug–Sep (Elgood 1982).

85.   ACCIPITER OVAMPENSIS
      (I.157)   Ovampa Sparrow-Hawk   AfM/NB
Rare intra-African migrant, mainly Jul–Dec, to northern savanna. Collected Gambaga, Dec (Hartert 1899a); probable sightings Mole, Aug–Sep (Harvey & Harrison 1970) and Tamale, 4 Sep (E. Hall). Seen at "close quarters after killing a rat", 10 May, Accra (N. Wood). This early record is consistent with migration from the south (Elgood 1982).

86.   ACCIPITER TOUSSENELII (= MACROCELIDES)
      (I.163)   West African Goshawk   RB
Common resident (*A. t. macrocelides*) within the forest region (M. Horwood, Holman 1947); collected Mampong (5) in Ashanti, and Ejura, Feb (Lowe 1937). Sporadic records for Mole Game Park (Harvey & Harrison 1970; Greig-Smith 1976a), but probably resident.
Breeding. Female with slightly enlarged ovaries: Ejura, 16 Feb (Lowe 1937). Eggs and young: Akropong, Akwapim, Dec to late Feb (C. M. Morrison). Immature: Wenchi, Jan (Russell 1949a).

87.   MELIERAX (= MICRONISUS) GABAR
      (I.165)   Gabar Goshawk   R(B)
Not uncommon resident in northern savanna, south along dry eastern corridor to Accra Plains, and westwards to Cape Coast (R. B. Payne). Sporadic records throughout the year at Accra. No records from within the forest area.
Breeding. Unrecorded. In Nigeria, Apr–Jul (Elgood 1982).

88.   MELIERAX METABATES
      (I.166)   Dark Chanting-Goshawk   R(B), AfM?/(B)
Uncommon resident (*M. m. metabates*), but widespread in more open savanna in north (M. Horwood), occasional Mole, Aug (Harvey & Harrison 1970); an influx

into northern Ghana from further north apparently occurs in mid dry season, Jan–Mar (Bannerman 1953). Collected in the north, 25 Nov (D. Lamm). Only 2 records in south: Ho in Volta Region, 17 Aug (N. Wood); Weija near Accra, 7 Jan (N. Wood).

Breeding. Unrecorded. Breeds Mar and Apr at Sokoto and Zaria, Nigeria (Elgood 1982).

89. UROTRIORCHIS MACROURUS
(I.167)   Long-tailed Hawk   R(B)

A common resident, widespread in the forest zone and usually only seen when crossing roads (M. Horwood). Collected Dabocrom (Pel), Ejura and Mampong, Ashanti, Feb (Lowe 1937); also many were brought to Cockburn (1946).

Breeding. Unrecorded for West Africa.

Buteini

90. BUTASTUR RUFIPENNIS
(I.145)   Grasshopper Buzzard   AfM/NB

Common in northern savanna in dry season, Nov–Mar, due to influx from the north of non-breeding birds; some may remain throughout the year. Regular at savanna fires, Dec–Feb, birds moving south as far as Kete Kratchi and Ho (M. Horwood, L.G.G.).

91. BUTEO AUGURALIS
(I.153)   Red-necked (Red-tailed) Buzzard   AfM/B, Afm/B?

Common dry season breeding visitor to savanna areas, widespread; some probably resident within the forest zone, although not at Tafo (M. Lockwood). Influx of breeding birds at coast apparent late Sep, majority leaving by early Jun, although some remain throughout the year.

Breeding. Nest construction: frequently now in pylons, Dec. Eggs and young: Jan to early May in both savanna and forest. Same nest site may be used in consecutive years. Nested Subri River Forest Reserve sometime in 1983 (M. F. Hodges, Jr).

92. BUTEO BUTEO VULPINUS
(I.149)   Steppe Buzzard   V, PM

One record: a bird ringed in Tunisia recovered Keta (Appendix 3). Recorded Ivory Coast, Liberia and Senegal (Thiollay 1977); one ringed Norrby, Sweden (63°26′N, 16°06′E) recovered close to Ghana border at Atakpame, Togoland (7°20′N, 01°08′E), 28 Feb 1968.

93. BUTEO RUFINUS
(I.151)   Long-legged Buzzard   V, PM

One record: 3 together, all of different colour phases, Abokobi, 30 Nov 1971 (Walsh & Grimes 1981). Recorded at the coast in Nigeria (Elgood 1982) and in the Ivory Coast (Thiollay 1977, 1985).

94. KAUPIFALCO MONOGRAMMICUS
(I. 138)   Lizzard Buzzard   RB, AfM/B

Not uncommon resident in wooded savanna, e.g. Mole in north, Abokobi and Shai Hills on the Accra Plains in the south, and forest edge, e.g. Akropong, Akwapim (C. M. Morrison). Influx of breeding birds in dry season augments the resident birds: Tumu, Oct–Feb (Sutton 1970); Northwest Ashanti, late Dec to early Jun (Russell 1949a); Tafo, Dec–Feb (M. Lockwood); Kumasi (Holman 1947);

Accra Plains, Nov–Apr. Not recorded Cape Coast nor Winneba (M. Macdonald), and avoids thick forest.

Breeding. Eggs: northwest Ashanti, late Apr; Accra Plains, Feb–Mar. Nestlings: northwest Ashanti, May (Russell 1949a). Fledglings: Accra Plains, one in old nest of *Accipiter badius,* 30 Jul (B. Smit).

Aquilini

95.   AQUILA RAPAX
(I.128)   Tawny Eagle   RB

Uncommon and local resident (*A. r. belisarius*) in wooded savanna, e.g. Mole (Greig-Smith 1976a); elsewhere in north a dry season visitor at fires, Dec–Jan. Occurs Tumu (Sutton 1970) and 2 sightings Ejura, Jan–Feb (Lowe 1937). Regular on the Accra Plains, Jan to late Mar (Grimes 1972a), also Aug (J. R. Marshall); one at Amedzofe, 12 Apr (N. Wood).

Breeding. Occupied nest on Accra Plains thought to contain eggs, Dec–Jan (J. R. Marshall *in* Bannerman 1951). Eggs: probably Oct-Feb (Bannerman 1953).

96.   AQUILA WAHLBERGI
(I.130)   Wahlberg's Eagle   R(B)

Not uncommon resident in wooded savanna in the north; some reach the Accra Plains, where both dark and light phases occur, and Keta, Sep–Apr (Holman 1947).

Breeding. Twigs being carried Kwabenya on Accra Plains, late Oct and early Nov (L.G.G.). In Nigeria, Jun–Sep, and Dec (Elgood 1982).

97.   HALIAEETUS (= CUNCUMA) VOCIFER
(I.147)   Fish Eagle   RB

Not uncommon resident, well distributed throughout the north along major river systems and larger lakes with wooded fringes; in recent years the Volta lake has provided ideal habitat. Sporadic at fish farm within Subri River Forest Reserve (M. F. Hodges, Jr), occasional along the coastal belt near Sekondi (Bannerman 1951) and several Weija, Dec 1982.

Breeding. Occupied nest: Mole, Sep 1974 (N. C. Davidson). Juvenile: Mole, mid Aug (Harvey & Harrison 1970).

98.   HIERAAETUS (= CASSINAETUS) AFRICANUS
(I.136)   Cassin's Hawk-Eagle   RB

Uncommon forest resident. One filmed, Feb 1971, by R. A. Honeywell and identified by F. Walsh; probably overlooked, as in recent years regularly seen Aug–Dec, Apr–Jun, at several forest reserves (Macdonald & Taylor 1977).

Breeding. Well grown chick, 10 Dec 1976, at Suhien Forest Reserve, and in Jun 1977 a recently fledged young in same nest. Considered by Macdonald & Taylor (1977) as a possible biannual breeder, but the above fledgling may have been the chick of 10 Dec (see Skorupa *et al.* 1985); alternatively it may have been from another nest and was roosting in the nest found by Macdonald & Taylor.

99.   HIERAAETUS DUBIUS (= AYRESI)
(I.132)   Ayres' Hawk-Eagle   RB

Rare resident, confined to forest and coastal region. Records of singletons: Achimota, 23 Nov (L.G.G.); Nakwa, 14 Jan; Brimsu reservoir, 2 Oct (M. Macdonald); Tafo (M. Lockwood). An immature female of unknown age found dying, 5 Jan 1973, at Legon (wing 378 mm, tail 200 mm, tarsus 76 mm, L.G.G.), now in BMNH, overlooked in Snow (1978).

Breeding. A fledgling captured near Ntubia (=Antubia), 100 miles NW of Dunkwa, was sent (4 Apr 1947) to London Zoo by B. J. Shaw and eventually identified as a female by D. A. Bannerman (Bannerman 1951); it died on 19 May 1950 (P. J. Olney).

100. HIERAAETUS PENNATUS
(I.133)   Booted Eagle   PM

Not uncommon Palaearctic migrant in small numbers in well wooded savanna in north, Dec–Apr (Thiollay 1977, Walsh & Grimes 1981); possibly overlooked. Occasional light phase birds reach the Accra Plains (B. Smit, M. McClelland, F. Walsh).

101. HIERAAETUS SPILOGASTER (=FASCIATUS)
(I.131)   African Hawk-Eagle   R(B)

Uncommon resident of the northern woodland savanna. Collected Gambaga, 24 Oct 1898 (Hartert 1899a), and Sa, 14 Jun 1943 (Cockburn 1946). Sightings at Tumu, 10 Nov, 27 Nov, 25 May (Sutton 1970) and many at Mole (Greig-Smith 1976a). Only one record from south: Shai Hills, Jan or Feb 1986 (I. Hepburn).
Breeding. Unrecorded. In Nigeria, nesting Dec (Elgood 1982).

102. LOPHAETUS (=LOPHOAETUS) OCCIPITALIS
(I.137)   Long-crested Hawk-Eagle   RB

Common resident throughout the woodland savanna, less frequent in clearings within the forest region (M. Horwood); occasional, both dry and wet season months, in Shai Hills (L.G.G.); also once at Keta, 22 Aug (Sutton 1970).
Breeding. Two well grown nestlings, Apr, at Nchirra, NW Ashanti (Russell 1949a).

103. POLEMAETUS BELLICOSUS
(I.134)   Martial Eagle   R(B)

Uncommon resident in some northern savanna areas e.g. Mole, elsewhere occasional; single birds Tumu, 21 Oct, 24 Nov, 9 May, 1 Jun (Sutton 1970). In the south singletons sighted, Jun–Sep, in Shai Hills (L.G.G.).
Breeding. Unrecorded. In Nigeria, Aug–Jan (Elgood 1982).

104. STEPHANOAETUS CORONATUS
(I.135)   Crowned Hawk-Eagle   RB

Uncommon forest resident but well distributed; distinctive call often heard (M. Horwood). Collected in the last century Cape Coast (E. T. Higgins) and Accra (?) (Edwards *in* Bouet 1955).
Breeding. Well grown young: Nchirra, NW Ashanti, Apr 1947 (Russell 1949a).

Milvini

105. AVICEDA CUCULOIDES
(I.121)   Cuckoo Falcon   Afm/B

Not uncommon resident, but locally distributed both in wooded savanna in north (presumably *A. c. cuculoides*) and in forest clearings and wooded savanna in south (presumably *A. c. batesi*); not seen in every month. Accra Plains, Jan–Sep; Tafo, Nov only (M. Lockwood); Tamale, Jan–Feb (E. Hall); Gambaga escarpment, Jan and Aug (F. Walsh). Collected Boutry (Pel); Ejura, 31 Jan; Mampong in Ashanti, 5 Feb (Lowe 1937) and Mole, 8 Nov (Appendix 5).

Breeding. Carrying foliage: Abokobi, Apr (Grimes 1972a). Female with 4 more eggs to lay: Mampong, Ashanti, Feb (Lowe 1937). Adult with juvenile: Shai Hills, 8 Sep (L.G.G.).

106. ELANUS CAERULEUS
    (I.124)   Black-shouldered Kite   RB
Common resident (*E. c. caeruleus*) in wooded savanna in north and east, and on the Accra Plains eastwards to Denu (Sutton 1965b), although Holman (1947) thought it rare at Keta. Occasional within forest clearings: Tarkwa, 2 Apr; Korforidua, Jan–Mar (M. Horwood); avoids true forest. Common at Winneba in Horwood's day but now only occasional (Macdonald 1979a).
    Breeding. Nest building: Denu, Feb (Sutton 1965b). Nesting: Tono dam, Dec 1981 (R. Passmore). Eggs: Accra Plains, Dec–Feb (Grimes 1972a).

107. ELANUS (=CHELICTINIA) RIOCOURII
    (I.122)   Swallow-tailed Kite   AfM/NB
Not uncommon intra-African migrant, Nov–May, to northern dry savanna, particularly near Gambaga and Bawku, and south to Salaga and Wenchi. Not yet recorded from Mole (Greig-Smith 1976a). Collected Gambaga, 22 Jan 1899 (Hartert 1899a), Wenchi, 21 Jan (Lowe 1937), the latter incorrectly plotted in Snow (1978).

108. MACHEIRHAMPHUS (=MACHAERHAMPHUS) ALCINUS
    (I.125)   Bat-eating Buzzard or Bat Hawk   RB
Uncommon resident (*M. a. anderssoni*), locally distributed in savanna woodland; has occurred Shai Hills, Achimota, and Densu river in south and Tamale (Holman 1947) in north. Occasional Cape Coast (M. Macdonald), and in forest clearings; at Korforidua found in swallow roost (M. Lockwood). Avoids true forest (M. Horwood).
    Breeding. Juvenile: Mampong in Ashanti, 8 Feb (Lowe 1937).

109. MILVUS MIGRANS
    (I.123)   Kite (Black Kite)   Afm/B, PM
Abundant resident (*M. m. parasitus*) throughout, but only a few in south, Jun–Sep. Breeding birds arrive at Tafo and the coast late Sep. Southward migration of *parasitus* and presumably Palaearctic migrants (*M. m. migrans*) visible at Tumu late Sep (Sutton 1970).
    Palaearctic birds ringed in Spain (3), Switzerland (3), Germany (2) and France (1) have been recovered in Ghana (Appendix 3, Fry 1982).
    Breeding. Nest construction begins late Oct, nests often on electricity pylons. Nesting Tono dam, May (R. Passmore). Eggs: Accra Plains, Korforidua, and Akropong in Akwapim, Jan–Apr; Cape Coast, Sep–Feb (Macdonald 1979b).

110. PERNIS APIVORUS
    (I.126)   Honey-Buzzard   PM
Not uncommon Palaearctic migrant, widespread in both forest clearings and savanna, but mainly within forest zone, Nov–May; Mole, Oct (R. B. Payne). Some may remain in wet season; one, normal phase, Lake Bosumptwi, 24 Aug (N. Wood). Collected Boutry (Pel), "Denkere" (Aubinn) and Goaso, 18 Dec (Lowe 1937).
    Birds ringed in Sweden (7), Germany (2) and Holland (1) recovered within the forest region.

SAGITTARIIDAE

111. SAGITTARIUS SERPENTARIUS
(I.99)   Secretary Bird   AfM/NB

An uncommon nonbreeding visitor, Dec–Mar, in northern treeless dry savanna; sporadic records at Mole, Pong Tamale, Kete Kratchi and Yapei. A single at Shai Hills, 23 Mar 1974, was seen after the passing of a line storm (K. Rice); another in dry season at Kumasi (Holman 1947).

FALCONIDAE

112. FALCO ALOPEX
(I.118)   Fox Kestrel   AfM/NB?

Not uncommon non-breeding visitor from north, Nov–Mar, to northern savanna (8°–10°N), particularly along escarpments (Thiollay 1977) and at isolated rocky hills (Brown 1970). Often present at grass fires (F. C. Holman *in* Bannerman 1951, Sutton 1970). Collected Gambaga escarpment, Dec, by Giffard (Hartert 1899a) and Alexander (1902).

Breeding. Unrecorded, but Gambaga escarpment and any isolated rocky hills are likely sites. In more northern latitudes of West Africa breeds Mar at the end of its dry season stay (Brown 1970, Elgood 1982).

113. FALCO ARDOSIACEUS
(I.119)   Grey Kestrel   RB, Afm/B

Not uncommon in wooded savanna throughout, locally distributed and seasonal in coastal belt from Cape Coast eastwards to Keta. Resident in the north at Tumu (Sutton 1970) and Mole (Greig-Smith 1976a), but possibly not in every year (Taylor & Macdonald 1978a), and in the south at Legon and Shai Hills (Grimes 1972a), although records are few Jun–Sep. Absent Cape Coast, Dec–Feb (Macdonald 1979a); only one recorded Jan–Jul 1964, Denu (Sutton 1965b), but regular at Keta in Holman's day (Holman 1947).

Breeding. Eggs: C/3, Accra and Keta Plains, Jan–Mar (Holman 1947, Grimes 1972a). Dependent young: Cape Coast, 16 May 1977 (Macdonald 1979b).

114. FALCO BIARMICUS
(I.108)   Lanner   RB, Afm?

Uncommon resident (*F. b. abyssinicus*) in savanna throughout, often near villages; more common in coastal region east of Cape Coast, and in forest clearings near savanna areas, e.g. Akropong in Akwapim (C. M. Morrison). Regular at Cape Coast but seasonal, with more records Feb–Apr (Macdonald 1979a). Moderately common in north in Holman's day (Holman 1947), but not recorded in recent years at Tumu and only once at Mole, 9 Apr (Sutton 1970, Greig-Smith 1976a, Taylor & Macdonald 1978a). Collected Wenchi, 19 Jan, and Ejura, 5 Feb (Lowe 1937). Once recorded at sea off Accra, bird coming aboard ship (Sharland 1955).

Breeding. Nestlings: Accra Plains, mid Feb (J. R. Marshall *in* Bannerman 1951); Tamale, mid Apr. Flying young: Tamale, May (Holman 1947).

115. FALCO CHICQUERA
(I.115)   Red-necked Falcon   R?(B), AfM/NB?

Rare, probably resident (*F. c. ruficollis*), but locally distributed in drier more open treeless savanna in north; possibly overlooked. Sightings only at Gambaga

(Bannerman 1930), Jirape, 31 Oct (Sutton 1970), Tono dam, Jun (R. Passmore) and Mole, mid Aug (Harvey & Harrison 1970). Greig-Smith (1976a) thought it possibly a wet season non-breeding visitor to Mole.

Breeding. Unrecorded. In Nigeria, Jan–Mar (Elgood 1982).

116. FALCO CUVIERI
(I.110)   African Hobby   RB

Not uncommon resident in some areas of wooded savanna, e.g. Mole in north, Accra Plains in south; elsewhere seasonal. Commonest falcon Denu, Dec–Mar (Sutton 1965a,b), but only 3 sightings at Cape Coast, Jan–Mar (Macdonald 1979a); regular at Akropong in Akwapim, both dry and wet season months (C. M. Morrison), and at Mampong in Ashanti during Lowe's stay (Lowe 1937).

Breeding. Immatures on wing: Legon, no date (B. Smit, M. McClelland).

117. FALCO NAUMANNI
(I.117)   Lesser Kestrel   V, PM

Rare Palaearctic migrant, only 2 records: Mole, Jan (Maze 1971); 8 together at Yapei, 24 Apr 1973 (Thiollay 1977). Stated to occur in Ghana (Bannerman 1953, Serle *et al.* 1977), but source not traced.

118. FALCO PEREGRINUS
(I.107)   Peregrine   PM, RB

Uncommon, in open country at Coast (Accra) and inland. Most records, Oct–May, probably concern the Palaearctic migrant (*F. p. calidus*). Wet season records Accra (B. Smit) and sightings by Holman (1947) at Akim Oda, probably refer to African resident (*F. p. minor*), which has been collected at Axim (Bannerman 1930).

Breeding. Copulation observed, Akim Oda (Holman 1947).

119. FALCO SUBBUTEO
(I.109)   Hobby   V, PM

Rare Palaearctic migrant, only 3 certain records: one at Legon, 5 Mar 1973 (B. Smit *in* Walsh & Grimes 1981); one Mole, 6 Apr 1976 (Taylor & Macdonald 1978a); one Kibi, 20 Jan 1986 (R. E. Scott *et al.*). Other sightings by B. Smit at Legon in the dry season 1970–71 were considered to be this species.

120. FALCO TINNUNCULUS
(I.116)   Kestrel   PM, R(B)

Owing to the close similarity of *F. t. tinnunculus*, a Palaearctic migrant, and *F. t. rufescens*, an African resident, their status is uncertain. All dry season records, Nov–Mar, in open country throughout, probably refer to *tinnunculus*; occasional Cape Coast (M. Macdonald) and Kumasi (F. C. Holman *in* Bannerman 1951). African *rufescens* collected Ejura, 29 Jan 1935 (Lowe 1937).

Breeding. Unrecorded. In Nigeria, Mar–May (Elgood 1982).

Birds ringed in Holland (1) and Tunisia (1) have been recorded in Ghana. Moreau (1972) also reports a Czech-ringed bird recovered in Ghana, but the data are not traceable.

[FALCO VESPERTINUS
(I.112)   Red-footed Falcon (Red-legged Kestrel)

Regular sightings of small numbers over marshy areas at Mole in early part of dry season, Oct–Dec, were thought to be of this species (Greig-Smith 1976a), but this remains uncertain. Majority of records in Nigeria and all in Ivory Coast coincide with the spring migration, Feb–Apr (Elgood 1982, Thiollay 1985).]

PHASIANIDAE

Phasianinae

121. COTURNIX CHINENSIS (= EXCALFACTORIA ADANSONII)
(I.194)   Blue Quail   AfM/(B)

Locally not uncommon (*C. c. adansonii*) in moist grassy areas during the wet season, May–Jul, on the Winneba and Accra Plains. An African breeding migrant with a probable east–west movement; 15–20 pairs flushed near Winneba, 13 Jun 1973, but none there Dec 1973 (L.G.G.). Many collected, Jun and Jul, on Accra Plains (Bannerman 1930, Bouet 1955). Significantly only dry season records for Cape Coast and Sekondi — singles 24 Jan and 3 Feb respectively (M. Macdonald, Holman 1947). The late J. Hall examined "bewildered birds that had flown into houses" at Cape Coast, time and date unknown. In Ivory Coast common in savanna from coast northwards, mostly Nov–May, but some also in wet season (Thiollay 1985).

Breeding. Unrecorded. Very small young: Lagos, Nigeria, 3 Jul (Elgood 1982).

122. COTURNIX COTURNIX
(I.192)   Quail   PM

Uncommon Palaearctic migrant (*C. c. coturnix*), Oct–Mar, in scrub savanna, particularly in cassava farms, in coastal areas just west and north of Accra (Bannerman 1951, 1953). Occasional in forest clearings, e.g. Kumasi (F. C. Holman *in* Bannerman 1951), but not yet recorded from the north; probably overlooked.

123. COTURNIX DELEGORGUEI
(I.193)   Harlequin Quail   V, AfM?/NB

Vagrant (*C. d. delegorguei*), only one record. One shot, 4 Jan 1948, on the Accra Plains by Col. W. J. Brimble (C. M. Morrison); skin not preserved. In Nigeria, data suggest a southward movement in Dec, the middle of the dry season (Elgood 1982). A dry season migrant to the Ivory Coast (Thiollay (1985).

124. FRANCOLINUS AHANTENSIS
(I.188)   Ahanta Francolin   RB

A common resident (*F. a. ahantensis*), widespread in mature and secondary forest and in thickets in coastal areas from Cape Coast to western edge of Accra Plains. Occasional outside forest region: located in teak plantation at Kpandu (M. Horwood).

Breeding. Eggs: C/3, 4 or 5, late Dec to Jan. Small Young: Akropong, Akwapim, 22 Mar (C. M. Morrison). Half grown broods, Feb–Apr (M. Horwood).

125. FRANCOLINUS ALBOGULARIS
(I.179)   White-throated Francolin   RB

Locally not uncommon resident (*F. a. buckleyi*), in northern woodland savanna and along forest/savanna boundary, extending south to Ho and the Accra Plains. Not located yet in coastal areas west of Accra.

Breeding. Birds collected Ejura, Feb, had enlarged gonads (Lowe 1937). Pair with young (quail size): Tamale, 21 Oct (M. Horwood).

126. FRANCOLINUS BICALCARATUS
(I.183)   Double-spurred Francolin (Bushfowl)   RB

The commonest bushfowl (*F. b. bicalcaratus*), resident in most types of savanna, within forest clearings (e.g. Kumasi, Tafo) and forest/savanna edge; locally abundant near cultivation in coastal areas east of Elmina. Only located 3 times, however, at Tumu between Sep 1968 and Jul 1969 (Sutton 1970).

Breeding. Season extended. Eggs: Oct–June. Sparrow size young: Oct. Half grown young: Oct, Nov, Jan and Jun (M. Horwood, Macdonald 1979b).

127. FRANCOLINUS LATHAMI
(I.173)   Forest Francolin   RB

Not uncommon resident (*F. l. lathami*) throughout the forest region and locally in coastal thicket near Cape Coast and western edge of Accra Plains. Collected in many localities within the forest region but also near Accra in Feb (Bouet 1955) and near Legon, 30 Apr 1966 (Appendix 5).

Breeding. Eggs: Feb (M. Horwood).

128. PTILOPACHUS PETROSUS
(I. 195)   Stone-Partridge   R(B)

Locally not uncommon resident (*P. p. petrosus*), mainly but not always on rocky outcrops in savanna areas throughout the north and southward to the Accra Plains; not yet recorded west of Accra.

Breeding. Unrecorded. A wet season breeder in Nigeria (Elgood 1982).

Numidinae

129. AGELASTES MELEAGRIDES
(I.200)   White-breasted Guinea-Fowl   R(B)

A very rare forest species now greatly endangered and confined to undisturbed forest; probably now extinct within Ghana (Collar & Stuart 1985). In recent years was located in groups of 6–8, near Axim and Bia forest reserve (M. Horwood) and near Asankrangwa (L.G.G.) in western region. Two, captured in early 1960's, were sent to Berlin Zoo (Raethel 1965). In former days collected near Dabocrom (Pel), and 4–5 sighted, 1930, near Bopa, east (not west as *in* Bannerman 1953) of the Tano river (D. Cooper *in* Bannerman 1953).

Breeding. Unrecorded in West Africa.

130. GUTTERA EDOUARDI
(I.198)   Crested Guinea-Fowl   RB

Not uncommon widespread resident (*G. e. verreauxi*) within the forest zone, mainly in small groups. Occasional on Accra Plains and in Shai Hills (one shot, 24 Feb 1973). More regular there and on Winneba Plains in the last century (Ussher 1874). Collected Goaso and Ejura, Jan and Feb (Lowe 1937).

Breeding. Eggs: Jan–Feb. Female, collected 17 Feb, had 3 more eggs to lay (Lowe 1937).

131. NUMIDA MELEAGRIS
(I.197)   Guinea-Fowl   R(B)

Locally not uncommon resident (*N. m. galeata*) in wooded savanna throughout north, often occurring in flocks of 50–100; numerous at Tumu (Sutton 1970). Widespread domestication makes it difficult to assess status in southern areas but occurs Abutia Kloe in Volta region, and collected last century in "fantee country" (Bannerman 1930).

Breeding. Unrecorded. West African data suggest an extensive breeding season, peaking Jun–Oct.

TURNICIDAE

132. ORTYXELOS MEIFFRENII
(I.330)   Quail-Plover   AfM/B

Uncommon dry season breeding visitor, Dec–Mar, to coastal strip from Winneba westwards to Takoradi (Lamm & Horwood 1958). Not recorded in northern savanna nor in Volta region (M. Horwood); probably an intra-African migrant moving to more northern latitudes in wet season after breeding.

Breeding. Two newly hatched young, Elmina, in dry season (Lamm & Horwood 1958).

133.   TURNIX HOTTENTOTTA (= NANA)
(I.329)   Black-rumped Button-Quail   V

Vagrant, 2 records (*T. h. nana*): a skin, no date, marked Accra (Bannerman 1931: 487) and one sighting at Mole, April (Maze 1971).

134. TURNIX SYLVATICA
(I.328)   Button Quail   R(B)

Not uncommon, presumed local resident (*T. s. lepurana*) in open grassland in coastal areas east of Cape Coast, more common on Winneba and Accra–Keta Plains (D. Lamm). Records are sporadic and cover both dry and wet season months (Nov, Jan, Feb, Mar, Jun) and might indicate seasonal movement. Many collected in last century in coastal districts; no record from the north but probably overlooked.

Breeding. Unrecorded. In Nigeria, eggs, Jul; chicks, Jan and Apr (Elgood 1982).

GRUIDAE

Balearicinae

135. BALEARICA PAVONINA
(I.225)   Crowned Crane   AfM/NB

Uncommon non breeding visitor (*B. p. pavonina*), Dec–Jun, to wetlands in the north, much less common now than in earlier years. Along the Volta river, north of Yegi, groups of c. 12 were often located in Pomeroy's day, and Holman considered it common throughout the north (Bannerman 1931, 1951); c. 40 Pong Tamale, 1 Oct 1956 (M. Horwood). Occasional on the Accra Plains in 1930's but no recent records; southern records may have been escapes.

RALLIDAE

Rallinae

136. CANIRALLUS OCULEUS
(I.203)   Grey-throated Rail   R(B)

A rare resident (*C. o. oculeus*) along streams and marshes within the forest region. Most records are of collected specimens: Boutry river (Pel), Cape Coast (Higgins), Akwapim (Riis) and Ejura, Goaso and Mampong in Ashanti, Dec–Feb (Lowe 1937). One sighting in marshy area of forest in Obuasi district (M. Horwood).

Breeding. Unrecorded. In West Africa, at least Nov–Jun (MP&G).

137. CREX CREX
(I.205)   Corn Crake   PM

Rare Palaearctic migrant, possibly vagrant, only one record: a female collected, 13 Feb 1966, on the University campus at Kumasi (Dahm 1969).

138. CREX (= CRECOPSIS) EGREGIA

(I.206)   African Crake   RB

Not uncommon resident in dry savanna covered with low bush and patchy grass in coastal areas, in forest clearings, and in the north (Holman 1947). Usually avoids wet areas, but one netted Suhien sewage farm (M. Lockwood) and 5 Kasu lagoon, 5 · May (N. Wood). Found at Cape Coast, mainly Dec–May, and regular but probably seasonal at Winneba (Macdonald 1979a and *in lit.*); one near Weija, 1 Jun 1968 (L.G.G.). In Nigeria there is a northward movement in the rains (Elgood 1982).

Breeding. Eggs: C/4, cassava farm, 26 Apr 1947 (Russell 1949a); C/5 Tamale, no date (Holman 1947).

139. GALLINULA ANGULATA

(I.221)   Lesser Moorhen   AfM/B

Not uncommon wet season breeding visitor, mainly Jun–Sep, to coastal lagoons, marshes and wetlands but also north to Yendi and Bolgatanga (F. Walsh). Occurred at Kumasi during Holman's day but no recent records. After breeding, Elgood (1982) suggests a migration to south of the equator, but in Ivory Coast is present in all months (Thiollay 1985).

Breeding. Attributed nests, C/3, in wet season, 100 miles west of Accra in Keta area (Holman 1947). Nest building: Cape Coast, 15 Jun 1976. Nestlings: Cape Coast, 9 Jul 1978 (Macdonald 1979b).

140. GALLINULA CHLOROPUS

(I.220)   Moorhen   RB

Uncommon resident (*G. c. meridionalis*) in fresh water pools and along rivers with copious vegetation along banks. Locally distributed, numbers are subject to change from year to year. Common at Keta in 1942, but few in 1943 (Holman 1947). More recently in south, no records Denu (Sutton 1965b), Cape Coast (M. Macdonald) nor Tafo (M. Lockwood). In the north, not recorded Tumu (Sutton 1970) nor anywhere by Holman (1947) but occasional, Feb–Mar, Tamale (E. Hall) and Jan–Feb in White Volta valley (F. Walsh). Resident populations occur at a flooded quarry in the centre of Accra (Grimes 1972a) and at Mole (Greig-Smith 1976a).

Breeding. At Accra breeds throughout the year except during peak of wet season; 6 pairs (one trio) present 1974 (N. Wood). Breeding Keta, June: 15 eggs in one nest laid by 3 females (Holman 1947). Juvenile: Kpota, near Ada, 22 May 1976 (Macdonald 1979b).

141. HIMANTORNIS HAEMATOPUS

(I.202)   Nkulengu Rail   R(B)

Not uncommon resident (*H. h. haematopus*) along stream and marshy areas within the forest zone. The onomatopoeic call frequently heard at dusk and throughout night at Tarkwa, Mpraeso, Sefwi and other forest reserves (M. Horwood). Collected Dabacrom (Pel), Akwapim (Riis) and by Ussher (Bannerman 1931).

Breeding. Unrecorded in West Africa (MP&G).

142. LIMNOCORAX FLAVIROSTRA

(I.207)   Black Crake   RB

Common resident in forest and savanna wetlands bordering pools, rivers and sewage farms, and margins of lagoons in south.

Breeding. Eggs: C/4, Panbros saltpans, Accra, Keta and Kasu (Ke) lagoons, Jun (N. Wood). Chicks: Cape Coast, Mar (Macdonald 1979b). Half grown young: Kasu lagoon, May (N. Wood); Tafo, Sep (M. Horwood). Juveniles: Cape Coast, Oct (Macdonald 1979b).

143. PORPHYRIO (= PORPHYRULA) ALLENI
(I.219)   Allen's Gallinule   RB, Afm?
Not uncommon resident in reed beds and densely vegetated swamps in some coastal areas, elsewhere a probable migrant, but movement and direction obscure. At Tumu first seen 15 Jan and then regular until the wet season, Aug (Sutton 1970); at Mole, Apr–Aug (Greig-Smith 1976a); at Vea dam, 3 on 29 Jun and 1 on 3 Aug 1977 (F. Walsh). Occasional at Cape Coast, but absent in some years, and once Winneba, 8 May (M. Macdonald); in marsh along Ankobra river (A. J. M. Smith). Near Accra and Keta recorded in both wet and dry seasons and assumed resident.
Breeding. Extended. Eggs in ovaries: near Ada, 23 Jun 1956 (Lamm & Horwood 1958). 2 adults, 2 yearlings, 2 juveniles: Opintin river, 19 Jan 1974 (Wood 1977). Juvenile: Cape Coast, 7 Mar 1976 (Macdonald 1979b). Snow (1978) records breeding in wet season only, followed by a migration to lower latitudes.

144. PORPHYRIO PORPHYRIO (= MADAGASCARIENSIS)
(I.218)   Purple Gallinule   Afm?/B
Uncommon and very local, status uncertain (*P. p. madagascariensis*), found in wetlands bordering fresh water lakes in coastal region from Cape Coast eastwards to Keta but records sporadic. At Brimsu reservoir, near Cape Coast, Feb and Apr only (Russell 1949b), but no records since (M. Macdonald). At Keta common, Jun–Aug 1942, but none 1943 (Holman 1947); At Denu only one record, 24 Feb (Sutton 1964); present at lakes south of Ningo hill on Accra Plains, May 1974 (G. Vanderstichelen, N. Wood); up to 50 in marsh at Weija, 19 Nov 1985 (R. Broad). In north, only recorded at Tono dam, Apr 1982 (R. Passmore).
Breeding. Eggs: C/4, Keta, Jul 1942 (Holman 1947).

145. PORZANA MARGINALIS
(I.208)   Striped Crake   Afm?/B
Status uncertain, uncommon in wetlands and rice paddies in coastal strip from Cape Coast (Macdonald 1979a) eastwards to Keta; June records only but possibly overlooked due to secretive habits. In the north, one probable sighting, 2 Dec 1972, at Vea dam (F. Walsh). Collected near Big Ada, 23 Jun 1956 (Lamm & Horwood 1958).
Breeding. Eggs in oviduct: Big Ada, 23 Jun (Lamm & Horwood 1958).

[PORZANA PORZANA
(I.209)   Spotted Crake
No records of this Palaearctic migrant, but likely to occur; 3 sightings at Lagos, Nigeria, Jan–Feb (Elgood 1982), and one near Abidjan, Ivory Coast, Apr (Thiollay 1985).]

146. SAROTHRURA ELEGANS
(I.217)   Buff-spotted Crake (Pigmy Rail)   ?
One possible record from SW Ghana in Wassaw Region (near Tarkwa). Collins (1955) attributes the persistent, oft repeated, night call of a forest bird to this species. His description, however, does not tally completely with that of Keith *et al.* (1970). It occurs in Ivory Coast (Thiollay 1985) and Nigeria (Elgood 1982).

147. SAROTHRURA PULCHRA
    (I.216)   White-spotted Crake (Pigmy Rail)   RB
Locally common resident (*S. p. pulchra*) in most swampy areas within forest, forest clearings and secondary growth. During wet season, May–Jun, found in isolated forest patches on Accra Plains. Call easily mimicked by humans and any individual birds in the locality immediately respond and approach caller.
    Breeding. 4 nests, some with eggs, Opintin forest reserve, May–Jul (N. Wood). At Enugu in Nigeria, Sep–Dec (Elgood 1982).

    [SAROTHRURA RUFA
    (I.214)   Red-chested Crake
No records, but likely to occur as it has been recorded in Togoland (Erard & Vielliard 1977) and is thought to occur in Ivory Coast (Thiollay 1985).]

HELIORNITHIDAE

148. PODICA SENEGALENSIS
    (I.224)   Finfoot   R(B)
    Not uncommon resident (*P. s. senegalensis*) on shaded rivers and edges of reservoirs within coastal and forest zone, and along southern tributaries of the Black Volta and edges of Volta lake (M. Horwood, G. Vanderstichelen, F. Walsh). Collected Yegi, Ankobra river (Bannerman 1931), and Mampong in Ashanti, 3 Feb 1935 (Lowe 1937). In the north sighted along the White Volta at Pwalugu, 5 Dec 1972 (F. Walsh) and collected at Gambaga, 20 Dec 1898 (Hartert 1899a).
    Breeding. Unrecorded. Bird collected by Lowe would soon have begun breeding (Bannerman 1951).

OTIDIDAE

149. EUPODOTIS (= LISSOTIS) MELANOGASTER
    (I.235)   Black-bellied Bustard   Afm/B
    Not uncommon local resident in the more wooded grassland areas on the Accra Plains, recorded all months (J. R. Marshall), but dry season breeder visitor to Winneba (M. Horwood); not recorded Cape Coast (M. Macdonald). Occurs throughout the northern savanna and south to Kete Kratchi but status uncertain, possibly moving northwards after breeding in dry season. Not recorded Tumu (Sutton 1970), seasonal at Mole (Greig-Smith 1976a), sporadic at Tono dam, Aug and Dec (R. Passmore) and wet season records only, Jun–Aug, at Bolgatanga (F. Walsh). One, 5 Sep, on rocky pavement at Kwahu Tafo near Mpraeso within the forest region suggests movement (Sutton 1970).
    Breeding. Male in courtship display: east of Shai Hills, May (Macdonald 1979b). Egg shells: Winneba, Easter 1956 (M. Horwood). Juvenile Kwabenya, Accra Plains, Mar 1970 (P. Grubb).

150. EUPODOTIS SENEGALENSIS
    (I.232)   Senegal Bustard   R(B)
    Uncommon resident (*E. s. senegalensis*) in open savanna with scattered scrub in the far north; occurs Tono dam in all months (R. Passmore), also between Navrongo and Bawku (M. Horwood); only recorded once, however, 29 Dec 1970, near Bolgatanga (F. Walsh). Collected Binduri, south of Bawku (Alexander 1902) (mapped as Gambaga in Snow 1978). Bouet (1955) mentions a skin collected, Feb, by Lowe at Mampong, Ashanti, but this is not listed in Lowe (1937).
    Breeding. Unrecorded. In Nigeria, Jun–Oct (Elgood 1982).

151. NEOTIS DENHAMI

    (I.230)   Denham's Bustard   AfM/NB?

Status uncertain; a probable dry season non-breeding visitor, not uncommon (*N. d. denhami*) in woodland savanna north of the forest in dry season, but often sporadic: Kintampo, Jan–Feb (Cockburn 1946); NW Ashanti, late Dec to mid May (Russell 1949a); Bolgatanga, Dec–Jun (F. Walsh); once, 13 Nov, Tumu (Sutton 1970). Ghana data consistent with the observations in Nigeria of visible migration northwards in May, and southward Oct–Dec (Elgood 1982). Two records in south during wet season; singletons, Winneba, 9 Jun 1973, and in Botany gardens, Legon, 8 and 11 Jun 1966 (L.G.G.).

152. OTIS (= ARDEOTIS) ARABS

    (I.229)   Arabian (or Sudan) Bustard   AfM/NB

A rare dry season visitor (*O. a. stieberi*) to open grasslands in the far north, often with *Neotis denhami* (Lowe 1937). M. Horwood only recorded it occasionally at Bawku.

JACANIDAE

153. ACTOPHILORNIS AFRICANA

    (I.240)   Jacana (Lily-trotter)   RB

Abundant resident in permanent swamps and shallow pools with floating vegetation, in both savanna and forest regions, less common in brackish waters in coastal area. Local movement away from drying pools to permanent ones occurs in north (Holman 1947).

Breeding. Season probably extended, but mainly wet season. Eggs: Cape Coast, Jun–Sep (Macdonald 1979b); C/4, Pong Tamale, 9 Aug (F. C. Holman *in* Bannerman 1931). Chicks: in southern areas, May–Aug (G. Cansdale, M. Lockwood, N. Wood). Half grown young: in north, Nov–Dec (P. Greig-Smith, M. Horwood).

ROSTRATULIDAE

154. ROSTRATULA BENGHALENSIS

    (I.265)   Painted Snipe   Afm?/(B)

Status uncertain. Uncommon wet season visitor (*R. b. benghalensis*), mainly Apr–Sep, to wetlands and lake edges in coastal belt from Panbros saltpans west of Accra eastwards to Keta (Holman 1947, Grimes 1972a) but records are sporadic. One dry season record Denu, 15 Jan 1964 (Sutton 1965b). Occasional Kumasi, Nov–Mar (Holman 1947). In the north most records are in dry season: Yeji, Dec; Nalerigu, Mar; Tumu, 28 Mar, 26 Apr (Sutton 1970); Tamale reservoir, 8–9 in Mar 1975, 4–6 in Feb 1980 (E. Hall); Mole, Apr; however, at Vea dam small numbers, 1–4, late Jul to end Oct, max 30 in Nov and Dec, then singles sporadically Jan and Feb (F. Walsh).

Breeding. Unrecorded. At Lagos, Nigeria, Jun–Aug (Elgood 1982).

HAEMATOPODIDAE

155. HAEMATOPUS OSTRALEGUS

    (I.262)   Oyster-catcher   PM

Rare Palaearctic migrant (*H. o. ostralegus*), sporadic at coastal lagoons, saltpans and river estuaries, early Aug to Mar. First recorded in early 1950's (Bannerman 1953), with only 10 sightings between 1960 and 1986: Accra area 14 Aug 1968, 8 Aug

1971, Aug 1973 and Nov 1973; a single, Shama, Mar 1978 (M. Macdonald); Nakwa lagoon, 25 Nov 1985; Takoradi, 4 Dec 1985; Esiama, 17 on 30 Nov 1985, 14 in Jan or Feb 1986; Kikam, 3 in Jan or Feb 1986 (R. Broad, A. J. M. Smith, A. Nuoh).

RECURVIROSTRIDAE

156. HIMANTOPUS HIMANTOPUS
   (I.264)   Black-winged Stilt   RB, PM
   Common resident (*H. h. himantopus*) in coastal lagoons and saltpans, particularly near Accra and Cape Coast. At Cape Coast flocks up to 23 in April may represent return passage of Palaearctic birds (Macdonald 1978a). Occasional at Tafo, Nov–Mar, within the forest region (M. Lockwood). Northern records mainly in dry season, Nov–Apr, but some present Tamale reservoir, Mar–Oct (J. Callow).
   Breeding. First recorded breeding 24 May 1939, between Teshie and Labadi, near Accra (P. I. Lake *in* Bannerman 1951); now a regular breeder. Eggs: Accra area, mainly Apr–Jul. Young chicks: Nungua, 5 Feb 1957; Densu river, 3 Feb 1957 (M. Horwood). Not recorded breeding at Cape Coast (Macdonald 1979b).

157. RECURVIROSTRA AVOSETTA
   (I.263)   Avocet   V, PM
   A vagrant, presumably from the Palaearctic (*R. a. avosetta*). Only 3 records: 1–2 at Panbros saltpans west of Accra, 14 Jun to end Aug 1968, and c. 5 there on 6 Mar 1973; Elmina, 11 Jan 1976 (Macdonald 1978a). The late date in 1968 suggests a more local origin than the Palaearctic (see Elgood 1982).

BURHINIDAE

158. BURHINUS (=OEDICNEMUS) CAPENSIS
   (I.238)   Spotted Thicknee   AfM/NB?
   Uncommon intra-African migrant (*B. c. maculosus*), to open wooded savanna in the far north; all records are in the dry season, Nov–Feb, the non-breeding season. Collected Gambaga, 20 Dec, by Giffard (Hartert 1899a), and Bole and Lawra, Jan (Lowe 1937). One killed by car at Bulinga, 3 Nov 1971 (F. Walsh).
   Breeding. Unrecorded. One female collected Lawra, 17 Jan, had enlarging sexual organs (Lowe 1937); Lowe thought it would soon have been nesting. In Nigeria, breeds Mar–May (Elgood 1982).

159. BURHINUS (=OEDICNEMUS) SENEGALENSIS
   (I.237)   Senegal Thicknee   R?(B)
   Not uncommon at lagoons near Accra and eastwards to Togo border, along shores of inland reservoirs in savanna region, and on cultivated land in forest clearings. Status uncertain: in the north recorded mainly late Oct to early Apr, but from Aug at Tono dam (R. Passmore); in the south mainly Jan–Apr, but some in May. No records at the peak of the rains, but possibly overlooked. Elgood (1982) considered it resident in Nigeria.
   Breeding. Unrecorded. Breeds mainly in wet season, Mar–Aug, in Nigeria (Elgood 1982).

160. BURHINUS (=OEDICNEMUS) VERMICULATUS
   (I.239)   Water Thicknee   R?(B)
   Very uncommon (*B. v. buttikoferi*) at lakesides and along rivers both north and south of the forest. Probably resident, but status uncertain as *B. vermiculatus* and *B. senegalensis* are so similar in the field. In the south: recorded Accra by Bourdillon

(Bannerman 1951); Nungua, Feb (D. Lamm); Kasu lagoon, c. 7, 5 May (N. Wood). In the north: Buipi Volta ferry, 3 pairs, 25 Mar (Sutton 1965b); Yapei, c. 3, 23/24 Oct (N. Wood).

Breeding. Unrecorded in West Africa.

GLAREOLIDAE

Cursorinae

161. CURSORIUS (= RHINOPTILUS) CHALCOPTERUS
(I.296)   Violet-tipped (or Bronze-wing) Courser   AfM/(B)

Very uncommon, in the northern savanna, often on recently burnt ground; possibly overlooked due to nocturnal habits. Probably an African breeding migrant that moves northwards after breeding. Recorded Tamale, Yapei, Tono dam and Mole, Dec to mid May. Collected Mole, 31 Dec, 10 Jan, 19 Mar.

Breeding. Unrecorded. In Nigeria, small young, Feb–Mar (Elgood 1982).

162. CURSORIUS TEMMINCKII
(I. 295)   Temminck's Courser   R?B

Not uncommon, probably resident in open grassland and on playing fields on the Accra Plains and east to Keta; recorded only sporadically. At Achimota regular on playing fields, mid Jul to Nov, dispersing to open burnt grassland Jan–Mar; flocks have reached up to 27 in Jul, more often 5–6. Fewer records from the north: Tamale, Nov–May (Holman 1947, F. Walsh); Tumu, 1 on 24 Nov and 4 on 25 Nov (Sutton 1970); Bolgatanga, 6 Dec 1970; Bawku, 28 Nov 1970 (F. Walsh).

Breeding. Chick with adults: Tono dam, Feb 1982 (R. Passmore). Juveniles: Keta, 31 Aug (F. C. Holman *in* Bannerman 1951).

163. PLUVIANUS AEGYPTIUS
(I.301)   Egyptian Plover (Crocodile-bird)   R(B)

Not uncommon resident, often in flocks of 10–20, on sandy river banks north and east of the forest belt, south to Kete Kratchi. Occasional at irrigation dams at Tamale and Mole; at Vea dam, Aug to early Oct only (F. Walsh); at Tono dam, Sep only (R. Passmore). Subject to local movement due to water level changes.

Breeding. Unrecorded. In northern Nigeria, at end of the dry season, Feb–May (Elgood 1982).

Glareolinae

164. GLAREOLA (= GALACHRYSIA) CINEREA
(I.300)   Grey Pratincole   V

Vagrant. Located in 2s or 3s on sand banks on Volta river in Ussher's day; the only recent sighting is at Sakumo lagoon, near Tema, 6 Sep 1956 (D. W. Lamm). Collected Gambaga, 27 Oct, by Giffard (Hartert 1899a) but not located by Alexander (1902); possibly overlooked. Volta lake has removed much suitable habitat.

Breeding. Unrecorded. In Nigeria, Mar–May (Elgood 1982).

165. GLAREOLA NORDMANNI
(I.298)   Black-winged Pratincole   PM

Rare Palaearctic migrant, probably overlooked due to similarity to common resident *G. pratincola*. Only 2 records: reliably sighted at Panbros saltpans, flock of c. 10, 8 Mar (N. Wood); and Thomas (1966) lists it for Nungua; no records in north.

166. GLAREOLA (=GALACHRYSIA) NUCHALIS
(I.299)   White-collared Pratincole   RB

Not uncommon resident (*G. n. liberiae*) in colonies of 20–30 on exposed rocks of rivers; subject to local movements with rise and fall of water levels. The Volta lake has flooded the sites from Yegi south to Kete Kratchi where Alexander (1902) found them common. More recently, 1943–1954, found on Prah river within forest zone (M. Horwood); possibly overlooked on other main rivers.

Breeding. Eggs: on rocks in Prah river at Sekyere Hamang (5°10′N, 1°35′W), Dec 1943 (M. Horwood).

167. GLAREOLA PRATINCOLA
(I.297)   Pratincole   Afm/B

Locally very common (*G. p. fulleborni* = *boweni*) in the coastal region at lagoons, saltpans and irrigation dams. Subject to seasonal movements, but timings and numbers vary considerably from year to year. Cape Coast, Dec–Jun; max 50, Feb–Apr in 1975, 30 in 1976 (Macdonald 1978a). At saltpans west of Accra and elsewhere on Accra Plains, absent in most years from early Oct to early Feb (Grimes 1972a, Gass 1957), but c. 15, 28 Oct 1968, c. 80, 18 Dec 1968, c. 50, 29 Dec 1973 and some Jan 1968 and 1969. Max 100–200, late May to early Jul. Most adults appear to leave saltpans during Aug, the juvs in Sep. Few records in the north: Tumu, singles 20 Oct, 26 Apr (Sutton 1970); Tamale, singles 23 Dec (Holman 1947) and 15 Apr 1974 (E. Hall); c. 10, 29 Apr–10 May, 40 km north of Tamale (F. Walsh); Vea dam singles or twos, Oct–Feb (F. Walsh); Tono dam, Feb only (R. Passmore).

Breeding. Eggs: C/2, at saltpans west of Accra and Keta, Apr–Jul (Holman 1947, Grimes 1972a). Juveniles: Cape Coast, Apr–May 1977. Dependent young: Kpota near Ada, 22 May (Macdonald 1979b).

CHARADRIIDAE

168. CHARADRIUS (=LEUCOPOLIUS) ALEXANDRINUS
(I.245)   Kentish Plover   PM

Vagrant from the Palaearctic (*C. a. alexandrinus*), only 7 records, all coastal, but possibly overlooked inland: Winneba, one on 10 Feb 1970 (A. J. M. Smith, N. P. E. Langham) another on 9 Oct 1986 (I. Hepburn); Amminsa lagoon near Mankesim, one on 25 Nov; Sakumo lagoon near Tema, one on 14 Nov; Songaw lagoon near Ada, 3 on 28 Nov; Kikam-Bobrana, 3 on 30 Nov, singles on 8 and 10 Jan 1986 (RSPB expeditions). Coastal and inland records for Nigeria (Elgood 1982).

169. CHARADRIUS DUBIUS
(I.243)   Little (or Lesser) Ringed Plover   PM

Not uncommon Palaearctic migrant (*C. d. curonicus*) to shores of inland lakes and some coastal lagoons and saltpans, mainly Oct to early Apr. Local in coastal area: Iture, Cape Coast, regularly c. 12 mid Nov to late Dec, then fewer, rising to peaks of 32 and 17 on 5 Feb and 23 Feb respectively (Macdonald 1978a); Accra, sporadic records at inland fresh water reservoirs (Grimes 1972a); recorded once at Denu, 6 on 25 Jan (Sutton 1965a). Inland records; Kumasi, c. 10 in Dec and 2 mid Jan (Moorhouse 1968); Tafo, one netted (M. Lockwood — Appendix 1) and one 13 Feb 1977 (Macdonald 1978a). More regular at Vea dam in north: first recorded 25 Sep, c. 3–4 in autumn, c. 15 in early Feb (F. Walsh).

170. CHARADRIUS (=AFROXYECHUS) FORBESI
(I.248)   Forbes' Plover   RB, Afm/B

Not uncommon throughout the northern savanna but locally distributed: Tumu, dry season only, early Nov to mid May (Sutton 1970); Mole, resident in marshy areas of Game Park, often in flocks of 6–8 on burnt ground in dry season (Greig-Smith 1976a). Collected Wenchi and Lawra (=Laura), Jan (Lowe 1937) and recorded south to Kete Kratchi, Feb and Mar (M. Horwood). Occasional within forest zone, e.g. Kumasi. Previously more regular in coastal belt, Sekondi to Cape Coast (G. E. Shelley in Bannerman 1931), Accra, Nov to mid Mar in 1950s and Keta (Holman 1947, Grimes 1972a). No coastal records in recent years (Grimes 1972a, Macdonald 1978a).

Breeding. Eggs: on bovals (flat treeless areas, bearing a layer of short herbs and grasses, on which pools form in the rainy season) at Mole, Jul 1974, 1975. Pullus: Mole, 25 Aug 1975 (Greig-Smith 1977b).

171. CHARADRIUS HIATICULA
(I.242)   Ringed Plover   PM

A common Palaearctic migrant (*C. h. tundrae*) to coastal lagoons and shores of fresh water reservoirs and lakes throughout, mainly early Sep to early May with some remaining all the year at coastal lagoons. An influx occurs early Aug at Panbros saltpans; numbers remain c. 10 or less in autumn, but increase to c. 60 in Mar and Apr. Pre-migratory flocks are very vocal and depart in a NE direction from the pans in late Apr (Grimes 1972a, 1974b). A similar pattern is observed at Cape Coast (Macdonald 1978a). In the north is a passage migrant: Vea dam, early Sep to end of Oct, and again in Jan and Feb (F. Walsh); Tamale, Sep–Dec, and early Mar, max number 10 (E. Hall). Regular in dry season at Kumasi sewage farm (Moorhouse 1968) and netted at Tafo (M. Lockwood).

Birds ringed in Norway (2), Sweden (7), Germany (1), Poland (1) and UK (2) have been recovered in Ghana.

172. CHARADRIUS (=LEUCOPOLIUS) MARGINATUS
(I.244)   White-fronted Sand-Plover   RB

Locally not uncommon (*C. m. hesperius*) at lagoons at Accra and eastwards to Keta but less common than in Holman's day, when flocks often reached 40–50 (Holman 1947). Previously common at Cape Coast and other locations west of Accra (G. E. Shelley, J. M. Winterbottom in Bannerman 1931); no recent records at Cape Coast (Macdonald 1978a). No inland records but possibly overlooked.

Breeding. Eggs: C/2, at edges of lagoons, mainly Apr–Sep (Holman 1947). Chicks: 2 with adults, Labadi beach east of Accra, 17 Jan (F. Walsh).

173. CHARADRIUS (=LEUCOPOLIUS) PECUARIUS
(I.246)   Kittlitz's Sand-Plover   RB

Locally not uncommon resident (*C. p. pecuarius*) at lagoons, saltpans and fresh water dams at Accra and eastwards to Keta. Previously occurred at Cape Coast (Shelley in Bannerman 1931) but not recorded there in 1970's (Macdonald 1978a), and only 2 records at Nakwa, flocks of 11 and 10 on 4 and 16 Oct 1977 respectively (M. Macdonald 1979a). Three at Anyako, 7 Feb, and 2 on 12 Mar, Denu (Sutton 1965b), but more frequent in Holman's day (Holman 1947). In the north status uncertain: a dry season visitor to Tamale, max c. 20 (Holman 1947); but no recent records there (E. Hall); occurs Tono dam, Jan only (R. Passmore); in contrast there are wet season records from Mole (N. C. Davidson in Greig-Smith 1976a).

Breeding. Eggs: C/2, Keta, Apr–Sep (Holman 1947). Chicks: Panbros saltpans, west of Accra, 26 Jun 1970 (L.G.G.).

174. CHARADRIUS (= AFROXYECHUS) TRICOLLARIS
(I.247)   Three-banded Plover   V
The only certain record (*C. t. tricollaris*) is of one adult and 2 immature birds seen
by J. R. Marshall and K. M. Guichard on 9/10 Feb 1945 on the cricket oval of
Achimota school (Bannerman 1951). No records in coastal areas west of Ghana but
one from Mali (Snow 1978). In Nigeria possibly a non-breeding migrant from East
Africa (Elgood 1982).

175. PLUVIALIS DOMINICUS/PLUVIALIS APRICARIUS
(Not in MP&G/I.251)   Lesser Golden Plover/Golden Plover   V
Vagrant, only 4 records all singletons: Nungua, 2 Apr 1966 (presumed to be *P. d.
fulvus* from the Palaearctic — White 1970) (M. Edmunds & A. Lelek *in* Grimes
1972a); Nakwa lagoon, 4 Oct 1977 (presumed American nominate form *P. d. dominicus*) (Macdonald 1987b); Totope, near Songaw lagoon, 16 Jan 1986 (identified as *P.
apricarius*) (R. E. Scott, D. Daramani); Sakumo lagoon, 14 Oct (C. H. Gomersall).
P. apricarius has occurred Sao Thome (MP&G) and has been recorded in The
Gambia, but Gore (1981) considers that these sightings in The Gambia might well
have been *P. dominicus* as they are difficult to distinguish in the field. Following
Gore, they are not separated here.

176. PLUVIALIS (= SQUATAROLA) SQUATAROLA
(I.252)   Grey Plover   PM
Not uncommon Palaearctic migrant in small numbers, c. 10 or less, to lagoons,
sandy beaches and shores of fresh water dams in coastal region. Recorded in each
month but numbers fewer (c. 2–3) Jun and Jul. Arrivals reach Accra early Aug, but
not until Oct to Cape Coast (Grimes 1972a, 1974b, Macdonald 1978a). Occasional
at Kumasi, 6 Nov (Moorhouse 1968) and once at Mole, Apr (Maze 1971).
Birds ringed in Sweden (1) and UK (2) have been recovered in Ghana.

177. VANELLUS (= XIPHIDIOPTERUS) ALBICEPS
(I.258)   White-headed Plover   AfM/(B)
Present day status uncertain; in last century not uncommon seasonally on sand
banks of Ankobra, Jan–Mar, and Prah rivers within the forest region and along the
Volta river northwards to Kete Kratchi and Gambaga (Bannerman 1931). In
Nigeria it is absent from the southern rivers, Jun–Aug (Elgood 1982) and
Bannerman (1953) implies the same for Ghana; but at Cape Coast reservoir regular
in 1940s, flocks up to 12, May–Sep (Russell 1949b), though only once recorded
there by Gass (1954), 4 on 23 Sep 1950, and no recent records (M. Macdonald). In
the north recorded sporadically, mainly in dry season: Tono dam, May and
Aug–Nov (R. Passmore); occasional Tamale reservoir (Bannerman 1951); Vea dam,
end Sep (F. Walsh); Mole, 2 on 20 Dec; not recorded Tumu (Sutton 1970). Only one
wet season record, 28 Jun, at Navrongo far from any large river (Sutton 1970).
Giffard collected a male, 14 Mar, at Gambaga (Hartert 1899a).
Breeding. Unrecorded. In Nigeria, south to Onitsha, Feb–May, Benin, Mar–May
(Elgood 1982).

178. VANELLUS (= STEPHANIBYX) LUGUBRIS
(I.254)   Senegal Plover   R(B), Afm
Locally common in coastal areas from Elmina eastwards to Accra Plains, frequenting open grass plains and playing fields. Few records from northern savanna
but recorded in both dry and wet season (F. Walsh, R. Passmore). In the south
recorded all months and presumed resident but status uncertain due to nocturnal
movements. In early 1960s, a frequent nocturnal visitor to playing fields at Legon,

birds departing at dawn to open areas of the Accra Plains and eastwards to Shai hills, where they occur during the day. No nocturnal visits to Legon in 1970s, presumably through reduction of playing field areas. Occasional records of flying birds, up to 6 together, at Abokobi and along Akwapim hills, Aug (L.G.G). Collected Elmina, Apr (Blissett), Akwapim (Riis), Accra, Apr and Aug (Aubinn and Reichenow respectively).

Breeding. Unrecorded. In Nigeria, pair with chicks Lagos, 22 Sep (Elgood 1982).

179. VANELLUS (= AFRIBYX) SENEGALLUS
  (I.259)   Wattled Plover   RB

Not uncommon resident (*V. s. senegallus*), scattered throughout the northern savanna, particularly where there are irrigation dams and wetlands, south to Kete Kratchi, Ho and the Accra Plains. Ussher (Sharpe 1872a) thought it a visitor to Accra Plains, Jun to early Oct, but now locally resident at larger irrigation dams which were not present in Ussher's day. Not recorded in coastal areas west of Accra (M. Macdonald). In north occurs Vea dam, Aug–Dec (F. Walsh) and Tono dam, Aug–May (R. Passmore), where probably resident.

Breeding. Mole, mid Jul 1974 and 1975 (Greig-Smith 1977b); Tamale reservoir, C/4 21 May; Accra Plains, Apr and May. This conflicts with the statement in Snow (1978) that it breeds mainly in the dry season, but agrees with the data from Nigeria (Elgood 1982).

180. VANELLUS (= HOPLOPTERUS) SPINOSUS
  (I.255)   Spur-winged Plover   R?(B)

Uncommon along shores of reservoirs and irrigation dams in northern savanna, status uncertain, but presumed resident: records, mainly all singletons, are only sporadic. Recorded Tamale reservoir, Dec, Mar and Oct (Holman 1947, E. Hall); Pong Tamale, 24 Nov 1937 (Holman 1947); Bolgatanga, 29 May, 22 Jul, 5 Aug; Vea dam, mid Dec (F. Walsh) and Tono Dam, Dec–Apr (R. Passmore). Only one coastal record; a single at Nungua, no date (N. Gardiner *in* Thomas 1966).

Breeding. Unrecorded. In Nigeria, Mar–May (Elgood 1982).

181. VANELLUS (= ANOMALOPHRYS) SUPERCILIOSUS
  (I.257)   Brown-chested Wattled Plover   V, AfM/NB

Vagrant intra-African migrant to savanna woodland in dry season. Only one record: Count Zech collected it at Kete Kratchi, Jan (Reichenow 1902, Serle 1956). No records further west of Ghana, but breeds in Nigeria, Jan–Feb (Serle 1956).

182. VANELLUS (= SARCIOPHORUS) TECTUS
  (I.260)   Black-head Plover   AfM/(B)

Uncommon, mainly dry season visitor (*V. t. tectus*) to dry open savanna with little grass cover, Nov–May, from latitudes further north in West Africa. Recorded Tumu throughout dry season, up to 4 seen sporadically (Sutton 1970); Bolgatanga, pairs, Nov–Jun (F. Walsh); occurs Tono dam, Nov, Dec and Jan (R. Passmore). Collected Tumu, 19 Jan (Lowe 1937).

Breeding. Unrecorded. In Nigeria, mostly Mar–May (Elgood 1982).

SCOLOPACIDAE

Tringinae

Numeniini

183. LIMOSA LAPPONICA
(I.290)   Bar-tailed Godwit   PM
Uncommon Palaearctic migrant (*L. l. lapponica*), mainly Aug–May, to saltpans, lagoons and shore line from Sekondi (M. Horwood) eastwards to Keta, where Holman recorded 200 on 31 Oct; more often 1–4 together (Holman 1947, Grimes 1972a, Macdonald 1978a). Occasional in some years at saltpans, Jun and Jul. Only one inland record; Tono dam, Oct (R. Passmore).

184. LIMOSA LIMOSA
(I.289)   Black-tailed Godwit   PM
Uncommon passage migrant (*L. l. limosa*) from the Palaearctic, both coastal and inland. Coastal records at Accra and Cape Coast, 3 or less, Jul–Oct, but at Keta, 24–32 in Dec and Jan (Holman 1947). Passage less marked in spring: Accra, Mar (Grimes 1972a); Denu, 29 May (Sutton 1965a); not recorded Cape Coast (Macdonald 1978a). In north only recorded at Vea dam: 1 on 22 Jul, then from 2–9 regularly until early Oct, and 7–9 in late Nov to early Dec (F. Walsh).

185. NUMENIUS ARQUATA
(I.291)   Curlew   PM
Not uncommon Palaearctic migrant to coastal areas, mainly *N. a. arquata*, though *N. a. orientalis* has been collected at the mouth of the Nakwa (= Naqua) river (Bannerman 1931). Few records at Cape Coast, but regular passage at Panbros saltpans, early Aug to early Sep, some flocks reaching 60. Numbers in dry season smaller, flocks of 10–15. The majority leave by May, but some remain all summer (Grimes 1972a, Macdonald 1978a). Inland records: Kumasi, a pair Dec 1925 (F. C. Holman *in* Bannerman 1931); Bibiani golf course, 28–30 Nov 1952 (M. Horwood).

186. NUMENIUS PHAEOPUS
(I.292)   Whimbrel   PM
Common Palaearctic migrant (*N. p. phaeopus*) to coastal lagoons, river mouths and saltpans along coast east of Takoradi, mainly Aug to early May although some remain throughout the year; more common than *N. arquata*, perhaps by a factor of 3 or more. Numbers increase at Panbros saltpans early Aug, flocks of 12–60, then decrease but increase again to c. 50 in Apr prior to overland migration in a NE direction. The pre-migratory flights are quite marked in Apr (Grimes 1972a, 1974b, Macdonald 1978a). One inland record: Mole, 3 on 21 Aug (Harvey & Harrison 1970).
Birds ringed in UK (2) have been recovered in Ghana.

Tringini

187. TRINGA ERYTHROPUS
(I.286)   Spotted or Dusky Redshank   PM
Common Palaearctic migrant to lagoons and saltpans in coastal areas east of Cape Coast, less common at inland wetlands. Numbers at any given locality fluctuate during winter due to local movements. Recorded Cape Coast, mainly Oct–Mar (Macdonald 1978a), but at saltpans west of Accra birds in partial breeding dress arrive late Aug to early Sep and reach c. 800 in Nov and c. 2000 by Dec. In Apr many

are in breeding dress and flocks leave saltpans in a NE direction (Grimes 1969b, 1972a, 1974b). Inland records: Kumasi sewage farm, 3 from 19 Oct to 18 Dec (Moorhouse 1968); Tamale reservoir, 1 on 22 Nov 1975, 12 on 12 Dec 1975 and small flocks (20 or less) Feb and Mar (E. Hall); Vea dam, singles late Sep, Oct, 4 or less Nov, Dec, and occasional flocks (20–25) Jan and Feb (F. Walsh). Bannerman (1953) states that *T. erythropus* "can be considered an accidental visitor" in West Africa and refers to "considerable" flocks of *T. totanus* in the Keta area, though elsewhere mainly singly and distinctly local. Present data suggest that *totanus* may have been misidentified, although changes in status of the 2 species cannot be excluded (Macdonald 1978a).

188. TRINGA FLAVIPES
(Not in MP&G)   Lesser Yellowlegs   V
Vagrant from Nearctic: one at Elmina, 1 Dec 1985 (E. Dunn, A. Grieve, R. Broad). Also recorded from Nigeria (Elgood 1982).

189. TRINGA GLAREOLA
(I.283)   Wood Sandpiper   PM
Common Palaearctic migrant throughout, at edges of pools, sewage farms, reservoirs, lagoons and saltpans, mainly mid Aug to early May, but in some years recorded each month. Earliest dates: Vea dam, 22 Jul (F. Walsh); Mole, 27 Jul (Harvey & Harrison 1970); saltpans west of Accra, 19 Jul. Fresh autumn arrivals are vocal and in small flocks of 10 or less, but up to c. 80 in Aug and Sep at Accra and Vea dam. One flock (c. 40) observed leaving saltpans, 1810 GMT 26 Aug 1970, in a NE direction (Grimes 1972a). Spring departures are NE from Accra area (Grimes 1974b). Numbers at Vea dam reach c. 200 in Feb (F. Walsh).
Birds ringed in Sweden (6), Poland (1) and Germany (1) have been recovered in Ghana.

190. TRINGA (= ACTITIS) HYPOLEUCOS
(I.281)   Common Sandpiper   PM
Common Palaearctic migrant; singletons occur throughout at any small reservoir, sewage farm, lagoon or wetland, mainly Aug–Apr, some remaining throughout the year at saltpans on coast and inland at Mole (Moorhouse 1968, M. Lockwood, F. Walsh). Flocks of 4–15 occur inland and on coast during spring and autumn migrations (Harvey & Harrison 1970, Grimes 1972a, Macdonald 1978a, F. Walsh).
Birds ringed Finland (2) and Sweden (3) have been recovered in Ghana.

191. TRINGA (= GLOTTIS) NEBULARIA
(I.288)   Greenshank   PM
Common Palaearctic migrant to lagoons and saltpans in coastal areas, mainly Aug–May but flocks of 1–5 may remain Jun and Jul. Less common inland, but widely distributed at edges of reservoirs and wetlands throughout, occasionally within the forest belt at Kumasi sewage farm and Tafo reservoir (Moorhouse 1968, M. Lockwood). At saltpans west of Accra, flocks reach 60–200 in Aug and again in Apr prior to migration. Initial departure directions from saltpans are NE (Grimes 1972a, 1974b).
Birds ringed in Sweden (1), Germany (2), and Holland (1) have been recovered in Ghana.

192. TRINGA OCHROPUS (= OCROPHUS)
    (I.282)   Green Sandpiper   PM
Uncommon Palaearctic migrant, mainly late Oct to early May, to edges of fresh water lakes and wooded streams throughout. Occasional at Cape Coast (Macdonald 1978a), but regular in Accra area (Grimes 1972a). Usually in flocks of 1–4, but one at Panbros saltpans, 2 Jun 1973, reached 50–60 (L.G.G.). Subject to local movement at inland sites, but regular at Tafo (M. Lockwood) and Kumasi sewage farm. Earliest records at Vea dam, 19 Aug, then occasional throughout the winter (F. Walsh).

193. TRINGA (= GLOTTIS) STAGNATILIS
    (I.287)   Marsh Sandpiper   PM
Not uncommon Palaearctic migrant, mainly Aug to late Apr, to coastal lagoons and saltpans. At Accra and Keta more regular and in larger numbers — up to 40 together in Oct, decreasing to c. 10 in Apr — than at Cape Coast (Holman 1947, Grimes 1972a, Macdonald 1978a). Occasional at fresh water reservoirs and sewage farms inland, usually 1–2, but regular at Vea dam, where spring passage is more marked than autumn passage (F. Walsh). Collected Sekondi by Pel (SMNH).

194. TRINGA TEREK (= XENUS CINEREUS)
    (I.280)   Terek Sandpiper   V, PM
Vagrant Palaearctic migrant, at the western edge of its wintering range. 2 records: singletons, Panbros saltpans, 31 Jan 1974 (N. Wood); Korle river mouth, Accra, 17 Nov 1985 (E. Dunn, A. Grieve, R. Broad).

195. TRINGA TOTANUS
    (I.285)   Redshank   PM
Uncommon Palaearctic migrant (*T. t. totanus*), mainly Aug to early May, but some are recorded all year, at saltpans, lagoons and freshwater reservoirs in coastal region (Grimes 1972a, Macdonald 1978a). Less frequent at inland sites: Tamale, 23 Dec, 6 Mar, 22 Mar (Holman 1947, E. Hall); Tumu, 27 Mar (Sutton 1970); Mole, 23 Aug (Harvey & Harrison 1970); Pwalugu, 16 Dec and Nalerigu, 12 Jul (F. Walsh); Tono dam, Dec–Feb (R. Passmore). See also *T. erythropus*.
    Birds ringed in Sweden (2) have been recovered in Ghana.

Arenariinae

196. ARENARIA INTERPRES
    (I.279)   Turnstone   PM
Not uncommon Palaearctic migrant (*A. i. interpres*), mainly early Aug to late May, to shore line, lagoons and saltpans, some remaining throughout the northern summer (Grimes 1972a, Macdonald 1978a). An influx to the coast at Accra occurs early Aug, and probable passage through Cape Coast late Aug; highest numbers (up to 24) at Cape Coast usually Feb.
    Birds ringed in Sweden (1), Finland (1), UK (2) and Namibia (1) have been recovered in Ghana. The Namibia record is the only recovery in Ghana of a bird ringed in southern Africa.

Phalaropinae

197. PHALAROPUS FULICARIUS
(I.293)   Grey Phalarope   V, PM
Vagrant from the Palaearctic. 2 inland records: one on a reservoir at Obuase
Goldmine, 30 miles south of Kumasi, 3 Apr 1967; another at Kumasi sewage farm,
20 Nov 1966 (Moorhouse 1968). No inland records for Nigeria (Elgood 1982), but 3
in Ivory Coast, Jan–Mar (Thiollay 1985).

Gallinagoninae

198. GALLINAGO (= CAPELLA) GALLINAGO
(I.266)   Common Snipe   PM
Not uncommon Palaearctic migrant (*G. g. gallinago*) throughout, to wetlands at
edges of reservoirs, streams and lagoons, mainly Oct to mid Apr with isolated
records in May at Accra; usually in groups of 1–3. Records in the north: Tamale, 1–3
Oct–Feb but 20 on 6 Mar (E. Hall); arrives Vea dam mid Sep, up to c. 15 early Oct,
then up to 10 until late Jan, but 2 peaks of 32 and 26 in Feb (F. Walsh). An increase
in numbers occurs in northern wetlands of Nigeria during the spring passage,
Mar–Apr (Elgood 1982).

199. GALLINAGO (= CAPELLA) MEDIA
(I.267)   Great or Double Snipe   PM
Uncommon Palaearctic migrant, mainly Oct–Mar, to wetlands in the north,
occasionally to coastal areas, e.g. Accra and Cape Coast (Grimes 1972a, M.
Macdonald). One record Kumasi (Moorhouse 1968) and one netted Tafo (M.
Lockwood). Less numerous in north than *G. gallinago*. Arrives Vea dam early Aug,
max 28 mid Aug, then 1–9 from Sep to early Feb, increasing up to 16 late Feb
(F. Walsh). A similar pattern occurs in Nigeria (Elgood 1982).

200. GALLINAGO (= LYMNOCRYPTES) MINIMA
(I.269)   Jack Snipe   PM
Uncommon Palaearctic migrant to wetlands bordering reservoirs in the north,
Nov–Apr. Only one record in the south: a single at Nungua dam, 2 Apr 1966 (M.
Edmunds & A. Lelek *in* Grimes 1972a). Arrives Vea dam early Nov, up to 9 occur-
ring mid Nov, then regularly 1–2 until early Feb, thereafter increasing up to c. 14
(F. Walsh).

201. LYMNODROMUS GRISEUS
(Not in MP&G)   Short-billed Dowitcher   V
One sighting at Iture, 8 km west of Cape Coast, 24 Oct 1976 (Macdonald 1977c) is
the only record for West Africa and is accepted for this check-list. *L. griseus* is
difficult to distinguish from the Long-billed Dowitcher *L. scolopaceus,* which is
more common in the Western Palaearctic than *L. griseus*; T. Inskip, of ICBP,
considers the details given by Macdonald are insufficient to make the identification
certain.

Calidrinae

202. CALIDRIS (= CROCETHIA) ALBA
(I.277)   Sanderling   PM
Not uncommon Palaearctic migrant, Aug to early May, to sandy shores, coastal
lagoons and saltpans at Cape Coast, Accra and Keta (Holman 1947, Sutton 1970,

Grimes 1972a, Macdonald 1978a). Birds arrive at Panbros saltpans during late Jul (e.g. 9 on 29 Jul 1970), and early Aug, 2–10 birds; but main passage occurs Sep, c. 80 in 2nd week, and Oct, c. 170 in 1st week. In spring, 40–80 in Mar and Apr (Grimes 1972a). Only one inland record: 2 for 10 days, Nov 1965, at Kumasi sewage farm (Moorhouse 1968).

Birds ringed in UK (4) have been recovered in coastal areas of Ghana.

203. CALIDRIS (= EROLIA) ALPINA
   (I.271)   Dunlin   V, PM

Rare Palaearctic migrant (*C. a. alpina*). Only 5 certain records: singletons in breeding dress at Panbros saltpans west of Accra, 7 May 1971 and 16 Jun 1973 (Grimes 1972a, D. Tulloch & G. Vanderstichelen); one Elmina, 12–14 Mar 1978 (Macdonald 1978c); one Apam, 4 Dec 1985 (A. Grieve, D. Daramani); one Sakumo lagoon, Tema, 14 Jan 1986 (B. Scott). The record of c. 30 at the saltpans, 6 Sep 1968, by an Oxford group of students remains uncertain (Grimes 1972a).

204. CALIDRIS CANUTUS
   (I.274)   Knot   PM

Uncommon Palaearctic migrant (*C. c. canutus*) to coastal areas: singletons Dixcove, 21 Nov 1970 and Iture (5°06′N, 1°20′W), 25 Oct 1970 (D. James); Teshie, 3 on 21 Aug 1943 (J. R. Marshall, Flt. Lt. Farmer *in* Bannerman 1951); c. 30 with *C. minuta* at saltpans, Accra, 7 Oct 1970 (Grimes 1972a); several at Tema, Oct and Jan (D. Lamm, F. Walsh).

205. CALIDRIS FERRUGINEA (= EROLIA TESTACEA)
   (I.270)   Curlew Sandpiper   PM

A common and regular Palaearctic migrant, mainly Aug–Apr, at saltpans and lagoons near Accra; occasional Jun and Jul (Grimes 1972a). In marked contrast, rare and irregular at Ituri, Cape Coast; only 7 records, max count 9, during 96 visits extending over 15 months (Macdonald 1978a). Birds in partial breeding dress arrive Panbros saltpans, Accra late Jul/early Aug (c. 20 on 4 Aug 1966, c. 800 on 2 Aug 1968, c. 60 on 29 Jul 1970) and numbers remain high, 100–150, throughout northern winter (Grimes 1972a). Numbers in Jun and Jul at Panbros are sporadic and fluctuate: e.g. 1968, c. 25 on 21 Jun, c. 120 on 28 Jun, c. 37 on 29 Jun and 4 on 16 Jul. Occasional inland at Kete Kratchi, Kumasi, early Oct to Nov (Moorhouse 1968) and Tamale, 3 on 8 Apr 1979 (E. Hall). At Vea dam, autumn passage only, mid Aug to end Nov, max c. 35 mid Oct, except a singleton early Feb (F. Walsh).

One bird ringed in Sweden was recovered at Keta.

206. CALIDRIS FUSCICOLLIS
   (Not in MP&G)   White-rumped Sandpiper   V

Rare vagrant from the Nearctic. Only one record: one on 4 Dec 1985 at Apam (E. Dunn, A. Grieve, R. Broad). Recorded once at Cape Town and once in Namibia (Ryan 1981).

207. CALIDRIS (= EROLIA) MINUTA
   (I.272)   Little Stint   PM

An abundant Palaearctic migrant, Aug to early May, to coastal lagoons, creeks and saltpans, and inland reservoirs and sewage farms. Birds arrive at Panbros saltpans, Accra each year at end Jul or early Aug, numbers peak 2nd week Sep and remain high, c. 100–150, in Oct, thereafter decreasing to c. 20 or less (Grimes 1972a); at Cape Coast numbers peak in Nov (Macdonald 1978a). Numbers increase prior to spring migration: c. 300 on 2 Mar and c. 170 on 3 Mar at Apam (J. M. E. Took);

c. 100 on 9 May at Denu (Sutton 1970). Inland records: Kumasi, late Nov to mid Dec (Moorhouse 1968); Tamale, up to 30, Dec–Mar, 1 on 4 Apr (E. Hall); Vea dam, first recorded 20 Aug, with small peaks (c. 20) late Sep to early Oct, mid Dec (c. 29) and early Feb (c. 45) (F. Walsh). Commoner inland than on coast in Nigeria (Elgood 1982).

208. CALIDRIS (= EROLIA) TEMMINCKII
(I.273)   Temminck's Stint   PM

Uncommon and irregular Palaearctic migrant, Oct–Apr, to edges of larger reservoirs and irrigation dams mainly in the north, but some records within forest zone and along coast. Records in north: Tamale, 3 Apr 1938 (Holman 1947); Vea dam, c. 4, 11–17 Oct and 3 from 10–16 Jan (F. Walsh). Coastal records, all singletons: Nungua, no date (N. Gardiner *in* Thomas 1966); Korle lagoon, Accra, 1 Oct 1979; Anhwian saltpans, 5 Nov 1979 (E. Dunn, A. J. M. Smith). Occasional at Kumasi sewage farm, c. 4 early Oct to Nov (Moorhouse 1968).

209. TRYNGITES SUBRUFICOLLIS
(Not in MP&G)   Buff-breasted Sandpiper   V

Vagrant from the Nearctic. Only one record: a singleton at Sakumo lagoon near Tema, 4 Dec 1985 and again on 14 Jan 1986 (RSPB expeditions). Previously recorded in West Africa only in Sierra Leone (Field 1974), but on 4 other occasions in Africa as far south as Zululand (Robson & Robson 1979).

210. PHILOMACHUS PUGNAX
(I.278)   Ruff & Reeve   PM

Uncommon, max c. 10, but regular Palaearctic migrant in south, early Aug to mid Apr, to Panbros saltpans (Bannerman 1953, Grimes 1972a); in contrast, only 3 records at Cape Coast, 3 on 1 Nov, singletons on 7 Nov and 1 Dec (Macdonald 1978a). Occasional at Kumasi sewage farm, late Oct (Moorhouse 1968) and Mole (Greig-Smith 1976a). Commoner in north, regular at Vea dam from early Aug, numbers building up to 200+ by early Feb (F. Walsh); occurs Tono dam, Dec–Mar (R. Passmore).

No ringing recoveries.

STERCORARIIDAE

211. STERCORARIUS PARASITICUS
(I.302)   Richardson's (or Arctic) Skua   V

Not uncommon migrant from Holarctic. Sighted Takoradi harbour, 4 on 3 Dec 1985 (R. Broad); Elmina, 6 on 27 Jan 1986 (R. E. Scott *et al.*); one caught Jamestown harbour, Accra 12 Oct 1979 (E. Dunn). Some of the frequent sightings of *Stercorarius* species off Cape Coast were thought to be this species (M. Macdonald).

Birds ringed in Finland (1) and UK (2) have been recovered off Prampram, Apam and Takoradi, Dec–Jun.

212. STERCORARIUS POMARINUS
(I.303)   Pomatorhine (or Pomarine) Skua   PM

Not uncommon Holarctic migrant, Aug–Mar, regular in groups of 10 or less, in off-shore waters and near harbour entrances; often captured by fishermen for food (M. Horwood, E. Dunn, A. J. M. Smith, L.G.G.). Collected by Ussher (3), Blissett (1) and Shelley (1) in last century (Bannerman 1931).

213. STERCORARIUS SKUA
    (Not in MP&G)   Great Skua (or Bonxie)   V, PM?
Vagrant. Sightings, presumed to be the Palaearctic race *S. s. skua*: singletons seen regularly in 1970 off the breakwater of Tema harbour, Jan–Feb; another some 20 km south of Tema in same period (A. J. M. Smith, N. Langham). Not seen in coastal surveys in 1979 or 1985/86 (E. Dunn).

LARIDAE
Larinae

214. LARUS CIRRHOCEPHALUS (= CIRROCEPHALUS)
    (I.307)   Grey-headed Gull   V, AfM/NB
Vagrant to coastal waters and shoreline. 6 records: off Accra, 10 Apr (J. M. Winterbottom *in* Bannerman 1931); Labadi beach, Accra, Dec (D. W. Lamm); Tema harbour, 25 Jun (M. Edmunds); Panbros saltpans, 20 Jul (M. Edmunds, I. Taylor), 2 on 8 Jan 1986; Keta, one on 18 Jan 1986 (R. E. Scott *et al.*).

215. LARUS FUSCUS
    (I.305)   Lesser Black-backed Gull   PM
A not uncommon Palaearctic migrant, mainly mid Sep to early Apr with stragglers Jul and Aug, to saltpans and lagoons west of Accra and eastwards to Keta (Holman 1947, Grimes 1972a). Usually 10–40 together, but once 160–200, Dec. Not recorded from Cape Coast (M. Macdonald). One record inland at Kumasi (Cansdale 1948).
Nominate *fuscus* ringed in Sweden (3) have been recovered at Keta.

216. LARUS MINUTUS
    (Not in MP&G)   Little Gull   V
Vagrant, all immatures and singletons: Panbros saltpans, 14 Nov 1985 (E. Dunn, A. Grieve, R. Broad), 19 Jan 1986 (A. J. M. Smith); Sakumo lagoon west of Tema, 10 Jan 1986 (R. E. Scott *et al.*). Up to 5 recorded exceptionally, Jan–Feb 1969 and Dec–Jan 1970, at Lagos, Nigeria (Elgood 1982); also recorded Sierra Leone (Field & Owen 1969) and Angola (Sinclair 1974).

217. LARUS RIDIBUNDUS
    (I.308)   Black-headed Gull   PM
Uncommon Palaearctic migrant, Dec–Mar, mainly to saltpans and lagoons west of Accra and eastwards to Keta. Not recorded in 1950s (D. W. Lamm), numbers increasing in the 1960s from singletons to up to c. 20 in Jan 1967 and subsequently (Grimes 1972a; RSPB expedition 1986). Rare inland; only 2 records, at Vea dam, singletons on 28 Dec 1970 and 6 Dec 1971 (F. Walsh).

218. LARUS (= XEMA) SABINI
    (I.309)   Sabine's Gull   V
Vagrant. Only one record: 1 adult and 1 immature 24–32 km south of Tema, Nov 1979 (E. Dunn, A. J. M. Smith).

Sterninae

219. ANOUS STOLIDUS
    (I.325)   Noddy   V
Vagrant. 2 records (*A. n. stolidus*): one collected off the Ghana coast, a skin in BMNH obtained by R. B. Sharpe from H. Whitely (Bannerman 1931); one sighting

thought to be this species. Tema, 14 Nov 1985 (E. Dunn, R. Broad). Breeds on islands in the Gulf of Guinea.

220. ANOUS TENUIROSTRIS (= MEGALOPTERUS MINUTUS)
(I.326)   White-capped or Black Noddy   V

Vagrant (*A. t. atlanticus*). Only 2 records: one with flock of *Sterna nigra* at saltpans west of Accra, 1430 GMT on 21 Oct 1973 — earlier in the day there had been a rain squall off the coast (J. H. Franklin); one inshore at Elmina, 10–15 Apr 1978 (M. Macdonald).

221. STERNA ALBIFRONS
(I.318)   Little Tern   RB, PM

Not uncommon resident (*S. a. guineae*) in coastal areas near Accra eastwards to Keta (Holman 1947, Grimes 1972a). Only a wet season visitor, Apr–Sep, to Cape Coast (Macdonald 1979a); occasional on the Volta river from its mouth to Akosombo dam. Large counts in Nov 1985 (240, 282) at Panbros may have included *S. a. albifrons* from the Palaearctic (E. Dunn).

Breeding. Eggs: C2/3, saltpans at Cape Coast, Accra, Tema and Keta, Jun to early Oct (Bourdillon 1944, Holman 1947, Grimes 1972a, Macdonald 1979b). Nests well dispersed at Accra, but in contrast at Keta, 70 pairs were breeding in 4 separate colonies (Holman 1947), but information on density of nests not given.

A bird ringed in Sweden has been recovered at Keta and also the Javan subspecies *S. a. sinensis*. (Grimes 1978b).

222. STERNA ANAETHETUS
(I.321)   Bridled Tern   V

Vagrant. Only 2 records: singleton off Elmina, 14 Mar 1978 (Macdonald 1979a); another at Panbros saltpans, 7 Nov 1979 (A. J. M. Smith).

223. STERNA BALAENARUM
(I.319)   Damara Tern   AfM/NB

Transequatorial migrant to the Ghana coastline, May–Aug, from breeding grounds in southwestern Africa. Groups of up to c. 40 at Kedzi and Cape St Paul (Sutton 1965b) and regularly seen off-shore (Robins 1966).

224. STERNA BENGALENSIS
(Not in MP&G)   Lesser Crested Tern   V

Vagrant. Only 4 sightings: Tema, 3+ on 8 Oct 1979 (E. Dunn, A. J. M. Smith); Panbros, one, possibly 2, 2 Nov 1979 (A. J. M. Smith), one 15 Nov 1985 (E. Dunn); Old Ningo (5°44′N, 0°11′E), one 18 Nov 1985 (E. Dunn). These are the first records for the Guinea coastline, although a regular winter visitor to The Gambia from the Mediterranean (Gore 1981).

225.   STERNA DOUGALLII
(I.315)   Roseate Tern   PM

Not uncommon Palaearctic migrant *S. d. dougallii*), Sep–Mar, to lagoons, saltpans and inshore waters. Previously overlooked in West African waters (Bourdillon 1944; Bannerman 1951), and only recognised in coastal waters of Ghana in 1970, although ringing recoveries date from 1950. Large day roosts of 700–1000 on breakwater at Tema harbour, Jan/Feb 1970 (A. J. M. Smith, N. P. E. Langham), but now (1986) numbers greatly reduced (E. Dunn). Night roosts of few hundred birds form before and after dark at saltpans west of Accra, Oct (E. Dunn,

A. J. M. Smith). Easily caught by local boys, numbers caught being high when sardine catches are high (Dunn 1981, Dunn & Mead 1982).

At least 182 birds ringed in UK and Eire have been recovered in Ghana.

226. STERNA FUSCATA
(I.320)   Sooty Tern   V

Vagrant (probably all *S. f. fuscata*). Only 10 records: 2 out of 3 terns collected 15 Jul 1956, at Sakumo lagoon, Tema (Lamm & Horwood 1958); one found dead, Nov 1969, at Nyanyanu, west of Accra (W. Pople); one with 200 *Sterna nigra* at saltpans west of Accra, 11 Apr 1974 (L.G.G.). The remaining 7 records are of juveniles ringed as chicks on Dry Tortugas off southern Florida, USA (Robertson 1969; see Appendix 3).

227. STERNA HIRUNDO
(I.313)   Common Tern   PM

Common Palaearctic migrant (*S. h. hirundo*) along the entire coastline and off-shore waters, many remaining throughout the summer months (Langham 1971). Day and night movements in autumn, taking place inshore late Aug, peaking 2nd week Sep, were readily detected by radar, but not the spring movements, which must take place further off-shore (Grimes 1977b). Daily movements of all *Sterna* spp. are linked with oceanic upwellings that occur off the Ghana coast, beginning May/Jun, and the consequent build up of sardine populations. Most birds leave land roosts before dawn, spend the day foraging at sea and return to roosts before and after dusk. Daylight counts at lagoons and saltpans are not, therefore, representative of the number of *Sterna* spp. wintering in the coastal areas (Grimes 1977b).

At least 293 birds ringed in western Europe and 5 in Poland have been recovered along the coast of Ghana.

228. STERNA HYBRIDA (= CHLIDONIAS LEUCOPAREIA)
(I.324)   Whiskered Tern   PM

Uncommon Palaearctic migrant (*S. h. hybrida*), Dec–Apr, to saltpans and lagoons at Accra eastwards to Keta; only one record at Cape Coast, 11 Jan 1976, but possibly overlooked (M. Macdonald). In breeding dress by late Mar, and flocks reach c. 200 (Wink 1976). Inland sightings only at Vea dam, 1–3 from 10 Sep to 15 Oct (F. Walsh).

Birds ringed in France (3) and Spain (2) have been recovered at Keta and inland at Osudoku and Nkawkaw (Mees 1977).

229. STERNA (= CHLIDONIAS) LEUCOPTERA
(I.323)   White-winged Black Tern   PM

Uncommon and irregular Palaearctic migrant, late Oct to early May, to coastal areas from Cape Coast eastwards to Keta and Denu. Recorded Keta, c. 10 on 10 May 1942 (Holman 1947); Cape Coast, 3–26 Apr 1953 (Gass 1957); Denu, 9 May 1964 (Sutton 1965b); Sakumo lagoon west of Tema, 15 on 10 Jan 1986 and 20 on 14 Jan 1986 (R. E. Scott *et al.*). Regular inland at Vea dam, end Aug to Mar, numbers less than 5 (F. Walsh); also occurs Tono dam in same period (R. Passmore, J. Stewart).

230. STERNA MAXIMA
(I.317)   Royal Tern   AfM/NB

Common non-breeding visitor (*S. m. albididorsalis*) to inshore waters and coastal lagoons; particularly common at saltpans at Cape Coast, Accra and Keta. Birds arrive from breeding grounds end Aug; counts at Panbros saltpans reach c. 400 late

Sep and remain high until early Nov; many depart in Apr but some remain throughout the year. Over 1000 counted along the Ghana coastline, Nov–Dec 1985 (E. Dunn, A. Grieve, R. Broad). In 1970s and 1985 numbers were much larger than those in 1950s (max 10–12) (Gass 1954). Breeds in The Gambia and northwards to Mauritania, May–Jul (MP&G).

One chick ringed at Banc d'Arguin, Mauritania, has been recovered in Ghana.

231. STERNA (=CHLIDONIAS) NIGRA
(I.322)   Black Tern   PM

An abundant Palaearctic migrant (*S. n. nigra*) to inshore waters and coastline, many remaining throughout the year; also on larger inland reservoirs as far north as Tamale (F. C. Holman *in* Bannerman 1951). Hundreds congregate at spillway of the Volta dam at Akosombo whenever flood gates are open. Autumn passage occurs early Aug and peaks in 2nd and 3rd week Sep. Night roosts, containing 1000s of birds, form at Panbros saltpans before and after dark and are vacated before dawn (Grimes 1972a, 1974f). A flock (c. 30) drifted eastwards from Panbros, 6 Aug 1970, gaining height by fluttering into the SW breeze; 15 minutes later it was still climbing and drifting eastwards just before it was lost from view.

Birds ringed in Sweden (1), Holland (2), Mauritania (2) and Ivory Coast (2) have been recovered in Ghana.

232. STERNA (=GELOCHELIDON) NILOTICA
(I.311)   Gull-billed Tern   PM

Uncommon Palaearctic migrant (*S. n. nilotica*) to larger coastal lagoons and saltpans at Accra and eastwards to Keta. Sporadic records, Aug–Feb, usually 1–3, but flock of 20 at Denu, 18 Jan (Sutton 1965b). One inland record: one on 18 Sep 1976 at Tamale reservoir (E. Hall).

233. STERNA PARADISAEA (=MACRURA)
(I.314)   Arctic Tern   PM

A not uncommon Holarctic migrant to coastal waters and lagoons, particularly during autumn migration, Aug–Oct; present in small numbers throughout winter months. Birds in their second summer move into the Gulf of Guinea from Antarctic waters (Langham 1971).

At least 18 ringed in Finland and UK have been recovered in Ghana.

234. STERNA SANDVICENSIS
(I.316)   Sandwich Tern   PM

Very common Palaearctic migrant (*S. s. sandvicensis*) to inshore waters, lagoons and saltpans, many remaining throughout the year (Langham 1971). Autumn migration begins Aug, reaching a peak mid Sep. Little or no movements take place along the coast of Ghana in spring (Grimes 1977b). Night roosts form, before and after dark, at Panbros saltpans and are vacated before dawn.

At least 548 birds ringed in western Europe (84% in UK) have been recovered in coastal districts since the first known record in 1911 (Bannerman 1931).

235. STERNA TSCHEGRAVA (=HYDROPROGNE CASPIA)
(I.312)   Caspian Tern   PM, AfM/NB?

Not uncommon, probably mainly Palaearctic migrant, Sep–May, to larger lagoons at Keta, Denu and Ada (Holman 1947, Sutton 1965b, 1970). Occasional at Panbros saltpans, Accra, but only one record further west, 3 in Mar 1978 at Dixcove (M. Macdonald, A. J. M. Smith). Inland records: Tamale, 22 Nov 1975 (E. Hall);

Vea dam, 3 Oct 1972 (F. Walsh). Birds from breeding grounds off Senegal and former Portuguese Guinea may occur in Ghana.

Birds ringed in Finland (16) and Sweden (18) have been recovered at Keta, but also inland.

RHYNCHOPIDAE

236. RHYNCHOPS (= RYNCHOPS) FLAVIROSTRIS

(I.327)   Scissor-billed Tern or Skimmer   R(B)

Locally not uncommon resident at the Panbros saltpans and lagoons west of Accra, occasional and sporadic elsewhere; recorded near mouth of the Volta river (H. T. Ussher *in* Bannerman 1931) and inland at Yegi (A. W. J. Pomeroy *in* Bannerman 1931) and Sugu in the north, 7 May 1971 (F. Walsh); not recorded at Keta (Holman 1947, Sutton 1965a, 1970). Numbers and status at Panbros changed in 1966/67 when saltpans were enlarged; not recorded there by D. W. Lamm and M. D. I. Gass in 1950s; occasional before 1967, but regular afterwards, counts usually 20–40 in 1968, 60–70 in 1970 (Grimes 1972a). In 1979, 94 on 13 Oct (E. Dunn); a large influx on 8 Nov 1979 occurred after a rain storm (A. J. M. Smith) with c. 100 still present 10 Nov 1979 (E. Dunn).

Breeding. Unrecorded. Courtship flight: Panbros, Jul. In Nigeria, Apr–May (Elgood 1982).

PTEROCLIDIDAE

237. PTEROCLES QUADRICINCTUS

(I.335)*   Four-banded Sandgrouse   AfM/B

Not uncommon intra-African migrant in the drier open savanna in the far north; recorded Bawku, Gambaga and Nangodi end Oct to late Apr (M. Horwood, F. Walsh), Tumu, early Nov to Mar (Sutton 1970) and south to Mole (Greig-Smith 1976a). In wet season, moves northwards. Collected by Giffard at Gambaga, 1 Jan and 3 Mar (Hartert 1899a), and by Alexander (1902).

Breeding. One juvenile, 3 Mar 1898, Gambaga (Hartert 1899a). Breeds Nigeria, Oct–May (Elgood 1982).

*Named *Eremialector quadricinctus* by MP&G.

COLUMBIDAE

238. COLUMBA GUINEA

(I.337)   Speckled Pigeon   RB

Surprisingly, only an uncommon local resident (*C. g. guinea*) in some urban areas, records often sporadic. Not recorded Tumu (Sutton 1970), Mole (Greig-Smith 1976a) nor Bolgatanga (F. Walsh), but present Navasco (c. 15 miles northwest of Bolgatanga) Sep 1977 (J. F. Monk). Regular Tono dam (R. Passmore) and present at Vea dam, Mar and Aug 1972 and 1977, but not at other times (F. Walsh). Regular at Tamale in dry season in Holman's day, but fewer records now (E. Hall). At Gambaga only few, Nov–Apr, but larger flocks during early rains (Alexander 1902). Collected Navrongo, 21 Jan (Lowe 1937), Gambaga, 28 Aug (Hartert 1899a).

Breeding. Nest building: Jirape, 30 Oct (Sutton 1970). Eggs: C/2 Kumbungu, Nov (Holman 1947). Female collected by Lowe, 21 Jan, had just finished laying.

239. COLUMBA LIVIA
(I.336)   Rock Pigeon   R(B)

Very localised (*C. l. gymnocyclus*); only recorded along the Gambaga escarpment. Collected Gambaga by Giffard, 28 Aug (Hartert 1899a) and Alexander (1902); recent sightings at Nakpanduri, 18/21 Mar 1964 (Sutton 1965b). Not recorded in Nigeria (Elgood 1982) nor Ivory Coast (Thiollay 1985).

Breeding. Unrecorded. In West Africa, probably Apr–Jul (MP&G).

240. COLUMBA MALHERBII (= TURTUROENA IRIDITORQUES)
(I.342)   Gabon Bronze-naped Pigeon   R(B)

Uncommon resident (*C. m. iriditorques*) in canopy of both mature and secondary forest; easily overlooked if voice is not known. Not uncommon, 12–14 Jan, along the Asukawkaw river in the Volta Region (F. Walsh). Collected Aburi (H. T. Ussher *in* Bannerman 1931), Mampong in Ashanti and along the Afram river (Lowe 1937). Sighted at Opintin Gallery forest, 2 Nov 1974 (N. Wood).

Breeding. Unrecorded. In Liberia: eggs, Mar; females with large ovaries, Apr, Jul and Sep; Nestling, 29 Mar (Colston & Curry Lindahl 1986).

241. COLUMBA UNICINCTA
(I.341)   Afep Pigeon   R(B)

Rare resident of forest canopy. Few records: Akim-Oda, a flock of 6 feeding in canopy at forest edge, Oct (G. Cansdale); Bia National Park, song and display flight, 6–9 Apr 1977 (Taylor & Macdonald 1978b). Collected Ejura, Ashanti, 30 Jan (Lowe 1937).

Breeding. The male collected by Lowe was in breeding condition.

242. OENA CAPENSIS
(I.353)   Namaqua (or Long-tailed) Dove   AfM/(B)

A local, not uncommon intra-African migrant, Sep–May, throughout northern savanna, south to Kete Kratchi and Salaga (R. E. Crabbe). Moves northwards at the beginning of the rains in May after breeding.

Breeding. Unrecorded. In Nigeria, Oct–Apr (Elgood 1982).

243. STREPTOPELIA DECIPIENS
(I.349)   Mourning Dove   R(B)

Status uncertain, probably not uncommon local resident (*S. d. shelleyi*) in the more arid savanna areas in north, but few records. Considered resident at Mole by Greig-Smith (1976a), but few records in Mar and Apr (Maze 1971, M. Edmunds, L.G.G.) and in some years none (Taylor & Macdonald 1978a). Not recorded Tumu (Sutton 1970), Bolgatanga (F. Walsh), nor at Tamale (Holman 1947, E. Hall). No records in south, but occurs at coast in Nigeria (Elgood 1982) and in Togo at Lome (Browne 1980)

Breeding. Unrecorded. Breeds almost all months in Nigeria (Elgood 1982).

244. STREPTOPELIA ROSEOGRISEA (= DECAOCTO)
(I.351)   Pink-headed (or Rose-grey) Dove   V

Vagrant. One sighting: 2 (*S. r. roseagrisea*) on 5 Apr 1976 at Mole (9°22′N) (Taylor & Macdonald 1978a). This is well south of its normal range in West Africa, although in Nigeria it has occurred as far south as Funtua (11°32′N, 7°18′E) (Elgood 1982).

245. STREPTOPELIA SEMITORQUATA
(I.347)   Red-eyed Dove   RB

An abundant resident at forest edge and in well wooded savanna throughout the north, southwards through the Volta Region to the Accra — Ho — Keta Plains and westwards along the coastal strip to Sekondi. Absent from open savanna with few trees, e.g. Denu and Keta in the SE and Bawku in NE, where it is replaced by *T. vinacea,* and from within forest clearings e.g. Kumasi and Tafo (M. Lockwood). Collected along the Ankobra river, near Axim (Bannerman 1931).

Breeding. Extended. Birds in breeding condition collected Feb (Lowe 1934). Eggs: in south and north, Aug. Nestlings: at Legon and Achimota, mid Dec (Grimes 1972a).

246. STREPTOPELIA (=STIGMATOPELIA) SENEGALENSIS
(I.352)   Laughing Dove   RB

Abundant resident (*S. s. senegalensis*) throughout, apart from the forest region, frequenting towns, villages gardens and farms. Not recorded Tafo (M. Lockwood) nor Kumasi (Holman 1947).

Breeding. Extended. Eggs: C/2, Accra and Legon, in most months, one nest used for 5 consecutive clutches between May 1971 and Feb 1972 (Grimes 1972b); in coastal strip west of Cape Coast, eggs, Aug–Feb (Macdonald 1979b). Peak in breeding occurs in dry season, Nov–Feb.

247. STREPTOPELIA TURTUR
(I.344)   Turtle Dove   PM

Uncommon Palaearctic migrant (probably all *S. t. turtur* although North African *S. t. arenicola* might occur) in the north, Oct–Apr. Singletons recorded Bolgatanga and Vea dam (F. Walsh); a flock of c. 50, Apr, near Lawra (Wink 1976). Collected Mole Game Reserve, Oct and Nov. The increase in rice cultivation in the north may help concentrate numbers in the future.

248. STREPTOPELIA VINACEA
(I.350)   Vinaceous Dove   RB

Abundant resident in all types of savanna throughout the north, south along the dry eastern border of Ghana to the Accra Plains. A vagrant at Winneba, Dec, and not recorded further west along coastline (M. Macdonald). Large flocks, 1000–2000, may form at end of dry season (Apr) in the north, e.g. Tamale (E. Hall) and at Kintampo (Taylor & Macdonald 1978a). Absent from forest clearings, but overlaps with *S. semitorquata* along forest edge at the base of the Akwapim scarp.

Breeding. Surprisingly, only one record; breeding Ejura, Feb (Lowe 1937). Elsewhere in West Africa, in most months (MP&G, Elgood 1982).

249. TRERON (=VINAGO) AUSTRALIS
(I.362)   Green (Fruit) Pigeon   RB

Common resident (*T. a. sharpei*) throughout forest zone, in primary and second-ary forest, in clearings and at forest edge. Extends northwards into the savanna zone along riverine forest and southwards to the coastal strip. Often congregates in large flocks, up to several hundred, at ripening *Ficus* spp. (Lowe 1937). Frequently trapped for food.

Breeding. Nest building: Accra Plains, 20 Nov (L.G.G.); Tafo, May and Oct (M. Lockwood). Eggs: Worawora, Sep (C. M. Morrison); Wenchi, Jan (Lowe 1937).

250. **TRERON (= VINAGO) WAALIA**
      (I.360)   Bruce's Green Pigeon (Yellow-bellied Fruit-Pigeon)   RB
Common resident throughout wooded savanna in the far north, where it replaces
T. australis, although both overlap in savanna further south. Often in large flocks at
fruiting *Ficus* spp; major local movements of the dove occur due to the differing
fruiting times of the *Ficus* spp (Bannerman 1953). Although Holman (1947 and *in*
Bannerman 1931, 1951) reported it a vagrant at Kumasi and occasional at Keta,
there are no recent records.
   Breeding. Extended. Nest/eggs: Bawku, Dec (A. W. J. Pomeroy *in* Bannerman
1931); Pong Tamale, Apr and May (Walsh 1981); in north, Nov and Dec (Holman
1947). Fledgling: Mole, Oct (Genelly 1968).

251. **TURTUR ABYSSINICUS**
      (I.356)   Black-billed Blue-spotted Wood-Dove (Black-billed Wood-Dove)
                                                                          RB
Common resident in northern wooded savanna, often in cassava plantations,
extending southwards through the Volta Region to the Accra–Ho–Keta Plains.
Throughout its southern range is sympatric with *T. afer*; east of the Volta river at
Keta the 2 species occur in approximately equal numbers, but west of the river *afer* is
more numerous (Holman 1947, D. W. Lamm *in* Grimes 1972a). In coastal strip west
of Accra, it is rare: occasional at Sekondi (Holman *in* Bannerman 1951) but only
twice at Cape Coast; one shot by Buckley (Bannerman 1931), and one sighted, 22
Feb 1977 (M. Macdonald). Absent from within large forest clearings.
   Breeding. Eggs: C/1–2, Kwabenya, May (P. Grubb); Winneba, July (F. Walsh);
Navrongo, Aug (F. Walsh). In Nigeria a dry season breeder, Oct–Mar (Elgood
1982).

252. **TURTUR AFER**
      (I.355)   Blue-spotted (or Red-billed) Wood-Dove   RB, Afm?
Common resident in secondary forest, farmland and large forest clearings (e.g.
Tafo, Kumasi) throughout, avoiding mature forest. Extends northwards into well
wooded savanna areas along riverine forest, where it overlaps in approximately
equal numbers with *T. abyssinicus.* The smaller numbers recorded in some years at
Mole at end of dry season, Apr, suggest a movement southwards as the dry season
progresses (Taylor & Macdonald 1978a).
   Breeding. Mar–Oct, mainly Jul and Aug (Holman 1947), nest sites often in
cassava and maize plantations. Nest building: Accra, 23 May 1976. Egg in oviduct:
Cape Coast, 6 Jan 1977. Nestling: Cape Coast, 17 Jun 1976 (Macdonald 1979b). In
Nigeria, Oct–Mar (Elgood 1982).

253. **TURTUR BREHMERI (= CALOPELIA PUELLA)**
      (I.358)   Blue-headed Dove   R(B)
Uncommon shy resident (*T. b. infelix*), probably now confined to mature lowland
forest reserves, possibly less common now than in early part of century, but easily
overlooked (Macdonald & Taylor 1977). Collected Dabocrom (Pel), Akwapim
(Riis), Cape Coast (Higgins), Prahsu and Fumsu (Alexander), Mampong in Ashanti
(Lowe 1937).
   Breeding. The male collected by Lowe, 25 Feb, was "just about to breed".

254. **TURTUR (= TYMPANISTRIA) TYMPANISTRIA**
      (I.354)   Tambourine Dove   R(B)
Common resident in both mature and secondary forest, forest edge and coastal
thicket, often associated with cassava plantations within forest zone. Reaches

Hohoe and Amedzofe in Volta region (Sutton 1970). Collected Sekondi (Pel, Lowe), Cape Coast (Higgins), Ejura and Mampong in Ashanti (Lowe) (Bannerman 1931, 1951).

Breeding. Unrecorded. Nesting material being carried; Kumasi, no date (Holman 1947); Akropong in Akwapim, 5 Sep (C. M. Morrison). In Nigeria, juv, 8 Jun and 2 adults with squab, 25 Feb (Elgood 1982).

PSITTACIDAE

255. AGAPORNIS PULLARIA
(I.407)   Red-headed Lovebird   R(B)

Uncommon resident (*A. p. pullaria = guineensis*) in wooded savanna and riverine forest throughout north, and south via the Volta Region to the Accra — Ho — Keta Plains and westwards along the coastal strip to Cape Coast (Gass 1954, Grimes 1972a, Greig-Smith 1976a). Rarer now than during the last century when it was common in coastal villages (Ussher 1872). Usually seen in small groups, 6–12, but pairs in wet season at Denu (Sutton 1965b) and at Mole (M. Horwood).

Breeding. Unrecorded. Eggs and juv in Nigeria, Oct (Elgood 1982).

256. AGAPORNIS SWINDERNIANA
(I.408)   Black-collared Lovebird   R(B)

A rare forest species (more akin to *A. s. swinderniana* of Liberia than *A. s. zenkeri* of the Camerouns — Snow 1976); probably now confined to forest reserves. Collected, 10 Feb 1902, by B. Alexander, probably at Hweremasi (6°46′N, 1°24′W) (Snow 1976). Recent sightings: Bia National Park and Kakum and Pra Suhien Forest Reserves, groups of up to 10 feeding on fig seeds in mature and secondary forest and in forest clearings (Macdonald & Taylor 1977, Macdonald 1980e).

Breeding. Unrecorded in West Africa (Elgood 1982).

257. POICEPHALUS GULIELMI
(I.402)   Red-headed (Red-crowned) Parrot   RB

Not uncommon resident (*P. g. fantiensis*) in mature and secondary forest throughout forest zone and in larger forest clearings, e.g. Tafo (M. Lockwood), Mpraeso (Sutton 1970). Regular in Bia National Park, often in flocks of c. 30 at dawn and dusk (Taylor & Macdonald 1978b); flocks of c. 10 or less, Wassaw district and Asankrangwa, Mar and Apr (M. Horwood).

Breeding. Young on wing: Tafo, in May (M. Lockwood).

258. POICEPHALUS ROBUSTUS
(I.401)   Brown-necked Parrot   RB

Not uncommon resident (*P. r. fuscicollis*) in mature wooded savanna, e.g. Mole (Greig-Smith 1976a), Kete Kratchi (M. Horwood), and forest edge, e.g. Mampong in Ashanti (Sutton 1970); occasional Kumasi (L.G.G.) and one probable flock (c. 30), no date, Tafo (M. Lockwood). Subject to local movements, at least in some years, in the northern savanna (Macdonald 1978d).

Breeding. Pair investigating nest-holes: Mole, mid Jul and Aug (Greig-Smith 1977b).

259. POICEPHALUS SENEGALUS
(I.404)   Yellow-bellied (or Senegal) Parrot   RB

A common resident throughout the wooded savanna north of the forest, south through the Volta Region to the Accra — Ho — Keta Plains, usually in flocks of 10–12 but occasionally larger (c. 30). Seasonal at Tono dam, Apr–Dec (R.

Passmore). At Legon, numbers increased between 1960 and 1975 as planted trees matured (Grimes 1972a). White recognises 2 races, nominate *senegallus* in the north, and *versteri* in the south, the latter having a scarlet rather than orange abdomen.

Breeding. Eggs: Legon, Jun. Fledglings: Legon, Aug (Grimes 1972a). Prospecting nest holes at Mole, Jul and Aug (Greig-Smith 1977b).

260. PSITTACULA KRAMERI
(I.406)   Rose-ringed (or Long-tailed) Parrakeet   R(B)

Not uncommon resident (*P. k. krameri*), although subject to local movements, in open wooded savanna throughout the north and southwards through the Volta Region to the Accra — Ho — Keta Plains, usually in groups of 10 or less, but large flocks may gather in guinea-corn plantations in north (Alexander 1902).

Breeding. Investigating possible nest holes: Mole, Jul and Oct–Dec (Greig-Smith 1977b).

261. PSITTACUS ERITHACUS
(I.400)   Grey Parrot   RB

Uncommon local resident (*P. e. erithacus*) throughout the forest zone, mainly confined to forest reserves but occasional in forest clearings, e.g. Tafo (M. Lockwood), Mpraeso, Kade and Kumasi (L.G.G.). Large numbers were sold in 1870s at Cape Coast and Accra (Ussher 1872) and this practice continues unabated and illegally until the present day, illegal export by now having greatly reduced the Ghanaian population. In 1940s Horwood occasionally located flocks of 500–1000, near Bekwai, and has occurred at Atebubu, Kete Kratchi (J. M. Winterbottom) and Ejura (Lowe 1937). In contrast, is now locally distributed and only 2s and 3s were recorded at Bia National Park in 1970s (Taylor & Macdonald 1978b).

Breeding. No precise data; young fledglings for sale from Mar onwards.

MUSOPHAGIDAE

262. CORYTHEOLA CRISTATA
(I.395)   Great Blue Turaco (Blue Plantain-eater)   R(B)

Not uncommon resident, in groups of 3–10, in mature and secondary forest and occasional in riverine forest attached to the main forest block. Occurred throughout the forest zone in Ussher's day and was collected near Accra (Ussher 1872) and Kete Kratchi (Count Zech) in the last century. Occurred at Ejura in the 1930s (Pomeroy) and as late as the 1950s was common, particularly in secondary forest containing a canopy of *Musanga smithii* (M. Horwood). In contrast, recent records are fewer and mainly from forest reserves near Mpraeso, Kibi, Tarkwa, Kade and Bia National Park (L.G.G., Macdonald & Taylor 1977).

Breeding. Unrecorded. In Nigeria probably irregular; juvenile with down, Nov, and female with oviduct egg, May (Elgood 1982).

263. CRINIFER PISCATOR
(I.396)   Grey Plantain-eater   RB

A common and widespread resident throughout mature woodland savanna north of the forest belt, southwards through the Volta Region to the Accra — Ho — Keta Plains, less common in the Sudan zone around Bawku, only recorded Tamale, Oct–Jun (J. Callow) and sporadic at Tumu (Sutton 1970). Although not present in coastal belt west of Accra in last century (Ussher 1874), it is now a common resident at Cape Coast and Winneba (J. Hall, M. Macdonald).

Breeding. Nuptial display: Mole, Jul. Copulation: Mole, mid Aug (Greig–Smith 1977b). Nest building: Legon, Apr. Eggs: Legon, Nov–Dec. Fledglings: Legon, Oct and Feb (L.G.G.).

264. MUSOPHAGA VIOLACEA
(I.393)   Violet Turaco (Violet Plantain-eater)   R(B)

Not uncommon local resident in riverine forest north of the forest zone and southwards in woodland through the Volta Region to wooded inselbergs on the Accra — Ho — Keta Plains; absent from the more open savanna in the north and south, only recorded once at Tumu (Sutton 1970). Although collected by Ussher at Cape Coast and located at Sunyani (J. M. Winterbottom *in* Bannerman 1933), there are no other records from within the forest zone and no recent records from Cape Coast (M. Horwood, M. Macdonald).

Breeding. Unrecorded. Stated to be Apr at Gambaga (Alexander 1902) but no specific data. In Nigeria, nestling and juveniles, Jun–Nov (Elgood 1982).

265. TAURACO (=TURACUS) MACRORHYNCHUS
(I.388)   Black-tip Crested Turaco   R(B)

Uncommon resident (*T. m. macrorhynchus*) in mature and secondary forest, particularly when *Musanga smithii* is dominant (M. Horwood). Less common now than previously; Horwood found it common and widely distributed in 1950s. Outside the forest region is replaced by *T. persa*.

Breeding. Unrecorded. In Cameroun *T. m. verreauxii* (Red-tip Crested Turaco) breeds Jun–Aug (MP&G).

266. TAURACO (=TURACUS) PERSA
(I.385)   Guinea Turaco   R(B)

Not uncommon resident (*T. p. persa*) in mature and secondary forest, forest clearings, and well wooded savanna just north of the forest and south through the Volta Region to inselbergs on the Accra — Ho — Keta Plains and coastal thicket west of Accra. Sympatric with *T. macrorhynchus* within the forest, but the latter is restricted to the forest. At Legon, numbers increased between 1960 and 1970 as trees matured and formed a closed canopy (Grimes 1972a). Collected Axim, Sekondi, Cape Coast and located Kumasi (F. C. Holman), Sunyani (J. M. Winterbottom), Ejura and Mampong in Ashanti (Lowe 1937).

Breeding. Unrecorded. In Cameroun, Aug (MP&G).

CUCULIDAE

Cuculinae

267. CERCOCOCCYX MECHOWI
(I.367)   Dusky (or Mechow's) Long-tailed Cuckoo   R(B)

Uncommon resident of mature forest; no sightings, but easily located through distinctive calls. Regularly heard at Atewa, in reserves north of Cape Coast and in the western Region (L. Cole). A skin labelled 'Commendah' (Bannerman 1933) may well refer to present day Kommendah west of Cape Coast.

Breeding. Unrecorded in West Africa (MP&G).

268. CERCOCOCCYX OLIVINUS
(I.368)   Olive Long-tailed Cuckoo   R(B)

Rare resident of mature forest; only known from skins: collected "Fanti country" and near Kumasi by F. C. Holman (Bannerman 1933, 1951).

Breeding. Unrecorded. No certain record anywhere in West Africa; a possible host is *Stizorhina frazeri* (Elgood 1982).

269. CHRYSOCOCCYX (=LAMPROMORPHA) CAPRIUS
(I.375)   Didric Cuckoo   RB, Afm/B

Seasonally common in forest clearings, forest edge and wooded savanna throughout. Although mainly recorded in wet season there are dry season records, which makes its status uncertain. Regularly heard at Tafo in most months (M. Lockwood, L.G.G.), at Akropong Jan–May and Jul–Nov (C. M. Morrison), but is only regular in wet season at Kumasi after mid Feb (S. Woodell) and at Denu, on the coast, after Mar (Sutton 1965). In the north, a wet season visitor to Mole, May–Sep (Greig-Smith 1976a), but present at Tumu, Sep–Jul (Sutton 1970). Resident at Accra and Cape Coast, but few are recorded between late Aug and mid Oct (Grimes 1972a, Macdonald 1979a).

Breeding. In coastal districts mainly wet season, Mar–Jul, when its main host *Ploceus cucullatus* breeds, but more prolonged in forest region. Young on wing: Tafo, Nov and Jan (M. Lockwood).

270. CHRYSOCOCCYX CUPREUS
(I.374)   Emerald Cuckoo   R(B)

A common resident (*C. c. cupreus*) of mature and secondary forest throughout, reaching Amedzofe and Hohoe in the Volta Region (L.G.G.), easily located through calls. Not recorded north of the forests although northward movements occur in Nigeria (Elgood 1982). A skin collected by Giffard and named *Chrysococcyx cupreus* (Bodd) by him is plotted as this species in Snow (1978). However, the name used by Giffard (Hartert 1899a) is according to Bannerman (1933: 114) a synonym of *C. caprius*.

Breeding. Unrecorded. In Nigeria, female with oviduct egg, 13 May (Elgood 1982). In Liberia, oviduct eggs, Aug–Sep (Colston & Curry-Lindahl 1986).

271. CHRYSOCOCCYX FLAVIGULARIS
(I.377)   Yellow-throated Green Cuckoo   ?

A rare forest species. Only one record; a skin collected at Elmina (Shelley 1879). Collected at 3 separate locations in southwest Togoland near Ghana border (Bannerman 1931).

Breeding. Unrecorded from anywhere in its range (MP&G).

272. CHRYSOCOCCYX (=LAMPROMORPHA) KLAAS
(I.376)   Klaas' Cuckoo   RB, Afm/B

Seasonally not uncommon in mature and secondary forest, forest clearings, and wooded savanna throughout the north, south to the Accra — Ho — Keta Plains and west through coastal thicket zone. Calling birds may be heard, Jul–Apr, within forest zone (M. Horwood, Taylor & Macdonald 1978b), but Holman (Bannerman 1933) found it often absent for months at Kumasi. In coastal districts, mainly Jan–Aug, occasional at other times (Grimes 1972a, M. Macdonald). Although considered a wet season visitor, May–Sep, to Mole and Tono dam, there is one dry season record in Jan (Maze 1971).

Breeding. Eggs, no date, obtained from nests of *Prinia subflava, Zosterops senegalensis* and *Lamprotornis caudatus* (Pomeroy *in* Bannerman 1933, Holman 1947). Seen being mobbed by *Eremomela badiceps* and *Cinnyricinclus leucogaster* (M. D. I. Gass).

273. CLAMATOR GLANDARIUS
(I.371)   Great Spotted Cuckoo   Afm/B, PM?

Not uncommon seasonally in wooded savanna in north, but records are sporadic; less common on the Accra — Ho — Keta Plains, and occasional in coastal strip westwards to Cape Coast. Records in north: Tumu, 1–3, Dec–May (Sutton 1970); Bolgatanga, Oct–Jun (F. Walsh). Records in south: Legon, Dec–Jun (Grimes 1972a, L.G.G.); Denu, Jan–Mar (Sutton 1965b); Winneba and Cape Coast, Dec–Feb (J. R. Marshall, D. James, M. Macdonald). The presence of Palaearctic migrants are probable but not proven.

Breeding. Fledglings: one being mobbed at Achimota by *Corvus alba,* Jun; another at Legon by *Lamprotornis purpureus.* Juveniles: Keta, Nov (F. C. Holman *in* Bannerman 1933); Legon, Feb (M. Edmunds, P. Grubb *in* Grimes 1972a).

274. CLAMATOR JACOBINUS
(I.373)   Black and White (or Pied) Cuckoo   Afm/(B)

Locally uncommon intra-African migrant (*C. j. pica*) to mature wooded savanna in north, May–Sep (Greig-Smith 1976a). Elsewhere records (all singletons) are few: Tumu, 12 Jun; Navrongo, 28 Jun (Sutton 1970); Legon, 10 Feb 1968, and 25 Jul 1971 (Grimes 1972a).

Breeding. Unrecorded. In Nigeria, juveniles fed by hosts (*Turdoides plebejus, Pycnonotus barbatus*), Jun and Jul (Elgood 1982).

275. CLAMATOR LEVAILLANTII (= CAFER)
(I.372)   Levaillant's Cuckoo   Afm/B, RB

Not uncommon but irregular intra-African migrant to wooded savanna near Bolgatanga (F. Walsh) and Tamale (J. Callow), mainly in wet season, May–Nov, but considered resident at Mole (Greig-Smith 1976a). Probably resident on the Accra Plains, single birds Sep–Feb, often in pairs Mar–Aug; but mainly a dry season visitor, Nov–Feb at Cape Coast (M. Macdonald). Occasional within forest clearings at Tafo (M. Lockwood), Kumasi, Feb (B. Woodell) and Mampong in Ashanti (Lowe 1937).

Breeding. Female with oviduct egg: 15 Feb (Lowe 1937). Juvenile with host (*Turdoides plebejus*): Legon, Jun and Jul (Grimes 1972a, L.G.G.); Achimota, 3 Nov (M. D. I. Gass); Agogo, 7 Jan (M. D. I. Gass).

276. CUCULUS CANORUS CANORUS
(I.363)   Cuckoo (European Cuckoo)   PM

Rare Palaearctic migrant to forest clearings, savanna and coastal strip east of Cape Coast. Very few sightings, all uncertain due to similarity of *canorus* with *C. c. gularis*: Kumasi, Jan (Holman *in* Bannerman 1951); Tumu, 22 Sep, 12 Feb (Sutton 1970); Bia Game Park (Taylor & Macdonald 1978b). Those collected in Ghana (3♂♂, 2♀♀) are small and overlap in size with the cuckoos that breed in Iberia and the Maghreb (Moreau 1972: 183). The same is true for all other Palaearctic cuckoos collected in West Africa, and Moreau points out that this is "perhaps the clearest example on the African continent of the segregation of local breeding populations in winter".

277. CUCULUS CANORUS GULARIS
(I.363)   African (or Yellow-billed) Cuckoo   Afm/B

Not uncommon intra-African migrant to wooded savannas in north, mainly in wet season, Mar–Aug (F. Walsh, E. Hall, J. Callow, Sutton 1970). Dry season records: 3–4 together at Kete Kratchi, 27–29 Jan (M. Horwood); one, Feb, at Tumu (Sutton 1970). In south, on the Accra Plains regularly recorded and very vocal,

Jan–Aug, occasional during rest of year, twice in Oct and Nov (Grimes 1972a, L.G.G.). In contrast, only one record for Cape Coast, 6 Jun 1977 (M. Macdonald). Movements eastwards across the Accra Plains, involving 1–3 birds in late Jul, may have been migration (L.G.G.).

Breeding. Nestling: Legon, in nest of *Corvinella corvina,* May (Grimes 1979b). Immatures: Legon, Jun and Aug (L.G.G.).

278. CUCULUS CLAMOSUS (= CAFER)
(I.366)   Black Cuckoo   R(B), AfM/NB?

Not uncommon resident (*C. c. gabonensis*), in mature and secondary forest (Taylor & Macdonald 1978b), forest clearings, e.g. Kumasi, Tarkwa and Tafo, forest edge, e.g. Abokobi, Akropong in Akwapim. The status of the savanna race *C. c. clamosus* is uncertain and it may only be a non-breeding migrant (White 1970). Occurs in coastal savanna at Winneba, no dates (M. Horwood), and on the Accra Plains, records in each month, but most records of calling birds Mar–Jun (Grimes 1972a, L.G.G.). Recorded Salaga, no date (R. E. Crabbe), but no other records in northern savanna; probably overlooked. Collected Elmina (Blissett) and in "Denkera" (Ussher 1874) in last century.

Breeding. Unrecorded. In southern Africa it parasitises shrikes (Serle *et al.* 1977).

279. CUCULUS SOLITARIUS
(I.365)   Red-chested (or Solitary) Cuckoo   R(B)

Not uncommon resident (*C. s. solitarius*) of mature and secondary forest. No records outside forest region except one at Kete Kratchi, no date (R. E. Crabb) and one near Accra, 1 Jun 1965 (M. Edmunds *in* Grimes 1972a). M. Horwood found it common within the Ghana forests but never located it in savanna in the north, although he did so in Nigeria. Possibly overlooked in the north, as a northward movement is apparent in Nigeria, Apr–Sep (Elgood 1982).

Breeding. Unrecorded. In Cameroun, Aug (MP&G).

280. PACHYCOCCYX AUDEBERTI (= VALIDUS)
(I.370)   Thick-billed Cuckoo   V?

Only 3 records: one collected (A. H. Booth) at Odumasi Krobo, 9 Feb 1952 (Lamm & Horwood 1958); singletons sighted, Amedzofe, 8 Mar (Sutton 1965b), and Tafo, no date (M. Lockwood).

Phaenicophaeninae

281. CEUTHMOCHARES AEREUS
(I.384)   Yellow-bill   RB

Common resident (*C. a. flavirostris*) in mature and secondary forest throughout forest zone, occasional in riverine forest at Hohoe and Kete Kratchi and regular in thickets in the Shai Hills, at Abokobi (both on the Accra Plains) and in coastal region west of Accra. No records in the north but possibly overlooked.

Breeding. Eggs: C/2, Kumasi, Mar (Holman 1947); Odumasi Krobo, 17 May (C. M. Morrison).

Centropinae

282. CENTROPUS LEUCOGASTER
(I.379)   Black-throated (or Great) Coucal   RB

Uncommon resident (*C. l. leucogaster*) in both mature and secondary forest and in coastal thicket, eastwards to Akwapim hills; more often heard than seen, often calling at night. Alexander (1902) recorded it at Prahsu (within the forest region), which Bannerman (1933) initially placed north of the forest but later corrected (Bannerman 1951).

Breeding. A captured bird at Kumasi, 10 Aug 1947, promptly laid an egg (G. Cansdale *in* Bannerman 1951). Stated to be Oct by Alexander (1902), but no data provided.

283. CENTROPUS MONACHUS
(I.381)   Blue-headed Coucal   R(B)

Not uncommon resident (*C. m. fischeri*), although status and distribution is uncertain due to similarity in field with *C. senegalensis*. (In some places in Nigeria it is ecologically separated from *senegalensis,* preferring wetter thickets and edges of marshes than *senegalensis*.) Probably widely but locally distributed in suitable habitat in savanna zone north, east and south of the forest region. Collected Accra (Ussher), in Akwapim (Riis) and at Pong on the Accra Plains (Alexander 1902). Bannerman (1933) incorrectly stated that Pong was in the northern territories.

Breeding. Unrecorded. In Cameroun, May–Sep (MP&G).

284. CENTROPUS SENEGALENSIS
(I.382)   Senegal Coucal   RB

Common resident (*C. s. senegalensis*) in thickets and scrub throughout the savanna north of the forest, east and south to the Accra — Ho — Keta Plains, and westwards in coastal thickets reaching Axim (M. Horwood, M. Macdonald). Present in forest clearings, but absent within mature forest. The melanic (rufous) form (*'epomidis'*) has been collected at Boutry (Pel), in "fantee country" (Ussher *in* Bannerman 1933), and in central Region (Bannerman 1951). One albino near Shai Hills, May (L.G.G.).

Breeding. Nesting: Mole, Jul and Aug (Greig-Smith 1977b). Fledglings: Accra Plains and Cape Coast, Apr–Jun (Grimes 1972a, Macdonald 1979b).

285. CENTROPUS TOULOU (= GRILLII)
(I.378)   Black (-bellied) Coucal   Afm/B

Not uncommon breeding migrant to coastal areas, mainly wet season, May–Aug, as far west as Axim where Horwood found it more common than *senegalensis*; occurs Kumasi Sewage Farm, Apr (M. F. Hodges, Jr), occasional in dry season at Nakwa, 18 Dec (Macdonald 1979a) and Sekondi, Jan (Holman 1947). Locally distributed in wetlands in the north, most records in wet season Jul–Sep, but considered resident at Mole (Greig-Smith 1976a). At Keta most birds disperse after breeding to unknown destinations (Holman 1947).

Breeding. Eggs: C/3–4, Keta, Jul–Sep (Holman 1947). Immatures with adults: in marshes at Panbros, Apr–Jun (Grimes 1972a). Birds holding territories: Mole, Jul–Aug (Greig-Smith 1977b).

TYTONIDAE

286. TYTO ALBA
(I.473)   Barn Owl   RB

Common resident (*T. a. affinis*) in suburbs of larger towns such as Accra, Kumasi, Cape Coast in south and Tamale, Bolgatanga and Salaga in north, also in wooded savanna at Mole (Greig-Smith 1976b) and north of Tamale (F. Walsh). Collected in Akwapim (A. Swanzy) and Kete Kratchi (Count Zech).

Breeding. Eggs: Accra, Oct and Nov (Gass 1954). Fledglings: Legon, late Nov and Dec (L.G.G.); Bolgatanga, late Jan (F. Walsh).

STRIGIDAE

Buboninae

287. BUBO AFRICANUS
(I.492)   Spotted Eagle-Owl   R(B)
Common resident (*B. a. cinerascens*) in both mature and secondary forest (M. Horwood), forest clearings, forest edge, and wooded savanna throughout north (Sutton 1970, F. Walsh) and on the western edge and inselbergs of the Accra Plains (Grimes 1972a). One record Cape Coast, Jan (M. Macdonald), occasional at Sekondi (Holman *in* Bannerman 1951). Collected Achimota (V. T. Foote and A. H. Booth *in* Grimes 1972a).
Breeding. Unrecorded. In Nigeria, Dec–Apr (Elgood 1982).

288. BUBO LACTEUS
(I.493)   Verreaux's (or Milky) Eagle-Owl   R(B)
Rare resident, probably overlooked, in wooded savanna north of the forest belt. Only 2 records: ♂ collected Kwobia, some 30 km or so west of Yendi (Alexander 1902); a certain sighting Mole, 3 Sep (Harvey & Harrison 1970).
Breeding. Unrecorded. In Nigeria, Jan–Mar (Elgood 1982).

289. BUBO LEUCOSTICTUS
(I.495)   Akun Eagle-Owl   R(B)
Rare resident in lowland forest, only known from skins. Collected Dabocrom (Pel), in Akwapim (Riis), "Denkere" (location unknown today — Ussher 1874) and Mampong in Ashanti (Lowe 1937).
Breeding. Unrecorded. Nestling: Liberia, Feb (MP&G). Juvenile with much down on body: Liberia, Jul (Colston & Curry-Lindahl 1986).

290. BUBO POENSIS
(I.496)   Fraser's Eagle-Owl   R(B)
Uncommon resident (*B. p. poensis*) of mature and secondary forest throughout forest region. Collected Cape Coast, Dabocrom (Pel), "Denkere" (location unknown today) and "Fantee" (Bannerman 1933), Mampong and Goaso (Lowe 1937), and more recently at Ayimensah at the foot of the Akwapim ridge below Aburi (D. W. Lamm). Recorded Akim Oda (M. Horwood), Kumasi (F. C. Holman *in* Bannerman 1951), and recently at Cape Coast, 3 Jul 1977 (M. Macdonald).
Breeding. Unrecorded. In Nigeria, captive bird laid an egg on 11 Oct (Elgood 1982). In Liberia, females with enlarged ovaries, Jan, Sep, Nov; juveniles, Jun and Aug (Colston & Curry-Lindahl 1986).

291. BUBO SHELLEYI
(I.494)   (Shelley's) Banded Eagle-Owl   R(B)
Rare forest resident, only known from skins. Two collected "Denkere" (location unknown today — Sharpe & Ussher 1872). Occurs in both the Upper and Lower Guinea forests
Breeding. Unrecorded anywhere in its range (MP&G).

292. CICCABA (= STRIX) WOODFORDII
(I.478)   African Wood-Owl   RB
Not uncommon resident (*C. w. nuchalis*) in mature and secondary forest and forest edge throughout forest region, often singly on roadsides after dark (M. Horwood). Collected Cape Coast (M. F. Blissett), along the Afram river near

Mpraeso (M. Horwood), and in the Asankrangwa and Atewa forest reserves (L.G.G.).

Breeding. Eggs: C/1, Kumasi, Feb (Holman 1947). Juvenile: Goaso and Mampong in Ashanti, Jan and Feb (Lowe 1937).

[GLAUCIDIUM CAPENSE ETCHECOPARI (not in White)
(I.488)   Barred Owlet
Recorded from 17 mature and/or secondary forested areas in Ivory Coast, in some places considered common (Thiollay 1985). Likely to occur in Ghana.]

293. GLAUCIDIUM PERLATUM
(I.486)   Pearl-spotted Owlet   R(B)
Uncommon local resident (*G. p. perlatum*) confined to mature woodland savanna in north and south through the Volta region to inselbergs on the Accra–Ho Plains, but occurs in older suburbs of Accra, Achimota and Legon; not recorded in coastal areas west of Accra (M. Macdonald) nor in drier open savanna near Keta (Sutton 1965b). Occurs Tono dam, Sep only (R. Passmore).
Breeding. Unrecorded. In Nigeria, egg in oviduct, Apr (Elgood 1982).

294. GLAUCIDIUM TEPHRONOTUM
(I.487)   Red-chested (Yellow-legged) Owlet   RB
Rare resident (*G. t. tephronotum*) of mature forest, only known from skins. Initially described from a specimen labelled 'South America' but correctly surmised by Bannerman (1933) to be from West Africa. Collected Mampong in Ashanti, 25 Feb (Lowe 1937); trapped during daylight in mature forest west of Sefwi Wiawso, no date (Jeffrey 1970). Occurs Liberia (Thiollay 1985), but not east of Ghana; in Cameroun *G. t. pycrafti* has been collected (White 1970).
Breeding. The female collected by Lowe had just finished laying.

295. LOPHOSTRIX (= JUBULA) LETTI
(I.483)   Akun Scops (or Maned) Owl   R(B)
Very rare resident of mature and fringing forest. Only one record: collected at Mampong in Ashanti, 18 Feb 1934 (Lowe 1937). Occurs in Ivory Coast (Thiollay 1985) and in Cameroun (Louette 1981b), but not in Nigeria (Elgood 1982).
Breeding. Unrecorded. Young in Cameroun, Dec (MP&G). A pair with a full grown young in Liberia, 19 Feb (Colston & Curry-Lindahl 1986).

296. OTUS ICTERORHYNCHUS (= ICTERORHYNCHA)
(I.481)   Sandy Scops Owl   R(B)
Uncommon resident (*O. i. icterorhynchus*) of mature forest and forest edge. Collected in "fantee" (= Fanti *in* Bannerman 1933) by Ussher (Shelley 1873), Bibianaha, 100 km west of Kumasi, 1912 (Bannerman 1933) and Tafo, Apr 1942 (G. Cansdale *in* Bannerman 1951). Sighted by Holman at Kumasi (Bannerman 1951). Occurs in Ivory Coast (Thiollay 1985), Liberia (Colston & Curry-Lindahl 1986) and Cameroun (Louette 1981b), but not in Nigeria (Elgood 1982).
Breeding. Unrecorded. Unknown throughout its range (MP&G).

297. OTUS (= PTILOPSIS) LEUCOTIS
(I.482)   White-faced Scops Owl   RB
Not uncommon resident (*O. l. leucotis*) in wooded savanna in north, south through the Volta Region to the wooded inselbergs on the Accra–Ho–Keta Plains and westwards to Cape Coast along the coastal belt. Occurs in older suburbs of Accra, Achimota and Legon, but not from Tafo within the forest.

Breeding. Eggs: C/3, Legon, Oct–Jan; Puolagu, Jan; Keta, Oct (Holman 1947). Nestlings: Legon, Oct–Feb (Grimes 1972a, L.G.G.).

298. OTUS SCOPS
      (I.479)   Scops Owl   RB, PM
Not uncommon resident (*O. s. senegalensis*) in wooded savanna throughout north, south through the Volta Region to the inselbergs on the Accra–Ho–Keta Plains and suburbs of Accra, Achimota and Legon; not recorded in coastal belt west of Accra (M. Macdonald). The Palaearctic *O. s. scops* occurs, but is only known from a skin collected near Legon by Booth (Lamm & Horwood 1958).
Breeding. Eggs: C/3, near Accra, 28 Feb (Shelley & Buckley 1872).

299. SCOTOPELIA PELI
      (I.497)   (Pel's) Fishing Owl   R(B)
Rare resident in mature forest bordering large rivers both within and just north of the forest region. Collected in last century at Boutry River (Pel), Kete Kratchi (Count Zech *in* Reichenow 1897) — data overlooked in Snow (1978). One recent sighting, 3 Jul 1975 at Bui rapids (F. Walsh). Occurs in both Upper and Lower Guinea forest blocks (MP&G).
Breeding. Unrecorded. In Nigeria, nesting Aug and Oct; pullus, Feb (Elgood 1982).

300. SCOTOPELIA USSHERI
      (I.498)   (Ussher's) Rufous Fishing Owl   R(B)
Rare resident of mature forest, only 2 records; type specimen, location uncertain, collected by Aubinn for Ussher (Bannerman 1933); another at Dunkwa, May 1941 (G. Cansdale *in* Bannerman 1951). Only occurs in the Upper Guinea forest block (MP&G).
Breeding. Unrecorded. No records anywhere within its range (MP&G).

CAPRIMULGIDAE

Caprimulginae

301. CAPRIMULGUS BINOTATUS
      (I.512)   Brown (Dusky) Nightjar   R?(B)
Rare probable resident in undergrowth of mature forest. Type specimen collected Dabocrom (Pel). No other records until early 1970s; sighted on several occasions in the Ahanta Forest Reserve (5°23′N, 2°28′W) (L. Cole). There are 2 map positions given in Snow (1978), one of which is an error and the other incorrectly placed (P. R. Colston). Not recorded with certainty elsewhere in the Upper Guinea forest (Thiollay 1985) but present in the Congo forests and Cameroun (MP&G).
Breeding. Unrecorded in West Africa (MP&G).

302. CAPRIMULGUS (= SCOTORNIS) CLIMACURUS
      (I.515)   Long-tailed Nightjar   RB, Afm/NB
Not uncommon widespread resident (*S. c. sclateri*) in coastal areas from Cape Coast to Accra (Macdonald 1976a, Grimes 1972a), and also at Mole in the north (Greig-Smith 1976a). In addition, occurs as a non-breeding migrant from more northern latitudes to the savanna in northern Ghana, larger forest clearings, e.g. Kumasi, Tarkwa, Mpraeso and Wiawso, and to the coastal region where numbers are noticeably higher in the dry season than the wet season. In the far north of Nigeria, there is a paler population *C. c. climacurus,* which is thought resident

(Elgood 1982); but pale specimens collected at Accra have also been allocated to *climacurus* (Bannerman 1933, 1953).

Breeding. Extended. Eggs: C/2, Tema, Dec (Captain & Mrs Furnival); Prampram, 10 May (C. M. Morrison); C/1 Accra, 26 Sep (A. Honeywell); Cape Coast, 25 Apr (Macdonald 1979b). Dependent young: Cape Coast, 20 Mar. Juvenile: Cape Coast, 9 Jul (Macdonald 1979b).

303. CAPRIMULGUS EUROPAEUS
(I.500)   (European) Nightjar   V, PM

Rare Palaearctic migrant (*C. e. europaeus*). Only 2 records: collected at Keta, 21 Dec 1942 (Holman 1947); one good sighting at Cape Coast University, 4 Jan 1976 (M. Macdonald).

[CAPRIMULGUS FOSSII
(I.508)   Gabon Nightjar

Although Bannerman (1953) includes Cape Coast and Accra within the West African range of this nightjar, both White (1970) and Snow (1978) exclude West Africa from its range; earlier skins thought to be *fossii* are now considered to be *climacurus* (P. R. Colston). In spite of this, however, M. Macdonald is confident of sighting *fossii* on 16 May 1976 at Cape Coast. Dead birds picked up in Ivory Coast (Thiollay 1985) were thought to be *fossii*, but as there were no other skins available for comparison these records need confirmation (J.-M. Thiollay).]

304. CAPRIMULGUS INORNATUS
(I.505)   Plain Nightjar   AfM?/(B), Afm

Uncommon seasonally in northern savanna probably throughout, and in larger forest clearings; very few records and status uncertain. Many probably, as elsewhere in West Africa, move to the southern edge of the Sahara at the beginning of the rains (May) and return south after breeding there (Bannerman 1953). A dry season visitor to Kumasi (Holman *in* Bannerman 1951), but present both dry and wet season months at Mole (Greig-Smith 1976a). Sighted at Keta by Holman, and one at Legon, 1 Jan 1972 (M. Edmunds *in* Grimes 1972a). A dry season migrant in Ivory Coast (Thiollay 1985) and Nigeria, but some present in all months at Lagos, Nigeria (Elgood 1982).

Breeding. Unrecorded. In Nigeria, fledgling, Apr (Elgood 1982).

305. CAPRIMULGUS NATALENSIS
(I.506)   White-tailed Nightjar   R(B)

Locally uncommon resident (*C. n. accrae*) in grassland on Accra Plains; no other records. Type specimen collected at Accra (Smith *in* Shelley 1875); others at Christianborg, a part of Accra, Dec 1879, at Ninquah, which is probably present-day Nungua east of Accra (Bannerman 1933), and Quaminfio, between Accra and Legon, 11 Feb (Shelley & Buckley 1872). More recently (Feb 1955, May and June 1956) collected at Labadi and near Shai Hills (D. W. Lamm). Recorded through its distinctive call notes at Accra, 13 Oct 1942 (J. Chapin).

Breeding. Unrecorded. In Nigeria, eggs, Apr and May (Elgood 1982).

306. CAPRIMULGUS PECTORALIS (= NIGRISCAPULARIS)
(I.501)   Dusky (Black-shouldered) Nightjar   ?

Status unknown; only one record (presumably *C. p. nigriscapularis*); the calls of 2 birds at Cape Coast, 10 Jan 1971, agreed with description given in MP&G for the species (D. James). Resident and widespread in secondary forest in Nigeria (Elgood

1982), isolated records in Sierra Leone (Snow 1978), but not recorded in Ivory Coast (Thiollay 1985).

307. CAPRIMULGUS RUFICOLLIS
(I.503)   (North African) Red-necked Nightjar   V, PM
Rare Palaearctic migrant. Only one record: collected Gambaga, 28 Mar 1901 (Alexander 1902). Occurs in Ivory Coast (Thiollay 1985), but no records from Nigeria (Elgood 1982).

[CAPRIMULGUS RUFIGENA
(I.502)   Rufous-cheeked Nightjar
The occurrence of *C. rufigena* at Goaso (Lowe 1937, Snow 1978) was based on a wrong identification; the skin is a female *climacurus* collected 22 Dec (Chapin 1939, Bannerman 1951, Snow & Louette 1981). The only West African records are from Northern Nigeria (Elgood 1982).]

308. CAPRIMULGUS TRISTIGMA
(I.504)   Freckled Nightjar   R(B)
Locally uncommon resident (*C. t. sharpei*) on rocky outcrops and escarpments in the northern savanna. Type specimen collected Gambaga, 22 Feb (Alexander 1901). Flushed from Konkori escarpment in Mole, 12 Jan, and also at Nakpanduri (Sutton 1970). Probably overlooked in the north.
Breeding. Unrecorded. In Nigeria, eggs, Jan and May (Elgood 1982).

309. MACRODIPTERYX LONGIPENNIS
(I.513)   Standard-winged Nightjar   AfM/B
A not uncommon intra-African breeding migrant to open savanna throughout north, late Oct to late Mar, south to the Accra Plains and Cape Coast, mainly Dec–Feb (Grimes 1972a, M. Macdonald), but one Cape Coast, 13 Oct (RSPB Film Unit); also occurs on grass-dominated inselbergs within the forest zone (Woodell & Newton 1975)
Breeding. Eggs: C/2, Kumasi, Jan (Woodell & Newton 1975). Males in display: Legon and Mole, Feb and Mar respectively (Greig-Smith 1977b, L.G.G.).

[MACRODIPTERYX (=COSMETORNIS) VEXILLARIUS
(I.514)*   Pennant-winged Nightjar
The record of this transequatorial migrant, mapped in Snow (1978), is of a single-ton sighted at Accra, early Feb 1933 (M. J. Field *in* Bannerman 1933). This is unacceptable (P. R. Colston agrees) as the bird is difficult to identify in the field when in non-breeding dress, and this remains the only record as well as the date being exceptionally early (earliest date for Nigeria is 5 Apr, Elgood 1982).
*Named *Semeiophorus vexillarius* by MP&G.]

APODIDAE

Apodinae

Chaeturini

310. CHAETURA CASSINI
(I.605)*   Cassin's Spinetail   R(B)
Uncommon resident, recorded regularly within the last 2 decades, often with *Chaetura sabini,* over forest clearings at Kade (Sutton 1965b), Tafo (M. Macdonald),

Lake Bosumptwi (N. Wood), Subri River Forest Reserve (M. F. Hodges, Jr) and Bia National Park (Taylor & Macdonald 1978b); possibly overlooked previously, but records may represent a westward extension of its range.
Breeding. Unrecorded in West Africa.
*Named *Neafrapus cassini* by MP&G.

311. CHAETURA MELANOPYGIA
(I.604)*   Ituri Mottled-throated (Chapin's) Spinetail   R(B)
A not uncommon resident, recorded regularly within the last 2 decades over forest clearings, cocoa farms and reservoirs within the forest region; numbers at Tafo have built up since the first sighting there on 26 Feb 1972 (Macdonald & Taylor 1977, Taylor & Macdonald 1978b). A ♀ trapped at Tafo (in BMNH) was similar to nominate race in Cameroun (Lockwood *et al.*). More common than *C. cassini* at Daboase, Kade, Akwatia, Subri River Forest Reserve (M. F. Hodges, Jr) and Bia National Park (Sutton 1965b, M. Macdonald). The data suggest a westward extension of its range.
Breeding. Unrecorded from within West Africa (MP&G).
*Named *Telacanthura melanopygia* by MP&G.

312. CHAETURA SABINI
(I.607)   Sabine's Spinetail   R(B)
Not uncommon resident over forest clearings and reservoirs throughout the forest region; the commonest spinetail at the Bia National Park (Taylor & Macdonald 1978b); occasional over forest/savanna boundary north of Kumasi (F. Walsh). The early sightings by Lowe (1937) were overlooked in Snow (1978).
Breeding. Unrecorded; season probably prolonged (MP&G).

313. CHAETURA USSHERI
(I.603)*   Mottled-throated Spinetail   RB, Afm
Not uncommon resident (*C. u. ussheri*) throughout the northern savanna, usually in groups of less than 10 but occasionally up to 30 (Sutton 1970). Seasonal on the Accra Plains, mainly Jan–Sep, and westwards to Cape Coast, May–Jul (Grimes 1972a, M. Macdonald). Data overlooked in Snow (1978).
Breeding. Entering nest hole: May (Alexander 1902). Nesting: Tono dam, Aug (R. Passmore). Nests: Cape Coast Castle, Jul (Ussher 1874). Nestlings: Mampong Quarry, Accra Plains, mid Mar (Grimes 1972a); Dixcove, 10 Mar (Macdonald 1979b); near Navrongo, 28 Jun (Sutton 1970).
*Named *Telacanthura ussheri* by MP&G.

Apodini

314. APUS (=MICROPUS) AEQUATORIALIS
(I.598)   Mottled Swift   Afm/(B)
Uncommon, probably resident (*A. a. lowei*) at the Mampong Quarry on the Shai Hills, recorded in each month but not always present; large temporary influx, c.1000 or more, with *Apus melba,* over the western edge of the Accra Plains, 5 Mar 1975, was associated with an unusually late return of harmattan conditions at the coast (Grimes 1974d). Elsewhere only recorded at Tumu in May (Sutton 1970).
Breeding. Probably extended; suspected breeding at Mampong Quarry in vertical crack in rock face, but not proven (L.G.G.). Unrecorded in West Africa (MP&G).

315. APUS (=COLLETOPTERA) AFFINIS
(I.599)   Little Swift   RB

The commonest swift in Ghana (*A. a. affinis*), resident, numerous and widespread throughout in towns and villages, particularly within the forest region. Breeding and roosting colonies often reach 1000 or more. Occurs Mole only in wet season, May–Sep (Greig-Smith 1976a). Dusk flights of tightly wheeling flocks of 15–30, that reach high altitudes are a common sight over large towns.

Breeding. Extended. Nest construction: Akropong in Akwapim, Nov and Dec (C. M. Morrison); Cape Coast, Jul; Gambaga, Apr; Wa, Jan. Eggs: Tafo, May; Cape Coast, Aug and Oct. Nestlings: Tafo, Sep; Cape Coast, Jan and Feb (Macdonald 1979b).

316. APUS (=MICROPUS) APUS
(I.589)   Common Swift   PM

Common Palaearctic migrant (*A. a. apus*), much more numerous during the spring migration, Mar–May, than in autumn, sporadic only in 'winter', usually just before or after line squalls. Autumn passage: Bolgatanga, 6 on 19 Aug; Vea dam, 20 seen on 21 Aug (Walsh & Grimes 1981); Tumu, 22 Sep (Sutton 1970). Spring passage northwards: Amedzofe, 17 May (M. Horwood); Tumu, many thousands 21 Mar, flocks of 20–200 on 26 Mar, 7, 15 and 25 May, singles on 26, 27 May and 25 Jun (Sutton 1970). Westward migration along Akwapim ridge, 7 Apr (C. M. Morrison) and over Osu, Accra on 9 May (M. Horwood). Small numbers over clearings in primary forest within Bia National Park, early Apr (Taylor & Macdonald 1978b).

317. APUS (=MICROPUS) BATESI
(I.595)   Black Swift   R?(B)

Rare, probably resident, status uncertain due to lack of information. A possible sighting at Kade, Apr (Sutton 1965b); certainly sighted on 3 occasions at Subri River Forest Reserve: singletons on 26 Aug and 25 Dec, 4 on 4 Sep (Macdonald & Taylor 1977). Recorded in both Upper and Lower Guinea (Serle *et al.* 1977).

Breeding. Unrecorded. In Cameroun, May–Sep (MP&G).

318. APUS (=MICROPUS) CAFFER
(I.600)   White-rumped Swift   RB

Uncommon but local resident (*A. c. streubelii*) in northern savanna, recorded Tumu, Larabanga and Mole, south through Volta Region to the Accra Plains and westwards along coast to Nakwa, but not at Cape Coast (M. Macdonald). Often associated with breeding colonies of *Hirundo abyssinica* in south. Occasional within forest clearings, e.g. Tafo (M. Lockwood). At Mole an irregular wet season visitor, Jul–Sep (Greig-Smith 1976a)

Breeding. Using nests of *Hirundo semirufa* at Wenchi, 23 Jul (F. C. Holman), and nests of *Hirundo abyssinica* at Abokobi, Mar–Jun (Grimes 1972a). Nestlings: Abokobi, Jun and Sep (L.G.G.).

319. APUS (=MICROPUS) MELBA
(I.597)   Alpine Swift   V, PM

Vagrant from the Palaearctic (*A. m. melba,* though other races from East Africa may occur). Only twice recorded. Small flocks of c. 30 appeared with *Apus aequatorialis* over the western sector of the Accra Plains, 5 Mar 1975, during the re-occurrence of harmattan conditions at the coast (Grimes 1974d). Another flock, c. 300, with *Apus apus* and *Delichon urbica* was seen over Amedzofe, Mar (Walsh & Grimes 1981).

One bird ringed in Switzerland recovered in the Volta Region.

320. APUS (= MICROPUS) PALLIDUS
(I.590)   Mouse-coloured (Pallid) Swift   PM
Uncommon Palaearctic migrant, sight records only. Probably *A. p. brehmorum*,
which breeds in the Palaearctic, but could be nominate *pallidus*, which breeds in the
northern Sahara. Suspected Tumu (Sutton 1970); singleton with 50 *Apus apus* 25
miles north of Tamale, 29 Apr, and 2 at Mole, 19 Dec (F. Walsh & Grimes 1981);
singletons Cape Coast with *Apus apus* and *Apus affinis,* 30 Nov and 28 Apr
(Macdonald 1978c); 300 at Prang, 17 Mar, and 5 at Gambaga, 4 Apr (Wink 1976).

321. CYPSIURUS PARVUS
(I.602)   Palm Swift   RB
Common resident found wherever favoured species of palms occur. In the south
the darker race *C. p. brachypterus* often associates with coconut (*Cocus*), Oil Palm
(*Elaeis*) and Royal Palm (*Oreodoxia regia*), but also with *Borassus* palm on the
Accra Plains; in the northern savanna the nominate race *C. p. parvus* associates with
Borassus palm.
Breeding. Nesting: Akropong, Nov (C. M. Morrison); Mole, Jul; Kumasi, no date
(F. C. Holman *in* Bannerman 1933); Legon, May–Jul (Grimes 1972a).

COLIIDAE

322. COLIUS STRIATUS
(I.516)   Speckled (Bar-breasted) Mousebird   R?(B)
Not uncommon (*C. s. nigricollis*) in the Mole Game Park; seen regularly in small
numbers, c. 5 or less (Greig-Smith 1976a). No other records, possibly overlooked,
and no records west of Ghana.
Breeding. Unrecorded. At Jos in Nigeria, eggs, Apr–May and Aug (Elgood 1982).

TROGONIDAE

323. APALODERMA NARINA
(I.520)   Narina's Trogon   R(B)
Not uncommon (*A. n. constantia*) in mature forest, more frequently heard than
seen (M. Horwood, Taylor & Macdonald 1978b). Collected "Denkere" (locality now
unknown), Oct (Sharpe & Ussher 1872) and in Akwapim (Riis *in* Reichenow 1872).
Breeding. Unrecorded. No records within West Africa (MP&G).

ALCEDINIDAE

Cerylinae

324. CERYLE (= MEGACERYLE) MAXIMA
(I.418)   Giant Kingfisher   R(B)
Uncommon local resident at edge of wooded reservoirs and rivers in coastal
region and northern savanna; mainly piscivorous. Sporadic coastal records Axim,
Sekondi, Cape Coast, Weija and Panbros saltpans, more regular in north at Tamale
reservoir (E. Hall), Mole (Greig-Smith 1976a), Nakpanduri (Sutton 1970), Yendi,
along Black Volta at Bui (F. Walsh) and south to Kete Kratchi and Volta region
(N. Wood). No records from within forest zone.
Breeding. Unrecorded. In Liberia and Cameroun, Dec and Jan (MP&G).

325. CERYLE RUDIS

(I.417)   Pied Kingfisher   RB

A common piscivorous resident (*C. r. rudis*) in coastal region and throughout northern savanna at all types of water edge with trees. Infrequent within forest region, e.g. Kumasi, but not recorded at Tafo (M. Lockwood). Abundant at coastal lagoons, particularly at Panbros saltpans, where food is plentiful and nest sites numerous. Subject to local movement in north when irrigation dams dry out; in some years, a wet season visitor to Mole, Apr–Sep (Greig-Smith 1976a).

Breeding. Excavating nest holes: Panbros saltpans, Apr–Jun (Grimes 1972a) and Aug (J. M. Winterbottom *in* Bannerman 1933).

Alcedininae

326. ALCEDO (=CORYTHORNIS) CRISTATA

(I.421)   Malachite Kingfisher   RB

Common resident at edge of reservoirs, irrigation dams, and rivers in northern savanna and, in addition, lagoons and saltpans in coastal region. Occasional within the forest zone, but more regular in larger forest clearings, e.g. Tafo and Kumasi. Food is insects and fish, taken from water.

Breeding. Occupying nest holes: Panbros saltpans, May–Jun. Fledglings: Keta, 29 Jul (F. C. Holman *in* Bannerman 1951); Cape Coast, 5 Jun (Macdonald 1979b).

327. ALCEDO (=CORYTHORNIS) LEUCOGASTER

(I.422)   White-bellied Kingfisher   R(B)

Uncommon resident (*A. l. bowdleri*) at edge of streams and reservoirs within mature and secondary forest. Netted in cocoa plantation, Tafo (M. Lockwood). Occurs Mampong in Ashanti (Lowe 1937), Abetifi (L.G.G.) and Bia National Park (Taylor & Macdonald 1978b). Not dependent on presence of water for food.

Breeding. Unrecorded. In Cameroun, Oct (MP&G).

328. ALCEDO QUADRIBRACHYS

(I.420)   Shining-blue Kingfisher   R(B)

Uncommon widespread resident (*A. q. quadribrachys*) at edge of reservoirs and slow running streams within the forest region and in riverine woodland along many northern rivers. Common along Nsukawkaw river, Jan 1972 — c. 50 pairs along 48 km of river (F. Walsh). Occasional in mangroves. Collected Dabocrom (Pel); Kete Kratchi (Count Zech). Food is a mixed diet, taken from water.

Breeding. Unrecorded. In Nigeria, entering nest hole, 5 Nov; young juvenile, 28 Oct 1969 (Elgood 1982).

329. CEYX (=MYIOCEYX) LECONTEI

(I.424)   Dwarf Kingfisher   R(B)

Rare resident found near streams within mature and secondary forest. Collected by Aubinn in "fantee country" for Ussher; netted Ahanta Forest Reserve, Jan 1969 (L. Cole), and Bia National Park (M. Rucks *in* Macdonald & Taylor 1977). Occurs near Jasikan (M. Horwood) and in the Subri River and Kakum Forest Reserve (M. Macdonald). Food, mainly insects.

Breeding. Unrecorded anywhere in West Africa (MP&G).

330. CEYX (=ISPIDINA) PICTA

(I.423)   Pigmy Kingfisher   RB

Common resident (*C. p. picta*), widespread in gardens, forest clearings, e.g. Akropong, Anum, Tafo, and in riverine forest. Seasonal in some areas: in far north, only a wet season visitor to Bolgatanga, May–Aug (F. Walsh), and in some years to Mole (Taylor & Macdonald 1978a), although Greig-Smith considered it resident and more common than the Malachite Kingfisher *Alcedo cristata*. In the south, a dry season visitor to Cape Coast, Nov–Feb (M. Macdonald), but resident in residential areas of Accra and Legon (proved by colour ringed individuals); numbers increase at Legon in dry season (Grimes 1972a). Insect food taken from both water and ground surfaces.

Breeding. Nesting: Legon, Apr–Jul (L.G.G.).

Daceloninae

331. HALCYON BADIA
(I.429)   Chocolate-backed Kingfisher   R(B)

Uncommon insectivorous resident in both secondary and mature forest; all recent records are from forest reserves. Collected in last century by Aubinn and by Ussher, at Mampong in Ashanti by Lowe (1937), and near Mpraeso (M. Horwood). Netted in Atewa Forest Reserve (L.G.G., N. Wood), and several sightings in Bia National Park (M. Macdonald).

Breeding. Unrecorded. Nigeria: a male in breeding condition, 12 Feb (Elgood 1982).

332. HALCYON CHELICUTI
(I.430)   Striped Kingfisher   RB, Afm

Locally not uncommon insectivorous resident (*H. c. chelicuti*) in savanna wood-land in the north, e.g. Mole, and south through the Volta Region to the Accra–Keta Plains. More numerous in the dry season at Denu (Sutton 1965b), and a few records Legon, Sep–Oct (Grimes 1972a). The coastal record west of Takoradi in Snow (1978) has not been traced; not recorded Cape Coast (M. Macdonald) nor at Winneba (M. Horwood, M. Macdonald, L.G.G.). Seasonal in the larger forest clearings; a dry season visitor to Kumasi, Nov–Mar (Holman 1947). Only present Tumu, Sep–Dec (Sutton 1970), but absent Bolgatanga, Sep–Jan (F. Walsh) and Tono dam, Sep–Dec (R. Passmore).

Breeding. Display and copulation: Mole, Jul–Aug; Legon, May–Jun (Grimes 1972a). Female collected Ejura, 23 Jan, had just finished laying (Lowe 1937).

333. HALCYON LEUCOCEPHALA
(I.428)   Grey-headed Kingfisher   Afm/B

Not uncommon (*H. l. leucocephala*) seasonally in savanna woodland in both northern and southern areas; more common in the north. Occurs within large forest clearings e.g. Kumasi, Begoro, Anum, Oct–Apr (Holman 1947, L.G.G.), and in forest outliers on the Accra Plains, Nov–Jan (Grimes 1972a, L.G.G.). Occurs both dry and wet season months in northern savanna, but mainly in dry season at Tono dam, Feb–May (R. Passmore) and Mole, Nov–Apr; common Mole in December (Sutton 1970), but only one record in Aug (Harvey & Harrison 1970). Collected Elmina, Apr (Blissett); Gambaga, Nov and Apr (Giffard *in* Hartert 1899a); Goaso and Wenchi, Dec and Jan (Lowe 1937); Kete Kratchi, Jan, Apr and May (Count Zech *in* Bouet 1961). Probably subject to the same migration/breeding cycle as found in Nigeria (Elgood 1982). In Nigeria some birds in some years move from the forest zone into the Guinea savanna to breed, Mar–May, then move further north into Niger, Jun–Sep, and return south in Oct. Diet, mainly insects.

Breeding. Many pairs entering nest holes in roadside ditches between Hohoe and Kpandu, 19 Feb (M. Horwood). Juvenile collected near Gambaga, 1 Jul (Giffard).

334. HALCYON MALIMBICA
(I.426)   Blue-breasted Kingfisher   RB

Not uncommon resident (*H. m. forbesi*) in coastal belt west of Accra, and at forest edge and larger forest clearings, e.g. Kumasi, Tafo, and in riverine forests in north; particularly common at Mole and along the White Volta (F. Walsh). Occasional within mature forest at Bia National Park (Taylor & Macdonald 1978b). Mainly wet season visitor, Apr–Jul, to the forest outliers on the Accra Plains. Diet varied, mainly insectivorous.

Breeding. Eggs: C/4, Kumasi, Mar (Holman 1947). Display flights: Legon, Mar–Jun (L.G.G.). Breeding in north, Apr (Alexander *in* Bannerman 1933).

335. HALCYON SENEGALENSIS
(I.425)   Woodland (or Senegal) Kingfisher   RB, Afm/B

A common resident in coastal regions from Accra westwards, in closed forest and forest clearings, e.g. Kumasi, Tafo (M. Lockwood). Widespread, but mainly wet season, May–Nov, in northern savanna, but only Sep and Oct at Tumu (Sutton 1970). Both insectivorous and piscivorous.

Breeding. Display flights begin Legon and Tafo, Mar/Apr. Eggs in ovary: Weija, 13 Mar (D. W. Lamm). Nesting: Mole, Jul and Aug (Greig-Smith 1977b). Fully fledged young: Kumasi, 20 Oct (G. Cansdale *in* Bannerman 1951); Tafo, Nov (M. Lockwood).

MEROPIDAE

336. BOMBYLONAX BREWERI
(I.447)   Black-headed Bee-eater   R(B)

Rare forest species. Only 2 records: one collected in riverine forest along Affram river, and another pair sighted the same day, 6 Feb 1952 (M. Horwood) (date incorrect *in* Bannerman 1953). Data not included in Snow (1978).

Breeding. Unrecorded. Nigeria, 3 adults feeding nestlings, 23 Mar (Elgood 1982).

337. MEROPS (= AEROPS) ALBICOLLIS
(I.437)   White-throated Bee-eater   AfM/NB

A common non-breeding migrant, usually in flocks of 20–30, throughout the south, with clear north to south migration. Occurs Accra Plains, coastal belt west of Accra and within forest zone, mainly late Oct to late May. Dates of first arrivals at coast range from 20 Oct to 1 Nov (C. M. Morrison, Gass 1963, D. W. Lamm, M. Macdonald, L.G.G.). Most birds leave the south at end May, with stragglers remaining until end Jun. A passage migrant at Mole (Greig-Smith 1977a), Tono dam (R. Passmore) and near Bolgatanga (F. Walsh), moving south in Oct and Nov and northwards in May. Sporadic at Tumu, Oct–Jan (Sutton 1970).

338. MEROPS APIASTER
(I.431)   (European) Bee-eater   PM

Not uncommon Palaearctic migrant, Sep–May, to the Accra–Ho Plains, less frequent in northern savanna and occasional only in coastal areas around Cape Coast (R. B. Payne); absent from forest region. Numbers that winter on the Accra Plains have increased within the last 2 decades; only twice recorded by Gass (1963), but flocks, c. 20 or less, are now regular late Oct to end Mar (L.G.G.), particularly in cassava plantations in the thicket zones of the Accra Plains. Only recorded twice at Tumu, c. 20 on 29 Sep and 2 on 14 May (Sutton 1970), and only occasional at Mole, Oct (R. B. Payne).

339. MEROPS BULOCKI (= MELITTOPHAGUS BULLOCKI)
(I.442)   Red-throated Bee-eater   RB

Common resident (*M. b. bulocki*) in the northern savanna south to Kete Kratchi, but locally distributed along wooded streams with high banks and in erosion gullies. At Tumu only recorded Oct (Sutton 1970).

Breeding. Breeding colonies: Nakpanduri, 18 Mar (Sutton 1970); along Tamale–Yendi road, 2 Jan; Yegi–Tamale road, 12 Sep; Yapei, 30 Oct; along stream north of Gambaga, 24 Nov (M. Horwood). Many adults netted Mole, Jul and Aug, in post breeding moult; range of live weights 20–26 g (Oxford student data *in* Fry 1970).

340. MEROPS (= MELITTOPHAGUS) GULARIS
(I.445)   Black Bee-eater   RB

Not uncommon resident (*M. g. gularis*) of forest edges, clearings and often near water or on telegraph wires along forest roads, but occasionally within mature and secondary forest, e.g. Subri River Forest Reserve (M. F. Hodges, Jr), Bia National Park (C. Martin). Elsewhere records are sporadic: Dixcove, 16 Sep (Sutton 1970), Takoradi, Mar; Yegi (Pomeroy); Sunyani (J. M. Winterbottom). Only one record outside forest region: a singleton near Ada, 2 Feb 1986 (B. Scott). Collected Mampong in Ashanti and Goaso, Jan–Feb (Lowe 1937).

Breeding. Eggs: C/3 and young in nestholes, Dec to early Apr (Holman 1947, M. Horwood). Possibly double brooded (M. Horwood); one pair nested in hole in ground in cassava farm.

341. MEROPS (= DICROCERCUS) HIRUNDINEUS
(I.446)   Swallow-tailed Bee-eater   RB

Uncommon, local resident (*M. h. chrysolaimus*) in mature wooded savanna in north, but locally distributed; records sporadic, probably due to local movements. Resident in small numbers at Mole; present Tumu, late Nov to end Jun (Sutton 1970); Bolgatanga, Dec–May (F. Walsh). Moves southwards to Accra–Ho–Keta Plains in dry season, Sep to end Feb (D. W. Lamm, L.G.G.); occasional in clearings in coastal thicket west of Accra, Oct (Gass 1963), but not recorded at Winneba nor at Cape Coast (M. Macdonald). Collected Gambaga (Giffard *in* Hartert 1899a); Ejura, Feb (Lowe 1937).

Breeding. Juveniles: with adults just west of Accra, 13 Oct 1957 (Gass 1963); at Mole, Jul (Greig-Smith 1977b).

342. MEROPS MALIMBICUS
(I.434)   Rosy Bee-eater   AfM/NB

Not uncommon non-breeding migrant to forest clearings, forest edge and throughout coastal region eastwards to Shai Hills, Denu and Keta, mainly dry season, Oct–Mar. Occasional at end of rains, Jul–Sep, at Weija, Akropong (C. M. Morrison), Subri River Forest Reserve (M. F. Hodges, Jr) and Brimsu reservoir (Horwood 1964, Gass 1963). Absent from south, Apr–Jun, which is its breeding season. Only once recorded at Mole in wet season; no records Tumu (Sutton 1970), Bolgatanga nor Tamale (F. Walsh). No breeding colonies have been found and it is possible that it migrates to breeding areas in Nigeria. A rare visitor to Ivory Coast (Thiollay 1985).

343. MEROPS (= MELITTOPHAGUS) MUELLERI
(I.444)   Blue-headed Bee-eater   R(B)

Rare resident (*M. m. mentalis*) of mature forest and forest edge. Only 2 recent records: one in a forest reserve south of Tarkwa, and a pair in reserve north of Cape Coast (M. Horwood). Collected in "fantee" country in last century (Aubinn).

Breeding. Unrecorded. In Nigeria, young being fed 24 Apr (Elgood 1982); Cameroun, Jan (MP&G)

344. MEROPS NUBICUS.
(I.435)   Carmine Bee-eater   Afm/B

Common migrant (*M. n. nubicus*) throughout northern savanna, frequent at grass fires, and south through the Volta Region to the Ho–Keta Plains reaching the coast at Keta (Holman 1947); recently reported in Shai Hills west of the Volta river (D. Daramani). Mostly absent, May–Sep, but some remain at Mole, Bolgatanga, Navrongo, Tamale and Gambaga (Gass 1963, Sutton 1970, F. Walsh). Located just north of Gambaga and thought to breed there, Jul (Gass 1963).

Breeding. Large colony located along bank of small stream at Mole, 25–30 Mar 1964 (Sutton 1965b), but no records since and overlooked by Greig-Smith (1977b). In Nigeria, Apr–Jun (Elgood 1982).

[MEROPS ORIENTALIS
(I.433)   Little Green Bee-eater

It is thought best to omit the claim by Maze (1971) of a sighting at Mole, Apr, as this remains the only record, and the normal habitat is the Sudan and Sahel zones (Snow 1978). However, it occurs in Burkino Fasso just north of the Ghana border at Bawku, where the Sudan zone enters Ghana (F. Walsh).]

345. MEROPS (= MELITTOPHAGUS) PUSILLUS
(I.439)   Little Bee-eater   RB, Afm

Not uncommon resident (*M. p. pusillus*) throughout the northern savanna, southwards through the Volta Region to the Accra–Ho–Keta Plains, and west-wards along coast to at least Sekondi. Often found in marshy areas and at edges of reservoirs, but also in drier cultivated land and open grassland, e.g. Winneba and Nakwa. Numbers increase in coastal areas during dry season, Sep–Apr, but records are sporadic (Gass 1963, Grimes 1972a). In late 1970s, regular at Cape Coast end Sep to end Nov, then absent until Feb and then regular until Jun (Macdonald 1979a). In the north resident at Bolgatanga (F. Walsh) and Mole (Greig-Smith 1976a), but at Tumu and Tono dam, Oct–May only (Sutton 1970, R. Passmore). Occasional in forest clearings, e.g. Tafo in dry season (M. Lockwood).

Breeding. Eggs in nest holes in roadside bank, Sekondi, mid Mar to May (Holman 1947); 6 juveniles with 2 adults Nungua, 7 Apr (Gass 1963).

346. MEROPS SUPERCILIOSUS (= PERSICUS)
(I.432)   Madagascar (or Blue-cheeked) Bee-eater   AfM/NB

Rare non-breeding intra-African migrant (probably *M. s. chrysocercus*) to northern savanna, but possibly overlooked elsewhere. Only recorded Tumu reservoir: 6 on 10 Nov, 10 on 20 Nov, 4 on 15 Jan, 10 on 12 Feb, and 2 on 19 May (Sutton 1970). Occurs in Ivory Coast as far south as 9°N (Thiollay 1985).

CORACIIDAE

347. CORACIAS ABYSSINICA
(I.410)   Abyssinian Roller   AfM/NB

A not uncommon dry season migrant, mainly mid Oct to end May, but stragglers to Jul, in wooded savanna throughout north, south to Kete Kratchi and Ho (M. Horwood, F. Walsh, Sutton 1970). Occasional at height of dry season, Jan and Feb, near Keta and in forest clearings, e.g. Kumasi (F. C. Holman *in* Bannerman 1951).

Often found at bush fires. Migrates northwards to Sahel zone at the beginning of the rains in May.

348. CORACIAS CYANOGASTER
(I.414)   Blue-bellied Roller   R?(B), Afm

Uncommon, status uncertain due to patchy distribution and sporadic records. Absent in northern savanna, Sep to end of Jan, but regular from mid Oct to mid Jan in the Volta region from Ho to Kete Kratchi (M. Horwood). Collected, however, at Gambaga, Nov and Jan (Hartert 1899a) and occurs Mole, where it is probably a passage migrant Dec and again in wet season (Greig-Smith 1977a). Occurs in every month at forest edge on the Accra Plains and is probably resident; occasional at Winneba, Feb (M. Macdonald). A pair in forest clearing, Apr, near roadside 25–40 km northwest of Kumasi (L.G.G.).

Breeding. Unrecorded. Breeds in The Gambia, May–Jul (MP&G, Gore 1981).

349. CORACIAS GARRULUS
(I.409)   European Roller   PM

Rare Palaearctic migrant (*C. g. garrulus*): one in forest clearing Akim Oda, 21 Feb (G. Cansdale *in* Bannerman 1951); another Mole, 6 Apr (Macdonald 1978c); 13 birds hawking at an emergence of termites, 30 Mar, 72 km north of Tamale (F. Walsh).

350. CORACIAS NAEVIA
(I.413)   Rufous-crowned Roller   Afm/B

Locally not uncommon seasonal migrant (*C. n. naevia*) in both open and wooded savanna, but status and movements uncertain. Recorded each month on the Accra—Ho—Keta Plains, usually perched on telegraph poles along main roads, but more common in wet season, Mar–Jul (Sutton 1965b, Grimes 1972a). No records in coastal strip west of Accra (M. Macdonald). Widespread but sporadic in northern savanna, mainly Sep–Mar (Sutton 1970, M. Horwood), but also Apr and May at Tono dam (R. Passmore); absent from Bolgatanga (F. Walsh) and considered a passage migrant at Mole (Greig-Smith 1977a).

Breeding. Rolling courtship display Kwabenya and Abokobi on Accra Plains, Mar and Sep (Grimes 1972a, L.G.G.).

351. EURYSTOMUS GLAUCURUS (=AFER)
(I.415)   Broad-billed Roller   RB, Afm/B

Common (*E. g. afer*), but seasonal in all types of savanna with large trees from the coast at Accra northwards through the Volta Region. Occasional within forest, e.g. Atewa Forest Reserve (N. Wood), and forest clearings (Lowe 1937). Mainly a dry season visitor to the coastal strip west of Accra, reaching Dixcove (D. James) and Axim, Nov–Apr; only one record Cape Coast in wet season, 10 Jul (Macdonald 1979a). More numerous on Accra Plains in dry season. Resident at Mole (Greig-Smith 1976a), regular in the Asukawkaw valley (F. Walsh), but only twice recorded Tumu, 5 Oct and 18 Jun (Sutton 1970) and not recorded Bolgatanga (F. Walsh).

Breeding. Eggs/young: Achimota, May–Jul (Grimes 1972a); Akropong, Mar (C. M. Morrison). Juvenile collected Gambaga, Oct (Hartert 1899a, Bouet 1961).

352. EURYSTOMUS GULARIS
(I.416)   Blue-throated Roller   RB

Not uncommon resident (*E. g. gularis*), widespread in both mature and secondary forest, forest clearings and cocoa farms (Holman 1947, M. Horwood, M.

Lockwood). Collected Wassaw, Mar (Blissett); Aburi, Sep (Reichenow 1872); Ejura and Goaso, Dec–Feb (Lowe 1937).

Breeding. Eggs: C/3, Kumasi, Feb–Apr (Holman 1947). Juvenile collected Aburi, Sep (Reichenow 1872). Immatures: Kumasi, May–Sep (M. D. I. Gass).

UPUPIDAE

353. UPUPA EPOPS
(I.466)   European Hoopoe (Hoopoe)   AfM/(B), PM

Uncommon dry season breeding visitor, Nov–Apr, to wooded savanna in north, south to Kete Kratchi (M. Horwood, F. Walsh, Gass 1954); only occasional at Tumu (Sutton 1970). No records during wet season, May–Oct. Both African *U. e. senegalensis* and Palaearctic *U. e. epops* occur Mole (Taylor & Macdonald 1978a) and probably elsewhere.

Breeding. Unrecorded. In Nigeria, Jan–Mar (Elgood 1982).

PHOENICULIDAE

354. PHOENICULUS (=SCOPTELUS) ATERRIMUS
(I.470)   Black (or Lesser) Wood-Hoopoe   R(B), Afm

Locally uncommon, probably resident (*P. a. aterrimus*) in wooded savanna and riverine forest, but elsewhere in north sporadic. Only recorded 3 times at Tumu, Oct–Dec (Sutton 1970) and occasionally at Tamale. Greig-Smith (1976a) considered it resident at Mole but Taylor & Macdonald (1978a) thought it moved south into Mole at the end of the dry season. Occurs Jasikan, Apr, and Kete Kratchi, May (M. Horwood) and in both dry (Dec–Jan) and wet season (Jun) months also in the forest outliers on the Accra—Ho—Keta Plains; probably resident in small numbers. One record Achimota forest reserve, another at Aburi gardens, 3 Nov (N. Wood).

Breeding. Unrecorded. Immature netted Mole, Jul (Harvey & Harrison 1970). In Nigeria, young in nest April (11°N); Lake Chad area, probably May and Jun (Elgood 1982).

355. PHOENICULUS BOLLEI
(I.469)   White-headed (Buff-headed) Wood-Hoopoe   RB

Widespread and not uncommon resident (*P. b. bollei*) of mature and secondary forest throughout forest zone, keeping to the tops of the canopy. Bannerman (1931) accepted the Accra record of J. M. Winterbottom, but the record is to be doubted.

Breeding. Eggs: C/2 in nest hole 35 m above ground, May–Jun (Holman 1947). A pair visiting nest hole 35 m up in *Celtis soyauxii*, 24/25 Apr (M. Horwood).

356. PHOENICULUS (=SCOPTELUS) CASTANEICEPS
(I.471)   Forest (Chestnut-headed) Wood-Hoopoe   R(B)

Not uncommon resident (*P. c. castaneiceps*) of mature forest, forest clearings, e.g. Kade (Sutton 1970), particularly in the Central Region. Distribution similar to *bollei*. Bannerman (1931) mentions an Accra record but this is doubtful — the bird may have been brought there by a collector.

Breeding. Unrecorded, but display flight, 19 May (M. Horwood). No records anywhere in Africa.

357. PHOENICULUS PURPUREUS (=ERYTHRORHYNCHUS)
(I.468)   Green Wood-Hoopoe (or Kakelaar)   RB, Afm

Locally common resident (*P. p. guineensis*) of savanna woodland and riverine forest in north, becoming more common southwards through the Volta Region to the Accra—Ho—Keta Plains (Grimes 1972a). Not recorded in coastal strip west of Accra (M. Macdonald, L.G.G.). At Mole, numbers in wet season exceed those in dry season, and some may move south in dry season (Taylor & Macdonald 1978a). Only recorded twice at Tumu, 5 Oct and 28 Jan (Sutton 1970). Numbers at Legon and Achimota have changed since the 1940s; considered a dry season migrant, Nov–Apr, by J. R. Marshall (Bannerman 1951), but resident after late 1960s when planted trees were mature and formed areas of continuous canopy.

Breeding. Prolonged and cooperative, up to 6 helpers recorded; consecutive clutches laid in same nest hole 1969–1975 (Grimes 1975b). Eggs: Legon, Dec, Feb, May and Sep; Yegi area, Jan (A. W. Pomeroy *in* Bannerman 1933). Nestlings Legon, Mar, Apr, May; Mole, May.

BUCEROTIDAE

358. BUCORVUS ABYSSINICUS
(I.465)   Abyssinian Ground Hornbill   RB

Uncommon local resident in wooded savanna in north, south to Kete Kratchi. Not recorded Tumu (Sutton 1970), but located between Wenchi and Bole (Lowe 1937). No records Ho — Keta Plains, but occasional in Shai Hills on the Accra Plains. Collected there in last century (Pel), sighted in Nov 1956 (D. W. Lamm) and irregularly since in dry season, Oct–Feb (Capt & Mrs Furnival, G. Vanderstichelen, L.G.G., RSPB Film Unit). Bannerman (1931) and Bouet (1961) refer to an Aburi record by Buckley & Shelley (1872), but the only hornbill listed by them for Aburi is *Tropicranus albocristatus*.

Breeding. Near Tono dam, Navrongo, a male with large red wattles and blue bare skin, carrying bolus of leaves near likely nest hole in a baobab, 2 Sep 1977; female, smaller and with no wattles present with male (J. F. Monk).

359.   BYCANISTES CYLINDRICUS (= ALBOTIBIALIS)
(I.450)   Brown-cheeked (or White-thighed) Hornbill   RB

Uncommon resident (*B. c. cylindricus*) of both mature and secondary forest, and forest clearings in mainly the Central and Western Regions; often in parties of up to 6. Collected Goaso, Dec (Lowe 1937). Less common now than in 1960s, probably due to cutting down of mature forest.

Breeding. Male taking food to nest hole, 20 Jan (M. Horwood); male collected by Lowe would soon have been breeding.

360.   BYCANISTES FISTULATOR
(I.449)   Piping Hornbill   R(B)

A common resident (*B. f. fistulator*) in mature and secondary forest, often in vocal groups of up to 10, and in forest outliers in the Volta Region (M. Horwood). The range of *fistulator* extends eastwards into Nigeria as far as the Niger river; east of this *B. f. sharpii* occurs. Most authors (White 1970, MP&G, Serle *et al.*) recognise the Niger river as the boundary between the 2 forms, and intermediates have been collected there. Bannerman (1953), however, accepts the record of Lowe (1937), who heard *B. f. sharpii* along the Afram river, near Ejura where he had collected *fistulator*. However, Lowe neither saw nor collected *sharpii* in Ghana, and his record does seem doubtful, since the range extension westward from the Niger river is great. Recently, however, Macdonald & Taylor (1977) claim good sightings of *sharpii* at both Atewa and Worobong Forest reserves, which gives more credence to Lowe's record. Nevertheless, *sharpii*'s presence in Ghana still needs confirmation as the above remain the only records west of the Niger.

Breeding. Unrecorded. In Zaire prolonged, beginning Jan (MP&G).

361. BYCANISTES SUBCYLINDRICUS
(I.452)   Black-and-White-Casqued (or Grey-cheeked) Hornbill   R(B)

Prior to early 1960s a common forest resident (*B. s. subcylindricus*) throughout forest zone, particularly along the southern scarp of the Voltaian basin, often up to 50 together (M. Horwood), and in the Central and Western Regions. Collected Ejura and Goaso, Jan and Feb (Lowe 1937). The fewer records since 1960s probably reflect the gradual destruction of the forests.

Breeding. Unrecorded. Prolonged in tropical Africa, mainly Mar–Jul (MP&G).

362. CERATOGYMNA ATRATA
(I.455)   Black-casqued Hornbill   RB

Not uncommon resident of the canopy, preferring mature rather than secondary forest, widespread in the Sefwi district, south to Axim and eastwards to Cape Coast (M. Horwood). In the Bia National Park more numerous than *C. elata* (Taylor & Macdonald 1978b). Often feeds in same tree as *C. elata* and *B. cylindricus* (M. Horwood).

Breeding. Nestling, Nov (Russell 1949a), later identified as a female.

363. CERATOGYMNA ELATA
(I.454)   Yellow-casqued Hornbill   RB

Previously not uncommon resident, often in groups of 6–12, in mature and secondary forest throughout forest zone, except the southern scarp forest of the Voltaian basin (M. Horwood, D. James), occasional in forest outliers at Kete Kratchi (R. E. Crabbe). More recently, less common due to gradual destruction of forests. Occurs Kade (Sutton 1965b), Cape Coast reservoir (L.G.G.), Subri River Forest Reserve (M. F. Hodges, Jr) and Bia National Park (Taylor & Macdonald 1978b).

Breeding. Feeding of an incubating bird in 2 separate nest holes in *Terminalia superba,* 14 and 16 Jan 1953 (M. Horwood); a fully fledged young, 30 Apr 1954 (M. Horwood).

364. TOCKUS (= LOPHOCEROS) CAMURUS
(I.463)   Red-billed Dwarf Hornbill   R(B)

Rare resident (*T. c. pulchrirostris*) of mature forest. Relatively few records: Kumasi (F. C. Holman *in* Bannerman 1951); Dunkwa and near Mount Ajuanema at Mpraeso (M. Horwood); Juaso, 9 Oct 1942 (J. Chapin); Bia National Park (Taylor & Macdonald 1978b); Subri River Forest Reserve (M. J Hodges, Jr). Collected Mampong in Ashanti, 25 Feb (Lowe 1937).

Breeding. Male collected by Lowe was in breeding condition. Unrecorded in West Africa. In northern Congo, probably Aug to Nov (MP&G).

365. TOCKUS (= LOPHOCEROS) ERYTHRORHYNCHUS
(I.457)   Red-billed Hornbill   R(B)

Not uncommon resident (*T. e. erythrorhynchus*) of the drier more open wooded savanna in the far north near Navrongo and Bolgatanga, eastwards to Bawku and south to Gambaga and Nakpanduri (Sutton 1965b, F. Walsh, L.G.G.). Only recorded once at Tumu, 4 Feb (Sutton 1970); not recorded at Mole (Greig-Smith 1976a).

Breeding. Unrecorded. In northern Nigeria, Sep–Nov (Elgood 1982).

366. TOCKUS FASCIATUS (= LOPHOCEROS SEMIFASCIATUS)
(I.460)   Pied (or Allied) Hornbill   RB

A very common resident (*T. f. semifasciatus*) in both mature and secondary forest,

forest clearings and riverine forest, in which it ranges northwards into the savanna; equally common in coastal areas west of Accra. Occasional Achimota, Legon and Shai Hills, mainly wet season Apr–Oct, but resident in thickets and forest patches along the foot of the Akwapim scarp (Grimes 1972a, L.G.G.).

Breeding. Eggs: C/1, Jan–Apr (Holman 1947); nest holes usually c. 10 m above ground. Occupied nest hole University of Kumasi, Feb (B. Woodell).

367. TOCKUS (= LOPHOCEROS) HARTLAUBI
   (I.462)   Black Dwarf Hornbill   RB

Not uncommon resident (*T. h. hartlaubi*) of mature and secondary forest; solitary and easily overlooked due to its habit of sitting motionless while visually searching for insects (M. Horwood) which are caught on the wing in much the same way as a flycatcher feeds (Sutton 1970). Collected Ejura, Feb (Lowe 1937); near Kumasi, 8 May (Cockburn 1946).

Breeding. Well formed eggs (4) in ovary of female collected by Lowe, Feb.

368. TOCKUS (= LOPHOCEROS) NASUTUS
   (I.456)   Grey Hornbill   RB, AfM/B

Seasonally common (*T.n. nasutus*), mainly Oct–May, throughout the northern savanna, and south through the Volta Region to the Accra—Ho—Keta Plains. Occasional at Winneba but no records further west along coast (M. Macdonald). In northern savanna visible migration occurs southwards Oct and Nov and north-wards in Jun (Genelly 1968, Sutton 1970, F. Walsh, L.G.G.); at Mole some are sedentary. A resident population occurs on the Accra Plains, which is augmented by an influx of migratory birds at the beginning of the dry season, Oct. A loose flock of 20–30 was observed moving eastwards across the Accra Plains, 19 Jun (L.G.G.). Found at forest edge at Akropong in Akwapim, Jan–Mar; first recorded there in 1945 when forest trees were greatly reduced (C. M. Morrison).

Breeding. At Legon, late Dec to Jun, same nest hole used in consecutive years; data suggest double broods (Grimes 1972a).

369. TROPICRANUS ALBOCRISTATUS
   (I.453)   White-crested Hornbill   RB

Not uncommon resident (*T. a. macrourus*) in mature and secondary forest throughout forest zone and forest edge, ranging into the Volta region and reaching Amedzofe (M. Horwood, C. M. Morrison); rare at Cape Coast (M. Macdonald). Often seen crossing main roads within the forest region (L.G.G.).

Breeding. Active at nest hole Dodowa on Accra Plains, 16 Oct 1971 (Grimes 1972a). Fledgling: Mampong, Ashanti, 25 Feb (Lowe 1937).

CAPITONIDAE

370. BUCCANODON DUCHAILLUI
   (I.540)   Yellow-spotted Barbet   R(B)

Not uncommon resident (*P. d. duchaillui*) in mature and secondary forest throughout forest zone, often in plantations, particularly near the Oil Palm *Elaeis guineensis*; not recorded along the southern scarp of the Voltaian basin, but probably overlooked (L.G.G.) and rare at Cape Coast (M. Macdonald).

Breeding. Unrecorded. In Nigeria nestlings, Jan (Elgood 1982). In Liberia, juvenile just out of nest, 7 Nov (Colston & Curry-Lindahl 1986).

371. GYMNOBUCCO CALVUS
(I.535)   Naked-faced Barbet   RB

Common resident (*G. c. calvus*) of mature and secondary forest and forest clearings throughout forest region; range extends into the Volta region, and is particularly common in the Amedzofe area (Sutton 1965b).

Breeding. Extended and colonial. Active colonies: Kumasi (F. C. Holman *in* Bannerman 1933); Goaso and Mampong, Jan (W. P. Lowe *in* Bannerman 1951); Aburi, 15 Feb (L.G.G.); Tafo, Mar–Sep (M. Lockwood). Juvenile collected Mampong in Ashanti, Feb (Lowe 1937). *Indicator minor conirostris* often occurs at breeding colonies (M. Horwood).

372. GYMNOBUCCO PELI
(I.536)   Bristle-nosed Barbet   R(B)

Not uncommon resident (*G. p. peli*), sympatric with *G. calvus* and possibly equally abundant, although the 2 are not easily distinguished in the field. First collected at Dabocrom in c. 1857 (Pel).

Breeding. Surprisingly unrecorded. In Nigeria, nesting in same tree as *G. calvus* Jun (Elgood 1982).

373. LYBIUS (= POGONORNIS) BIDENTATUS
(I.525)   Double-toothed Barbet   RB

Not uncommon resident (*L. b. bidentatus*) of forest outliers on the Accra — Ho — Keta Plains extending northwards to Kete Kratchi. Occurs in forest edge along the Akwapim range and at Ejura to the north of the forests. Occasional in coastal belt as far west as Cape coast (Lowe 1937, Grimes 1972a, M. Horwood, M. Macdonald). No records further north than the lower stretches of the White Volta (Alexander 1902); not recorded Tumu, Mole, Gambaga nor Bolgatanga.

Breeding. Nesting: Accra airport, Jun; Legon, Nov (Grimes 1972a, L.G.G.); Cape Coast, Apr (Macdonald 1979b). Adult carrying food Legon, 8 Sep (L.G.G.).

374. LYBIUS (= POGONORNIS) DUBIUS
(I.523)   Bearded Barbet   RB

Not uncommon resident in wooded savanna throughout north and in urban gardens in larger towns, e.g. Tamale, occasionally as far south as Yegi. In the north it replaces *L. bidentatus* of southern Ghana.

Breeding. A pair with 2 young at nest hole near Tamale, 30 June (M. D. I. Gass). In Nigeria, Mar–Jul (Elgood 1982).

375. LYBIUS (= TRICHOLAEMA) HIRSUTUS
(I.532)   Hairy-breasted Barbet   RB

Not uncommon resident (*L. h. hirsutus*) of mature and secondary forest, forest edge and forest clearings throughout forest zone, particularly in the Central and Western Regions. Occurs Amedzofe area in Volta Region. Collected Mampong in Ashanti, 19 Feb (Lowe 1937).

Breeding. Female collected by Lowe had 2 more eggs to lay, Feb. Nesting: Amedzofe, late Mar (Sutton 1970).

376. LYBIUS VIEILLOTI
(I.529)   Vieillot's Barbet   RB

Common resident (*L. v. rubescens*) of the Accra — Ho — Keta Plains and throughout wooded savanna in north; regular Winneba in coastal belt but only occasional at Cape Coast (L.G.G., M. Macdonald). Once recorded at Akropong in Akwapim, 10 Jun (C. M. Morrison). Duetting is heard at Legon, Nov–Jun.

Breeding. Nesting: Kintampo, Mar (Alexander 1902); Legon, Mar–Jun (L.G.G.). Nestlings: Shai Hills, 29 May (Macdonald 1979b).

377. POGONIULUS ATRO-FLAVUS (=ERYTHRONOTOS)
(I.543)   Red-rumped Tinker-bird   R(B)

Not uncommon resident of mature and secondary forest, but also forest clearings, e.g. Kumasi; the known localities — Lake Bosumptwi, Agogo, Akropong in Akwapim and Mampong in Ashanti — suggest that it has a wide distribution. Collected Mampong in Ashanti, Feb (Lowe 1937).

Breeding. Unrecorded. In Nigeria, breeding begins mid Mar; in Cameroun, Feb (Elgood 1982).

378. POGONIULUS BILINEATUS (=LEUCOLAIMA)
(I.544)   Lemon-rumped Tinker-bird   RB

A common resident (*P. b. sharpei*) of the northern forest/savanna boundary and riverine forest. Occurs on the Accra — Ho Plains, mainly in forest outliers and the thicket zone along the base of the Akwapim scarp, and in coastal belt westwards to Cape Coast. Less frequent within the forest and forest clearings, e.g. Kumasi, Tafo.

Breeding. A male collected, 13 Feb, by Lowe (1937) was in breeding condition. Nesting: Kibi, 20 Jan (B. Scott, A. J. M. Smith).

379. POGONIULUS CHRYSOCONUS
(I.542)   Yellow-fronted Tinker-bird   RB

Common resident (*P. c. chrysoconus*) in wooded savanna throughout north and south through the Volta Region to the Accra — Ho — Keta Plains, frequent also in residential areas. Occasional at Cape Coast (M. Macdonald) and in larger forest clearings, e.g. Kumasi, but not recorded Tafo (M. Lockwood). In the last century both Ussher (1874) and Alexander (1902) found it rare near Accra, but in the 1930s it was common (J. M. Winterbottom).

Breeding. Extended at Legon: a pair, presumably the same, reared broods from nest holes in the same flamboyante tree in Oct/Nov, Dec/Jan, Mar/Apr and May/Jun in both 1969 and 1970. Young in nest holes Botanical gardens, Legon; Oct, Dec, Jan, Mar (Grimes 1972a, L.G.G.).

380. POGONIULUS SCOLOPACEUS
(I.547)   Speckled Tinker-bird   R(B)

Widespread common resident (*P. s. scolopaceus*) of mature and secondary forest, cocoa plantations and thickets throughout forest zone; the frequency of its calls suggests that it is locally abundant.

Breeding. Inspecting nest holes Tafo, Feb (M. Lockwood). In Nigeria, feeding young in most months, Feb–Nov (Elgood 1982). In Liberia, young taken from nest, 30 Jan (Colston & Curry-Lindahl 1986).

381. POGONIULUS SUBSULPHUREUS
(I.546)   Yellow-throated Tinker-bird   RB

Widespread and not uncommon resident (*P. s. chrysopygus*) in mature and secondary forest, forest clearings, e.g. Kumasi, and forest edge, e.g. Akropong in Akwapim (C. M. Morrison); absent from costal region. Collected Mampong in Ashanti, 30 Dec (Lowe 1937) and 15 Jan (D. W. Lamm).

Breeding. The female collected by Lowe had just finished laying; the one collected by Lamm had well developed eggs in ovary.

382. TRACHYPHONUS (= TRACHYLAEMUS) PURPURATUS

(I.550)   Yellow-billed Barbet   RB

Common widespread resident (*T. p. goffinii*) of mature and secondary forest, often in shade trees of Cocoa plantations; occasional forest edge along Akwapim hills, but more frequent in the Amedzofe range (C. M. Morrison). Collected Mampong in Ashanti, 11 Feb (Lowe 1937).

Breeding. Female collected by Lowe had one more egg to lay; nesting Akropong in Akwapim, Nov (C. M. Morrison).

INDICATORIDAE

383. INDICATOR EXILIS

(I.555)   Least Honey-Guide   R(B)

Rare resident (*I. e. exilis*) of mature forest and forest edge; known mainly from skins, but recently sighted at Cape Coast and in Komenda Forest Reserve (M. Macdonald). The 2 males collected at Mampong in Ashanti by Lowe (1937: 653) were initially identified as *I. e. willcocksi* (now given specific status — see Species No. 387), but are now known to be *I. e. exilis* (Chapin 1962, Snow 1978, D. W. Snow).

Breeding. Unrecorded. In Nigeria a captive female laid an egg, 20 Nov (Elgood 1982). A known host species in Kenya is *Pogoniulus billineatus* (Friedmann 1955: 227). In Liberia, females with large yolk in ovary, Nov; another that had just laid, Aug (Colston & Curry-Lindahl 1986).

384. INDICATOR INDICATOR

(I.551)   Black-throated Honey-Guide   RB

Uncommon resident throughout the northern savanna from Tumu in the west (Sutton 1970) to Gambaga in the east; records mostly sporadic, but regular at Mole, particularly in the wet season, when birds are invariably in pairs (Harvey & Harrison 1970). Occasional in the Volta region, but more regular on the Accra Plains at Legon, Achimota and in the Shai Hills (Grimes 1972a, L.G.G.).

Breeding. Juveniles: Tumu, 20 Sep (Sutton 1970). Immatures: Mole, Jul and Aug (Greig-Smith 1977b). Known hosts are mainly kingfishers, bee-eaters, wood-hoopoes, barbets and woodpeckers (Friedmann 1955: 139).

385. INDICATOR MACULATUS

(I.553)   Spotted Honey-Guide   R(B)

Rare resident (*I. m. maculatus*) of mature and secondary forest, but also forest clearings and forest outliers. Collected in last century at Kete Kratchi (Count Zech); at Kwissa between Bekwai and Prasu (= Prahsu) (Alexander 1902); and by Pel (SMNH), probably near Dabocrom. Recently trapped in old vegetable garden, Tafo (M. Lockwood), and in the Ahanta Forest Reserve (L. Cole). Occurs in Sabri Forest Reserve and Bia National Park (M. Macdonald).

Breeding. Unrecorded. In Cameroun, breeding condition, Nov (MP&G). Host species unknown, but thought to be barbets and woodpeckers (Friedmann 1955). In Liberia, female with distended oviduct, Mar; another with large ovary and yolks, Nov (Colston & Curry-Lindahl 1986).

386. INDICATOR MINOR

(I.554)   Lesser Honey-Guide   R(B)

Probably uncommon resident (presumably all *I. m. senegalensis*) throughout the northern savanna; sporadic records at Gambaga and Bolgatanga (F. Walsh), but considered resident at Mole (Greig-Smith 1976a). Collected Bole, Jan (Lowe 1937) and netted Nangodi Bridge, Nov (F. Walsh). Only one record in south; a female netted Legon, 24 Dec 1971 (Grimes 1972a). In the forest zone *I. m. conirostris* (formerly *I. conirostris* and subspp.) has been collected at Ejura and Mampong in Ashanti (Lowe 1937), and at Ahanta Forest Reserve, Jan 1969 (L. Cole).

Breeding. Unrecorded. 4 adults present at breeding colony of *Gymnobucco peli*, date unknown (M. Horwood). Known hosts are mainly kingfishers, bee-eaters, barbets and woodpeckers (Friedmann 1955). In Liberia, a female with a distended oviduct, Nov (Colston & Curry-Lindahl 1986).

387. INDICATOR WILLCOCKSI
        (I.556)   Willcock's Honey-Guide   R(B)
Rare resident (*I. w. willcocksi*) of the forest zone. Only one record: the type specimen, a female, was collected at Prahsu (=Prasu), Oct (Alexander 1901, 1902), and was initially placed as a subspecies of *I. exilis,* but later given specific status (Chapin 1962).

Breeding. Unrecorded anywhere in West Africa. Host species unknown.

[MELICHNEUTES ROBUSTUS
        (I.559)   Lyre-tailed Honey-Guide
In West Africa, known from the Tai Forest Reserve and Mount Nimba in Ivory Coast (Thiollay 1985), and east of the Niger river in Nigeria (Elgood 1982). Its presence in southwest Ghana would not be surprising, but its very distinctive vocal display has never been heard in Ghana.]

388.   MELIGNOMON EISENTRAUTI (not in White)
        (Not in MP&G)   Serle's Honey-Guide   R(B)
Rare resident of mature forest. Only one probable record: one good sighting thought to be this species in Kakum Forest Reserve, 2 Oct 1977 (Macdonald 1980e). A skin collected by W. Serle in Cameroun, initially thought to be a juvenile *M. zenkeri,* was later identified as *eisentrauti* after the latter's discovery on Mount Nimba by A. D. Forbes-Watson (Colston 1981). A specimen was collected by Eisentraut a little before Serle's, but was only later found in the Musee Royal, Tervuren, Belgium (Louette 1981).

Breeding. Unrecorded anywhere in West Africa. Host species unknown.

389. PRODOTISCUS INSIGNIS
        (I.562)   Cassin's Honey-bird (Sharp-billed Honey-bird)   RB
Rare resident (*P. i. flavodorsalis*) of both forest and forest/savanna boundary, mainly known from skins collected by Lowe (1937): a female at Goaso, 28 Dec; another at Ejura, 2 Feb; a male at Goaso, 1 Jan. Occasional Subri River Forest Reserve (M. F. Hodges, Jr). More widespread in lowland forest in Nigeria (Elgood 1982).

Breeding. The female collected at Goaso had a soft-shelled egg in oviduct. Known hosts in other parts of Africa are flycatchers, warblers and white-eyes (Friedmann 1955).

[PRODOTISCUS REGULUS
        (I.561)   Wahlberg's Honey-bird
No records for Ghana, but found on Mount Nimba in Liberia (Thiollay 1985, Colston & Curry-Lindahl 1986), in Nigeria (Elgood 1982) and Togo (de Roo *et al.* 1971); likely, therefore, to occur in Ghana.]

PICIDAE

Jynginae

390. JYNX TORQUILLA
    (I.587)   Wryneck   PM
Rare Palaearctic migrant (*J. t. torquilla*) to forest clearings, e.g. Kumasi, Mampong in Ashanti, wooded savanna in north and coastal belt west of Accra; probably overlooked. Collected Lawra, 17 Jan (Lowe 1937); netted Mampong in Ashanti, 27 Dec (F. Walsh); occasional at Mole (Greig-Smith 1977a); singletons at Kumasi, 20 Nov and 25 Feb (M. D. I. Gass) and at Cape Coast, 6 Mar 1976 (M. Macdonald).

Picuminae

391. VERREAUXIA AFRICANA
    (I.586)   Golden-brown Piculet   R(B)
Rare resident. Only one sight record, which was accepted by Snow (1978): a female and a possible juvenile seen together at Akutuase, 27 Jan 1977 (Macdonald & Taylor 1977). This is the first record for Upper Guinea, apart for one in Nigeria (Bannerman 1933) which Elgood (1982) rejected.
Breeding. Unrecorded. In Cameroun, probably Nov–Mar (MP&G).

Picinae

392. CAMPETHERA ABINGONI
    (I.573)   Golden-tailed Woodpecker   R(B)
Uncommon resident (*C. a. chrysura*) in riverine forest at Mole, "seen regularly in small numbers" (Greig-Smith 1976a). One netted at Mole weighed 55·0 g (Appendix 7). There are no other records for Ghana. It has not been recorded in Nigeria (Elgood 1982) nor in Ivory Coast (Thiollay 1985), but occurs Senegal, Gambia, Guinea-Bissau (Portuguese) (Bannerman 1953, Gore 1981).
Breeding. Unrecorded in West Africa (MP&G).

393. CAMPETHERA CAILLIAUTII (= PERMISTA)
    (I.565)   Green-backed Woodpecker   R(B)
Rare resident (*C. c. permista*) of forest edge; mainly known from 19th century skins. Collected Abokobi and "Kafaba" (present location along the Akwapim scarp unknown) (A. Reichenow), and Aburi (T. E. Buckley); both locations are at the western edge of its range in West Africa. Also at Yegi (Snow 1978), but source not traced. A juvenile female collected at Aburi (BMNH) is a hybrid of this species with *C. maculosa* (Snow 1978). One sighting of a female in secondary forest near Kumasi (M. D. I. Gass).
Breeding. Unrecorded in West Africa. In Zaire, Mar–May (MP&G).

394. CAMPETHERA CAROLI
    (I.566)   Brown-eared Woodpecker   R(B)
Rare resident of mature and secondary forest; very little known of its distribution. Collected Cape Coast (Ussher 1874), but data overlooked in Snow (1978). Recent sightings at Cape Coast and in mature forest to the north of Cape Coast (D. James).
Breeding. Unrecorded. In Cameroun, Jan–Feb (MP&G).

395. CAMPETHERA MACULOSA
(I.564)   Golden-backed Woodpecker   R(B)

Rare resident of mature and secondary forest, mainly known from skins. Collected Prahsu (Alexander 1902); Aburi (T. E. Buckley); Ejura and Mampong in Ashanti (Lowe 1937). Occurs Akropong in Akwapim (C. M. Morrison), near Kumasi (M. D. I. Gass) and Bia National Park (Taylor & Macdonald 1978b). A juvenile female collected at Aburi (BMNH) is a hybrid of *maculosa* and *cailliautii* (Snow 1978).

Breeding. Unrecorded in West Africa (MP&G). One at nest hole, 22 May; excavation of nest holes, Aug and Sep (M. D. I. Gass).

396. CAMPETHERA NIVOSA
(I.567)   Buff-spotted Woodpecker   R(B)

Uncommon resident (*C. n. nivosa*) in coastal thicket from Axim to Accra and inland in mature forest and forest edge, often found in cocoa plantations. Regularly netted at Tafo in cocoa plots (M. Lockwood); recorded frequently at Cape Coast (D. James, M. Macdonald) and once in Bia National Park (Taylor & Macdonald 1978b).

Breeding. Unrecorded. In Nigeria, C/1 mid Apr (Elgood 1982).

397. CAMPETHERA PUNCTULIGERA
(I.572)   Fine-spotted Woodpecker   RB

Locally not uncommon resident (*C. p. punctuligera*) in wooded savanna in north, south through the Volta Region to wooded inselbergs on the Accra—Ho—Keta Plains and in older residential areas of Accra, Achimota and Legon. Occurs Tono dam, Aug and Sep (R. Passmore); only once recorded at Tumu, 21 Nov (Sutton 1970), and no records at Winneba nor at Cape Coast (M. Macdonald).

Breeding. Eggs: Legon, Dec and Jan. Nestlings: Legon, 22 Mar (Grimes 1972a).

398. DENDROPICOS FUSCESCENS
(I.574)   Cardinal Woodpecker   R(B)

Rare resident (*D. f. lafresnayi*) of wooded savanna in north and forest edge in the south, probably overlooked. Collected in Akwapim (A. Reichenow), Kpong (=Pong) on the Accra Plains and Kete Kratchi (B. Alexander 1902). Infrequent records at Mole (Greig-Smith 1976a) and once at Gambaga (R. B. Payne).

Breeding. Unrecorded. In Nigeria, breeding activity Oct–Apr (Elgood 1982).

399. DENDROPICOS GABONENSIS (=LUGUBRIS)
(I.578)   Melancholy Woodpecker   R(B)

Not uncommon resident (*D. g. lugubris*) probably throughout the forest zone. Regular in secondary forest at Cape Coast (M. Macdonald), Kwahu Tafo and Aduamoah near Mpraeso (Sutton 1970). Occasional in wooded savanna on the Accra Plains (Grimes 1972a, L.G.G.). Type specimen collected in Akwapim in 1857 and several more in scattered areas up to 1902 (Bannerman 1933). Collected in riverine forest at Wenchi (Lowe 1937).

Breeding. Unrecorded. In Sierra Leone, young in Apr (MP&G).

400. DENDROPICOS OBSOLETUS
(I.579)*   Brown-backed Woodpecker   RB

Not uncommon resident (*D. o. obsoletus*) in mature woodland savanna in north and south to Kete Kratchi, occasional in residential areas of major towns, e.g.

Tamale. Only twice recorded Tumu; 1 on 29 Nov and 2 on 8 Dec (Sutton 1970). Collected Gambaga, Jan and Mar (Giffard).

Breeding. Nesting: Ejura, Feb (Lowe 1937); Mole, Nov (Greig-Smith 1977b).

*Named *Ipophilus obsoletus* in MP&G.

401. MESOPICOS GOERTAE
(I.581)   Grey Woodpecker   RB

Common widespread resident (*M. g. centralis = agmen*) throughout the northern savanna, south through the Volta Region to the Accra—Ho—Keta Plains, but not in coastal region west of Accra; much attracted to older residential areas with mature trees, e.g. Accra, Legon.

Breeding. Nesting: Legon, Dec–Feb, often in abandoned termite hills, but more usually in trees (Grimes 1972a); Tumu, late Nov (Sutton 1970). Female collected Wenchi, 20 Jan 1934, had just finished laying (Lowe 1937); female with egg in oviduct, no date, Krobo Hill (D. W. Lamm).

402. MESOPICOS PYRRHOGASTER
(I.582)   Fire-bellied Woodpecker   RB

Not uncommon resident of mature and secondary forest, and forest clearings throughout forest zone; its drumming calls are a conspicuous sound of the forests. Occurs Amedzofe in east and occasionally at Cape Coast (M. Macdonald). Collected Goaso, Ejura and Mampong in Ashanti (Lowe 1937).

Breeding. Nesting: Akropong in Akwapim, 15 Aug; Abetifi, Jan (C. M. Morrison). Noisy young in nest hole: Atewa Forest Reserve, 29 Dec 1972 (L.G.G.). Pair watched at nest hole, end July to end Aug (M. D. I. Gass).

PASSERINES

EURYLAIMIDAE

403. SMITHORNIS CAPENSIS
(I.609)   African (or Delacour's) Broadbill   R(B)

Rare resident (*S. c. delacouri*) of undergrowth within secondary and mature forest, but also in riverine forest just north of forest/savanna boundary. Netted within forest reserve 50 km north of Cape Coast (D. James); collected twice at Ejura, a male on 26 Jan and a female on 5 Feb (Lowe 1937). Possibly more common than data suggest.

Breeding. Unrecorded. In Cameroun, May (MP&G).

404. SMITHORNIS RUFOLATERALIS
(I.610)   Red-sided Broadbill   R(B)

Not uncommon resident (*S. r. rufolateralis*) of forest zone. Collected in last century in the Wassaw area near Tarkwa and at Fumso (Bannerman 1936). Many recent sightings in forest reserves at Sefwi and Kwahu districts (M. Horwood), near Cape Coast (D. James), in Bia National Park (N. C. Davidson), and in the Subri, Pra Suhien and Aduamoah reserves (M. Macdonald).

Breeding. Unrecorded. In Cameroun, Dec and Jan (MP&G).

PITTIDAE

405. PITTA ANGOLENSIS
(I.613)   African Pitta   R(B)

Rare resident (*P. a. pulih*) of forest floor and thickets bordering the forest zone. Collected in last century near Accra, Cape Coast, near Tarkwa (Wassaw district) and in Akwapim (Bannerman 1936). One collected at Achimota, 4 Mar 1937, by D. Gillett is in Zoology Department at Legon (Appendix 5).

Breeding. Unrecorded. In Cameroun, Sep (MP&G).

ALAUDIDAE

406. EREMOPTERIX LEUCOTIS
(I.631)   Chestnut-backed Sparrow-Lark   AfM/(B)

Not uncommon (*E. l. melanocephala*) dry season African migrant, Oct–May, from drier areas north of Ghana to savanna areas north of about 10°N. Occurs Gambaga, Lawra, Navrongo, Mole and along the Tamale/Bolgatanga road (F. Walsh). Flocks of 30–50 in Oct on areas of burnt grass at Tumu and thereafter regular until May (Sutton 1970). Song flight, Jan, at Lawra and Navrongo; immatures seen by Alexander (1902).

Breeding. Unrecorded. Elsewhere in West Africa, mainly Nov–Mar (MP&G), but also Oct in Nigeria (Elgood 1982).

407. GALERIDA CRISTATA
(I.629)   Crested Lark   R(B)

Resident, abundance uncertain. Regular (*G. c. senegallensis*) in small numbers at Mole (Greig-Smith 1976a), where it is confined to bovals (areas of shallow soil covered with short herbs and grasses). Probably overlooked elsewhere in north with similar habitat.

Breeding. Unrecorded. In northern Nigeria, mainly Nov–Mar, once in May (Elgood 1982).

408. GALERIDA (= HELIOCORYS) MODESTA
(I.630)   Sun Lark   RB

Not uncommon resident (*G. m. modesta = G. m. giffardi*) widespread in the north in treeless savanna containing rocky outcrops. Frequent near houses and on areas of short cut grass e.g. football pitches at Lawra and Tumu (Lowe 1937, Sutton 1970). Collected at Gambaga (Hartert 1899a), Wa, 15 Jan and Lawra, 18 Jan (Lowe 1937) and Yendi (M. Horwood), but not recorded from Mole (Greig-Smith 1976a). Occurs in flocks in May (Alexander 1902).

Breeding. Gambaga, female with fully developed eggs in oviduct, 29 Dec (Alexander 1902); 2 males with enlarged gonads, Jan (Lowe 1937); song flight at Vea dam, 29 Jun (F. Walsh). In Nigeria, nests mainly Oct–Nov (Elgood 1982).

409. MIRAFRA NIGRICANS (= PINAROCORYS ERYTHROPYGIA)
(I.624)   Red-tailed Bush-Lark   AfM/(B)

Uncommon dry season African migrant (*M. n. erythropygia*), Nov–Apr, with a patchy distribution in northern savanna. Collected at Gambaga by Giffard (Hartert 1899a), Salaga by Alexander (1902) and Wenchi (Lowe 1937). Sporadic records at Sugu and Bolgatanga, Mar–Apr (F. Walsh), Kete Kratchi (D. W. Lamm) and Tumu, 10 Nov (Sutton 1970), but no records Mole (Greig-Smith 1976a). Probably moves northwards out of Ghana to Sahel zone during rains; one straggler at Denu, 5 Aug (Sutton 1970), is the only record in the south.

Breeding. Unrecorded, although the male collected, 10 Jan, by Lowe (1937) had just finished breeding. In Nigeria, nest in Jan; young in Apr (Elgood 1982).

410. MIRAFRA RUFOCINNAMOMEA (= BUCKLEYI)
(I.619)   Flappet Lark   RB, Afm/B

The commonest lark (*M. r. buckleyi*), resident in all lightly wooded savanna in north and in coastal savanna east of Winneba, but not recorded at Cape Coast (J. B. Hall, M. Macdonald). Local movements may occur in north in some years — Greig-Smith (1976a) considered it resident at Mole, but subsequent data suggested it left Mole at end of the dry season (Taylor & Macdonald 1978a). The flapping song flight occurs regularly during wet seasons, but also after rain storms in the drier months.

Breeding. Mainly in wet seasons: Gambaga, Jun (Alexander 1902); Legon and Shai Hills, May–Jul (L.G.G.). At Zaria, Nigeria, also breeds in dry months (Elgood 1982).

HIRUNDINIDAE

411. DELICHON URBICA
(II.1022)   House Martin   PM

Not uncommon Palaearctic migrant (*D. u. urbica*), Oct–May, mainly over northern savanna, only occasionally over the forest and southeast coastal region; usually in mixed flocks with swifts (*Apus* spp.) and swallows (*Hirundo* spp.). Flocks at Mole and Tumu are of 20 or less Oct, reaching 100–200 Nov and several hundred in Dec, thereafter generally decreasing to 20 or less; but at Mole flocks may again reach 300–400 in Mar, as at Salaga sometimes. Few records in south: Shai Hills, 19 Mar (I. Taylor); Keta, 28 Jan (Holman 1947); Amedzofe, Jan (L.G.G.); Bia National Park, 8 Apr (Taylor & Macdonald 1978b).

412. HIRUNDO ABYSSINICA
(II.1008)   Striped Swallow   RB, Afm/B

Common resident (*H. a. puella*) in both savanna and larger forest clearings throughout, but subject to regular movements in certain localities, some movements possibly to areas outside Ghana. In the north mainly a wet season visitor, mid Mar to late Jul, but has occurred Feb at Ejura (Lowe 1937). In the coastal belt from Cape Coast eastwards to Accra Plains flocks regularly occur Feb–Jul, only sporadically in other months and none Aug and Oct (Gass 1954, Grimes 1972a). Present every month at Tafo, minimum numbers in Jul after breeding (M. Lockwood).

Breeding. Nest building at beginning of rains, the dates varying with local rainfall pattern. In south: eggs and nestlings, Mar–Jul; in north, May–Aug (Gass 1954, Sutton 1970, Grimes 1972a, Macdonald 1979b, L.G.G.). Old nests often used by *Apus caffer* in Sep after swallow has nested.

413. HIRUNDO AETHIOPICA
(II.998)   Ethiopian Swallow   RB, Afm/B

Not uncommon local resident (*H. a. aethiopica*) in the coastal region from Cape Coast eastwards to Accra Plains, but numbers increase Mar–Apr and stay high until Sep–Oct, which suggests a migrant population; records in dry season months are sporadic (D. James, R. B. Payne, Grimes 1972a). In the north occurs Tamale and Sugu (F. Walsh) May–Jul; not located elsewhere in north, but possibly overlooked. No records prior to mid 1960s; present data represent an extension westwards of its range from N. Nigeria and east of the Niger (White 1961).

Breeding. Cape Coast, Winneba, Panbros and Shai Hills, Apr–Jun; nests placed under bridges.

414. **HIRUNDO DAURICA** (= RUFULA)
    (II.1004)   Red-rumped Swallow   AfM?/(B)
    Locally not uncommon (*H. d. domicella*) and widespread, particularly near reservoirs, in northern savanna, but status uncertain. Occurs every month at Tumu reservoir (Sutton 1970), but elsewhere in north considered mainly a wet season visitor (F. Walsh). Occurs Mole, Jul–Aug (Greig-Smith 1976a); Bolgatanga, Apr–Sep (F. Walsh). Occasional in dry season at Mole in Dec, Nakpanduri, Mar (Sutton 1965b) and Tamale, Feb. In the south at Weija, Panbros and Achimota recorded in most months, probably resident (D. W. Lamm, L.G.G.), but only occasional at Cape Coast (D. James, M. Macdonald), Kumasi, Feb (B. Woodell) and once at Tarkwa, 16 Jun (M. Horwood).
    Breeding. Nest building Panbros saltpans and Madina, near Legon, Mar–Apr (Grimes 1972a, L.G.G.).

415. **HIRUNDO FULIGULA** (= PTYONOPROGNE RUFIGULA)
    (II.1021)   African Rock Martin   RB
    Common widespread resident (presumably *H. f. bansoensis*) of rocky outcrops in northern savanna and on inselbergs on the Accra Plains and eastwards to Keta, but also around villages within forest region, particularly along the southern escarpment from Akropong to Mampong Ashanti. Occurs Agogo (J. Chapin, G. Cansdale), Mpraeso (L.G.G.), Tafo (M. Lockwood), Akropong and Wesley College, Kumasi (C. M. Morrison). Bannerman (1939) separated *bansoensis* from the lighter lowland forest race *rufigula*.
    Breeding. Within forest: nest building Agogo, mid Sep (G. Cansdale). Eggs and nestlings: Agogo, Jun and Nov; Mpraeso, May and Oct; Kibi, 9 Jul; Akim Oda, 19 Dec (G. Cansdale). Immatures with adults: Agogo, 9 Oct (N. B. Collins, J. Chapin). On the Accra Plains, May–Jun and Oct (L.G.G.). Often double brooded in quick succession (Bannerman 1939).

416. **HIRUNDO (PSEUDHIRUNDO) GRISEOPYGA**
    (II.1009)   Grey-rumped Swallow   R?B, Afm
    Locally not uncommon (presumably *H. g. griseopyga,* which occurs in Nigeria) in northern savanna, possibly resident. Recorded Dec, Jan, Apr and Jun at scattered localities in north (F. Walsh), but at Mole only at end of dry season (Taylor & Macdonald 1978a) or not at all (Greig-Smith 1976a). Within forest region only recorded over lake at Tafo, no date (M. Lockwood). At Asutsuare on the Accra Plains, a strong northwestward passage occurred 29 Jan. Taylor & Macdonald (1978a) thought it moved into Ghana, although they do not specify its provenance, during the dry season, but perhaps not regularly.
    Breeding. An immature at Tafo, 29 Jan (Macdonald 1979a).

417. **HIRUNDO LEUCOSOMA**
    (II.999)   Pied-winged Swallow   R?B, Afm/B
    Locally not uncommon and possibly resident near towns and villages in the northern savanna, rare within the forest region; also occurs in some coastal districts, regularly at Sekondi, at least in the dry season (Holman 1947), and recorded each month at Cape Coast and eastwards to Accra Plains, but birds always apparently on the move (Macdonald 1979a). At Winneba, Akropong in Akwapim, on the Accra Plains and at Keta and Denu is mainly a wet season visitor, early Mar to Jul (Holman 1947, Sutton 1965, Grimes 1972a), with occasional records Oct (M. Horwood). In the north regular at Tamale (E. Hall), sporadic at Tumu, Nov–May (Sutton 1970), and, in marked contrast, at Mole and Bolgatanga only in wet season,

Jul–Sep (Greig-Smith 1976a, F. Walsh). Collected Axim and in other coastal towns in last century (Bannerman 1939).

Breeding. Keta, wet season May–Jun (Holman 1947); Achimota, May (D. W. Lamm). Fledglings: Winneba, 11 Jun (L.G.G.).

418. HIRUNDO NIGRITA

(II.1001)   White-throated Blue Swallow   RB, Afm/B

Not uncommon resident of rivers and streams within the forest region, particularly along the rivers Ancobra, Tano, Birrim and Offin in the southwest (M. Horwood). Occurs away from rivers at Tarkwa and Akim Oda where seasonal (Holman 1947); also occasionally outside main forest belt at Kete Kratchi (R. E. Crabbe). Flock of 12 on telegraph wires, 7/8 Sep, at Tarkwa may have been migrating (M. Horwood).

Breeding. Either extended or 2 breeding seasons. Eggs, C/3, Akim Oda, Jun and Aug. Nestlings: Akim Oda, 21 Jan (Holman 1947). The same nest site — a broken nest of *Hirundo semirufa* — was used in both Jan and following Jun.

419. HIRUNDO RUSTICA

(II.993 & 994)   Swallow (& Red-chested Swallow)   PM, RB

Abundant Palaearctic migrant (*H. r. rustica*) to forest clearings throughout forest zone, mainly Sep to early May, earliest date 29 Jul, Kumasi (Gass 1957) and latest, 3 Jun, Cape Coast (D. James). Northward movement over coastal areas, Apr, suggests passage from southern latitudes, but there is no ringing data to confirm this (Walsh & Grimes 1981, Taylor & Macdonald 1978a); flocks often occur along Akwapim hills, Apr, after rainstorms. In the north occurs with *H. r. lucida* but in smaller numbers, late Sep to early May; few records at Mole (Greig-Smith 1976a). Large wintering roosts within the forest region, one at Tafo estimated at a million birds was regularly occupied late Sep to early May (M. Lockwood).

The African race (*H. r. lucida*) occurs mainly in the northern savanna; status is uncertain — an abundant resident at Tumu (Sutton 1970), it is only a wet season visitor, Jun–Aug, to Mole and Tamale (Greig-Smith 1976a, E. Hall), but recorded at Bolgatanga, Feb–Aug (F. Walsh).

Breeding. *H. r. lucida*: nesting Nakpanduri, Mar (Sutton 1965b); visiting nest sites Mole, Jul (Greig-Smith 1977b).

Birds ringed in Belgium (10), Holland (4), UK (5), France (10), Germany (2), Luxembourg (1), Ireland (1) and Spain (1) have been recovered in Ghana. An albino was trapped, Dec 1975.

420. HIRUNDO SEMIRUFA

(II.1006)   Rufous-chested Swallow   RB, Afm/B

Locally not uncommon resident (*H. s. gordoni*) in coastal districts, easily confused with *Hirundo senegalensis*. Within forest region status uncertain; resident Subri River Forest Reserve (M. F. Hodges, Jr), seasonal Kumasi, Mar–Oct (Holman *in* Bannerman 1939), but at Tafo, where it has been netted, dry season only (M. Lockwood). In the north at Mole, considered a wet season migrant, Aug (Greig-Smith 1976a), but occurs in early rains, May, at Bolgatanga (F. Walsh).

Breeding. Nest building: Panbros and Cape Coast, Apr, during early rains; Subri River Forest Reserve, Jun. Nestlings: Panbros, late Aug (L.G.G.).

421. HIRUNDO SENEGALENSIS

(II.1005)   Mosque Swallow   RB, Afm/B

Common resident (*H. s. senegalensis*) scattered throughout the northern savanna (F. Walsh, Sutton 1970), but only a wet season visitor to Mole (Greig-Smith 1976a);

usually associated with baobabs. In the coastal region from Sekondi eastwards to Accra Plains and Akwapim hills, *H. s. saturatior* is resident, but at Denu numbers increase after Feb just before breeding season (Sutton 1965a). Within the forest region recorded once only, at Akim Oda (Holman 1947).

Breeding. Extended; in coastal region mainly in wet season, Apr–Jul, but nest building Oct and Jan at Legon and Mampong quarry in Shai Hills. Nests placed under eaves but occasionally in rock crevices or holes in baobabs. Eggs: C2/3, Jul (L.G.G.).

422. HIRUNDO SMITHII
(II.1002)   Wire-tailed Swallow   RB

Not uncommon resident (*H. s. smithii*) at scattered localities throughout the northern savanna, usually near streams and reservoirs. More common at Mole in wet season, Jul–Sep, but occurs also in dry season; only occasional at Tumu (Sutton 1970). Resident within the forest zone at Tafo and recorded most months on the Accra Plains. In coastal region, extends eastwards to Nyanyanu, between Winneba and Accra, but not recorded Cape Coast (M. Macdonald).

Breeding. In north: Nakpanduri, Mar; Mole, Aug and Dec (Greig-Smith 1977b, Sutton 1965a). Nestlings: Zongoiri rapids, 21 May; Pwalugu, 16 May (F. Walsh). In south: nest building Labadi, 15 Apr (D. W. Lamm); mixed breeding colony with *H. abyssinica* and *Apus affinis* at Nyanyanu, 30 Jan (B. Scott, A. J. M. Smith).

423.   HIRUNDO SPILODERA (= LECYTHOPLASTES PREUSSI)
(II.1012)   Preuss's Cliff Swallow   RB, Afm

Locally not uncommon resident (*H. s. preussi*) wherever there are streams with rocky overhangs suitable as nest sites, mainly north of the forest zone and at Kete Kratchi before the formation of the Volta Lake. Once netted at a mixed swallow roost at Suhien within the forest zone (M. Lockwood); present at the Volta river at Asutsuare on the Accra Plains, 6 May (Macdonald 1979b).

Breeding. Nests packed together on under surface of an overhang, often above water. Active colonies along the Volta north of Gambaga, May–Jun, and south of Yegi, under bridge over the Pra river, 30 Dec. Nest building Tamale, Mar (F. Walsh). Gass (1954) found a breeding colony of c. 100 pairs at Kete Kratchi from Jan onwards, the nests being regularly swept away by floods May–Jun after breeding. Birds at Asutsuare, May, appeared to be prospecting nest sites below a bridge (M. Macdonald).

424. PSALIDOPROCNE NITENS
(II.1027)   Square-tailed Rough-wing Swallow   R(B)

Not uncommon resident (*P. n. nitens*) of forest clearings and forest edge, often in the company of *Psalidoprocne obscura* and *Hirundo leucosoma* (M. Horwood), but distribution is patchy. Records sporadic at any one locality; often in flocks of 20–30 at Anum, Sekondi, Begoro, Agogo, Tarkwa, Mpraeso (C. M. Morrison, N. Horwood, J. Chapin, Sutton 1970, L.G.G.); numerous at Atewa forest reserve, Aug–Sep (N. Wood), although not always present. At Tafo occurs every month at the reservoir (M. Lockwood). One positively identified at Mole, 4 Aug, consorting with *Psalidoprocne obscura* (Harvey & Harrison 1970). In last century occurred at Cape Coast Castle and Fort Victoria (collected by Ussher 1874), but no recent records (M. Macdonald). Collected, Jul 1966 (L. Cole), in forest reserve at 5°23′N, 2°28′W.

Breeding. Unrecorded. In Cameroun, Jan–Jul (MP&G).

425. PSALIDOPROCNE OBSCURA
    (II.1026)   Fantee (Fanti) Rough-wing Swallow   R?B, Afm
Not uncommon, but distribution patchy and seasonal, in forest clearings and forest edge in flocks of 20 or less. Inland from Cape Coast is mainly a dry season visitor, end Sep to end Mar, but there are several wet season sightings, May–Jun, of birds possibly on passage (Macdonald 1979a). In contrast, M. Horwood located them frequently at forest edges, Jun–Sep, and once saw birds apparently on the move at Korforidua. In north, mainly wet season, Jun–Sep, at Mole (Greig-Smith 1976a), but also Jan (Maze 1971, though not seen then by Macdonald 1979a), Mar (Sutton 1965b) and Apr (Macdonald 1979a). Collected Gambaga by Giffard (Hartert 1899a). Available data suggest movement by some populations southwards from the savanna in dry season.
    Breeding. Nesting in banks along the Takoradi/Cape Coast road, 1964, month uncertain (L.G.G.).

426. RIPARIA CINCTA
    (II.1018)   Banded Martin   AfM/NB?
Status of *R. c. cincta* is uncertain. Ussher (1874) collected one of a pair in Aug on the Volta river and Gass (1954) recorded 8–10 on 5 Nov over a grass fire on the Accra Plains. This conforms to the data from Nigeria, where it is mainly present May–Nov (Elgood 1982), although there are coastal records for Nigeria in Feb and Mar. In contrast, it occurs today intermittently, not every year, in coastal districts near Winneba, Dec–May (Macdonald 1979a). Macdonald concluded it was a non-breeding dry season visitor.

427. RIPARIA PALUDICOLA
    (II.1017)   African Sand Martin   R?(B), Afm?
Uncommon, probably local, resident (*R. p. minor*) in the far northern savanna, singly or in flocks of 20 or less at scattered localities in all months Oct–May, but possibly overlooked rest of year. Occurs White Volta valley near Sugu, along the Bolgatanga/Tamale road, at Pwalugu and Gambaga (Holman 1947, F. Walsh, I. Taylor, M. Macdonald, R. B. Payne).
    Breeding. Unrecorded. In Nigeria north of latitude 7°N, Oct-Feb (Elgood 1982).

428. RIPARIA RIPARIA
    (II.1015)   Sand Martin   PM
Uncommon Palaearctic migrant (*R. r. riparia*), likely to appear anywhere in the northern savanna, or within forest clearings or in coastal district, often with *Hirundo rustica*. In the north at Tumu an autumn and spring migrant, earliest and latest dates 20 Oct and 21 May (Sutton 1970). At Mole, largest numbers (c. 200) in Oct (R. B. Payne). Recorded in southeast at Keta, Nov and Jan (Holman 1947) and at Accra, 3 on 13 Nov (R. Broad). Regularly netted in swallow roost at Tafo, Jan–Feb 1978, ratio of martins/swallows 1 : 100. In contrast, only 2 trapped at the Tafo roost 1972–1976. A marked westerly movement of c. 200 occurred at Keta, 18 Jan (B. Scott).

MOTACILLIDAE

429. ANTHUS CAMPESTRIS
    (II.647)   Tawny Pipit   PM
Rare local Palaearctic migrant in the savanna of the far north (Walsh & Grimes 1981). Lowe (1937) collected it at Lawra, 17 Jan, and Navrongo, 21 Jan, and found them common and in pairs. In the south, occasional at Cape Coast (M. Macdonald); also singletons at Nakwa, 21 Jun (M. Macdonald), and on the Accra Plains, 21 Feb

(Wink 1976) and 8–10 Jan (R. Broad). The Jun date is late, but the identification certain.

430. ANTHUS CERVINUS
(II.656)   Red-throated Pipit   PM

Not uncommon Palaearctic migrant in small numbers to edges of coastal lagoons and irrigation dams, often with *Motacilla flava*. Regular at Cape Coast in dry season, Nov–Mar; also 2 at Winneba, 14 Jan (M. Macdonald). On the Accra Plains occurs Sakumo lagoon west of Tema, Dec–Jan (Lamm & Horwood 1958, R. Broad) and at Nungua, Mar–Apr (M. Edmunds). Inland, occasional on Tafo golf course where it has been ringed (Appendix 1, M. Lockwood), once 2 at Mole, 5 Apr (I. R. Taylor & M. Macdonald), but flocks of c. 30 often present mid Nov to Jan at Vea dam, where more common than *Anthus trivialis* (Walsh & Grimes 1981).

431. ANTHUS LEUCOPHRYS
(II.650)   Plain-backed Pipit   RB, Afm

Common local resident (*A. l. zenkeri*) in most types of open savanna and cultivation throughout north and south through the Volta Region to the Accra Plains and eastwards to Keta (Bannerman 1936, Sutton 1965b, 1970, Grimes 1972a, Greig-Smith 1976a), but only sporadic within Subri River Forest Reserve and at Cape Coast, Feb–Apr, where *A. l. gouldii* — a darker race found in coastal areas from Sierra Leone to Ivory Coast — may occur. Subject to local movements in coastal areas at least, e.g. numerous at Nakwa, 4 Oct, but only one present 12 days later (M. Macdonald).
Breeding. On Accra Plains, Feb–Jun; female with fully developed egg in oviduct, 20 Feb (D. W. Lamm).

432. ANTHUS NOVAESEELANDIAE (= RICHARDI)
(II.653)   Richard's Pipit   V

Vagrant. Only one certain sighting, on an area of open grassed flats on the Keta Plains north of Srogboe, 22 May 1976 (M. Macdonald, I. R. Taylor). Provenance uncertain, equally possibly from the Palaearctic (*A. n. richardi* occurs in Nigeria) or from Afrotropical populations, which are primarily montane grassland species (Elgood 1982).

433. ANTHUS SIMILIS
(II.649)   Long-billed Pipit   R?(B)

Very localised (race undetermined), only found on the grass covered summits containing rocky bluffs of Mt Game and 2 minor peaks at Amedzofe. Likely to occur in similar habitat on hills northeast of Amedzofe (Taylor & Macdonald 1979a).
Breeding. Unrecorded. In Cameroun, Mar (MP&G).

434. ANTHUS TRIVIALIS
(II.654)   Tree Pipit   PM

Common and widespread Palaearctic migrant (*A. t. trivialis*), Oct–Mar, on playing fields, farms and open areas of savanna throughout the north, in clearings within the forest region, and on the Accra Plains east to Keta; not recorded in coastal strip west of Accra (M. Macdonald). Often in flocks of 6–20, occasionally with *Motacilla flava*. Collected Ejura, 24 Jan (Lowe 1937); 2 collected on a cassava farm at Mampong in Ashanti, 27/29 Dec (F. Walsh); 25 ringed in roost of *Motacilla flava* at Tafo 1974–76 (Appendix 1, M. Lockwood). Less common in north than *Anthus cervinus* (F. Walsh).

435. MACRONYX CROCEUS
(II.658)   Yellow-throated Long-claw   RB

A widespread common resident, particularly on coast between Cape Coast and Keta (Sutton 1965b, Grimes 1972a, M. Macdonald) and northwards through the Volta region to Kete Kratchi, Salaga and Yendi (R. E. Crabbe). Very few records north of c. 10°N; not recorded Tamale (E. Hall), Mole (Greig-Smith 1976a), nor at Gambaga (Alexander 1902), and scarce at Lawra (Lowe 1937).

Breeding. Display flight: Accra Plains, April. Eggs: C/3 Winneba, 9 Jun; Accra Plains, Jun–Aug. Fledglings: Nakwa, 8 May (Macdonald 1979b).

436. MOTACILLA ALBA (= AGUIMP)
(II.637)   African Pied Wagtail   RB

Common resident (*M. a. vidua*) of villages throughout the forest region along streams and on playing fields and lawns. Numbers decrease north of the forest/savanna boundary — only occasional at Mole, Aug and Oct; Gambaga, Oct/Nov (R. B. Payne); rare north of Tamale towards Bolgatanga (F. Walsh). Also rare at Cape Coast (M. Macdonald) and west of Cape Coast, and absent from Accra Plains except at Dodowa at the base of the Akwapim hills and at Legon in the wet season, Jun (Grimes 1972a).

Breeding. Fledglings: Akropong, 19 May (C. M. Morrison); Tafo, Jun (M. Lockwood).

[MOTACILLA CLARA
Mountain Wagtail

C. M. Morrison is confident he saw one at a waterfall near Begoro, but it is usually considered a montane species, and the record needs confirmation, although there are 3 definite records in Ivory Coast as far south as c. 9°N (Thiollay 1985) and lowland records for Nigeria (Elgood 1982).]

437. MOTACILLA (= BUDYTES) FLAVA
(II.642, 645, 646)   Yellow Wagtails   PM

Very common Palaearctic migrant, even more so in south, to lake and lagoon edges, maintained parklands, playing fields and school and University campuses throughout, late Sep to early May. Most arrive in non-breeding dress, many attaining breeding dress late Mar onwards. Races that have been identified in southern Ghana are *flava* and *thunbergi*, the latter staying longest. Other races may occur, but not *M. f. flavissima*. In the north at Vea dam, numbers increase after late Sep to 20–30 in Nov, and to c. 60 Dec–Feb, then decreasing as rice paddies dry up. In contrast, is only occasional at Mole, and recorded only twice at Tumu, 10 Nov and 26 Mar (Sutton 1970). At Tafo, within the forest, birds arrive in second half of Dec, with 200–300 roosting in sugar cane and reeds bordering streams. Birds arrive earlier at Legon, presumably overflying the forest — earliest dates: 25 Sep 1962, 5 Oct 1966, 2 Oct 1968, 22 Sep 1970, 8 Oct 1971 and 21 Sep 1974. Numbers at Legon fluctuate in Apr, with numbers of *thunbergi* increasing, suggesting an origin further south.

Birds ringed in Sweden (5), Germany (1) and the Baltic (1) have been recovered in Ghana.

CAMPEPHAGIDAE

438. CAMPEPHAGA LOBATA (= LOBOTOS LOBOTUS)
(II.1039)   Wattled Cuckoo-Shrike   R(B)

Rare resident (*C. l. lobata*) of forest region. Previously known from 3 skins collected in Ghana, but now known from Mt Nimba, Liberia — 18 specimens 1967–

1971 (Colston & Curry-Lindahl 1986). Collected "interior of Fanti", c. 1875 (H. T. Ussher *in* Bannerman 1939), in "Ashanti" probably near Kumasi, 1884 (G. Lagden *in* Bannerman 1939) and Mampong, 22 Feb (Lowe 1937). An unconfirmed sighting during 1970s (M. Macdonald).

Breeding. Unrecorded anywhere in West Africa (MP&G).

439. CAMPEPHAGA PHOENICEA
(II.1032)   Red-shouldered Cuckoo-Shrike   R(B), Afm

Not uncommon local resident (*C. p. phoenicea*) in well wooded savanna in north and south, through the dry eastern corridor to the Accra Plains and westwards along the coast to Cape Coast and Elmina; also at forest edge and in the larger clearings, but only seasonally. At Kumasi only present in dry season (F. C. Holman *in* Bannerman 1939). In north regular at Tumu (Sutton 1970) and resident at Mole (Greig-Smith 1976a), but in the north near Bolgatanga only recorded in wet season, Jul–Sep (F. Walsh). In ones and twos at Legon, in the Shai Hills and thicketed areas near Abokobi in most months, probably resident (Grimes 1972a, L.G.G.).

Breeding. Unrecorded. In Nigeria, May–Sep (Elgood 1982).

440. CAMPEPHAGA QUISCALINA
(II.1034)   Purple-throated Cuckoo-Shrike   R(B)

Rare resident (*C. q. quiscalina*) of secondary forest and forest edge. Mainly known from skins collected in last century at "Denkere", Wassaw district and Aburi; more recently at Mampong and Ejura (Lowe 1937). Occurs Amedzofe (Sutton 1965b), Akropong (C. M. Morrison) and Subri River Forest Reserve (M. F. Hodges, Jr).

Breeding. Unrecorded, although the male collected, 6 Feb, at Ejura was about to breed (Lowe 1937). No other information (MP&G).

441. CORACINA (=CYANOGRAUCALUS) AZUREA
(II.1038)   Blue Cuckoo-Shrike   RB

Uncommon resident of both mature and primary forest, often in the canopy and probably, therefore, commoner than data suggest. Collected in Wassaw district (centred around Tarkwa), Kumasi, Prahsu and Fumso (Alexander 1902), at Ejura (Lowe 1937) and more recently in the Agyabura Forest Reserve in Kwahu; one found dead in the Pra Anum Forest Reserve in southern Ashanti (M. Horwood). Recent sightings at Kwahu Tafo (D. W. Lamm), Atewa Forest Reserve (L.G.G.), near Cape Coast, Subri River Forest Reserve (M. F. Hodges, Jr) and frequently in the Bia National Park (Taylor & Macdonald 1978b).

Breeding. A male collected at Ejura, 3 Feb, showed signs of breeding (Lowe 1937). Female feeding fledgling Subri River Forest Reserve, 15 May (M. F. Hodges, Jr).

442. CORACINA PECTORALIS
(II.1035)   White-breasted Cuckoo-Shrike   RB

Not uncommon local resident of well wooded savanna in the north reaching as far south as Ho through the dry eastern border with Togo (M. Horwood). Collected at Ejura and Bole, Jan–Feb, where it was fairly common; Salaga, Jul; Kete Kratchi, May; and Gambaga, Jan. Resident at Mole in small numbers (Greig-Smith 1976a), singletons seen regularly along Gambaga escarpment (Sutton 1970, L.G.G.), but no records at Tumu (Sutton 1970).

Breeding. A female collected at Ejura, 25 Jan, was about to lay (Lowe 1937). Elsewhere in West Africa, C/2 in the Gambia, Jun (Gore 1981).

PYCNONOTIDAE

443. ANDROPADUS ANSORGEI (=GRACILIS)

(II.719)   Ansorge's Greenbul   R(B)

Resident (*A. a. ansorgei*) of thickets and undergrowth within the forest zone. Difficult to distinguish from *A. gracilis,* its distribution and abundance is consequently uncertain; M. Macdonald considered it more common than *A. gracilis* at Cape Coast. No skins have been collected. One seen at Tafo, 29 Jan 1978 (F. Walsh). No other records.

Breeding. Unrecorded. In Nigeria, specimen in breeding condition, May and Dec (Elgood 1982).

444. ANDROPADUS CURVIROSTRIS

(II.720)   Cameroun Sombre Greenbul   RB

Not uncommon resident (*A. c. leoninus*) of thickets north of the forest/savanna boundary (Lowe 1937), equally common (*A. c. curvirostris*) in undergrowth in mature and secondary forest and in thickets of the coastal belt. Its distinctive calls reveal it as widespread in the south: Abokobi on the Accra Plains (L.G.G.), Akropong in Akwapim (C. M. Morrison), Atewa Forest Reserve (L.G.G.), but only occasional at Bia National Park (Taylor & Macdonald 1978b) and Cape Coast (M. Macdonald).

Breeding. Mampong, mid Feb (Lowe 1937).

445. ANDROPADUS GRACILIROSTRIS

(II.717)*   Slender-billed Greenbul   RB

Common resident (*A. g. gracilirostris*) of forest edge and clearing, often in undergrowth in groups of 6–8 (Lowe 1937); also in mature and secondary forest (Taylor & Macdonald 1978b). Collected at Prahsu and Fumso (Alexander 1902). Occurs Cape Coast (M. Macdonald), Tafo and along the foot of the Akwapim hills (M. Lockwood, L.G.G.).

Breeding. Female collected Mampong in Ashanti, 22 Feb, had just finished breeding (Lowe 1937).

*Named *Stelgidillas gracilirostris* by MP&G.

446. ANDROPADUS GRACILIS

(II.718)   Little Grey Greenbul   RB

Not uncommon resident (*A. g. extremus*) with a widespread distribution, usually in the middle canopy (Button 1964) of both primary and secondary forest, but also at forest edge. Collected at many sites within the forest region (Bannerman 1936). At Cape Coast less common than *A. ansorgei* (M. Macdonald).

Breeding. A female with oviduct egg, 12 Jun (D. W. Lamm). A male collected, 4 Jan, at Goaso was about to breed (Lowe 1937).

447. ANDROPADUS LATIROSTRIS

(II. 723)*   Yellow-whiskered Greenbul   R(B)

Common, widespread resident (*A. l. congener*) of mature and secondary forest, noisily active in canopy of small trees (Button 1964). Occurs Tafo, Atewa Forest Reserve, Mpraeso, Cape Coast and the Bia National Park (Taylor & Macdonald 1978b). One netted, 7 Jul, near Sefwi Wiasso (F. Walsh); collected Mampong in Ashanti (Lowe 1937).

Breeding. Unrecorded. In Nigeria, eggs in May (Elgood 1982). In Gabon, Dec–Mar in dry season (Brosset 1981b).

*Named *Stelgidocichla latirostris* by MP&G.

[ANDROPADUS (=ARIZELOCICHLA) MONTANUS
(II.713)   Mountain Little Greenbul
Hall & Moreau (1970) map a specimen on the Ghana/Togo border (Map 70), a record listed in MP&G. It is based on a skin collected at Klouto, 4 Jun 1950, by A. Villiers (Dekeyser 1951). There are several sub-montane forest patches in Ghana (Hall & Swaine 1976, 1981), but all attempts to confirm this particularly interesting record and trace the skin at the University of Dakar and in collections in Paris have failed. It seems certain that it was misidentified (A. Brosset), particularly as the record was not subsequently listed in Dekeyser & Derivot (1966, 1967).]

448.   ANDROPADUS VIRENS
(II.722)*   Little Greenbul   RB
Abundant widespread resident (*A. v. erythropterus = grisescens*) of the forest region in undergrowth within secondary and mature forests, often at forest edge and in thickets extending into savanna areas at the coast between Winneba and Accra (M. Macdonald, L.G.G.). Less common in wetter areas of forest in southwest; only twice recorded, in secondary forest, in the Bia National Park (Taylor & Macdonald 1978b).
Breeding. Mampong, Feb (Lowe 1937). Eggs: Akropong in Akwapim, C/2 on 23 May (C. M. Morrison); egg in oviduct, 3 Apr (D. W. Lamm).
*Named *Eurillas virens* by MP&G.

449.   BAEOPOGON INDICATOR
(II.695)   Honey-Guide (or White-tailed) Greenbul   RB
Not uncommon resident (*B. i. leucurus*), widespread in mature and secondary forest, usually in the canopy but also in undergrowth (Lowe 1937, Sutton 1965a, Brosset 1971a), often in groups of 4–7 (Button 1964). Collected Prahsu, Kumasi (Alexander 1902), Aburi and in the Wassaw (Tarkwa) area (Bannerman 1936).
Breeding. Nest building at Aburi, Aug (C. M. Morrison). Females collected at Mampong in Ashanti, Feb, had recently laid eggs (Lowe 1937).

450.   BLEDA CANICAPILLA
(II.690)   Grey-headed Bristle-bill   R(B)
Widespread and common resident of forest undergrowth in both mature and secondary forest. Occurs at forest edge at Akropong and Aburi on the Akwapim hills (C. M. Morrison), Tafo and Cape Coast (D. James, J. Karr, M. Macdonald). One netted, c. 5 Jul, was in heavy moult (F. Walsh). Subject to movements; one adult was found flying about in a lecture theatre at the University of Ghana at Legon, 21 Oct 1966 (Grimes 1972a).
Breeding. Unrecorded. In Nigeria, Jun (Elgood 1982).

451.   BLEDA EXIMIA
(II.689)   Green-tailed Bristle-bill   R(B)
Rare resident (*B. e. eximia*) of undergrowth in mature forest, until recently only known from skins collected in the last century (Bannerman 1936). Rare at Cape Coast, where birds located in canopy may have been migrants rather than foraging for food (M. Macdonald). Only once recorded in Bia National Park (Taylor & Macdonald 1978b); once netted in the Sukuma Forest Reserve, c. 5 Jul (F. Walsh).
Breeding. Unrecorded in West Africa (MP&G). In Gabon, C/2 in Feb–Mar (Brosset 1971a — the first description of its nest and eggs).

452. BLEDA SYNDACTYLA
(II.688)   Bristle-bill   R(B)
Rare resident (*B. s. syndactyla*) of thick undergrowth in both mature and second-
ary forest. Collected Mampong in Ashanti, 9 Feb (Lowe 1937) and in last century by
Aubinn (Bannerman 1936). Netted Asankrangwa, April 1965 (L.G.G.) and in the
Suhuma Forest Reserve, c. 5 Jul (F. Walsh). Several in bird army, Bia National Park
(Taylor & Macdonald 1978b).
Breeding. Unrecorded; possibly in any season (MP&G).

453. CALYPTOCICHLA SERINA
(II.721)   Serine Greenbul   R(B)
Rare resident of forest canopy of mature and secondary forest (Brosset 1971a).
Until recently only known from skins collected at Aburi, Kumasi (Alexander 1902),
"Fantee" and "Ashanti" (Bannerman 1936), but now known from mature forest in
Bia National Park (Taylor & Macdonald 1978b).
Breeding. Unrecorded in West Africa (MP&G). A male collected in Nigeria, Aug,
had enlarged testes (Elgood 1982).

454. CHLOROCICHLA (= PYRRHURUS) FLAVICOLLIS
(II.692)   Yellow-throated Leaf-love   R(B)
Rare resident (*C. f. flavicollis*) of thickets and wooded banks of streams in north-
ern savanna; regular at Mole in small numbers (Greig-Smith 1976a). Skins collected
at Makongo and Gambaga (Alexander 1902). No other records.
Breeding. Unrecorded. In northern Nigeria, May–Aug (Elgood 1982).

455. CHLOROCICHLA (= PYRRHURUS) SIMPLEX
(II.694)   Simple Greenbul (or Leaf-love)   RB
Common resident of undergrowth in secondary forest, forest edge (Kumasi and
Tafo) and in thicket at the coast from Sekondi eastwards to the Accra Plains and
Denu (Sutton 1965b). Recorded in wet season in thick orchard bush at Mole
(Harvey & Harrison 1970), but not listed by Greig-Smith (1976a). The third most
abundant bulbul after *Pycnonotus barbatus* and *Andropadus virens* at Akropong in
Akwapim (C. M. Morrison).
Breeding. Nest building: Cape Coast, Jul and Dec (Macdonald 1979b). Nestling:
Akropong, 18 Apr (C. M. Morrison). A female collected, 22 Feb, at Mampong had
one egg left in ovary (Lowe 1937).

456. CRINIGER (= TRICHOPHORUS) BARBATUS
(II.685)   Bearded Greenbul   RB
Not uncommon resident (*C. b. barbatus*) of thick undergrowth in mature and
secondary forest, but also in gallery forest at the coast near Winneba (N. Wood).
Mainly known from skins collected in the last century at Fumsu, Kwissa and
Dabocrom (Pel), but netted in 1950s at Kwahu Tafo (D. W. Lamm), and in Jul 1971
at Suhuma Forest Reserve (F. Walsh).
Breeding. Female collected, 3 Mar 1957, at Tafo had an egg in ovary (D. W.
Lamm). 2 juveniles collected, 5 Jul (F. Walsh).

457. CRINIGER (= TRICHOPHORUS) CALURUS
(II.686)   Thick-billed Red-tailed (or White-bearded) Greenbul   R(B)
Probably not uncommon resident (*C. c. verreauxi*) of undergrowth in mature and
secondary forest throughout the forest region, but easily overlooked. Mainly known
from skins collected at Axim, Fumso and Prahsu (Alexander 1902), Ejura and
Mampong (Lowe 1937) and Kumasi. Sighted at Tarkwa and in thick forest at

Amedzofe (Sutton 1965b), near Cape Coast and in the Bia National Park (Taylor & Macdonald 1978b).
Breeding. Unrecorded. The only record is Fernando Po, Nov (MP&G).

458. CRINIGER (= TRICHOPHORUS) OLIVACEUS
(II.687)   Yellow-throated Olive Greenbul   R(B)
Rare forest resident (*C. o. olivaceous*). Only known from a skin collected in "Fantee" by Aubinn (Bannerman 1936). Elsewhere known from The Gambia and Guinea, and recently netted in the Tai Forest Reserve in Ivory Coast (Thiollay 1985).
Breeding. Unrecorded. Female collected in Guinea, May, had small eggs in ovary (Bannerman 1936).

459. IXONOTUS GUTTATUS
(II.697)   Spotted Greenbul   R(B)
Uncommon local resident (*I. g. guttatus*) of mature and secondary forest, usually in canopy and, therefore, easily overlooked (Brosset 1971a). Collected near Kazarako(?), 4/5 Apr (Ussher 1874) and Aburi (Winterbottom *in* Bannerman 1936). At Sunyani, common in secondary growth forest (Bannerman 1936); 2 groups in mature forest in the Bia National Park (Taylor & Macdonald 1978b).
Breeding. Unrecorded. Nest building in southern Nigeria, Jun–Sep (Elgood 1982).

460. NICATOR CHLORIS
(II.1090)   Nicator   RB
Widespread common resident (*N. c. chloris*) of the middle stratum of mature and secondary forests. Also in gallery forests north of the forest region, and on the Accra Plains at Abokobi and Odumasi Krobo (C. M. Morrison, L.G.G.), but only occasional at Cape Coast (M. Macdonald). Collected at forest edge near most major towns within the forest region (Bannerman 1936). Located readily by its rich and loud song.
Breeding. Mampong, end of Feb, but no details (Lowe 1937). In Nigeria, males and females in breeding condition, Mar and May; female with an oviduct egg, 12 Jun (Elgood 1982).

461. PHYLLASTREPHUS ALBIGULARIS
(II.707)   White-throated Greenbul   R(B)
Resident (*P. a. albigularis*) in forest undergrowth and forest edge, often in mixed feeding flocks in mature forest; probably more widespread than records suggest. Occurs Tafo (L.G.G.), Brimsu reservoir near Cape Coast (M. Macdonald) and the UST campus at Kumasi (L.G.G.). Collected Mampong, 22 Feb (Lowe 1937) and netted Suhuma Forest Reserve, 7 Jul (F. Walsh).
Breeding. Unrecorded. In Nigeria, some specimens with enlarged gonads, Aug–Nov (Elgood 1982).

462. PHYLLASTREPHUS BAUMANNI
(II.706)   Baumann's Greenbul   R(B)
Rare resident (*P. b. baumanni*) of forest undergrowth and forest edge; probably more widespread and more abundant than records suggest. Collected Ejura, 16 Feb (Lowe 1937) and 2 netted at Cape Coast, 7 Jun (J. Karr, D. James); also seen at Bosusu, east of Mpraeso (D. James).
Breeding. Unrecorded. In Nigeria, female in breeding condition, Dec (Elgood 1982).

463. PHYLLASTREPHUS ICTERINUS
(II.710)   Icterine Greenbul   RB

Secretive resident (*P. i. icterinus*) of forest undergrowth. Until 1960s only known from a skin marked "Fanti" and a female collected at Mampong in Ashanti, 22 Feb (Lowe 1937). More recently collected at 5°23′N, 2°28′W near Nkwanta, 3 Sep 1966 (L. Cole) and 2 parties of c. 10 recorded in mature forest in the Bia National Park (Taylor & Macdonald 1978b).

Breeding. A female collected, 3 Sep, had 1·0 mm sized eggs in ovary (L. Cole).

464. PHYLLASTREPHUS (= PYRRHURUS) SCANDENS
(II.693)   Leaf-love   RB

A not uncommon resident (*P. s. scandens*) of forest edge and of riverine forest north of the forest/savanna boundry, often in flocks of c. 6. Occurs Jasikan and Amedzofe (Sutton 1965b), in gallery forest at Amanfro west of the Accra Plains (N. Wood) and Cape Coast (M. Macdonald). Singleton at Mole in riverine forest, 9 Aug (Harvey & Harrison 1970), but not listed by Greig-Smith (1976a). Collected Kete Kratchi, "Denkere" and Ejura (Bannerman 1936, Lowe 1937).

Breeding. Fledglings: Cape Coast, 2 Jan (M. Macdonald); Ejura, 16 Feb (Lowe 1937).

465. PYCNONOTUS BARBATUS
(II.684)   White-vented (Common Garden) Bulbul   RB

Abundant resident (*P. b. inornatus*) throughout, equally at home in dry savanna as it is within forest clearings and forest edge, but avoids continuous tracts of forest. Occurs within and near most, if not all, villages and regularly forms communal roosts of 50–60 birds in dry season, but occasionally these reach several hundred; at Tamale on 8 Feb 1987, 687 birds were counted leaving one roost between 0605 and 0640 hrs (F. Walsh).

Breeding. Extended, probably in nearly all months. Nest building: Cape Coast, Jul, Nov, Dec (M. Macdonald); Mole, Aug (Greig-Smith 1977b). Eggs and nestlings: C/2 Akropong in Akwapim, no date (C. M. Morrison); Accra Plains, May (Grimes 1972a); Mole, Jul (Greig-Smith 1977b). Fledglings: in south, Mar–Sep.

466. THESCELOCICHLA LEUCOPLEURUS
(II.691)   White-tailed Greenbul (Swamp Bulbul)   RB

Common and widespread, but local, resident, always in noisy groups of 6–8 usually in swampy areas within mature and secondary forest, forest clearings and forest edge. Collected at many sites throughout the forest region; known as the 'talky-talky-bird' in the various dialects (Lowe 1937).

Breeding. Probably cooperative. At Ejura, Feb (Lowe 1937).

LANIIDAE

Prionopinae

467. PRIONOPS (= SIGMODUS) CANICEPS
(II.1047)   Red-billed Shrike   RB

Not uncommon local resident (*P. c. caniceps*), widespread throughout areas of mature forest, usually in groups of c. 5–10 in the canopy (M. Horwood), also in gallery forest as far north as Kintampo (F. Walsh). Occurs in forests along the southern scarp of the Volta basin (C. M. Morrison), Atewa Forest Reserve (L.G.G.), Amedzofe and Afegame in the Volta region (Sutton 1965b, N. Wood), Tafo (M. Lockwood) and Bia National Park (Taylor & Macdonald 1978b).

Breeding. Mampong in Ashanti, a female collected 18 Feb had just finished laying (Lowe 1937).

468. PRIONOPS PLUMATA
(II.1044)   Straight-crested Helmet-Shrike   RB

Not uncommon resident (*P. p. plumata*) in well wooded savanna in north (Mole and Walewale), extending southwards through Hohoe, Ho and Anum in the Volta Region to inselbergs on the Accra Plains, always in family groups of 10–20. Occasional in older residential areas at Legon in Mar, Jun and Jul, but no records further west along the coast. Considered a partial migrant at Mole by Taylor & Macdonald (1978a) as they did not record it there in Apr, but in other years present in Mar and Apr (Greig-Smith 1976a, L.G.G.). Only once recorded at Tumu (Sutton 1970).

Breeding. Female collected Bole, 7 Jan, had just finished laying (Lowe 1937). Fledglings: Mole, Aug (Greig-Smith 1977b); Tamale, Mar (L.G.G.).

Malaconotinae

469. DRYOSCOPUS GAMBENSIS
(II.1073)   Puff-back   RB

Not uncommon resident (*D. g. gambensis*) in well wooded savanna in north, and south through the Volta Region to the Accra Plains (M. Horwood, Grimes 1972a). Occurs in forest edge at Cape Coast, Akropong in Akwapim (C. M. Morrison) and Kumasi (F. C. Holman *in* Bannerman 1939, B. Woodell).

Breeding. Eggs: Cape Coast C/1, 12 May (K. O'Carroll *in* Bannerman 1951). Dependent young: Legon, Aug–Oct (Grimes 1972a, L.G.G.); Mole, Sep–Oct (Greig-Smith 1977b). Breeding Apr, no data (Alexander 1902).

470. DRYOSCOPUS (=CHAUNONOTUS) SABINI
(II.1075)   Sabine's Puff-back   R(B)

Not uncommon resident (*D. s. sabini*) in mature and secondary forest, forest clearings and forest edge. Collected at many towns within the forest region from Axim and Cape Coast in south to Sunyani (J. M. Winterbottom *in* Bannerman 1939) and Kumasi inland (Holman 1947). Occasional in the suburbs of Accra.

Breeding. Unrecorded, but a pair in courtship display, 5 Jul at Tesano (N. Wood). In Nigeria, courtship display, Jun; male with enlarged gonads, Oct (Elgood 1982). On Mount Nimba, gonads moderately enlarged, Jun–Nov (Colston & Curry-Lindahl 1986).

471. LANIARIUS BARBARUS
(II.1063)   Gonolek (or Barbary Shrike)   RB

Common local resident (*L. b. barbarus*), confined to thickets in coastal region from Elmina to the Accra and Keta Plains and gardens of older residential areas of main towns (C. M. Morrison, D. James, M. Macdonald, Sutton 1965b, Grimes 1972a); extends northwards through the Volta region, widespread in riverine thickets (Greig-Smith 1976a, F. Walsh), but only sporadic at Tumu (Sutton 1970).

Breeding. Eggs: Legon, C/2 25 May; egg in oviduct, Apr (Alexander 1902). Fledglings: 3 with adults at Tesano, Accra, 2 Apr 1974 (N. Wood).

472. LANIARIUS FERRUGINEUS
(II.1067)*   Tropical Boubou (Bell Shrike)   R(B)

Not uncommon local resident (*L. f. major*) in thickets throughout the coastal belt from Axim to the Accra Plains, particularly its western edge and the inselbergs.

Not recorded within forest clearings such as Tafo and Kumasi. In the north less abundant, occurring Wenchi and Ejura (Lowe 1937), Mole in small numbers (Greig-Smith 1976a), Kete Kratchi (R. E. Crabbe), Tono dam in each month (R. Passmore), but not recorded Tumu (Sutton 1970) nor around Bolgatanga (F. Walsh). Duetting is most frequently heard in south during the rains, May–Jul (Grimes 1972a).

Breeding. Unrecorded. In Nigeria, incubating female, 10 Feb–7 Mar; C/2, 15 Jun (Elgood 1982).

*Named *L. aethiopicus* by MP&G.

473. LANIARIUS LEUCORHYNCHUS
(II.1065)   Sooty Boubou   R(B)

Uncommon secretive resident of undergrowth in mature and secondary forest and forest edge. Regularly recorded at Akropong in Akwapim (C. M. Morrison), but rare at Cape Coast although possibly overlooked (M. Macdonald). Occurs Kumasi (Holman *in* Bannerman 1939, C. M. Morrison) and netted Tafo in dry season, Nov–Feb (M. Lockwood).

Breeding. Unrecorded. In Liberia, Oct (MP&G). On Mount Nimba, females with enlarged ovaries, Mar and Nov (Colston & Curry-Lindahl 1986).

474. MALACONOTUS BLANCHOTI (= POLIOCEPHALUS)
(II.1086)*   Grey-headed Bush-Shrike (or Gladiator)   RB

Not uncommon local resident (*M. b. blanchoti*) in well wooded savanna in north, occurring Gambaga, Bole (Lowe 1937), Kete Kratchi, Salaga and Yendi (R. E. Crabbe), Mole (Greig-Smith 1976a) and Pong Tamale (F. Walsh). Not recorded from the Volta Region, but there is an established population at Achimota and Legon on the Accra Plains. At Cape Coast is only a rare vagrant in the dry season, Nov–Feb (M. Macdonald).

Breeding. Eggs: C/3 at Legon, 30 Jan 1972 and 16 May 1972 (B. Smit *in* Grimes 1972a). Fledglings: Legon and Achimota, Feb, May and Jul (Bannerman 1939, Grimes 1972a, L.G.G.). Juvenile with natal down still attached to head feathers, Accra, 2 Apr 1974 (N. Wood).

*Named *M. hypopyrrhus pallidirostris* by MP&G.

475. MALACONOTUS CRUENTUS
(II.1089)   Fiery-breasted Bush-Shrike   R(B)

Not uncommon resident of undergrowth of secondary forest and forest edge, widespread in the forest zone, but not recorded from the wetter forests of the southwest. Collected Cape Coast, Chama (Bannerman 1939) and Mampong in Ashanti (Lowe 1937). Occurs Amedzofe, Akropong in Akwapim (C. M. Morrison), Tafo (M. Lockwood) and in forest reserves north of Cape Coast (D. James). At Cape Coast, disorientated birds flew at night into houses, date not recorded (J. B. Hall).

Breeding. Unrecorded. In Cameroun, Aug (MP&G). On Mount Nimba, female with enlarged ovary and yolks, Jul and Nov; juvenile with much down, 29 Nov (Colston & Curry-Lindahl 1986).

476. MALACONOTUS LAGDENI
(II.1088)   Lagden's Bush-Shrike   V

Very rare vagrant. Only one record: the type specimen, collected in forests near Kumasi by Sir Godfrey Lagden. The only other records until recently were from montane habitat in eastern Congo, but is now known to occur on Mount Nimba (Hall & Moreau 1970, Colston & Curry-Lindahl 1986) and in the Tai Forest Reserve in Ivory Coast (Thiollay 1985).

Breeding. Unrecorded. In the Eastern Congo, a female had slightly enlarged ovaries, 29 Mar (Bannerman 1939).

477. MALACONOTUS (=CHLOROPHONEUS) MULTICOLOR
(II.1079)   Many-coloured Bush-Shrike   R?(B)

Previously not uncommon resident (*M. m. multicolor*) in canopy of secondary forest and forest edge. The scarlet-breasted form occurs Accra, Cape Coast and Mampong in Ashanti; the orange-breasted form at Kumasi, Makessim and interior of "fantee"; and the black-breasted mutant at Accra (Bannerman 1939). Present status unknown; a pair at Akropong in Akwapim and one at Amedzofe (C. M. Morrison).

Breeding. Unrecorded. In Nigeria, birds in breeding condition, Nov and Dec (Elgood 1982). On Mount Nimba, Liberia, male gonads very enlarged, Oct (Colston & Curry-Lindahl 1986).

478. MALACONOTUS (=CHLOROPHONEUS) SULFUREOPECTUS
(II.1081)   Sulphur-breasted Bush-Shrike   RB

Not uncommon resident (*M. s. sulfureopectus*) of the coastal thicket zone from Elmina and Cape Coast eastwards to the older residential areas of Accra and inselbergs on the Accra Plains. Not recorded in Volta region, nor within forest clearings, but occurs locally in the northern savanna at Mole (Greig-Smith 1976a) and Nakpanduri (Sutton 1970). At Legon, data suggest an influx of birds in the dry season, Nov–Feb (Grimes 1972a).

Breeding. Nest and eggs: C/2, Cape Coast, May and Jul (K. O'Carrol *in* Bannerman 1951); Achimota, 21 Jul. Juveniles: Mole, Jul and Aug (Greig-Smith 1977b).

479. NILAUS AFER
(II.1049)   Northern Brubru   RB, Afm

Not uncommon local resident (*N. a. afer*) of wooded savanna in north, occurring Ejura, Wenchi (Lowe 1937), Gambaga, Kintampo, Mole (Greig-Smith 1976a), Tumu (Sutton 1970) and Kete Kratchi (R. E. Crabbe). Local movements may occur in some years in the north (Taylor & Macdonald 1978a). Not recorded Cape Coast nor at Winneba (M. Macdonald), but a dry season visitor, end Oct to mid Mar, to residential areas at Legon and to inselbergs on the Accra Plains (Grimes 1972a).

Breeding. A female collected Wenchi, 14 Jan, had just finished laying (Lowe 1937). Juveniles at Mole, Jul and Aug (Greig-Smith 1977b).

480. TCHAGRA AUSTRALIS
(II.1077)   Brown-headed Bush-Shrike   RB

Not uncommon resident (*T. a. ussheri*) of thickets in coastal region from Cape Coast to western edge of the Accra Plains and its inselbergs. Occurs through the Volta region to Kete Kratchi, but not recorded further north either at Mole (Greig-Smith 1976a) or Tumu (Sutton 1970) or elsewhere. Local resident at forest edge and forest clearings at Akropong in Akwapim (C. M. Morrison), Tafo (M. Lockwood), and at Kumasi (F. C. Holman *in* Bannerman 1939, C. M. Morrison), where it frequented old cultivations and gardens.

Breeding. Nest and eggs: Kumasi, C/2–3, no date (F. C. Holman); C/2 Akropong, Jun; Kumasi, May (C. M. Morrison). Fledglings: Mampong Quarry on Accra Plains, 13 Jun (L.G.G.).

481. TCHAGRA (=ANTICHROMUS) MINUTA
    (II.1078)*   Black-cap Bush-Shrike   RB
Not uncommon resident (*T. m. minuta*) of long grass at the edges of thickets, forest and marshes in the coastal region from Cape Coast to the western edge and the inselbergs of the Accra Plains. Occurs Denu (Sutton 1965b) and along the Volta river reaching Kete Kratchi, Ejura (Lowe 1937), Kintampo (Bannerman 1939), and Mole, where it occurs in small numbers (Greig-Smith 1976a). No records at Tumu (Sutton 1970) nor in the far north (F. Walsh).
    Breeding. Dependent young Nakwa, at coast, 4 Oct (Macdonald 1979b).
    *Named *Bocagea minuta* by MP&G.

482. TCHAGRA SENEGALA
    (II.1076)   Black-headed Bush-Shrike   RB
A common resident (*T. s. senegala*) of disused cultivations, gardens and older residential areas throughout the coastal region from Axim to the Accra Plains (Grimes 1972a, M. Macdonald). Equally common and widespread throughout the northern savanna (Sutton 1970, Greig-Smith 1976a, F. Walsh).
    Breeding. Display flight most frequent in wet season, Apr–Jun in south and Jul–Sep in north. Dependent young: Legon, Apr (Grimes 1972a); Cape Coast, 22 Aug (Macdonald 1979b).

Laniinae

483. CORVINELLA CORVINA
    (II.1061)   Yellow-billed (Long-tailed) Shrike   RB
Common local resident (*C. c. togoensis*) in wooded savanna in north, occurring Mole (Greig-Smith 1976a), Bole (Lowe 1937), Gambaga and south through Kete Kratchi to the Keta and Accra Plains (Sutton 1965a, Grimes 1980). Only twice recorded at Tumu, 28 Jan and 4 Feb (Sutton 1970). In Ussher's day considered rare on the Accra Plains and only occasional in 1930s (J. M. Winterbottom *in* Bannerman 1939), but in 1970s common in older residential areas of Accra and Legon (Grimes 1980). Absent from Winneba and Cape Coast, although suitable habitat exists.
    Breeding. Cooperative. Fresh clutches (C/3, 4, 5) at Legon in all months except Nov (Grimes 1980). In the north, nesting Pong Tamale, Apr (F. Walsh). Juveniles: Mole, Jul (Greig-Smith 1977b).

484. LANIUS COLLARIS
    (II.1053)   Fiscal (or Fiscal Shrike)   RB
Not uncommon resident (*L. c. smithii*), restricted mainly to the coastal thicket zone from Takoradi to Winneba and locally in forest clearings. Occurs sporadically on the Accra Plains often in suburbs of Accra, and in bushy margins of marshes at Keta and Denu, mainly Apr–Oct, occasionally Dec–Mar (Sutton 1965a, Grimes 1972a, Macdonald 1980b, L.G.G.). Extends northwards to Kete Kratchi (Alexander 1902), but nowhere else except for some wet season records at Mole (Genelly 1968, Harvey & Harrison 1970), though not recorded there by Aberdeen students (Greig-Smith 1976a). In forest clearings occurs Akropong, Tafo, Korforidua (C. M. Morrison, M. Lockwood, L.G.G.) and Dixcove (Sutton 1970).
    Breeding. Cape Coast, Dec–Oct, with peak in egg laying possibly Jan (Macdonald 1980b). Dependent fledglings: Winneba and Apam, Jun; Tafo, Jan–Sep (M. Horwood, M. Lockwood, L.G.G.).

485. LANIUS EXCUBITOR
   (II.1050)*   Grey Shrike (Great Grey Shrike)   V
Vagrant (*L. e. leucopygos*). Only one record: a singleton at Tono dam in the far north, Mar and Apr 1982 (R. Passmore). Usually occurs in the Sahel zone or in thorn scrub to the north of Ghana, and the extension of its range southwards may be a result of the severe drought of the last decade.
   *Named *L. elegans* by MP&G.

486. LANIUS GUBERNATOR
   (II.1059)   Emin's Shrike   R?(B)
Rare, possibly resident in the drier savanna areas near Gambaga and Salaga and westwards to Tumu (Alexander 1902, Sutton 1970, R. E. Crabbe). Collected Gambaga (Alexander 1902). At Tumu sporadic singletons late Sep to early May; Mole, one on 12 Jan (Sutton 1970).
   Breeding. Unrecorded. Nigeria, fledglings with parents, 16 Jun (Elgood 1982).

487. LANIUS SENATOR
   (II.1060)   Woodchat Shrike   PM
Not uncommon, widespread Palaearctic migrant (*L. s. senator* and *L. s. badius*) throughout the northern savanna, early Oct to late May, and southwards through the Volta Region to the Accra and Keta Plains, Nov–Mar (Sutton 1965b, Grimes 1972a). Only 3 records west of Accra; one at Winneba and 2 at Cape Coast (M. Macdonald). Occurs in forest clearings at Kumasi (F. C. Holman, B. Woodell), Mampong, Akropong in Akwapim and Agogo (C. M. Morrison), Tafo (M. Lockwood) and Korforidua and Abetifi (M. Horwood). *L. s. badius* has been collected in the north and within forest clearings; *L. s. senator* at the coast at Accra, Abokobi and Weija, but also in the northern savanna (Bannerman 1939, D. W. Lamm).

MUSCICAPIDAE

Turdinae

488. ALETHE DIADEMATA (= CASTANEA)
   (II.844)   White-tailed Alethe   R(B)
Probably not uncommon resident (*A. d. diademata*) of undergrowth of mature and secondary forest. Secretive and difficult to detect, but often a member of bird armies. Until recently only known from skins collected at "Denkere", Wassaw (Tarkwa) district, and Prahsu (Bannerman 1936), but now known to occur Akropong, Akwapim (C. M. Morrison), Subri River Forest Reserve (M. F. Hodges, Jr) and in the Bia National Park (Taylor & Macdonald 1978b). Also netted at Kade (Sutton 1965b), Asankrangwa (L.G.G.), and in the Suhuma Forest Reserve, 5–7 Jul (F. Walsh).
   Breeding. Unrecorded. Cameroun, May–Sep (MP&G). On Mount Nimba, Liberia, females with enlarged ovaries, Jul–Sep; fledglings, Aug (Colston & Curry-Lindahl 1986).

489. ALETHE POLIOCEPHALA
   (II.845)   Brown-chested Alethe   RB
Secretive resident of undergrowth of mature forests (*A. p. castanonota*), abundance uncertain, but possibly not uncommon. Until recently only known from 5 skins collected in last century in "Fanti and Denkere" (Bannerman 1936), but recently collected in the Bronikron Forest Reserve, Sep 1966 (L. Cole).
   Breeding. Female with small oviduct eggs, 5 Sep (L. Cole).

490. CERCOMELA FAMILIARIS
(II.820)   Red-tailed Chat   RB

Local uncommon resident (*C. f. falkensteini*) in northern savanna zone, confined to scarps and hills. Only recorded Gambaga (Alexander 1902, L.G.G.), Bongo Hills (F. Walsh) and Mole (Greig-Smith 1976a). Probably overlooked.

Breeding. Nesting: Gambaga, Dec (Alexander 1902).

491. CERCOTRICHAS (= ERYTHROPYGIA) LEUCOSTICTA
(II.853)   Northern Bearded Scrub-Robin   RB

Uncommon resident (*C. l. leucosticta*) of thick forest undergrowth, distribution little known. The type specimen labelled "Accra", obtained c. 1883, remained the only record until the 1940s: Sekondi (Holman 1947), Akropong in Akwapim, Amedzofe (C. M. Morrison), though not recorded by Bannerman (1951). Netted Bronikron Forest Reserve, Jan (L. Cole) and sighted in Subri and Komenda Forest Reserves, Cape Coast and Bia National Park (Taylor & Macdonald 1978b).

Breeding. Fledgling at Akropong, 7 Jul (C. M. Morrison).

492. COSSYPHA ALBICAPILLA
(II.836)   White-crowned Robin-Chat   R(B)

Possibly not uncommon resident (*C. a. giffardi*) in thickets and riverine bush in the northern savanna. Collected Gambaga by Giffard (Hartert 1899a) and many sightings Mole (Greig-Smith 1976a), but none elsewhere and is probably overlooked.

Breeding. Unrecorded. Several pairs in territories at Mole in wet season, Jul–Sep (Harvey & Harrison 1970). Fledgling possibly *C. albicapilla* or *C. niveicapilla* Mole, Jul 1975 (Greig-Smith 1977b). In Nigeria, Jul (Elgood 1982).

493. COSSYPHA CYANOCAMPTER
(II.834)   Blue-shouldered Robin-Chat   R(B)

Uncommon resident (*C. c. cyanocampter*) of forest undergrowth, easily over-looked unless song in known. Type specimen collected Dabocrom (Pel) and others at Aburi, Cape Coast and Mampong in Ashanti (Bannerman 1936). Birds in song most months at Akropong in Akwapim, Anum, Begoro, Aburi (C. M. Morrison) and Agogo (J. Chapin). More recently, recorded at Cape Coast (M. Macdonald) and netted in the Bia National Park (C. Martin *in* Taylor & Macdonald 1978b).

Breeding. Unrecorded. In Cameroun, Oct (MP&G). On Mount Nimba, Liberia, female with enlarged ovary, Sep (Colston & Curry-Lindahl 1986).

494. COSSYPHA NIVEICAPILLA
(II.837)   Snowy-headed (Snowy-crowned) Robin-Chat   R(B)

Common resident (*C. n. niveicapilla*) of the coastal thicket zone from Elmina eastwards to the Accra Plains, often in thickets along paths and roads, but also in gardens of older residential areas of the major coastal towns. A superb and frequent mimicker of local bird songs during the wet season, Apr–Jul, and after rain (Grimes 1972a). Occurs in Volta region and is widespread in northern savanna, although less common than in south, at Gambaga, Salaga and Mole (Greig-Smith 1976a). In some years at Mole numbers decrease at the end of the dry season (Taylor & Macdonald 1978a) and at Tumu only recorded Jun (Sutton 1970). No records from within the main forest zone, apart from a skin marked "Denkere", but in Nigeria occurs in gardens within forest clearings (Elgood 1982).

Breeding. Unrecorded. In Nigeria in wet season, May–Aug (Elgood 1982).

[COSSYPHA POLIOPTERA
(II.832)   Grey-winged (White-browed) Robin-Chat
Recorded in wooded savanna and dense gallery forest in Nigeria (Elgood 1982), and also in Ivory Coast at heights above 1000 m (Thiollay 1985). It, therefore, may occur within Ghana.]

495. LUSCINIA MEGARHYNCHOS
(II.859)   Nightingale   PM
Very common Palaearctic migrant (*L. m. megarhynchos*), late Oct to Mar, to the coastal thicket zone from Cape Coast eastwards to Denu. Occurs in residential gardens at Legon and is particularly common in the thicket belt near Abokobi at the foot of the Akwapim hills (Shelley & Buckley 1872, Grimes 1972a). Widespread in forest zone at forest edge, clearings and overgrown plantations. Occurs Tafo (M. Lockwood), Begoro, Agogo, Amedzofe (C. M. Morrison), Kumasi, Mpraeso, Lake Bosumptwi (C. M. Morrison, L.G.G.) and Bia National Park (Taylor & Macdonald 1978b). Less common in the north, only recorded Mole (Greig-Smith 1976a), but possibly overlooked. In the south, song is heard from November onwards — territorial.

496. LUSCINIA SUECICA
(II.858)*   Bluethroat   PM
Uncommon Palaearctic migrant (subspecies unknown), located in rank and thorny vegetation on banks and ditches separating rice paddies at Vea dam, mid Nov to mid Jan, when paddies dried out and birds left the area. Only one other record, a male in rank grass, 2–3 m high, at the Kumasi sewage farm, 28 Jan (Walsh & Grimes 1981).
*Named *Cyanosylvia svecica* by MP&G.

497. MONTICOLA SAXATILIS
(II.808)   Rock-Thrush   PM
Uncommon Palaearctic migrant, sporadic and locally distributed. Occasional at Gambaga, but more regular in the Bolgatanga area (F. Walsh). Collected as far south as Ejura, 9 Feb (Lowe 1937), but not recorded Mole (Greig-Smith 1976a) nor at Tumu (Sutton 1970).

498. MONTICOLA SOLITARIA
(II.809)   Blue Rock-Thrush   PM
Uncommon Palaearctic migrant (*M. s. solitaria*), only found regularly at the Bongo Hills near Bolgatanga (F. Walsh). Stragglers have wintered at the Mampong quarry on the Accra Plains: a male from Nov 1971 to mid Mar 1972 with a second in mid Feb; another from Nov 1972 to end Feb 1973, and a female for a few days at end Mar 1973 (Wink 1976, Walsh & Grimes 1981).

499. MYRMECOCICHLA (= PENTHOLAEA) ALBÏFRONS
(II.821)   White-fronted Black Chat   RB
Uncommon resident (*M. a. frontalis*) locally distributed on open rocky savanna in north. Occurs Gambaga and near Yendi (Alexander 1902), Mole (Greig-Smith 1976a), Kete Krachi (R. E. Crabbe); Lowe (1937) collected it at Ejura. At Tumu only twice recorded, 4 on 10 May and 4 on 20 May (Sutton 1970).
Breeding. Nestling: Gambaga, Jan (Alexander 1902). Pair collected at Ejura, 24 Jan, was about to breed (Lowe 1937).

500. MYRMECOCICHLA   CINNAMOMEIVENTRIS   (=THAMNOLEA
    CORONATA)
    (II.823)   White-crowned Cliff-Chat   RB
Uncommon local resident (*M. c. coronata*) confined to rocky scarps in northern
savanna, but with an isolated population in the Shai Hills on the Accra Plains,
discovered in 1971 and not present in the 1950s when D. W. Lamm located *Cisticola*
aberrans in the same quarries. This population's origin is probably from the high-
lands of Togo. In the north, first located at Nakpanduri, May 1962 (L.G.G.), then
on the Konkori scarp in Mole in 1968 (Sutton 1970).
    Breeding. Nestlings: Mampong Quarry in Shai Hill, late May. Fledglings:
Mampong, Jul (Grimes 1972a).

501. NEOCOSSYPHUS POENSIS
    (II.807)   White-tailed Ant-Thrush   RB
Very rare resident (*N. p. poensis*) of forest undergrowth. Only 2 records: collected
in "Fanti" in last century (Bannerman 1936), and in the Bronikron Forest Reserve,
14 Sep 1966 (L. Cole).
    Breeding. Female collected, 14 Sep, had eggs in oviduct (L. Cole).

502. OENANTHE BOTTAE (=HEUGLINI)
    (II.817)   Heuglin's Red-breasted Wheatear (or Chat)   V
Vagrant. Only one record: a juvenile male (subspecies uncertain) collected at
Karaga, 5 May 1901 by B. Alexander (P. Colston). Though not in Alexander (1902),
included by Hall & Moreau (1970) and for Ghana by MP&G, but not by White
(1962). One record for Ivory Coast (Thiollay 1985), another for Togoland (Cheke
1982).
    Breeding. Unrecorded. In northern Nigeria, Jan–Apr (Elgood 1982).

503. OENANTHE OENANTHE
    (II.811)   Wheatear   PM
Uncommon Palaearctic migrant (*O. o. oenanthe*) mainly to open savanna in the
far north, often on burnt areas. Occurs Bolgatanga and Navrongo areas, early Nov
to late Mar (F. Walsh, R. Passmore), sporadically at Gambaga, Oct–Feb (Sutton
1965b, R. B. Payne), and rarely at Tumu, a singleton from 14 Jan to 19 Feb (Sutton
1970). In the south only one record; a singleton at the edge of a small lagoon,
midway between Accra and Apam (E. Dunn & A. J. R. Smith).

504. PHOENICURUS PHOENICURUS
    (II.857)   Redstart   PM
Not uncommon Palaearctic migrant (*P. p. phoenicurus*) to open wooded savanna
in north, often in gardens of older residential areas of Tamale and Bolgatanga.
Regular around Bolgatanga, early Nov to late Mar (F. Walsh), but sporadic at
Tamale, Yeji and Salaga (R. E. Crabbe), Mole (Greig-Smith 1976a) and Tumu
(Sutton 1970). Only one record from the south; a singleton in the Shai Hills, 29 Nov
1973 (L.G.G.).

505. SAXICOLA RUBETRA
    (II. 829)   Whinchat   PM
Widespread, locally common Palaearctic migrant, occurring within forest clearings such as Tafo, Kumasi and Tarkwa, also throughout the coastal thicket zone
from Cape Coast eastwards to the Accra and Keta Plains (Oct–Apr), and northwards through the Volta Region to northern savanna (late Sep to early May).

Frequently perches on telephone wires along roads and in cultivations. Adults are in breeding dress and singing in late Mar.

[SHEPPARDIA CYORNITHOPSIS
(II.841)   Akalat
Distribution in West Africa is discontinuous. *S. c. houghtoni* occurs in the Upper Guinea forest block as far east as Ivory Coast (15 records — Thiollay 1985), and *S. c. cyornithopsis* in the Lower Guinea forest block as far west as Cameroun. Thus *houghtoni* might well occur in Ghana.]

506. STIPHRORNIS ERYTHROTHORAX
(II.842)   Forest Robin   RB
Not uncommon resident (*S. e. erythrothorax*) of the forest floor vegetation, widespread within the forest region, but also occasionally in forest outliers on the Accra Plains. Type specimen collected Dabocrom (Pel), and others collected Mampong in Ashanti (Lowe 1937), Akropong in Akwapim and Anum (C. M. Morrison), Krobo Hill on the Accra Plains, 12 Feb 1957 (D. W. Lamm), Bia National Park (C. Martin *in* Taylor & Macdonald 1978b), and in the Bronikron Forest Reserve (L. Cole).
Breeding. Mampong, Feb (Lowe 1937).

507. STIZORHINA FRASERI (= FINSCHI)
(II.757)*   Finsch's Rufous Flycatcher*   RB
Uncommon resident (*S. f. finschi*) of forest floor vegetation, usually near streams and in overgrown cultivations; probably overlooked. Collected Accra in last century (Ussher 1874), the Monse Hills near Tarkwa (Alexander 1902), and Mampong in Ashanti (Lowe 1937) and Kwahu Tafo (D. W. Lamm). Occurs Tafo (L.G.G.), Amedzofe (Sutton 1970), Kumasi (F. C. Holman *in* Bannerman 1936) and in forest reserves north of Cape Coast (D. James).
Breeding. Eggs in ovary, 3 Mar 1959 (D. W. Lamm).
*Both Bannerman and MP&G place this species in flycatchers (Muscicapinae), hence the English name.

508. TURDUS PELIOS (= LIBONYANUS)
(II.796)*   Olive (or Kurrichane) Thrush*   RB
Widespread common resident (*T. p. saturatus*) of cultivations and residential gardens in towns throughout forest and savanna areas, also in the coastal thicket zone and riverine bush in the north. During F. C. Holman's 10 year stay at Kumasi, the thrush became as common as *Pycnonotus barbatus*. Less common at Denu on the coast, usually found in coco-nut palms in marshy areas (Sutton 1965b).
Breeding. Extended. Eggs: C/3 Legon, Apr–Aug (Grimes 1972a); C/3 Kumasi, Apr (C. M. Morrison). Nestlings and fledglings: Kumasi, 22 Feb (B. Woodell).
*Several names have been used for this species: *Turdus libonyanus* (Kurrichane Thrush) by Bannerman; *Turdus olivaceus* (Olive Thrush) by MP&G; while White includes it in *Turdus pelios,* to which MP&G give the name African Thrush.

509. TURDUS (= GEOKICHLA) PRINCEI
(II.804)   Grey Ground-Thrush   R(B)
Rare resident (*T. p. princei*) of forest floor. Only 2 records, both in the last century. Type specimen collected "Denkere" (probably the Tarkwa area of today) and one at Aburi in Akwapim (Sharpe 1873b, Bannerman 1936). Probably more common than appears, as it is widespread in Ivory Coast (Thiollay 1985).

Breeding. Unrecorded. In Nigeria a nest with C/3 in Aug was thought to be of this species (Elgood 1982). On Mount Nimba, Liberia, female with enlarged ova, Jun; another had recently laid 2 eggs, Aug (Colston & Curry-Lindahl 1986).

Timaliinae

510. PHYLLANTHUS ATRIPENNIS
(II.668)   Capuchin (or Black-winged) Babbler   R(B)

Not uncommon, widespread resident (*P. a. haynesi*) of thick undergrowth of forest and forest edge, usually in noisy groups of 12 or more, but secretive and difficult to observe. Many collected in last century at Kumasi, Dabocrom, Cape Coast, Sunyani and in Akwapim; the type specimen is labelled Accra (Bannerman 1936). Occurs Ejura (Lowe 1937) and Akropong in Akwapim (C. M. Morrison).

Breeding. Unrecorded. No records in Africa (MP&G).

511. TRICHASTOMA (=ILLADOPSIS) CLEAVERI
(II.679)*   Black-cap Illadopsis (Akalat)   R(B)

Uncommon resident (*T. c. cleaveri*) of the undergrowth of mature and secondary forest. Collected in "Fanti" in last century and located near Kumasi in parties of 6–8 (F. C. Holman *in* Bannerman 1936). Recently found in the Bia National Park (Taylor & Macdonald 1978b); probably overlooked.

Breeding. Unrecorded. In Nigeria, juveniles Jun and Aug (Elgood 1982). On Mount Nimba, Liberia, juvenile just out of nest, 8 Sep (Colston & Curry-Lindahl 1986).

*In White (1962: 162) *Malacocincla* is used for this genus, but he later corrects this to *Trichastoma* (White 1970: 296).

512. TRICHASTOMA (=ILLADOPSIS) FULVESCENS
(II.673)*   Brown Illadopsis (Akalat)*   R(B)

Not uncommon resident (*T. f. gularis* and, in eastern sector at least, *T. f. moloneyanus*) of dense thicket within the main forest belt, but more common in the coastal thicket zone from Cape Coast to the western edge of the Accra Plains. Collected Prahsu (Alexander 1902), Axim, Elmina, Abokobi and "Denkere" (Bannerman 1936) and Ejura (Lowe 1937). Occurs Amedzofe (Sutton 1965b) and has been netted at Tafo (M. Lockwood).

Breeding. Unrecorded. Liberia, female with enlarged ovary, Jun; another had finished laying, Oct (Colston & Curry-Lindahl 1986). Fledgling: Liberia, Jul; Cameroun, Apr, Jul, Sep–Nov (MP&G).

*White has grouped *gularis* and *moloneyanus* under *T. fulvescens,* which latter MP&G name Brown Illadopsis (II. 673); but MP&G give *moloneyanus* specific rank, *T. moloneyanus* (II.678 — Moloney's Illadopsis), placing *gularis* in *T. fulvescens.*

513. TRICHASTOMA (=ILLADOPSIS) PUVELI
(II.677)   Puvel's Illadopsis (Akalat)   R(B)

Resident, but distribution uncertain as it has been identified only recently in Ghana. Occurs in thickets at Abokobi,where song was regularly heard in the 1960s and 1970s, and identified as *T. rufescens,* being like that described in Bannerman (1953). However, Dr C. Chappuis has now identified a tape recording of the singer as *T. puveli* and confirms that he has netted a singing bird. Probably occurs elsewhere in the coastal region as it is the most widespread of the genus in Ivory Coast (Thiollay 1985).

Breeding. Unrecorded. No records anywhere in Africa (MP&G); gonads enlarged, Mount Nimba, Aug (Colston & Curry-Lindahl 1986).

514. TRICHASTOMA (= ILLADOPSIS) RUFESCENS
      (II.676)   Rufous-winged Illadopsis (Akalat)   R(B)
Not uncommon resident in the coastal thicket zone and forest edge, occasional in
forest outliers on the Accra Plains (Grimes 1972a, L.G.G.). Distribution overlaps
others' in the genus, but it occurs in more open thicket than the other species
(Grimes 1972a, M. Macdonald). Unlike *fulvescens* and *rufipennis, rufescens* is
solitary and spends much time on the ground (Lowe 1937).
      Breeding. Unrecorded. Sierra Leone, breeding condition, Apr; feeding young in
Dec (MP&G). On Mount Nimba, Liberia, females with enlarged ovaries, Apr and
Nov (Colston & Curry-Lindahl 1986).

515. TRICHASTOMA (= ILLADOPSIS) RUFIPENNIS
      (II.674)   Pale-breasted Illadopsis (Akalat)   RB
Not uncommon resident (*T. r. extrema*) of dense foliaged plants in undergrowth
of old cultivations and thickets in coastal region, seldom on the ground or on
branches of trees; always in small parties (Lowe 1937). Collected Axim, Goaso and
Mampong in Ashanti (Bannerman 1936) and netted Tafo in cocoa plantation (M.
Lockwood), Cape Coast (D. James) and near Kwahu Tafo (D. W. Lamm).
      Breeding. Female with eggs in ovary, 3 Mar 1957 (D. W. Lamm); egg in oviduct,
21 Apr 1965 (D. James).

516. TURDOIDES PLEBEJUS
      (II.661)   Brown Babbler   RB
Not uncommon resident (*T. p. platycircus*), widespread but locally distributed in
the northern savanna, extending southwards through the Volta Region to inselbergs
of the Accra Plains and older residential areas of Accra and Legon. In the north,
occurs Yendi (R. E. Crabbe), Mole (Greig-Smith 1976a), Tumu (Sutton 1970),
Tamale and Pwalagu (Holman 1947) and near Bolgatanga (F. Walsh). Occasional
in coastal areas west of Accra, but only once recorded at Cape Coast, 6 Dec
(M. Macdonald).
      Breeding. Cooperative and extended. Eggs: C/3 at Tamale, Apr (Holman 1947);
C/2 at Legon, 25 Apr (L.G.G.). Fledglings: Legon, 26 Aug 1972, 15 Dec 1972, 4 Jun
1973, 14 Dec 1974. One record of parasitism by *Clamator levaillantii,* May (Grimes
1972a, L.G.G.).

517. TURDOIDES REINWARDII
      (II.665)   Black-cap Babbler   RB
Not uncommon resident (*T. r. stictilaema*) with much the same distribution as *T.
plebejus,* but not as common nor as widespread in the north. In the south, occurs
Elmina (M. Macdonald), Legon and in thickets on inselbergs, but not recorded in
the Volta Region. In the north, regularly recorded at Mole (Greig-Smith 1972a), but
not recorded Tumu (Sutton 1970), Tamale nor in the Bolgatanga area (F. Walsh).
      Breeding. Cooperative. Female with oviduct egg at Weija, 18 Dec (D. W. Lamm).
Fledglings: Legon, 25 Mar 1970, 6 Jul 1970, 23 Apr 1973 (Grimes 1972a, L.G.G.).

Picathartinae

518. PICATHARTES GYMNOCEPHALUS
      (II.1139)   Yellow-headed Rockfowl   RB
Uncommon and very localised resident (*P. g. gymnocephalus*), requiring rocky
outcrops and caves within mature and secondary forest for nest sites, and dependent, therefore, on the local geology. Breeding colonies occur along the southern
scarp of the Volta basin and elsewhere in southern Ghana and northwest of Kumasi

(Grimes & Darko 1968). There are old sites at the foot of the Akwapim hills, close to the Accra to Aburi road.

Breeding. Colonial, with 2 breeding periods which coincide with main rains, Mar–Jun and Sep–Oct (Grimes 1964, Grimes & Darko 1968). E. Baumann discovered a nest in Jun 1894 at Apototsi which has been traditionally thought to be in Togoland, but is now probably to be identified with Awatotse in Ghana, a part of German Togoland before 1922 (Cheke 1986).

Sylviinae

519. ACROCEPHALUS ARUNDINACEUS
(II.877)   Great Reed Warbler   PM
Not uncommon Palaearctic migrant (*A. a. arundinaceus*), Nov–May, regular although locally distributed, mainly in swamp vegetation at edges of irrigation dams and sewage farms, but also in sugar cane plantations within forest clearings. Regular at Kumasi (F. C. Holman *in* Bannerman 1939) and Tafo (M. Lockwood — see Appendix 1), but in north only present at Vea dam, Nov–Jan (Walsh & Grimes 1981). Netted once at Denu, 1 May (Sutton 1965b) and likely to occur in sugar plantations on the Accra Plains. Not recorded Mole (Greig-Smith 1976a).

An Austrian ringed bird has been recovered at Tafo.

520. ACROCEPHALUS (= CALAMOECETOR) RUFESCENS
(II.892)*   Rufous Swamp (or Cane) Warbler   RB
Common resident (*A. r. rufescens*) in reed beds and marshes bordering mangrove swamps at Panbros and eastwards to Keta, where Holman (1947) found it common. Not recorded further west of Accra, but possibly overlooked, although its rich song would not go unnoticed. No other records apart from a singing bird (voice tape recorded) at Aburi gardens, 5 Oct (C. R. Watson) and sight records in reed beds near motel at Mole (Harvey & Harrison 1970), but not reported there since, where *A. scirpaceus* is irregular (Greig-Smith 1976a). The edges of the Volta Lake should provide suitable habitat for all *Acrocephalus* species in the future. One netted at Panbros, Jul, was of the nominate race (C. W. Benson).

Breeding. Keta and Panbros, Jun–Sep (Holman 1947, L.G.G.).

*Named *Calamocichla rufescens* by MP&G.

521. ACROCEPHALUS SCHOENOBAENUS
(II.882)   Sedge Warbler   PM
Regular and locally abundant Palaearctic migrant, mainly Oct–Apr; earliest record, at Vea dam, 24 Aug (Walsh & Grimes 1981). Occurs in rank growth at edges of irrigation dams, sewage farms and marshes. At Vea dam, up to 20 birds may give sub-song and hold territories from mid Nov within rice paddies; numbers fall to c. 6 after rice paddies are cut in Jan (F. Walsh). Occurs Kumasi sewage farm, Tafo (M. Lockwood), Tumu, Feb–Apr (Sutton 1970), Nakwa lagoon (M. Macdonald) and in *Typha* beds on the Accra Plains (Grimes 1972a).

Two birds ringed in UK have been recovered in Ghana.

522. ACROCEPHALUS SCIRPACEUS
(II.878)   Reed Warbler   PM
Not uncommon Palaearctic migrant (*A. s. scirpaceus*) in *Typha* beds, edge of marshes and irrigation dams, but also at sewage farms and in dry thicket on the Accra Plains. Regularly netted Tafo (Appendix 1), one netted in dry thicket within botanical gardens at Legon (12 Dec 1964) and another in *Typha* beds near Accra. In the north, irregular at Mole (Greig-Smith 1976a), and not recorded at Vea dam (F.

Walsh) or elsewhere. Occasionally occurs alongside *Luscinia suecica, Acrocephalus rufescens* and *A. schoenobaenus.*

Birds ringed in Sweden (1), Holland (1), France (1) and UK (1) have been recovered in Ghana. One bird ringed at Tafo was retrapped there a year later (Appendix 1).

523. APALIS FLAVIDA (= CANICEPS)
(II.911)   Yellow-chested Apalis   RB

Uncommon resident (*A. f. caniceps*) of forest edge, in coastal thicket zone and in riverine bush as far north as Du on the bend of the White Volta (F. Walsh). Occurs Akropong in Akwapim (C. M. Morrison), Cape Coast area (D. James, M. Macdonald) and Tewa Forest Reserve (N. Wood). L.G.G.'s record at Mole is now known to be incorrect (Greig-Smith 1976a).

Breeding. Akropong, fledgling being fed by parents, 14 Oct (C. M. Morrison).

524. APALIS NIGRICEPS
(II.914)   Black-capped Apalis   R(B)

Uncommon resident (*A. n. nigriceps*) of the lower canopy of mature and secondary forest, also in shade trees above cocoa plantations. Occurs Tewa Forest Reserve (N. Wood), in reserves c. 50 km north of Cape Coast (D. James), and Amedzofe (L.G.G.). Collected at Aburi (Shelley 1873), Prahsu (Alexander 1902) and Techiman near Wenchi (Lowe 1937).

Breeding. Unrecorded anywhere in West Africa (MP&G).

525. APALIS SHARPII
(II.917)   Sharpe's Apalis   RB

Not uncommon resident (*A. s. sharpii*), mainly in lower (5–25 m) canopy of mature forest. Occurs north of Cape Coast (D. James), in the Bia National Park, and is widespread in forests along the southern scarp of the Volta basin (Macdonald & Taylor 1977). Previously only known from a skin collected at an unknown locality in Ghana (Bannerman 1936).

Breeding. Bia National Park, a pair feeding 2 fledglings, 7 Apr (Macdonald & Taylor 1977).

526. BATHMOCERCUS (= EMINIA) CERVINIVENTRIS
(II.992)   Black-capped Warbler   R(B)

Rare resident (*B. c. cerviniventris*) of thick undergrowth of mature forests, often near streams. Only known from 2 skins collected in last century; one at "Denkere" and a male at Kwissa (Alexander 1902). Kwissa does not occur on current maps, but using the map in Alexander (1902) it would be near Dompoasi (6°18′N, 1°32′W).

Breeding. Unrecorded anywhere in West Africa (MP&G).

527. CAMAROPTERA BRACHYURA (= BREVICAUDATA)
(II.945)   Grey-backed Camaroptera   RB

Very common, widespread resident (*C. b. tincta*) throughout. Occurs in mature gardens and riverine bush throughout the northern savanna, equally abundantly in thickets at forest edge and in gardens of towns within the forest and coastal regions.

Breeding. Its remarkable pre-copulation display recorded Legon, 16 Jun, 9 Oct; Mole, Jul. Nest building: Akropong in Akwapim, 20 Aug (C. M. Morrison); Cape Coast, early May to early Jun (M. Macdonald). Juveniles: Mole, late Jul (Greig-Smith 1977b); Weija, 27 Dec (Grimes 1972a).

528. CAMAROPTERA CHLORONOTA

(II.944)   Olive Green (Green-backed) Camaroptera   R(B)

Common resident (*C. c. kelsalli*) of undergrowth and secondary growth within both mature and secondary forest, only occasional at Cape Coast (M. Macdonald). A secretive bird, but its prolonged cicada-like song — a repetition of a short whistled note lasting several minutes (Chapin 1953: 314) — indicates that it is widespread in forest reserves. Listed for Mole by Harvey & Harrison (1970), but its identification needs confirmation there and it is not included in Greig-Smith (1976a).

Breeding. Unrecorded. In Liberia, females with enlarged ovaries, Oct and Apr; a female had recently laid, Sep (Colston & Curry-Lindahl 1986).

529. CAMAROPTERA SUPERCILIARIS

(II.946)   Yellow-browed Camaroptera   RB

Not uncommon, widespread resident of undergrowth of forest edge, and of thickets and overgrown cultivations within forest clearings (Holman 1947). Collected Cape Coast, Prahsu (Alexander 1902), Mampong and Ejura in Ashanti (Lowe 1937), and occurs Akropong in Akwapim (C. M. Morrison), Tarkwa (Sutton 1965b) and Bia National Park (Taylor & Macdonald 1978b).

Breeding. Ejura, Feb (Lowe 1937); Akim Oda, C/3, no date (Holman 1947).

530. CISTICOLA ABERRANS (= EMINI)

(II.964)   Rock-loving Cisticola   RB

Locally common resident (*C. a. admiralis*), confined to rocky outcrops and scarps. In north occurs along the northern scarp of the Volta basin at Gambaga and Nakpanduri, on scarps in Mole (Greig-Smith 1976a) and in the Bongo hills near Bolgatanga (F. Walsh). Isolated populations occur on some inselbergs on the Accra Plains (Lamm & Horwood 1958, Grimes 1978a).

Breeding. Shai Hills, female with egg in ovary, 7 Oct (D. W. Lamm).

531. CISTICOLA BRACHYPTERA

(II.975)   Siffling Cisticola   RB

Common local resident (*C. b. brachyptera*) in north, occurring in well wooded savanna areas. Easily confused with *Cisticola rufa,* which overlaps its range in the northern savanna. Tops of trees, or a substitute such as a telegraph post, used as song posts are an essential part of its habitat. In the south, occurs in the coastal thicket zone eastwards to the Accra Plains, but is absent from large tracts of the Plains where grass is short and trees few. Collected Accra, Cape Coast, Kintampo, Kete Kratchi (Lynes 1930) and netted Tafo (M. Lockwood).

Breeding. Extended. Nest building at Nakwa, 14 Jan (M. Macdonald). Nestlings: Legon, Mar, Oct; Shai Hills, Jan, Aug. Territorial song, Mar–Oct, on Accra Plains (Grimes 1972a).

532. CISTICOLA CANTANS

(II.968)   Singing Cisticola   RB

Not uncommon resident (*C. c. swanzii*) of the northern savanna, but restricted to areas of a good mixture of grass and shrubs, as on old cultivations. More common in southern coastal zone, but local on the Accra Plains. Overlaps with *Cisticola erythrops* and within forest clearings with *C. lateralis*. Collected Accra, Cape Coast, Salaga and Gambaga (Lynes 1930). Occurs Kumasi (Holman 1947). Netted at Suhien near Tafo (M. Lockwood).

Breeding. Copulation observed near Legon, Mar (Grimes 1972a); singing males Mar–Oct. In northern Nigeria, Jun–Aug; in south, breeding condition, Oct (Elgood 1982).

533. CISTICOLA ERYTHROPS
(II.969)   Red-faced Cisticola   RB

Common, widespread resident (*C. e. erythrops*) in all savanna areas with rank grass, trees and shrubs, also forest clearings and throughout the coastal thicket zone. At Legon duetting song is heard in all months, but most frequently Mar–Oct. Collected Kumasi, Axim, Kete Kratchi (Lynes 1930) and regular at Tafo (M. Lockwood).

Breeding. Nest building: Cape Coast, Jun. Nestlings and fledglings: Accra Plains, Apr–Aug (Grimes 1972a, L.G.G.).

534. CISTICOLA EXIMIA
(II.958)   Black-backed Cisticola (Cloud-scraper)   RB

Not uncommon resident (*C. e. winneba*) in open grassland areas of the Winneba Plains (the type locality — Lynes 1930) and Accra Plains, which become water-logged in the wet season; also at edges of lagoons at Panbros. No records for either Keta Plains or northern savanna, but is probably overlooked unless flight song is known.

Breeding. Female collected by Lynes at Winneba had well developed egg in oviduct, May (Lynes & Vincent 1934). In Nigeria, large ova in ovary, 9 Jul; C/4, 15 Nov and fledgling, 15 Sep (Elgood 1982).

535. CISTICOLA GALACTOTES
(II.970)   Winding Cisticola   RB

Common local resident (*C. g. amphilecta*) wherever there are wetlands with reed beds, but absent from forest clearings, e.g. Tafo (M. Lockwood). Local and seasonal in the north, but more widespread in the coastal region from Cape Coast eastwards to the Accra Plains; also found in rank growth along drainage and sewage canals within Accra. At Vea dam and Yendi only present in wet season, Jun–Aug (F. Walsh).

Breeding. Eggs: C/2 Cape Coast, Jul–Aug (Pitman & Took 1973, M. Macdonald). Nestlings: Weija, 30 Nov; Cape Coast, 28 Nov. Dependent young: Cape Coast, 19 May (M. Macdonald).

536. CISTICOLA JUNCIDIS
(II.953)   Zitting Cisticola (or Fan-tailed Warbler)   RB

Common resident (*C. j. uropygialis*) within coastal thicket zone, on any waste ground, open areas with short grass and edges of cultivations. Song flight Accra Plains, Feb–Nov. Not recorded within forest clearings such as Kumasi and Tafo (M. Lockwood), and surprisingly few records in northern savanna. Not recorded Mole (Greig-Smith 1976a) nor near Bolgatanga (F. Walsh), but present Tumu, Jul–Aug (Sutton 1970).

Breeding. Nest building: Cape Coast, May–Jul, Dec. Nestlings: Sekondi, Aug (Macdonald 1979b).

537. CISTICOLA LATERALIS
(II.961)   Whistling Cisticola   RB

Not uncommon resident (*C. l. lateralis*) of forest edge and cultivations within the forest region, excepting the wetter forests of southwest. Occasional at Cape Coast and mainly occurs in wet season on inselbergs and in the northeast sector of the Accra Plains. In the north collected in woodland savanna at Bole, Ejura, Wenchi (Lowe 1937), Kintampo, Yegi and Kete Kratchi (Lynes 1930); occurs regularly at Mole (Greig-Smith 1976a). The loud melodious song is heard every month, most frequently in wet season.

Breeding. Nestlings and fledglings: Mole, Aug; Akwatia in Kwahu, 12 Jun (Macdonald 1979b).

538. CISTICOLA NATALENSIS
(II.974)   Croaking Cisticola   RB

Common resident (*C. n. strangei*) of savanna areas both north and south of the forest region where there is rank grass and scattered shrubs, often at edges of cultivations. Occasional in forest clearings at Akim Oda and Tafo (M. Horwood, M. Lockwood), but no recent records from Cape Coast (M. Macdonald). Collected Accra, Kpong, Cape Coast, Kete Kratchi, Salaga, Gambaga and Masarka (Alexander 1902, Lynes 1930).

Breeding. Holding territories at Legon and Mole during wet seasons, May–Jul and Jul–Sep respectively. Breeding Keta Plains in wet season, no dates (Holman 1947).

539. CISTICOLA RUFA
(II.977)   Rufous Cisticola   RB

Probably not uncommon resident of the drier savanna woodland in the north, but status uncertain as it is easily confused with *Cisticola brachyptera*. Absent from savanna areas in south where *C. brachyptera* occurs. Collected Gambaga, Batenga and Salaga (Lynes & Sclater 1934) and occurs Mole (Harvey & Harrison 1970)

Breeding. Mole, adults carrying food, Jul; feeding fledglings, late Nov (Greig-Smith 1977b).

540. CISTICOLA RUFICEPS
(II.979)   Red-pate Cisticola   R(B)

Uncommon resident (*C. r. guinea*) of grass savanna with scattered trees, but also in more wooded savanna with bushy undergrowth. Type specimen collected Kintampo (Alexander 1902), others at Gambaga, Masarka and Salaga (Lynes 1930, Lynes & Sclater 1934). Occurs Mole alongside *C. rufa* (Greig-Smith 1976a). No other records, but probably overlooked.

Breeding. Unrecorded, but is in breeding dress in wet season, Jun–Aug. In Nigeria, eggs in late Aug, fledgling in Oct (Elgood 1982).

541. EREMOMELA BADICEPS
(II.938)   Brown-crowned Eremomela   RB

Not uncommon resident (*E. b. fantiensis*) in middle and lower storeys of mature and secondary forest, forest edge and clearings, usually in small family parties. Occurs Begoro (C. M. Morrison), Mpraeso, Kade, Aburi, Tafo (L.G.G.) and Bia National Park (Taylor & Macdonald 1978b), but only occasional at Cape Coast (M. Macdonald).

Breeding. Adults with dependent young: Mpraeso, 27 Sep; Tafo, 28 Dec–2 Jan (L.G.G.).

542. EREMOMELA ICTEROPYGIALIS (=GRISEOFLAVA)
(II.933)   Yellow-bellied Eremomela   AfM?/(B)

Uncommon, possibly an African migrant (*E. i. alexanderi*) from the Sahel zone to northern savanna at end of the dry season, Feb–May, but records are too few to be certain. Recorded Mole on 4 dates in Aug, usually in small groups (Harvey & Harrison 1970), and singletons, 3–4 Apr (Taylor & Macdonald 1978a). Easily confused with *E. pusilla* and probably overlooked.

Breeding. Unrecorded. Birds in breeding condition in Mali, Jun and Jul, and Chad in Feb (MP&G).

543. EREMOMELA PUSILLA
(II.935)   Smaller Green-backed Eremomela   RB
Common resident (*E. p. pusilla*) of well wooded savanna throughout north, and south through the Volta Region to the Accra and Keta Plains and residential suburbs of Accra. Not recorded in forest clearings, absent from Cape Coast (M. Macdonald). Pre-dawn song markedly different from the daylight song (Grimes 1975a).
Breeding. Cooperative. Fledglings with more than 2 adults: Legon, 13 Apr, 11 Jun 1970, 16 Jun 1973, 7 Oct (Grimes 1972a, L.G.G.); Mole, Jul and Aug (Greig-Smith 1977b); Shai Hills, 15 Jun (L.G.G.), 29 May (M. Macdonald).

544. HIPPOLAIS ICTERINA
(II.871)   Icterine Warbler   PM
Rare Palaearctic migrant, although possibly overlooked. Netted at Denu, 1 May (Sutton 1965a). A skin collected at Aburi (Shelley & Buckley 1872) was subsequently lost from the BMNH (Bannerman 1939). A singleton at Mole, 4 Apr 1976 (Taylor & Macdonald 1978a).
A bird ringed in Belgium has been recovered in Ghana.

545. HIPPOLAIS PALLIDA
(II.872)   Olivaceous Warbler   PM
Uncommon, although regular, Palaearctic migrant (*H. p. opaca*) to scattered localities in northern savanna, Nov–Apr. Collected Gambaga, 4 Jan (Hartert 1899a), regular at Tumu early Nov to Feb (Sutton 1970), but at Bolgatanga occurs only Mar and Apr (F. Walsh). In the south only 4 records: singletons in suburbs of Accra, 14 and 27 Apr 1965, and at Achimota, 16 Jan and 14 Mar (M. Edmunds *in* Grimes 1972a).

546. HIPPOLAIS POLYGLOTTA
(II.870)   Melodious Warbler   PM
Uncommon Palaearctic migrant to northern woodland savanna. At Mole regular in small numbers, Oct–Apr, but confined to sites of abandoned villages where canopy is closed and higher than average (Greig-Smith 1977a). Scattered records elsewhere in north, Jan to early May (Walsh & Grimes 1981). Much more common in coastal areas, mid Oct to early Apr, particularly in older residential areas of Accra and Legon and on inselbergs. Occurs also in forest clearings at Tafo and Kumasi, Akropong in Akwapim and Anum (C. M. Morrison). Birds hold territories and song is heard from Oct. Collected Sekondi, Aburi, Ejura and Mampong in Ashanti (Lowe 1937).

547. HYLIA PRASINA
(II.1198)*   Green Hylia   RB
Common widespread resident (*H. p. superciliaris*) of undergrowth of mature and secondary forest throughout the forest zone, occasional in forest outliers, reaching Jasikan (F. Walsh) and regular in coastal thicket zone.
Breeding. Developing egg in ovary, 3 Jun (D. W. Lamm).
*Placed in Nectariniidae by Bannerman and MP&G.

548. HYPERGERUS ATRICEPS
(II.952)   Oriole Warbler (or Moho)   RB
Uncommon local resident of forest outliers in northern savanna zone, occurring south through the Volta region to inselbergs on the Accra Plains, but only occasional in coastal zone as far west as Elmina. Collected Accra, Pong, Cape Coast,

Elmina, Wassaw district near present day Tarkwa (Bannerman 1936), and Weija (D. W. Lamm).

Breeding. Nest construction: Weija, Jul (D. W. Lamm); Mole, Aug (Greig-Smith 1977b).

549. LOCUSTELLA LUSCINIOIDES
(II.876)   Savi's Warbler   PM

Rare Palaearctic migrant (*L. l. luscinioides*). Only recorded at Vea dam; 3 in rank vegetation in wetland, 4 and 6 Jan (Walsh & Grimes 1981). One collected, 6 Jan, was the nominate race; skin is now in BMNH.

550. MACROSPHENUS CONCOLOR
(II.948)   Grey Longbill   RB

Uncommon resident of undergrowth of mature and secondary forest throughout the forest zone. Collected Prahsu, Fumso and Kwissa (just south of Dompoasi) (Alexander 1902), Ejura, Goaso and Mampong in Ashanti (Lowe 1937). Occurs Cape Coast, (D. James, M. Macdonald) and Akropong in Akwapim (C. M. Morrison).

Breeding. End of Dec at Goaso, no details (Lowe 1937).

551. MACROSPHENUS FLAVICANS
(II.949)   Kemp's Longbill   R(B)

Resident of forest growth and probably not uncommon (*M. f. kempi*), but easily overlooked if calls are not known. Occurs regularly at Akropong in Akwapim (C. M. Morrison), and song recorded Atewa Forest Reserve on many occasions (L.G.G.). Singleton in mature forest at Bia National Park (Taylor & Macdonald 1978b).

Breeding. Unrecorded. In Liberia, female with yolks (6 and 8 mm) in ovary which was enlarged, Dec (Colston & Curry-Lindahl 1986).

552. PHOLIDORNIS RUSHIAE
(II.1199)   Tit-Hylia (Tiny Tit-Weaver)   RB

Not uncommon resident (*P. r. ussheri*) of lower canopy of mature and secondary forest throughout forest zone but also forest clearings, usually in family groups. Collected Fumso (Alexander 1902), Axim (W. P. Lowe *in* Bannerman 1949). Occurs in forest along southern scarp of the Volta basin, at Kumasi, Atewa Forest Reserve, Tafo, Aburi (L.G.G.) and Bia National Park (Taylor & Macdonald 1978b). Only occasional Cape Coast (M. Macdonald).

Breeding. Nest building: Bia National Park, 10 Apr (Taylor & Macdonald 1978b). Dependent fledglings: Aburi, 28 Dec; Tafo, Nov, late Dec, Jan; Atewa Forest Reserve, Dec, Jan (L.G.G.).

553. PHYLLOSCOPUS COLLYBITA
(II.896)   Chiffchaff   PM

Rare Palaearctic migrant (*P. c. collybita*), although probably overlooked. Netted Yegi, 6 Mar 1972 and one in song, 21 Feb, in a thicket clump near Teshie lagoon east of Accra (Wink 1976). Considered to occur at Mole, but identification not certain (Greig-Smith 1977a).

554. PHYLLOSCOPUS SIBILATRIX
(II.897)   Wood Warbler   PM

Probably not uncommon Palaearctic migrant, but easily overlooked as it keeps to the canopy at forest edges and clearings within mature and secondary forest, and also in well wooded savannas. Occurs on Accra Plains at Legon, Achomota and

Dodowa, Nov–Apr (Shelley & Buckley 1872, Grimes 1972a), at Akropong in Akwapim (C. M. Morrison), Tafo, Bia National Park (Taylor & Macdonald 1978b) and near Cape Coast (M. Macdonald). Song recorded from Nov onwards. At Pong Tamale in north, occurs only in spring, late Mar to early May (Walsh & Grimes 1981).

555. PHYLLOSCOPUS TROCHILUS
   (II.895)   Willow Warbler   PM
   Locally common resident (*P. t. trochilus*) to wooded savanna in north, mid Sep to early Apr (F. Walsh, Greig-Smith 1977a). Less common in forest clearings, but regular at Tafo (M. Lockwood), Akropong in Akwapim (C. M. Morrison) and in parklands, gardens and inselbergs on the Accra Plains. Only occasional at Winneba and not recorded at Cape Coast (M. Macdonald). Some song is heard at Legon from mid Oct onwards but is at its best Feb and Mar.
   A bird ringed in UK has been recovered in Ghana.

556. PRINIA (= HELIOLAIS) ERYTHROPTERA
   (II.988)   Red-wing Warbler   RB
   Not uncommon local resident (*P. e. erythroptera*) north and south of the forest region, occurring in overgrown cultivations, woodland savanna and areas with mixture of long grass and shrubs. Collected Accra, Cape Coast, Kete Kratchi, Gambaga and Salaga (Bannerman 1939). Occurs in the north at Tumu (Sutton 1970), and is common at Mole (Greig-Smith 1976a). Regular in western coastal areas on the Accra Plains and on inselbergs, but mainly only in wet season at Cape Coast (M. Macdonald).
   Breeding. Breeding dress: Legon, May and Jun; Mole, Jul. Nest building: Cape Coast, 3 Jun (M. Macdonald). Dependent fledglings: Accra Plains, May–Jul (Grimes 1972a, L.G.G.); Cape Coast, 13 Jun (M. Macdonald).

557. PRINIA SUBFLAVA
   (II.982)   Tawny-flanked Prinia   RB
   The most abundant resident warbler (*P. s. subflava*) throughout the northern savanna (F. Walsh, Sutton 1970, Greig-Smith 1976a). The southern race (*P. s. melanorhyncha*) is equally abundant in forest clearings, in the coastal thicket zone and on the Accra and Keta Plains.
   Breeding. Nest building: Accra, 23 May (Macdonald 1979b); Mole, Jul (Greig-Smith 1977b). Dependent young: Legon, Oct and Nov (L.G.G.).

   [SCHOENICOLA PLATYURA (= BREVIROSTRIS)
   (II.904)   Fan-tailed (Swamp) Warbler
   M. Macdonald sighted a bird which he is convinced was this species and not *Sphenoeacus mentalis,* in undergrowth in a forest clearing c. 40 km north of Cape Coast. As this is the only record and the species' known habitat in West Africa is montane grassland in Sierra Leone, Nigeria and Cameroun, the record is not included.]

558. SPHENOEACUS (= MELOCICHLA) MENTALIS
   (II.989)   Moustache-Warbler (Moustached Scrub-Warbler)   RB
   Not uncommon resident (*S. m. mentalis*) in northern savanna which contains a mixture of rank grass and shrubs, bordering irrigation dams and water courses. Regular at Mole (Greig-Smith 1976a), only occasional at Tumu, Dec and Feb (Sutton 1970). In the south, regular in wetter areas of the Accra Plains and on inselbergs, but sporadic at Winneba and no recent records at Cape Coast. In the

north, collected Sekwi(e), Daboya, Kete Kratchi, Gambaga, Ejura and Yegi (Alexander 1902, Lowe 1937), and in south at Pong, Accra and Cape Coast (Gordon 1847, Bannerman 1939).

Breeding. Nest building at Nakwa, 18 Jun (Macdonald 1979b).

559. SYLVIA ATRICAPILLA
(II.864)   Blackcap   PM

Rare Palaearctic migrant (*S. a. atricapilla*) although probably overlooked. Collected within forest region at Wenchi, 9 and 14 Jan, and in the vicinity of Lake Bosumptwi, 28 Feb (Lowe 1937). Singletons at Amedzofe, Dec (C. M. Morrison) and Tumu, 30 Nov (Sutton 1970).

560. SYLVIA BORIN
(II.863)   Garden Warbler   PM

Not uncommon Palaearctic migrant, often 3–4 feeding together, occurring regularly within forest zone at forest edge and in clearings, late Oct to late May (C. M. Morrison, M. Lockwood). Widespread in coastal thicket zone from Cape Coast eastwards to the western edge and inselbergs of the Accra Plains, Oct–Apr. One flew into a lighted window at Akropong in Akwapim at 2230 hrs, 6 Mar (C. M. Morrison). Fewer records in north, but regular at Mole (Greig-Smith 1976a, 1977a).

561. SYLVIA COMMUNIS
(II.862)   Whitethroat   PM

Uncommon Palaearctic migrant (*S. c. communis*), mainly to northern savanna. Recorded Tumu, Nov and Feb only (Sutton 1970), sporadically at Mole near marsh and in adjacent acacia scrub (Greig-Smith 1976a, 1977a), but is regular further north around Bolgatanga, early Dec to early Mar (F. Walsh). Collected Gambaga, 21 and 27 Jan, and Accra, 8 Feb (Bannerman 1939).

562. SYLVIETTA BRACHYURA
(II.925)   Crombec (or Nuthatch Warbler)   RB

Not uncommon local resident (*S. b. brachyura*) of woodland savanna throughout the north, ranging southwards via the Volta Region to inselbergs and drier thickets of the Accra Plains, but not further west. At Bolgatanga, only recorded Nov–Jan (F. Walsh).

Breeding. Nestlings and fledglings: Mole, Nov (Greig-Smith 1977b); Shai Hills, Mar (L.G.G.).

563. SYLVIETTA DENTI
(II.929)   Lemon-bellied Crombec   RB

Rare resident (*S. d. hardyi*) in undergrowth of secondary and mature forest. Collected Abrobonko, Fumsu, Kumasi and Mampong in Ashanti (Bannerman 1939). Netted Tafo (M. Lockwood) and sighted Bia National Park (Taylor & Macdonald 1978b).

Breeding. Holman describes a nest placed 12 m above ground at Kumasi, no dates (Bannerman 1939). In Liberia, a female had just laid, Sep (Colston & Curry-Lindahl 1986).

564. SYLVIETTA VIRENS
(II.928)   Green Crombec   RB

Not uncommon resident (*S. v. flaviventris*) of undergrowth of secondary and mature forest, also in plantations and forest edge, in coastal thicket zone and in thickets and inselbergs on the Accra Plains. Collected Axim, Sekondi, Kumasi,

Goaso and Prahsu (Bannerman 1939). Netted Tafo (M. Lockwood) and regular at Aburi and Akropong in Akwapim, at Anum, Begoro, and Amedzofe (C. M. Morrison).

Breeding. Nesting Kumasi, C/2 no dates (Bannerman 1939). Fledglings: Akropong, 24 Jan; Odumasi Krobo, Jan and Aug (C. M. Morrison).

Muscicapinae

565. ARTOMYIAS USSHERI
(II.752)   Ussher's Dusky Flycatcher   R(B)

Not uncommon forest resident at forest edge or in clearings, usually perched high on bare branch in canopy, often several together. Type collected Abrobonko (Ussher 1874); also collected at Fumsu, Kwissa (Alexander 1902), Aburi, Dunkwa and Mampong in Ashanti (Lowe 1937). Occurs north of Cape Coast (D. James), Bia National Park (Taylor & Macdonald 1978b), and throughout forest reserves in the Central Region (M. Horwood, D. W. Lamm).

Breeding. Unrecorded anywhere in West Africa.

566. BRADORNIS PALLIDUS
(II.739)   Pale Flycatcher   RB

Not uncommon resident (*B. p. modestus*) throughout woodland savanna of north, south through the Volta Region to inselbergs on the Accra Plains, in Akwapim hills (C. M. Morrison) and in coastal thicket at Winneba and Cape Coast (D. James, M. Macdonald), where it may be migratory (M. Macdonald). Type collected Abokobi on the Accra Plains (Shelley 1873) — not Kintampo as in Bannerman (1936), who is mistakenly followed by White (1963) and MP&G.

Breeding. Eggs: Atebubu, Apr (L.G.G.); Akropong, 28 May (C. M. Morrison); Shai Hills, eggs in ovary, 29 Apr (D. W. Lamm). Nestlings: Mole, May; Cape Coast, 16 May (Macdonald 1979b). Fledglings: Akropong, 8 May; Mole, Jul–Sep (Genelly 1968, Greig-Smith 1977b).

567. FICEDULA ALBICOLLIS
(II.727)*   White-collared Flycatcher   PM

Rare Palaearctic migrant (*F. a. albicollis*) to woodland savanna in north. Only 3 records in north: collected Gambaga, Nov and Jan (Hartert 1899a), and Bole, Jan (Lowe 1937). Also occasional in parkland on Accra Plains: singletons with *Muscicapa striata* 8 Oct 1970, 17 Nov 1970 and 23 Dec 1971 (Grimes 1972a).

*Named *Muscicapa albicollis* by MP&G.

568. FICEDULA HYPOLEUCA
(II.726)*   Pied Flycatcher   PM

Common Palaearctic migrant (*F. h. hypoleuca*), regular in woodland savanna in north, Oct to early May (F. Walsh, Greig-Smith 1977a), but only recorded in autumn at Tumu (Sutton 1970). Occasional Kumasi (F. C. Holman, B. Woodell) and in coastal areas at Cape Coast, Sep (R. B. Payne), Legon, 30 Dec, and Achimota, 27 Feb, 4 Mar and 17 Mar (M. Edmunds *in* Grimes 1972a). Easily confused with previous species in autumn.

*Named *Muscicapa hypoleuca* by MP&G.

569. FRASERIA CINERASCENS
(II.746)   White-browed Forest Flycatcher   RB

Resident of forest region, abundance uncertain as there are few records since the type was collected in "Fanti" (Hartlaub 1857). Regular Akropong in Akwapim (C. M. Morrison); probably overlooked.

Breeding. Nest construction: Akropong, Jan. Eggs: Akropong, 10 May. Dependent young: Akropong, 15 May (C. M. Morrison).

570. FRASERIA OCREATA
(II.745)   Forest Flycatcher   R(B)

Not uncommon widespread resident (*F. o. prosphora*) of both canopy and lower strata, often in groups of c. 5. Collected Prahsu, Fumsu and Kwissa (Alexander 1902). Frequent Atewa Forest Reserve (L.G.G.), in forest reserves north of Cape Coast (D. James) and in primary forest in Bia National Park (Taylor & Macdonald 1978b).

Breeding. Unrecorded. In Nigeria: female with egg in ovary, 31 Oct; dependent juvenile, 4 Oct (Elgood 1982).

571. MELAENORNIS EDOLIOIDES
(II.741)   Black Flycatcher   RB

Not uncommon resident (*M. e. edolioides*) of woodland savanna in north at Tumu (Sutton 1970) and Mole (Greig-Smith 1976a), south to Kete Kratchi and through the Volta region to inselbergs on the Accra Plains, also Akropong, Achimota and Weija (C. M. Morrison, Gass 1954). Occasional only Cape Coast (D. James) but no recent records (M. Macdonald). Regular Shai Hills, males in song, Jun–Oct (Grimes 1972a).

Breeding. Dependent young: Shai Hills, 28 Aug (L.G.G.); Mole, Jul (Greig-Smith 1977b); Gambaga, Jul (Hartert 1899a).

572. MUSCICAPA (= ALSEONAX) AQUATICA
(II.729)   Swamp Flycatcher   R(B)

Uncommon local resident (*M. a. aquatica*) in riverine habitat in north, regular Mole (Greig-Smith 1976a) in marshy areas, Sugu (F. Walsh), and collected Makongo (8°20'N, 0°38'W) — a village on road between Yegi and Salaga, probably now under the Volta Lake (Bannerman 1936); probably overlooked.

Breeding. Unrecorded. In Nigeria, nest thought to contain young, Mar (Elgood 1982).

573. MUSCICAPA CAERULESCENS (= ALSEONAX CINEREUS)
(II.736)   Ashy (or White-eyed) Flycatcher   R(B)

Resident (*M. c. nigrorum*) of forest edge and woodland, probably uncommon; few records and probably overlooked owing to similarity to others in the family. Collected in "Fanti" by Ussher, Aburi by Shelley and Kete Kratchi by Alexander (Bannerman 1936).

Breeding. Unrecorded. In Nigeria, building nest, Dec (Elgood 1982).

574. MUSCICAPA (= ALSEONAX) CASSINI
(II.735)   Cassin's Grey Flycatcher   R(B)

Not uncommon local resident at edges of streams, rivers and reservoirs within the forest region. Collected along Ancobra river (Burton & Cameron 1883), regular along most of the large rivers in Central Region and Kwahu (M. Horwood), at Tarkwa (Sutton 1970), and occasional at Brimsu reservoir, Cape Coast (L.G.G., M. Macdonald).

Breeding. Unrecorded. In Nigeria, Feb–Jun (Elgood 1982).

575. MUSCICAPA (= PEDILORHYNCHUS) COMITATA
(II.749)   Dusky Blue Flycatcher   RB

Not uncommon forest resident, widespread in secondary forest, forest edge and clearings. Collected Cape Coast (Shelley & Buckley 1872), Prahsu and Fumsu (Alexander 1902), Goaso (Lowe 1937), Axim, Kumasi and in Wassaw district, around Tarkwa (Bannerman 1936). Regular Akropong (C. M. Morrison), Akim Oda (M. Horwood), Tafo (M. Lockwood), Atewa Forest Reserve (N. Wood) and Bia National Park (Taylor & Macdonald 1978b).

Breeding. Regularly uses old nests of *Malimbus* species. Eggs: C/1, Akropong, 10 May. Active nests: Akropong, Jan, Mar, May, Jul (C. M. Morrison). Fledgling: Akropong, 12 Jun (M. Horwood).

576. MUSCICAPA (= ALSEONAX) EPULATA
(II.733)   Little Grey Flycatcher   R(B)

Uncommon resident of forest edge and clearing, widespread and usually in lower strata; also in gallery forest just north of forest/savanna boundary. Collected Aburi, Fumsu, Prahsu and near Tarkwa in Wassaw district (Bannerman 1936), and Ejura (Lowe 1937). Occurs Atewa Forest Reserve (N. Wood) and Tafo (F. Walsh).

Breeding. Unrecorded. Liberia, female with enlarged ovaries, Jan (Colston & Curry-Lindahl 1986).

577. MUSCICAPA GAMBAGAE
(II.725)*   Gambaga Dusky Flycatcher   R(B)

Uncommon resident of woodland savanna in north, few records. Easily confused with *Muscicapa striata*. Type collected at Gambaga (Alexander 1901), occasional Nangodi Bridge over Red Volta and Pong Tamale (F. Walsh), and possibly Mole (Taylor & Macdonald 1978a).

Breeding. Unrecorded anywhere in West Africa.

*Regarded as race of *Muscicapa striata* (II.725) by MP&G.

578. MUSCICAPA (= PARISOMA) GRISEIGULARIS
(II.737)   Grey-throated Tit-Flycatcher   RB

Recently discovered in Ghana, previously only known from east of the Niger (White 1963, Elgood 1982). Rare resident of mature forest and forest clearing, although probably overlooked previously due to similarity to other sympatric flycatchers. One adult and one juvenile collected in Cocoa plantation at Tafo, Feb (M. Lockwood), skins identified by BMNH. Also known now from Ivory Coast and Liberia (Thiollay 1985, Colston & Curry-Lindahl 1986).

Breeding. Previously unknown. Adult with young: Tafo, Feb (M. Lockwood). In Liberia, female with enlarged ovaries, Aug, Sep (Colston & Curry-Lindahl 1986).

579. MUSCICAPA (= ALSEONAX) OLIVASCENS
(II.730)   Olivaceous Flycatcher   R(B)

Rare resident of forest undergrowth, probably overlooked. Only one record; one collected in "Fanti" by Ussher (Bannerman 1936). Also occurs Ivory Coast and Liberia (Thiollay 1985, Colston & Curry-Lindahl 1986).

Breeding. Unrecorded. In Liberia, juvenile 14 Oct (Colston & Curry-Lindahl 1986).

580. MUSCICAPA STRIATA
(II.725)   Spotted Flycatcher   PM

Not uncommon Palaearctic migrant (only *M. s. striata* collected and identified, but *M. s. balearica* probably occurs). In north, mainly a passage migrant, regular in autumn, Sep–Oct (Sutton 1970, Greig-Smith 1977a, R. B. Payne). Overwinters in forest clearing at Kumasi, Jan–Apr (B. Woodell), but only occasional Tafo. Also in woodland on inselbergs and in older residential areas of Accra, Achimota and Legon (Grimes 1972a), and Akropong in Akwapim (C. M. Morrison). A passage migrant at Cape Coast (M. Macdonald). Apr records on Accra Plains probably involve birds on passage from further south (D. W. Lamm).

A bird ringed in UK has been recovered in Ghana.

581. MUSCICAPA (=PEDILORHYNCHUS) TESSMANNI
(II.750)   Tessmann's Flycatcher   R(B)

Rare forest resident, easily confused with sympatric *Muscicapa comitata*. Mainly known from skins collected Prahsu and Fumsu (Alexander 1902) and Goaso (Lowe 1937). Twice recorded Jukwa, near Cape Coast (M. Macdonald).

Breeding. Unrecorded anywhere in West Africa.

582. MYIOPARUS (=PARISOMA) PLUMBEUS
(II.738)   Grey Tit-Flycatcher   RB

Rare resident (*M. p. plumbeus*) of woodland savanna and riverine forest in north, e.g. Mole (Greig-Smith 1978a), occasional Tumu (Sutton 1970) and within forest clearings at Tafo (where one was netted in an overgrown vegetable garden — M. Lockwood), and Cape Coast (M. Macdonald). Collected Gambaga, Aug and Jan (Hartert 1899a) and Kete Kratchi (Alexander 1902).

Breeding. Juveniles: Mole, Jul (Greig-Smith 1977b).

Platysteirinae

583. BATIS MINIMA (=POENSIS*)
(II.764)   Fernando Po Puff-back Flycatcher   R(B)

Rare forest resident (*B. m. poensis*) of middle storey, although probably overlooked. Collected Sekondi and Aburi (Bannerman 1936). One recent sighting near Jukwa (M. Macdonald).

Breeding. Unrecorded. In Nigeria, males with enlarged testes, Jan and Jun (Elgood 1982).

*Now given specific status by Lawson (1984) as *Batis occultus*.

584. BATIS SENEGALENSIS
(II.770)   Senegal Puff-back Flycatcher   RB

Not uncommon resident, widespread in woodland savanna in north, often with *Eremomela*; regular Tumu (Sutton 1970) and Mole (Greig-Smith 1976a), and occurs Lawra, Kete Kratchi, Kintampo, Gambaga and White Volta Valley (Bannerman 1936, F. Walsh), as well as on inselbergs on Accra Plains, but unrecorded in coastal thicket zone (Grimes 1972a, M. Macdonald). Collected Ejura, Wenchi and Lawra, Jan–Feb (Lowe 1937).

Breeding. Female with egg in ovary: Shai Hills, 29 Apr (D. W. Lamm). Adult with dependent young: Mole, Aug and Sep (Greig-Smith 1977b).

585. BIAS MUSICUS
(II.759)   Black and White Flycatcher   RB

Not uncommon resident (*B. m. musicus*) of forest edge, clearings and thickets along streams within forest zone. Regular at Akropong (C. M. Morrison) and Weija (D. W. Lamm), also occurs Mampong in Ashanti (D. W. Lamm), Kumasi

(Holman) and occasionally inselbergs on Accra Plains (Grimes 1972a) and Jukwa (M. Macdonald).

Breeding. Female with egg in ovary: Mampong, 7 Mar (D. W. Lamm).

586. MEGABYAS FLAMMULATA
(II.758)   Shrike Flycatcher   RB

Not uncommon resident (*M. f. flammulata*) of undergrowth and middle storey of mature and secondary forest. Collected Aburi, Prahsu, Kintampo and in Akwapim (Bannerman 1936), and Ejura and Mampong in Ashanti (Lowe 1937). Regular Begoro and Amedzofe (C. M. Morrison, L.G.G., Sutton 1965b).

Breeding. Display flight: Amedzofe, Feb (L.G.G.). 2 breeding males collected Mampong, Feb (Lowe 1937). 2 females with one juvenile, collected 5 Mar (M. Horwood).

587. PLATYSTEIRA (= DYAPHOROPHYIA) BLISSETTI
(II.777)   Red-cheeked Wattle-eye   R(B)

Common widespread resident (*P. b. blissetti*) of dense undergrowth of mature and secondary forest and forest edge; also in coastal thicket zone and in thickets at Abokobi on the Accra Plains, and on some inselbergs. Bell-like song frequent Abokobi, Sep–Oct (Grimes 1972a) but also at other times. Type collected in Wassaw district near Tarkwa, others at Aburi (Bannerman 1936) and Ejura (Lowe 1937).

Breeding. Unrecorded. In Liberia, females with ova in ovaries, Apr (Colston & Curry-Lindahl 1986). In Nigeria, adults feeding young, Mar, and with juveniles, Jan (Elgood 1982).

588. PLATYSTEIRA (= DYAPHOROPHYIA) CASTANEA
(II.775)   Chestnut Wattle-eye   RB

Common widespread resident (*P. c. hormophora*) of lower storey in mature and secondary forest and forest edge. Collected Sekondi, Aburi, Prahsu, Fumsu (Alexander 1902, Bannerman 1936), and Mampong in Ashanti (Lowe 1937). Regular in forest clearings at Kumasi, Begoro, Anum, Mpraeso, Atewa Forest Reserve, Aduamoah (C. M. Morrison, L.G.G.), Kade (Sutton 1965b), Cape Coast, Atewa Forest Reserve and Bia National Park (Taylor & Macdonald 1978b).

Breeding. Adult with nesting material: Akropong, Dec (C. M. Morrison). Fledgling just out of nest: 21 Feb (Lowe 1937). Immature netted Sukuma Forest Reserve, 7 Jul (F. Walsh).

589. PLATYSTEIRA CONCRETA (= DYAPHOROPHYIA ANSORGEI)
(II.779)   Yellow-bellied Wattle-eye   R(B)

Rare resident (*P. c. concreta*) of forest undergrowth; only 2 records. Type thought to have been collected in Ghana (Hartlaub 1855a,b); a pair, the "brilliant orange-yellow throat and breast clearly visible in gloom", in lantana thicket near Lateh, 16 Oct (C. M. Morrison).

Breeding. Unrecorded. In Liberia, juvenile, 5 Feb (Colston & Curry-Lindahl 1986).

590. PLATYSTEIRA CYANEA
(II.771)   Wattle-eye   RB

Common resident (*P. c. cyanea*) of savanna woodland in north, and south through the Volta region to inselbergs on the Accra Plains, coastal mangroves and coastal thicket zone. Only occasional in some forest clearings, probably resident Sunyani and Kumasi (F. C. Holman, J. M. Winterbottom *in* Bannerman 1936), but not recorded Tafo (M. Lockwood).

Breeding. Dependent young/juvenile: Opintin Gallery Forest, 2 Nov (N. Wood); Mole, Aug (Greig-Smith 1977b); Cape Coast, 17 Jun (Macdonald 1979b).

Monarchinae

591. ERYTHROCERCUS MCCALLI
(II.755)   Chestnut-cap Flycatcher   RB

Not uncommon resident (*E. m. nigeriae*) of lower and middle storey of mature and secondary forest, usually in groups of 6–8 and often in mixed species flocks. Collected Kumasi, Goaso and Mampong in Ashanti (Lowe 1937, Bannerman 1953). Regular Agogo, Begoro, Mamfe (C. M. Morrison), in forest reserves in Kwahu district (L.G.G.), Tafo (M. Lockwood), Tarkwa (Sutton 1975b) and Bia National Park (Taylor & Macdonald 1978b); occasional Brimsu reservoir, Cape Coast (M. Macdonald).

Breeding. Family group with dependent young: Aduamoah, Jun (L.G.G.).

592. HYLIOTA FLAVIGASTER
(II.760)*   Yellow-bellied Flycatcher   R(B)

Uncommon resident (*H. f. flavigaster*) of the canopy of woodland savanna in north, regular Mole (Greig-Smith 1976a), occasional Tumu (Sutton 1970). Collected Gambaga, Kintampo (Alexander 1902), Ejura and Bole (Lowe 1937). Probably occurs through the Volta region — a pair collected in Shai Hills, 20 May (D. W. Lamm *in* Grimes 1972a). Often occurs with *Batis senegalensis*.

Breeding. Unrecorded, although a male had enlarged gonads, Shai Hills, 20 May (D. W. Lamm). In Nigeria, probably May–Jul (Elgood 1982).

*The genus *Hyliota* is placed in Sylviinae by Morony *et al.*, in Muscicapinae by Bannerman (1953), in Monarchinae, as given here, by White (1963), and in Muscicapidae by MP&G.

593. HYLIOTA VIOLACEA
(II.762)*   Violet-backed Flycatcher   R(B)

Not uncommon resident (*H. v. nehrkorni*) of middle storey of mature and secondary forest, particularly in open cultivated clearings such as cocoa farms. Type specimen labelled Accra (Hartlaub 1892); also collected Prahsu (Alexander 1902). Occurs throughout forests of the Central and Kwahu Regions (L.G.G.) and regular in reserves inland from Takoradi and Cape Coast (Macdonald & Taylor 1977). Known range extends to Liberia and Ivory Coast (Thiollay 1985, Colston & Curry-Lindahl 1986).

Breeding. Unrecorded anywhere in West Africa.

*See *Hyliota flavigaster*.

594. TERPSIPHONE (=TCHITREA) RUFIVENTER
(II.791)   Red-bellied Paradise Flycatcher   RB

Common resident (*T. r. nigriceps*) of lower storey and undergrowth of mature and secondary forest, cocoa plantations, forest clearings and forest edge, also riverine forest at Kete Kratchi (R. E. Crabbe). Collected Axim, Sekondi, Accra, Aburi, Fumsu and Prahsu (Alexander 1902, Bannerman 1936). Regular Akropong (C. M. Morrison), Cape Coast (M. Macdonald), Opintin Gallery Forest (N. Wood), Abokobi (L.G.G.), and netted Suhuma Forest Reserve (F. Walsh) and Achimota L.G.G.). At Bia National Park, a group of 12, Apr (Taylor & Macdonald 1978b).

Breeding. Female with egg in ovary: Mpraeso, 23 Apr (D. W. Lamm). Nest with young: Agogo, Apr (C. M. Morrison). Dependent juvenile: Opintin Gallery Forest, 8 Aug (N. Wood).

595. TERPSIPHONE (= TCHITREA) VIRIDIS
(II.787)   Paradise Flycatcher   RB, Afm
Common local resident (*T. v. ferreti*) of riverine forest in north, less common in
Volta Region and only occasional on inselbergs on the Accra Plains, at Legon and
Weija (D. W. Lamm *in* Grimes 1972a). Only recorded Tumu in wet season,
May–Jun (Sutton 1970). Not recorded in coastal thicket zone (M. Macdonald).
Breeding. Juvenile: Mole, Aug (Greig-Smith 1977b).

596. TROCHOCERCUS (= ERANNORNIS) LONGICAUDA
(II.780)*   Blue (Fairy) Flycatcher   RB
Not uncommon local resident (*T. l. longicauda*) of northern woodland savanna
and riverine forest, regular Mole (Greig-Smith 1976a), but not recorded Tumu
(Sutton 1970). Range extends south to inselbergs on the Accra Plains, sporadic
records covering both dry and wet season months (Grimes 1972a, L.G.G.). At Mole
perhaps less abundant in dry season (Taylor & Macdonald 1978a).
Breeding. Fledgling: Mole, Jul 1975 (Greig-Smith 1977b). In Nigeria, Jun–Aug in
Guinea zone (Elgood 1982).
*Placed in the genus *Elminia* by MP&G.

597. TROCHOCERCUS NIGROMITRATUS
(II.786)   Dusky Crested Flycatcher   R(B)
Resident, probably not uncommon in undergrowth of mature and secondary
forest; recently located Atewa Forest Reserve, Kakum Forest Reserve northwest of
Cape Coast, and Bia National Park (Macdonald & Taylor 1977). Now also known
from Liberia (Colston & Curry-Lindahl 1986) and Ivory Coast (Thiollay 1985).
Breeding. Unrecorded. In Cameroun, Apr (MP&G).

598. TROCHOCERCUS NITENS
(II.784)   Blue-headed Crested Flycatcher   R(B)
Rare resident (*T. n. reichenowi*) of forest undergrowth. Type collected "Fanti"
(Bannerman 1936); others collected Prahsu (Alexander 1902) and Mampong in
Ashanti (Lowe 1937). Occasional Akropong in Akwapim (C. M. Morrison); no
other records, but possibly overlooked.
Breeding. Unrecorded, although a male was in breeding condition, Mampong, 22
Feb (Lowe 1937). No records within West Africa.

REMIZIDAE

599. REMIZ (= ANTHOSCOPUS) FLAVIFRONS
(II.1101)   Yellow-fronted Penduline Tit   R(B)
Uncommon resident (*A. f. waldroni*) of lower storey of forest trees, but easily
overlooked and possibly more widespread and abundant than records suggest. Type
collected Goaso, feeding with numerous sunbirds (Nectariniidae), 15 Dec (Lowe
1937). Flock of 30 was disturbed in Kakum Forest Reserve feeding on debris from
old nests of the red ant *Oecophylla* sp. (Macdonald 1980e). Occurs in Liberia
(Colston & Curry-Lindahl 1986) and Ivory Coast (Thiollay 1985).
Breeding. Unrecorded. In Nigeria, breeding condition, Nov (Elgood 1982).

600. REMIZ (= ANTHOSCOPUS) PARVULUS
(II.1100)   Yellow Penduline Tit   RB
Not uncommon resident of northern savanna, regular Tumu (Sutton 1970) and
Mole (Greig-Smith 1976a), although numbers may diminish in some years at Mole
at end of the dry season (Taylor & Macdonald 1978a). No records in south, but

recently reported at the coast near Lome, on the Ghana/Togo border (Browne 1980).

Breeding. Nest building: Pong Tamale, Apr (F. Walsh). Female collected Bole, 10 Jan, had just finished laying (Lowe 1937).

PARIDAE

601. PARUS (= MELANIPARUS) FUNEREUS
(II.1096)   Dusky Tit   RB

Rare resident (*P. f. funereus*) of the upper storey of mature and secondary forest. Collected near Elmina, Sep 1861, by C. J. M. Nagtglas. Occurs Worobong Forest Reserve in Kwahu and Atewa Forest Reserve (Macdonald & Taylor 1977). No other records for Ghana, but known to occur in Ivory Coast (Thiollay 1985) and Liberia (Colston & Curry-Lindahl 1986).

Breeding. Dependent young: Worobong Forest Reserve, 20 Apr; Atewa Forest reserve, 21 May (Macdonald & Taylor 1977).

602. PARUS LEUCOMELAS (= MELANIPARUS NIGER)
(II.1094)   (White-shouldered) Black Tit   RB

Not uncommon resident (*P. l. guineensis*) usually in mixed flocks in savanna woodland in north, and south through Volta Region to Ho and inselbergs on the Accra Plains; no records in coastal thicket zone. Regular Tumu (Sutton 1970), Mole (Greig-Smith 1976a) and in northeast sector of Accra Plains (Grimes 1972a). Collected Wenchi, Bole and Ejura (Lowe 1937).

Breeding. Adults in breeding condition: Bole and Wenchi, Jan–Feb (Lowe 1937). Adults with dependent young: Gambaga, mid Apr (Alexander 1902); Mole, Jul (Greig-Smith 1977b).

CERTHIIDAE

603. SALPORNIS SPILONOTA
(II.1200)   Spotted Creeper   RB

Uncommon resident (*S. s. emini*) of woodland savanna in north, regular Mole (Greig-Smith 1976a), but at Tumu only late Sep to end Nov (Sutton 1970). Occasional Bole (Lowe 1937) and Kete Kratchi (D. W. Lamm). Collected Sekwi, Gambaga, Dokonkade (Alexander 1902) and Wenchi and Ejura (Lowe 1937).

Breeding. Female collected 14 Jan had 2 more eggs to lay (Lowe 1937).

NECTARINIIDAE

604. ANTHREPTES COLLARIS
(II.1188)   Collared Sunbird   RB

Common widespread resident (*A. c. subcollaris*) of secondary forest, forest edge and clearings, also in coastal thicket zone to western edge of Accra Plains at Abokobi, along Akwapim hills and on some inselbergs. Occasional in riverine forest just north of forest/savanna boundary, reaching Ejura.

Breeding. Extended. Nest building: Abokobi, 8 Mar; Shai Hills, 20 Jun; Opintin Gallery Forest, 26 Apr (N. Wood); Tafo, Oct (L.G.G.); Akwapim hills, Oct (C. M. Morrison). Eggs: C/2, Akropong in Akwapim, 2 Nov; Achimota, Jul (L.G.G.). Dependent young: Akropong, Aug, Dec (C. M. Morrison); Aburi, Nov and Feb (N. Wood, L.G.G.); Tafo, Jul (L.G.G.); Cape Coast, Apr (L.G.G.).

605. ANTHREPTES FRASERI
(II.1194)   Fraser's Scarlet-tufted Sunbird   R(B)
Locally not uncommon resident (*A. f. idius*) in canopy of mature and secondary
forest, easily overlooked. Collected Prahsu (Alexander 1902), Sunyani (J. M.
Winterbottom *in* Bannerman 1948) and near Mpraeso (M. Horwood). Common in
Bia National Park (Macdonald & Taylor 1978b).
Breeding. Unrecorded. In Nigeria, female in breeding condition, Apr and Nov
(Elgood 1982).

606. ANTHREPTES GABONICUS
(II.1197)   Brown Sunbird   R(B)
Not uncommon resident, mainly restricted to coastal mangrove and coconut
groves scattered along coast from the Volta River to Cape Coast (Grimes 1972a, D.
James); no recent records from Cape Coast (M. Macdonald). Occasional inland at
Opintin Gallery Forest (18 Jun — N. Wood) and Kete Kratchi (Alexander 1902).
Breeding. Unrecorded. In Nigeria, dry season, Jan (Elgood 1982).

607. ANTHREPTES LONGUEMAREI
(II.1191)   Violet-backed Sunbird   R(B)
Rare resident (*A. l. longuemarei*) of savanna woodland, little known. Several
collected Ejura, Jan–Feb (Lowe 1937). Occasional in acacia at Mole (Greig-Smith
1976a, F. Walsh); no other records.
Breeding. Male collected Ejura, 14 Feb, had just finished breeding (Lowe 1937). In
Nigeria, nest building, Feb and nestlings, 26 Feb (Elgood 1982).

608. ANTHREPTES (= HEDYDIPNA) PLATURA
(II.1156)   Pygmy Sunbird   AfM/(B)
Not uncommon intra-African migrant (*A. p. platura*) to northern savanna,
mainly mid Oct to Apr at Tumu (Sutton 1970) and Mole; but recorded 3 times Mole,
mid Aug (Harvey & Harrison 1970, Greig-Smith 1976a) and at Bolgatanga, end
Nov to mid Jan (F. Walsh).
Breeding. Unrecorded. In Nigeria, mostly Dec–Feb (Elgood 1982).

609. ANTHREPTES RECTIROSTRIS
(II.1189)   Green Sunbird   RB
Not uncommon resident (*A. r. rectirostris*), widespread in canopy of forest zone,
forest edge and clearings; regular Mpraeso (L.G.G.), and Tafo (M. Lockwood).
Collected near Tarkwa (Burton & Cameron 1883), Aburi (Shelley *in* Bannerman
1948), Goaso and Mampong in Ashanti, Dec–Feb (Lowe 1937).
Breeding. Female collected Goaso, 14 Dec, was incubating (Lowe 1937).

610. NECTARINIA (= CHALCOMITRA) ADELBERTI
(II.1175)   Buff-throated Sunbird   RB
Not uncommon resident (*A. a. adelberti*), widespread in mature and secondary
forest, forest edge and clearing, often feeding in *Bombax* spp., *Malacanthia olnifolia*
(Lowe 1937) and *Spathodia campanulata* (J. M. Winterbottom *in* Bannerman 1948).
Regular throughout the Akwapim Hills and southern scarp forests, in Central and
Ashanti Regions, and in forest clearings at Tafo (M. Lockwood) and Kumasi (B.
Woodell), although only Jan–Mar in Holman's day (Bannerman 1948). Occasional
in forests of the Western Region (Taylor & Macdonald 1978b) and outside forest
zone in wet season at Hohoe, Amedzofe (Sutton 1965b) and Legon (L.G.G).
Breeding. Nest building: edge of Lake Bosumptwi, 29 Dec (L.G.G.). Juveniles
moulting into adult plumage: Aug (M. Lockwood).

611. NECTARINIA (=CYANOMITRA) BATESI
(II.1183)   Bates' Sunbird   R(B)

Rare resident of forest zone; occasional at Jukwa (M. Macdonald), but probably overlooked through similarity with *N. seimundi*. No other records, but occurs Ivory Coast (Thiollay 1971, 1985) and in Nigeria (Elgood 1982).

Breeding. Unrecorded. In Nigeria, birds collected in breeding condition, Nov. Feb, Mar (Elgood 1982).

612. NECTARINIA (=CINNYRIS) CHLOROPYGIA
(II.1168)   Olive-bellied Sunbird   RB

The commonest forest sunbird (*N. c. kempi*), resident in secondary forest, forest edge and clearings and in coastal thicket zone; also at Abokobi and Dodowa and on inselbergs on the Accra Plains. Few records in forests of the southwest, only 2 in Bia National Park (Taylor & Macdonald 1978b).

Breeding. Nest building: Abokobi, 8 Mar; Shai Hills, 20 Jun, 20 Oct (L.G.G.); Tafo, Aug (M. Lockwood). Adults with dependent young: Akropong, 5 Sep, 24 Oct (C. M. Morrison); Aburi, 15 Feb (L.G.G.); Cape Coast, 12 Apr; Tafo, Feb and Sep (M. Lockwood).

613. NECTARINIA (=CINNYRIS) COCCINIGASTER
(II.1160)   Splendid Sunbird   RB

Common resident in coastal thicket zone, in residential areas of Accra and Legon, and on inselbergs on the Accra Plains (Grimes 1974c). Less common in north, regular Mole (Greig-Smith 1976a) and occurs Kintampo (Alexander 1902) and White Volta valley (F. Walsh); but rare Tumu: singletons 20 Oct and 16 Jan (Sutton 1970). No records from within forest zone. A large series collected Ejura, Wenchi and Goaso (Lowe 1937).

Breeding. In most months at Legon. Nest building: Legon, Jan, Mar, Apr, Dec. Eggs: C/2, Legon, Mar, Apr, Jun, Sep, Oct, Dec; Cape Coast, 17 Oct (M. Macdonald). Dependent young: Legon, Mar, Apr, May, Oct, Nov (L.G.G.); Cape Coast, Jul (M. Macdonald).

614. NECTARINIA (=CINNYRIS) CUPREA
(II.1159)   Copper Sunbird   RB

Common resident (*N. c. cuprea*) of coastal thicket zone and Accra Plains, extending northwards through Volta Region to savanna woodland. Mainly resident in north, e.g. Tamale and Mole (Greig-Smith 1976a), but seasonal Tumu, only in wet season, Jun–Sep (Sutton 1970).

Breeding. Males in breeding dress: Legon, late Feb to Oct (Grimes 1972a); Mole, Mar–Nov (Greig-Smith 1977b). Eggs: C/2, Legon, Jun and Jul (L.G.G.); Cape Coast, probably May–Sep (Macdonald 1979b). Dependent juveniles: Legon, May, Jun (L.G.G.).

615. NECTARINIA (=CYANOMITRA) CYANOLAEMA
(II.1181)   Blue-throated (Brown) Sunbird   R(B)

Not uncommon resident (*N. c. octaviae*) of mature and secondary forest, forest edge and clearing, regular Cape Coast (M. Macdonald), Tafo (M. Lockwood) and Mpraeso (L.G.G.). Occasional in woodland savanna at Mole in wet season, 12 Aug (Harvey & Harrison 1970), and Tamale (F. C. Holman *in* Bannerman 1948). Data for Mole omitted by Greig-Smith (1976a).

Breeding. Unrecorded. In Liberia, female with an enlarged ovary, Aug (Colston & Curry-Lindahl 1986).

616. NECTARINIA (=CHALCOMITRA) FULIGINOSA
(II.1172)   Carmelite Sunbird   R?(B)

Rare, possibly resident (*N. f. aurea*); previously confined to mangroves and cocoa plantations at mouth of Volta River and eastwards to Togoland, but no records since Ussher's day (Sutton 1970, Grimes 1972a, M. Macdonald) when moderately common; 8 collected along the Volta.

Breeding. Unrecorded. In Nigeria, nesting, 30 Nov; juveniles with adults, Oct and Nov (Elgood 1982).

617. NECTARINIA (=CINNYRIS) JOHANNAE
(II.1158)   Madame Verreaux's (=Johanna's) Sunbird   R(B)

Very rare resident (*N. j. fasciata*) of forest canopy and forest edge, mainly known from skins. Collected Fumsu and Prahsu (Alexander 1902), "Fanti" and "Denkera" (Ussher 1874) and Aburi (Shelley & Buckley 1872). Occurs in cocoa plantations at Tafo and netted there in garden (M. Lockwood), also Subri River Forest Reserve (M. F. Hodges, Jr).

Breeding. According to MP&G, Jun, but source not traced; no other records in West Africa (Bannerman 1953).

618. NECTARINIA (=CINNYRIS) MINULLA
(II.1169)   Tiny Sunbird   R(B)

Resident of forest clearings, but abundance uncertain due to similarity in field to *N. chloropygius,* probably rare. Only 2 old records: an immature collected by Aubinn for Ussher; another collected Aburi by T. E. Buckley, 21 Feb 1872, skin initially identified as *N. chloropygius* (Bannerman 1953).

Breeding. Unrecorded. Cameroun, Apr–Jun (MP&G).

619. NECTARINIA (=CYANOMITRA) OLIVACEA
(II.1182)   Olive Sunbird   RB

Common resident (*N. o. guineensis*) of coastal thicket zone, undergrowth of mature and secondary forest, forest edge and clearings, and thickets near Abokobi on the Accra Plains. Regular Kumasi (F. C. Holman *in* Bannerman 1948), Cape Coast (M. Macdonald) and Tafo (M. Lockwood); also occurs Sunyani (J. M. Winterbottom), Amedzofe and Bia National Park (Taylor & Macdonald 1978b). Collected Abrobonko (Ussher 1874), Aburi (Shelley & Buckley 1872), and Goaso, Lake Bosumptwi and Mampong in Ashanti, Dec–Feb (Lowe 1937).

Breeding. Fledglings: Tafo, May–Jul (M. Lockwood, L.G.G.).

620. NECTARINIA PULCHELLA
(II.1154)   Beautiful Sunbird   RB, Afm

Common resident (*N. p. pulchella*) of the savanna woodland and dry thorn scrub in north. Regular at Gambaga (Alexander 1902, L.G.G), Mole (Greig-Smith 1976a) and Bolgatanga (F. Walsh), but only seasonal at Tumu, Apr–Jun (Sutton 1970). Bannerman (1948) states that "Shelley secured specimens from within six miles of Cape coast". This record cannot be traced and the data are not included in the Atlas of Hall & Moreau (1970).

Breeding. Males in breeding dress in north, Apr–Oct. Nests: Mole, Jul–Sep (Greig-Smith 1977b).

621. NECTARINIA (=ANABATHMIS) REICHENBACHII
(II.1185)   Reichenbach's Sunbird   ?

Rare vagrant, status unknown. Recorded in mangrove swamp, 4 km west of Elmina, 24 Oct 1982 and along the edge of the River Hwini near Takoradi, 25 Sep

1982 and 5 May 1983 (M. F. Hodges, Jr). Ussher collected 2 at the mouth of the Volta (Sharpe 1870b, Bannerman 1948). Data used by White but not by Hall & Moreau (1970). In Nigeria, resident along rivers and lagoons in coastal areas from Lagos eastwards to the Congo (Elgood 1982, MP&G); occurs Ivory Coast (Eccles 1985).

622. NECTARINIA (=ANTHREPTES) SEIMUNDI
(II.1196)   Little Green Sunbird   R(B)

Uncommon resident (*N. s. kruensis*) of forest canopy and forest edge, mainly known from skins. Collected Sekondi. Axim, Ejura and Mampong (Lowe *in* Bannerman 1912a, Lowe 1937), Abrobonko and at 2 unknown sites earlier by Ussher (Bannerman 1948). Occurs Jukwa (M. Macdonald); no other recent records.

Breeding. Unrecorded, although a male was in breeding condition, Mampong, 21 Feb (Lowe 1937). In coastal Cameroun, adults in breeding condition, Jul and Nov (MP&G).

623. NECTARINIA (=CHALCOMITRA) SENEGALENSIS
(II.1176)   Scarlet-chested Sunbird   RB

The commonest sunbird of the woodland savanna north of the forest zone. Abundant and resident (*N. s. senegalensis*), often in feeding flocks of 20 in dry season. Collected at many sites in north, regular in gardens and cultivations of larger towns. Occasional in Shai Hills and other inselbergs on Accra Plains, in both wet and dry season (D. W. Lamm, Grimes 1972a); once at Cape Coast (D. James).

Breeding. Nest building: Pong Tamale, 31 Mar (F. Walsh). Eggs: C/2, Navrongo, 6 May (F. Walsh). Dependent young: Mole, mid Jul to late Aug (Greig-Smith 1977b); Mampong in Ashanti, 30 Sep (L.G.G.).

624. NECTARINIA (=CINNYRIS) SUPERBA
(II.1157)   Superb Sunbird   RB

Not uncommon resident (*N. s. ashantiensis*) of forest canopy and lower storeys, forest clearings and forest edge. Regular Mpraeso (L.G.G.), Kumasi (F. C. Holman), Sunyani (J. M. Winterbottom), Tafo (M. Lockwood), Kade (Sutton 1965b) and along Akwapim Hills (C. M. Morrison). Occurs Amedzofe and occasional Cape Coast (M. Macdonald). Collected Prahsu and Kwissa (Alexander 1902), Goaso, Ejura and Mampong in Ashanti (Lowe 1937) and earlier by Ussher (1874). Only one record in Bia National Park (Taylor & Macdonald 1978b) and once with *N. coccinigaster* at Legon, 7 Nov 1964 (M. Edmunds *in* Grimes 1972a).

Breeding. Nesting: Ashanti, end of Feb (Lowe 1937). Nest building: Mpraeso, Oct, Nov (L.G.G.). Eggs, C/2, Mpraeso, 10 Nov (L.G.G.). Juveniles: Tafo, Aug (M. Lockwood).

625. NECTARINIA (=CINNYRIS) VENUSTA
(II.1164)   Variable (Yellow-bellied) Sunbird   R(B)

Uncommon resident (*N. v. venusta*) of woodland savanna north of forest zone, regular Walewale (Sutton 1965b), but only occasional Mole (Greig-Smith 1976a). Male in breeding dress, Nov. Occasional at coast near Denu in wet season, May (Sutton 1965a). No other records.

Breeding. Unrecorded. In Nigeria, Oct–Jan; juveniles Lagos, May–Jul (Elgood 1982).

626. NECTARINIA (=CYANOMITRA) VERTICALIS
(II.1178)   Green-headed (or Olive-backed) Sunbird   RB

Uncommon local resident (*N. v. verticalis*) of coastal thicket zone, occurring from Axim eastwards to garden suburbs of Accra and Legon, and inselbergs on Accra

Plains. Regular Legon and Shai Hills (Grimes 1972a), but only occasional Cape Coast (M. Macdonald), although more regular in Ussher's day. In north less common, irregular Mole (Greig-Smith 1976a) and near Zongoiri in White Volta valley (F. Walsh).

Breeding. Copulation: Legon, 7 Oct (L.G.G.). Juveniles: Mole, Nov (Greig-Smith 1977b); Shai Hills, 30 Nov (L.G.G.).

ZOSTEROPIDAE

627. ZOSTEROPS SENEGALENSIS
(II.1141)   Yellow White-eye   RB

Common resident (*Z. s. senegalensis*), often in flocks of 5–10, in savanna woodland in north. Regular Mole, Tumu and Pong Tamale, also south through the Volta Region to Accra Plains on inselbergs and in parkland. Occurs throughout the coastal thicket zone and in larger forest clearings, e.g. Tafo (M. Lockwood), Kumasi and main towns along Akwapim hills (C. M. Morrison).

Breeding. Dependent young: Akropong in Akwapim, Jan and Jun (C. M. Morrison).

EMBERIZIDAE

628. EMBERIZA CABANISI
(II.1363)   Cabanis' Bunting   RB, Afm

Not uncommon resident (*E. c. cabanisi*), widespread in woodland savanna and in riverine habitat in north. Regular Mole, numbers increasing in dry season (Greig-Smith 1976a, 1977a), and Gambaga escarpment (L.G.G.). Collected Gambaga, Kintampo, Masarko, Sekwi, Kete Kratchi (Hartert 1899a), near Yendi (D. W. Lamm) and Mole (Fry 1970).

Breeding. Adults carrying food: Mole, early Sep (Greig-Smith 1977b).

629. EMBERIZA FORBESI
(II.1365)   Brown-rumped (Little) Bunting   R(B), Afm?

Not uncommon resident (*E. f. nigeriae*), widespread in abandoned cultivations and sparsely wooded savanna of north. Resident at Mole (Greig-Smith 1976a), but in some years fewer records at end of dry season suggest local emigration (Taylor & Macdonald 1978a).

Breeding. Unrecorded in West Africa.

630. EMBERIZA (=FRINGILLARIA) TAHAPISI
(II.1369)   (Cinnamon-breasted) Rock-Bunting   RB, Afm/B

Not uncommon resident (*E. t. goslingi*) of rocky outcrops in the far north, e.g. Bongo hills, Gambaga escarpment (M. Horwood, F. Walsh), but further south at Mole only a dry season breeding migrant (Greig-Smith 1976a). Collected Gambaga area (Hartert 1899a, Alexander 1902) and Lawra (Lowe 1937).

Breeding. Nesting: Gambaga and Lawra, Jan (Alexander 1902). Female with egg in ovary: 16 Jan (Lowe 1937).

FRINGILLIDAE

631. SERINUS (=POLIOSPIZA) GULARIS
(II.1353)   Streaky-headed Seed-eater   R(B)

Not uncommon resident (*S. g. canicapilla*) in savanna with scattered trees, widespread in north, often in millet and in flocks of c. 30 in Jan and Feb (Lowe 1937). Collected Bole, Tumu and Ejura (Lowe 1937).

Breeding. Unrecorded. In Nigeria, breeding condition, Jul (Elgood 1982).

632. SERINUS (= POLIOSPIZA) LEUCOPYGIUS
(II.1355)   White-rumped Seed-eater   R(B)

Uncommon resident (*S. l. riggenbachi*) of the far northern savanna, regular at Vea dam and Bolgatanga, in flocks of c. 30 in Mar and Apr; song in Jul (F. Walsh). These, the first records for Ghana, may indicate a recent southwards extension of its range. No other records.

Breeding. Unrecorded. In Nigeria, eggs, Jul, Aug and Dec (Elgood 1982).

633. SERINUS MOZAMBICUS
(II.1348)   Yellow-fronted Canary   RB

Common resident (*S. m. caniceps*), widely distributed throughout the northern savanna and found in most villages as a cage bird. Records at Kumasi are probably escapes as there are no other records within the forest region. Regular in Volta Region and south to woodlands and inselbergs on the Accra Plains. No records in coastal thicket zone west of Accra.

Breeding. Nest building: Mole, May. Courtship feeding: Mole, Aug. Dependent juveniles: Mole, Aug and Nov (Greig-Smith 1977b).

ESTRILDIDAE

634. AMADINA FASCIATA
(II.1302)   Cut-throat   AfM?/(B)

Status uncertain, possibly a dry season migrant (*A. f. fasciata*) to the drier open savanna of the far north; only 4 certain records: a male netted in garden at Tumu school, 23 Jan (Sutton 1970), a flock of 19 at Bolgatanga, 15 Jan 1973 (F. Walsh) and twice recorded in far north, 10–18 Feb 1983 (M. F. Hodges, Jr). Stated by Bannerman (1953) to occur in Ghana, but not in Bannerman (1949) and source of information has not been traced. Bannerman's data not used by Hall & Moreau (1970).

Breeding. Unrecorded. In Nigeria at Zaria, Jan (Elgood 1982).

635. AMANDAVA (= ESTRILDA) SUBFLAVA
(II.1334)*   Zebra Waxbill   R?(B), Afm?

Status uncertain as there are surprisingly few records, but possibly a not uncommon local resident (*A. s. subflava*) in moist grass savanna. Only recently recorded from Ghana, but undoubtedly overlooked (Bannerman 1953: 1483). In the south, 40 in a flock in cassava plantation at Denu, 19 May, and regular there Jun (Sutton 1965b); numerous at Atsutsuare, 29 Jan 1977 on the Accra Plains (M. Macdonald). In the north, c. 20 at Sugu, 9 May 1971, and 2 at Bolgatanga, 15 Jan 1973 (F. Walsh).

Breeding. Unrecorded. In Nigeria, eggs, Nov; adults with juveniles, Jan (Elgood 1982).

*Named *Neisna subflava* in MP&G.

636. ESTRILDA ASTRILD
(II.1323)   Waxbill   R?(B)

Status uncertain as records are few. Possibly local resident (*E. a. occidentalis*) in northwest savanna near border with Ivory Coast where it is widespread in the Guinea savanna zone (Thiollay 1985). Bannerman (1948, 1953), followed by White

(1963) and Goodwin (1982), accepted the records of J. M. Winterbottom, who considered it abundant at Kumasi within larger forest clearings, often in flocks of 20 or more and at Sunyani. The records need specimens for confirmation, but probably refer to *E. troglodytes*; they were not included in MP&G nor in Hall & Moreau (1970). The record at Denu by Sutton (1965b) is also open to question as he did not record *E. troglodytes* there. At Tumu, however, he recorded both *troglodytes* and *astrild*, the latter only once, 3 on 12 Feb. No other records.

Breeding. Unrecorded. In Cameroun, Nov (MP&G).

637. ESTRILDA (= URAEGINTHUS) BENGALA
(II.1339)   Red-checked Cordon-bleu   RB

The commonest resident astrild in north (*E. b. bengala*), widespread throughout the northern savanna zone, abundant Tumu (Sutton 1970), Tamale, Mole (Greig-Smith 1976a) and Bolgatanga (F. Walsh). Dalziel's (1922: 7) records for the Accra Plains may have been of escaped caged birds, for there are no recent records. Many collected Mole (Fry 1970).

Breeding. Nest building: Mole, May, Jul–Sep (Greig-Smith 1977b). Eggs: C/4 Mole, 28 Sep; Tamale, Aug (F. C. Holman). Egg in oviduct, Aug (Greig-Smith 1977b).

638. ESTRILDA (= LAGONOSTICTA) CAERULESCENS
(II.1322)   Red-tailed Lavender Waxbill (= Lavender Fire-Finch)   R(B)

Not uncommon resident in grassland savanna with scattered bushes or trees, also in abandoned farms. Regular Mole (Greig-Smith 1976a), in the Bongo Hills and Sisali valley (F. Walsh), but only occasional Tumu, Jan and Feb (Sutton 1970). Collected Gambaga, 30 Jul (Hartert 1899a), Bongo Hills, 19 Dec (D. W. Lamm) and Mole (Fry 1970).

Breeding. Unrecorded. In Nigeria, flocks and juveniles, Dec (Elgood 1982).

639. ESTRILDA LARVATA (= LAGONOSTICTA NIGRICOLLIS)
(II.1319)   Black-faced Fire-Finch   R(B)

Not uncommon resident (*E. l. togoensis*), widespread in north in grass savanna, abandoned farms and in rank growth near edge of water. Regular Mole (Greig-Smith 1976a) and Tumu (Sutton 1970). Collected Gambaga (Hartert 1899a, Alexander 1902), Ejura, Binduri, Bokonkade, Musarka (Alexander *in* Bannerman 1949), Bole, Lawra and Wa (Lowe 1937), Tamale reservoir and Tuluwe (M. Horwood) and Mole (Fry 1970). Occasional in forest clearings; collected Kumasi (Alexander *in* Bannerman 1949) and occurs Cape Coast, Sep and Nov (R. B. Payne).

Breeding. Unrecorded. In Nigeria, eggs Jul and Aug (Elgood 1982).

640. ESTRILDA MELPODA
(II.1327)   Orange-cheeked Waxbill   RB, Afm

The commonest estrild finch, an abundant resident occurring in northern savanna, forest clearings, coastal thicket zone and on Accra and Keta Plains. Often in flocks of c. 50 in Jul and Aug. Local movements occur in coastal thicket zone; numbers increase in Dec and remain high until Feb (Macdonald 1979a). Partial migrant Mole, numbers increasing in wet season (Greig-Smith 1977a).

Breeding. Dependent juveniles: Akropong in Akwapim, 3 Aug (C. M. Morrison); Mole, Nov (Greig-Smith 1977b).

641. ESTRILDA TROGLODYTES
(II.1325)   Black-rumped Waxbill   RB, Afm/B

Uncommon resident (*E. t. troglodytes*) in open grass savanna in north at Tumu

(Sutton 1970), Pong Tamale and in Red Volta Valley (F. Walsh), but not recorded Mole (Greig-Smith 1976a). Regular in thicket zone and on inselbergs on the Accra Plains, occasionally absent Jan and Feb (Gass 1954) — a wet season breeding visitor to coastal thicket zone, Mar–Nov (Macdonald 1979a). Collected Karaga, Kete Kratchi (Alexander 1902), near Dodowa, 22 Feb, and Ada, 22 Jun (D. W. Lamm).

Breeding. Nesting Cape Coast, May–Sep (Macdonald 1980a). Juveniles: Accra Plains, Aug and Sep (Gass 1954).

642. HYPARGOS (= MANDINGOA) NITIDULUS
(II.1308)   Green-backed Twin-spot   R(B)

Uncommon resident (*H. n. schlegeli*) of undergrowth of mature and secondary forest, often near water. Collected in "Fantee" by Nagtglas (Bannerman 1949), Mampong in Ashanti (Lowe 1937) and a specimen labelled Accra (Bannerman 1949). Netted Suhien sewage farm (M. Lockwood), Kumasi, May, and Cape Coast, 14 Jan (Gass 1954), and Bia National Park (C. Martin *in* Macdonald & Taylor 1977).

Breeding. Unrecorded. In Liberia, female with large ovary, Sep; juveniles, Sep (Colston & Curry-Lindahl 1986).

643. LAGONOSTICTA RARA
(II.1320)   Black-bellied Fire-Finch   R(B)

Not uncommon resident (*L. r. forbesi*) in northern savanna grassland with scattered trees and shrubs; also abandoned farms. Regular Mole, where common (Greig-Smith 1976a), and Sisali valley (F. Walsh). In south, occasional in coastal thicket zone; one in Opintin gallery forest west of Accra, 23 May (N. Wood), and thought to occur in thicket near Abokobi (Grimes 1972a). Collected Mole (Fry 1970).

Breeding. Unrecorded. In Nigeria, eggs in Jul; eggs in oviduct, Oct (Elgood 1982).

644. LAGONOSTICTA RUBRICATA
(II.1313)   African (Blue-billed) Fire-Finch   RB

Not uncommon resident (*L. r. polionota*), widespread in undergrowth of forest edge, clearings and along streams within forest region, occasional in Guinea Savanna zone. Regular at Cape Coast (Gass 1954, M. Macdonald), occasional Achimota and Weija (Gass 1954, D. W. Lamm) and Abokobi (Grimes 1972a). Type collected Cape Coast (Shelley 1873); also collected Ejura (Lowe 1937), Mampong in Ashanti (D. W. Lamm) and netted Suhien sewage farm (M. Lockwood). Only 2 records in northern savanna; one Mole, 21 Jul (Harvey & Harrison 1970), although not included by Greig-Smith (1976a); occasional Nakpanduri scarp (Sutton 1965b).

Breeding. Nest building: Cape Coast, 5 Jun 1976 (Macdonald 1979b). Female with eggs in ovary: 26 Jun 1955 (D. W. Lamm).

645. LAGONOSTICTA RUFOPICTA
(II.1317)   Bar-breasted Fire-Finch   RB

The most abundant resident fire-finch (*L. r. rufopicta*) in northern woodland savanna and in coastal thicket zone from Axim to the Accra Plains. Regular in gardens and farms at Legon and in suburbs of Accra, and in larger forest clearings. Collected in south at Axim, Sekondi and Cape Coast, and in north at Dokonkade (Alexander 1902) and Mole (Fry 1970).

Breeding. In south, is the host of *Vidua wilsoni,* nesting Cape Coast, May–Sep (Macdonald 1980a). Eggs: C/5 Opinten gallery forest, 25 Jul (N. Wood). Eggs in oviduct: Winneba, 27 Mar (D. W. Lamm); Mole, late Aug. Dependent young: Legon, Jun–Oct (Grimes 1972a, L.G.G.); Tafo, Aug (M. Lockwood).

646. LAGONOSTICTA SENEGALA
    (II.1316)   Red-billed (= Senegal) Fire-Finch   R(B)
Abundant resident (*L. s. senegala*), widespread in dry savanna woodland in north, also in farms and within villages. Regular Bolgatanga (F. Walsh), Tamale (F. Walsh) and Tumu (Sutton 1970). Collected Mole (Fry 1970), where in some years, numbers are fewer at end of dry season (Taylor & Macdonald 1978a). Reports sent to Bannerman (1949), suggested that *senegala* was widespread in coastal towns, but these must refer to *L. rufopicta,* although D. W. Lamm found it occasionally at Weija and along the Accra/Winneba road. Similarly, the record of *senegala* at Lome on the coast (Browne 1980) may probably be incorrect and should be *rufopicta,* for Browne doesn't include *rufopicta* in his list.
    Breeding. Unrecorded. In Nigeria, mainly May–Oct (Elgood 1982).

647. LONCHURA BICOLOR (= SPERMESTES POENSIS)
    (II.1278)   Black and White (Blue-billed) Mannikin   RB
Common resident (*L. b. bicolor*) of forest clearings and forest edge in tall grass, bushes and cultivations, often with *Lonchura cucullata*. Regular Akropong in Akwapim, Odumasi Krobo on Accra Plains (C. M. Morrison), Winneba, Cape Coast (M. Macdonald), Tafo (M. Lockwood), Abetifi and Amedzofe (L.G.G.). Collected Prahsu (Alexander 1902), Goaso (Lowe 1937), Elmina and Aburi (Bannerman 1949).
    Breeding. Nesting: Prahsu, Aug (Bannerman 1949); Akropong in Akwapim, Mar–Aug (C. M. Morrison). Egg in oviduct, Mampong in Ashanti, 3 Apr and 26 Jun (D. W. Lamm). Dependent young, Cape Coast, Jul and Aug (Macdonald 1979b). Juveniles: Tafo, Oct and Nov (M. Lockwood); Cape Coast, Oct–Dec (Macdonald 1979b).

648. LONCHURA (= SPERMESTES) CUCULLATA
    (II.1277)   Bronze Mannikin   RB
Common, often abundant resident (*L. c. cucullata*) throughout, often in family groups of c. 10. Widespread in coastal thicket zone, Accra and Keta Plains, within forest clearings, and throughout the northern Guinea savanna zone in farms, near villages and gardens of towns.
    Breeding. Extended, possibly in every month. Eggs: C/4, C/6 Cape Coast (Macdonald 1979b). Nesting Cape Coast, Mar–Jul (Macdonald 1980a). Dependent young: Legon, May, Jun and Oct–Jan (Grimes 1972a, L.G.G.); Tafo, Oct and Nov (M. Lockwood); Mole, Aug and Nov (Greig-Smith 1977b).

649. LONCHURA (= AMAURESTHES) FRINGILLOIDES
    (II.1280)   Magpie Mannikin   RB
Uncommon resident of forest edge and clearings, often with *L. bicolor* and *L. cucullata,* but less common then either. Regular Tafo (M. Lockwood), Kade (F. Walsh, L.G.G.), occasional Cape Coast (M. Macdonald) and Kumasi (F. C. Holman *in* Bannerman 1949). Has occurred in riverine forest at Asukawkaw, 3 Aug (F. Walsh).
    Breeding. Egg in oviduct: Akwatia, 8 Apr (D. W. Lamm). Juveniles: Cape Coast, 29 Oct (Macdonald 1979b); Kade, 10 Jul (F. Walsh).

650. LONCHURA MALABARICA (= EUODICE CANTANS)
    (II.1281)   Silver-bill   RB, Afm?
Uncommon local resident (*L. m. cantans*) in far north in rocky grassland savanna with scattered trees. Regular Bolgatanga, Mar–Nov and Jan (F. Walsh) and collected Bongo Hills, 17 Dec (D. W. Lamm). Occurs Tumu end of Sep and in

dry season (Sutton 1970), and Mole in Jan (Macdonald 1978d); these data suggest a movement southwards at end of the rains.

Breeding. Copulation: Bolgatanga, 25 Oct; Incubation: 3 Apr (F. Walsh). Nesting: under eaves of bungalow at Bawku, 14 Dec (M. Horwood).

651. NESOCHARIS CAPISTRATA
(II.1336)   Grey-headed Olive-back   R(B)

Rare local resident, mainly in riverine forest north of the forest/savanna boundary. Records are few: collected Kete Kratchi (B. Alexander, Dr Klose *in* Bannerman 1949); sporadic Mole (Greig-Smith 1976a).

Breeding. Unrecorded. In Nigeria, nest building, Jun and Jul (Elgood 1982).

652. NIGRITA BICOLOR
(II.1286)   Chestnut-breasted Negro-Finch   RB

Not uncommon resident (*N. b. bicolor*), widespread in lower storey of mature and secondary forest, forest clearings and forest edge. Collected Axim, Anum, Abrobonko, Sekondi, Aburi and Odumasi Krobo (Bannerman 1949), Goaso and Mampong in Ashanti (Lowe 1937). Occurs Tarkwa (Sutton 1965b), Tafo (M. Lockwood), Akropong in Akwapim, Amedzofe (C. M. Morrison), Subri River Forest Reserve (M. F. Hodges, Jr) and Bia National Park (Taylor & Macdonald 1978b); occasional Cape Coast (M. Macdonald).

Breeding. Nest building: Tafo, Mar and Apr (M. Lockwood); Mampong in Ashanti, Feb (Lowe 1937). Eggs: C/4 Kumasi, no date (F. C. Holman *in* Bannerman 1949); egg in oviduct Mampong in Ashanti, 20 Mar (D. W. Lamm). Juveniles: Tafo, Sep and Oct (M. Lockwood).

653. NIGRITA CANICAPILLA
(II.1284)   Grey-headed Negro-Finch   RB

Common resident (*N. c. emiliae*) of lower and middle storey, occasionally coming to ground, in mature and secondary forest, also forest clearings, forest edge, and in oil palm and cocoa plantations (G. S. Cansdale). Type collected "Fanti", others at "Denkere" (Ussher 1874), Aburi (Shelley & Buckley 1872), Prahsu, Dunkwa (Alexander 1902), Sekondi, Axim, Ejura, Goaso and Mampong in Ashanti (Lowe 1937). Regular Tafo (M. Lockwood), Cape Coast (M. Macdonald), Amedzofe (Sutton 1965b, L.G.G.), Subri River Forest reserve (M. F. Hodges, Jr) and Bia National Park (Taylor & Macdonald 1978b).

Breeding. Nesting: Mampong in Ashanti, Dec–Feb (Lowe 1937). Fledglings: Amedzofe, 22 Feb (L.G.G.); Tafo, Nov (M. Lockwood).

654. NIGRITA FUSCONOTA
(II.1287)   White-breasted Negro-Finch   RB

Uncommon resident (*N. f. uropygialis*), mainly in middle and upper storey of mature and secondary forest, but also undergrowth in forest clearings and riverine forest. Type collected "Fanti", other specimens at Mampong in Ashanti, Feb (Lowe 1937). Occurs Tafo (M. Lockwood), Amedzofe (L.G.G.), Ateiku in Central Region (M. Horwood), Subri River Forest Reserve (M. F. Hodges, Jr) and Bia National Park (Taylor & Macdonald 1978b); occasional Cape Coast (M. Macdonald).

Breeding. Nesting: Mampong in Ashanti, Feb (Lowe 1937).

655. NIGRITA LUTEIFRONS
(II.1285)   Pale-fronted Negro-Finch   ?

Status and abundance uncertain, possibly overlooked since it is very similar in the field to *N. canicapilla,* which is more common. Only one record; 2, probably a pair

(*N. l. luteifrons*), foraging in low secondary growth in partial clearing in forest at Amedzofe (Macdonald 1980e). Serle *et al.* (1977: 252) lists Ghana within its range, but source of their data has not been traced.

Breeding. Unrecorded. Cameroun, Jun; Fernando Po, Oct (MP&G).

656. ORTYGOSPIZA ATRICOLLIS
(II.1303)   Quail-Finch   RB

Not uncommon local resident in open sparsely grassed areas of coastal thicket zone and on Accra Plains (Grimes 1972a); race not known but possibly *O. a. ansorgei* which occurs in coastal areas from Guinea to Ivory Coast. In northern savanna *O. a. atricollis* occurs Tumu (Sutton 1970) and was collected at Gambaga (Alexander 1902); no other records there, but probably overlooked.

Breeding. Nesting: Tema at coast, Aug (Grimes 1972a).

657. PARMOPTILA WOODHOUSEI
(II.1282)   Flower-pecker Weaver-Finch   R(B)

Rare resident (*P. w. rubrifrons*) of lower storey in mature and secondary forest, often in mixed species foraging flocks. Type collected in "Denkere" by Aubinn (Shelley & Ussher 1872). Occurs in the forests of Ashanti (G. S. Cansdale *in* Bannerman 1953), Atewa Forest Reserve (L.G.G.), Subri River Forest Reserve (M. F. Hodges, Jr) and Kakum Forest Reserve (Macdonald & Taylor 1977). Previously thought to be restricted to Ghana, but now located on Mt Nimba (Colston & Curry-Lindahl 1986).

Breeding. Unrecorded. On Mt Nimba, Liberia: female with egg in oviduct, Apr; probably in breeding condition, Sep (Colston & Curry-Lindahl 1986).

658. PIRENESTES OSTRINUS
(II.1295–1296)*   Black-bellied Seed-cracker   RB

Not uncommon resident (*P. o. ostrinus*), widespread in undergrowth of mature and secondary forest, forest clearings and forest edge, often near water. Usually in pairs but occasionally flocks of 5–6. Regular at Atewa Forest Reserve (L.G.G.), Opintin Gallery Forest, west of Accra (N. Wood), and Tafo (M. Lockwood). Occurs in residential areas of Kumasi, May and Jun (Gass 1954), and occasionally Abokobi, Kwabenya (Grimes 1972a), Cape Coast (M. Macdonald) and Subri River Forest Reserve (M. F. Hodges, Jr). Collected Bibiani and Mampong in Ashanti (Lowe 1937); juvenile netted in *Motacilla flava* roost at Tafo (M. Lockwood).

Breeding. Nest building: Bibiani, 30 Oct (M. Horwood). Several nests with either eggs or nestlings, Opintin Gallery Forest, Aug (N. Wood).

*White does not separate *P. o. rochschildi* from *P. o. ostrinus,* which has a wider bill. Bannerman (1953) does, but MP&G treat them as separate species, *P. ostrinus* (1295 = Black-bellied Seed-cracker) and *P. rothschildi* (1296 = Rothschild's Seed-cracker).

659. PYTELIA HYPOGRAMMICA
(II.1310)   Yellow-winged Pytelia   R(B)

Rare local resident in thickets of coastal zone, also in savanna woodland in north. Type collected by Higgins in "Fanti" (Sharpe 1870a); also collected Abokobi (Shelley & Buckley 1872) and at Gambaga in north (Hartert 1899b). Occurs in Akwapim Hills, Opintin Gallery Forest — 8 together 20 Mar and 2 on 3 May (N. Wood); also at Teshie and on inselbergs on Accra Plains (D. W. Lamm, Grimes 1972a).

Breeding. Unrecorded. In Nigeria, C/3 Enugu, 18 Jan (Elgood 1982).

660. PYTELIA PHOENICOPTERA
(II.1309) Red-winged Pytelia   R(B)

Uncommon local resident (*P. p. phoenicoptera*) of grassland savanna with scattered shrubs and trees in Guinea Savanna zone. Sporadic Tumu, Nov, Dec and Feb (Sutton 1970), Sugu, Jan, Feb and Apr (F. Walsh). Collected Gambaga (Hartert 1899a, Alexander 1902) and at edge of Tamale reservoir, 2 on 21 Dec, 1 on 5 Jan (M. Horwood).

Breeding. Unrecorded. Nigeria, eggs Nov–Feb; egg in oviduct, 8 Sep (Elgood 1982).

661. SPERMOPHAGA HAEMATINA
(II.1291) Blue-bill   RB, Afm

Common resident (*S. h. haematina*) of undergrowth in mature and secondary forest, forest clearing and forest edge. Type collected c. 1805 in Ghana, others collected Prahsu (Alexander 1902), Mampong in Ashanti (Lowe 1937) and many other localities (Bannerman 1939). Regular at Opintin gallery forest (N. Wood), Bia National Park (Taylor & Macdonald 1978b) and in riverine forest in northeast sector of Accra Plains (Grimes 1972a). Occurs Amedzofe (Sutton 1965b), Dixcove (Sutton 1970), Weija, Worawora and Akropong (C. M. Morrison), Tafo (M. Lockwood), Korforidua (M. Horwood), Winneba and Cape Coast (D. James, M. Macdonald). 2 males killed by flying into a window pane during daylight hours suggest that local movements may occur: one was on Legon Hill, Feb 1966, the other in the Agricultural Department of the University of Ghana, 4 May (L.G.G.).

Breeding. Eggs: Opintin gallery forest, early Jun (N. Wood). Nestlings: Tafo, Sep (M. Lockwood).

PLOCEIDAE

Bubalornithinae

662. BUBALORNIS ALBIROSTRIS
(II.1201) Buffalo-Weaver   RB

Uncommon local resident (*B. a. albirostris*) confined to the Black Volta valley in the northwest extending south as far as Wa (F. Walsh).

Breeding. Breeding colonies: Lawra, 13 Oct 1956 (M. Horwood), 31 Oct 1968 (Sutton 1970); Bimbile, 12 Oct 1956 (M. Horwood); more recently 7 colonies located between Wa and Lawra, no date (F. Walsh).

Passerinae

663. PASSER GRISEUS
(II.1207) Grey-headed Sparrow   RB

Abundant local resident (*P. g. griseus*) in all coastal towns and villages and in many of the major towns throughout the forest region, also throughout the northern savanna where much more widespread today than previously. In 1900, Alexander located it as far north as Salaga, but not at Gambaga or elsewhere in the north. In contrast today, it is regular Bolgatanga, Tamale (F. Walsh), Tumu (Sutton 1970) and Mole, where numbers increase in the dry season (Greig-Smith 1977a), probably as a result of feeding flocks. Penetration into the forest zone has probably been via railways and major roads (C. M. Morrison *in* Bannerman 1949). In 1942 occurred Akropong and Bosusu in the Akwapim Region, but not to the north at Begoro, Anum, Worawora or Agogo (C. M. Morrison). Regular today in these towns, also Tafo (M. Lockwood).

Breeding. Nesting: Cape Coast in wet season, c. May–Jul (Macdonald 1979b); Tafo, where it uses old nests of *Hirundo abyssinica,* May (M. Macdonald); Legon, May (L.G.G.). Fledglings: Achimota, 26 Jan; Tafo, Jun; Legon, 19 Aug (L.G.G.).

664. PETRONIA (= GYMNORIS) DENTATA
    (II.1211)   Bush Petronia (Bush Sparrow)   RB, Afm?

Abundant local resident in the drier savanna with scattered trees and shrubs. The commonest bird at Tumu (Sutton 1970), regular Bolgatanga (F. Walsh), but considered a partial migrant at Mole where numbers increase in dry season (Greig-Smith 1977b), although this increase may be merely due to flocking and feeding. Collected Gambaga (Hartert 1899a), Karaga, Walewale (Alexander 1902) and Bole (Lowe 1937).

Breeding. Pairs entering nest holes: near Lawra, 24 Nov 1956 (M. Horwood); Bolgatanga, 3 Dec 1970 (F. Walsh). Carrying feather Bolgatanga, 19 Nov 1972 (F. Walsh).

665. PLOCEPASSER SUPERCILIOSUS
    (II.1203)   Chestnut-crowned Sparrow-Weaver   RB, Afm

Not uncommon resident of woodland savanna throughout north. Regular Mole (Greig-Smith 1976a), Bolgatanga (F. Walsh), Gambaga escarpment, but partial migrant Tumu where numbers increase in breeding season (Sutton 1970). Collected Gambaga, Masarka (Hartert 1899a, Alexander 1902) and Mole (Fry 1970). No records in south; Bannerman's (1949) reference to a specimen collected at Pong on the Accra plains by Alexander is not in the latter's 1902 paper and is omitted by Hall & Moreau (1970).

Breeding. Nest building: Mole, May to early Nov (Greig-Smith 1977b).

666. SPOROPIPES FRONTALIS
    (II.1212)   Speckled-fronted (Scaly-fronted) Weaver   R?B, Afm?/B

Status unknown (*S. f. frontalis*); only recorded recently (1975), at Mole, Oct–Dec (R. B. Payne, C. J. Risley *in* Greig-Smith 1976a). Usual range is in latitudes north of Ghana and this represents a southward extension.

Breeding. Nests: Mole, Oct 1975 (Greig-Smith 1977b).

Ploceinae

667. AMBLYOSPIZA ALBIFRONS
    (II.1260)   Grosbeak Weaver   Afm/B

Locally not uncommon (*A. a. capitalba*), seasonal and mainly confined to coastal thicket zone and larger forest clearings. Movements not completely clear. Occurs Cape Coast region, Jun to late Sep (exceptionally one on 25 Mar), with flock movements from northern sector in early Jun and westwards in Sep (Macdonald 1979a). Occurs Subri River Forest Reserve late Sep to late Nov and Mar (M. F. Hodges, Jr). Present Abokobi on Accra Plains, Feb–Jun, males in fresh breeding plumage May and Jun (Grimes 1972a), and Kumasi, May to at least Sep (Bannerman 1949, Gass 1954). Collected Cape Coast and Accra by Haynes (Bannerman 1949), Ejura on the Afram river, 30 Jan, the only record north of the forest zone (Lowe 1937), and netted Tafo, Nov (M. Lockwood). Birds probably first arrived at Kumasi in c. 1933 (F. C. Holman *in* Bannerman 1949). Stated by Macdonald (1979b) to occur within forest zone mainly Dec–Mar, but no details given and this is not consistent with all available data.

Breeding. Usually breeds in loose colonies, occasionally singly. Nest building: Kumasi, late Sep 1934 (Bannerman 1949). Eggs: Cape Coast, Aug (Macdonald

1979b); Kumasi, abandoned nest with egg, Sep (Bannerman 1949); Korforidua, Aug 1956 (M. Horwood). Nestlings: Korforidua, Aug (M. Horwood).

668. ANOMALOSPIZA IMBERBIS
(II.1306)   Parasitic Weaver   ?
Rare, status unknown. Only 2 records. In the north, a pair in a dry river bed at Sugu, 10 May 1971 (F. Walsh); in the south, one in thicket near Abokobi on Accra Plains, 23 May 1976 (M. Macdonald).
Breeding. Unknown in West Africa. Known to parasitise warblers (*Cisticola, Prinia*) and other small passerines.

669. EUPLECTES AFER (= AFRA)
(II.1270)   Yellow-crowned Bishop   RB
Common resident (*E. a. afer*) in marshy grassland, particularly near open stretches of water. Occurs within the coastal thicket zone, Accra and Keta Plains, and throughout the northern savanna, but not within forest clearings. Males in breeding dress: Panbros, Apr–Sep (Grimes 1972a); Denu from mid May (Sutton 1965b); Cape Coast from mid Apr (Macdonald 1979b); Tumu, Jun–Oct (Sutton 1970); Vea dam, mid Jul to mid Oct (F. Walsh), Mole, mid Jul to Sep (Greig-Smith 1977b).
Breeding. In wet season. Nest building and breeding territories: Mole, Aug (Greig-Smith 1977b). Nesting Accra Plains, Jun and Jul (L.G.G.).

670. EUPLECTES (= COLIUSPASSER) ARDENS
(II.1275)   Red-collared Widow-bird   ?
Status unknown, few certain records. One collected Wenchi (*E. a. concolor*) from a flock of mixed weaver species (Lowe 1937); also reported common, mid Oct, near Sunyani (J. M. Winterbottom), both records accepted as *E. ardens* by Bannerman (1949), but not included by Hall & Moreau (1970), who also exclude Bannerman's (1949) Togo data. The only other record is a singleton seen at Ankaful, near Cape Coast, 22 Feb 1977 (M. Macdonald).
Breeding. Nigeria, copulation, Oct; young just flying, Oct (Elgood 1982).

671. EUPLECTES HORDEACEUS (= HORDACEA)
(II.1266)   Black-winged Red Bishop   RB
Common resident (*E. h. hordeaceus*), scattered throughout the coastal thicket zone, Accra Plains, Volta Region and northern Guinea Savanna zone, in tall grass with scrub, cultivations, and often near water. Also in some larger forest clearings, e.g. Kumasi. Regular Mole (Greig-Smith 1976a) and Cape Coast, although males in breeding dress leave Cape Coast mid Jul and return in Oct and Nov (Macdonald 1979b). Seasonal Kumasi, Mar–Oct, and Tumu, Sep–Oct (Sutton 1970), but none Wenchi (Lowe 1937) nor Bolgatanga (F. Walsh), nor at Denu on the Keta Plains (Sutton 1965b). Only once at Tafo, male in breeding dress netted Dec (M. Lockwood). Often in mixed flocks with *Euplectes orix* but less common than *E. orix*.
Breeding. Nests in wet season. Males in breeding dress: Legon, Apr to late Oct (Grimes 1972a); Cape Coast, from late Apr (Macdonald 1979b). Active nests: west of Takoradi, 25 Jul, 6 Aug (M. Horwood). The departure of males still in breeding dress might mean that they first breed at the coast and then follow the rains northwards to breed elsewhere (Macdonald 1979b), a suggestion which also applies to males of *E. orix* and *E. macrourus,* both of which leave coastal areas while still in breeding dress.

672. EUPLECTES (= COLIUSPASSER) MACROURUS
(II.1272)   Yellow-mantled Widow-bird   RB, Afm

Common resident (*E. m. macrourus*), widespread in marshy areas with scrub and small trees throughout the coastal thicket zone, the Accra and Keta Plains, and northwards through the Volta Region to the northern savanna. Absent from forest clearings. Regular Mole (Greig-Smith 1976a), but seasonal Tumu, Sep–Jan and Jun and Jul (Sutton 1970) and mainly wet season at Sugu (F. Walsh). Some males in breeding dress leave coastal area in mid Jul and return in Oct and Nov (for possible implications see *E. hordaceus*). Outside breeding season forms mixed flocks (Lowe 1937, Greig-Smith 1978d).

Breeding. Nesting in wet season. Breeding dress: Accra Plains, late Mar to late Oct; Mole, Jul–Nov; Cape Coast, mid Apr to mid Oct.

673. EUPLECTES ORIX
(II.1265)   Red Bishop   RB

Common abundant resident (*E. o. franciscanus*) in grassland with shrubs and small trees, marshy areas with *Typha* and in cultivations, widespread throughout the coastal thicket zone, Accra and Keta Plains, and northwards through the Volta Region to the Guinea Savanna zone. Regular Accra Plains (Grimes 1972a), Tumu (Sutton 1970), Mole (Greig-Smith 1976a) and Bolgatanga (F. Walsh), seasonal Cape Coast (see *E. hordaceus* for details — Macdonald 1979b). Males in partial breeding dress form flocks of 100 or more in Aug on Accra Plains. More common than *hordaceus* and *macrourus*.

Breeding. Breeding dress: Accra Plains, mid Apr to mid Oct (Grimes 1972a); Cape Coast, from mid Apr (Macdonald 1979b); Mole, mid Jul to Sep (Greig-Smith 1977b). Eggs: Mole, Aug (Greig-Smith 1977b); Tamale, C/3 Aug; Nungua, nests in *Typha,* 16 Jun (L.G.G.).

674. MALIMBUS CASSINI
(II.1251)   Black-throated Malimbe   R?(B)

Status uncertain, but probably rare resident; few records only, all recent: at least 3 males feeding on fruit with *M. rubricollis, M. scutatus* and other species Tafo, 25 Jul 1976; 7 nests with entrance tunnels of lengths in the range 60–88 cm (mean 73 cm) collected at Tafo were thought to be of this species — the mean length for nests of *M. scutatus* is only 39 cm; and twice recorded Subri River Forest Reserve, 25 Dec 1976 and 6 Feb 1977 (Macdonald & Taylor 1977). Also another at Tafo, 30 Jan 1978) (F. Walsh, M. Macdonald). These records extend the previously known range of this weaver westwards by some 1100 km.

Breeding. Unrecorded other than the evidence of the nests.

675. MALIMBUS MALIMBICUS
(II.1248)   Crested Malimbe   R(B)

Not uncommon resident (*M. m. nigrifrons*) of lower storey in mature and secondary forest, widespread throughout forest zone. Collected Cape Coast, Aburi, Fumsu, Prahsu, and a skin marked Accra (Bannerman 1949). Regular Kade (Sutton 1965b), Subri River Forest Reserve (M. F. Hodges, Jr) and Tafo (M. Lockwood); occasional Cape Coast (M. Macdonald), Amedzofe (Sutton 1965b) and occurs Bia National Park (Taylor & Macdonald 1978b).

Breeding. Unrecorded. In Nigeria, nest building and juveniles, Feb (Elgood 1982).

676. MALIMBUS NITENS
(II.1250)   Gray's Malimbe (= Blue-billed Weaver)   RB

Common resident in lower storey, widespread in secondary and primary forest,

forest edge and clearings, often in oil palm near water. Regular in Akwapim hills, Kade, in gallery forest in coastal thicket zone, Tafo, Cape Coast, Kumasi, Subri River Forest Reserve (M. F. Hodges, Jr) and Bia National Park (Taylor & Macdonald 1978b). Collected at many locations throughout the forest zone (Bannerman 1949).

Breeding. Small colonies, 3–8 pairs; nests very often over water. Eggs: Opintin Gallery forest, 9 Oct (N. Wood); near Korforidua, 28 Sep. Fledgling just out of nest: Wenchi, 20 Jan (Lowe 1937).

677. MALIMBUS RUBRICEPS (= ANAPLECTES MELANOTIS)
(II.1259)   Red-headed Weaver   RB
Uncommon local resident (*M. r. leuconotus*) of northern woodland savanna. Regular along the Gambaga escarpment (L.G.G., Sutton 1965b), Pong Tamale (L.G.G.); occasional Mole, but not recorded Tumu nor Bolgatanga.

Breeding. Often nests in association with raptorial birds (Walsh & Walsh 1976). New nests: Buipe, no date (F. Walsh); Nakpanduri, 1 Apr 1963 (L.G.G.); Tampiong reservoir north of Tamale, 20 Dec 1956; Yapei, pairs at 3 nests, 10 Jan 1957 (M. Horwood).

678. MALIMBUS RUBRICOLLIS
(II.1249)   Red-headed Malimbe   RB
Common resident (*M. r. bartletti*) of middle and upper storey, widespread in secondary and mature forest. Regular Cape Coast (M. Macdonald), Akropong (C. M. Morrison), Kade and Amedzofe (Sutton 1965b), Abetifi (L.G.G.); occasional Tafo clearing (M. Lockwood), and near Hohoe in woodland savanna (Sutton 1965b). Collected at many sites throughout the forest zone (Bannerman 1949).

Breeding. Nest building: Mpraeso, 1 Nov 1968 (L.G.G.); Amedzofe, 31 Dec. Active nests: Aduamoah, Mar 1964 (L.G.G.).

679. MALIMBUS SCUTATUS
(II.1253)   Red-vented Malimbe   RB
Common resident (*M. s. scutatus*) of lower and middle storey, widespread in mature and secondary forest and forest edge, also gallery forest in coastal zone. Occurs Tafo (M. Lockwood), Akropong (C. M. Morrison), Kade and regularly at Subri River Forest Reserve (M. F. Hodges, Jr) and Bia National Park (Taylor & Macdonald 1978b). Collected at many sites within the forest zone (see Bannerman 1949). The wet season record at Mole (Harvey & Harrison 1970) is not accepted by Greig-Smith (1976a).

Breeding. Nest building: Dodowa, Mar (L.G.G.). Completed nest with adults present Tafo, Dec (M. Lockwood). Female had just finished laying Goaso, 30 Dec (Lowe 1937).

680. PLOCEUS (= MELANOPTERYX) ALBINUCHA
(II.1247)   White-naped Weaver   RB
Not uncommon resident (*P. a. albinucha*) of middle and upper storey of mature and secondary forest and forest clearing. Occurs in forests along the southern scarp of the Volta basin, in reserves north of Cape Coast (D. James) and occasionally at Cape Coast (M. Macdonald). Collected at Prahsu and Fumsu (Alexander 1902) and obtained Mampong in Ashanti (Lowe 1937).

Breeding. Immature: Mampong in Ashanti, 18 Feb (Lowe 1937). Dependent young: Tafo, Nov (L.G.G.).

681. PLOCEUS (= XANTHOPHILUS) AURANTIUS
(II.1229)   Orange Weaver   RB

Uncommon local resident (*P. a. aurantius*) confined to mangroves and coastal vegetation from Axim to Cape Coast, where it is rare (D. James, M. Macdonald, M. F. Hodges, Jr). First located Axim (Lamm & Horwood 1958) and then Cape Coast by Gass (1954) — data overlooked by Hall & Moreau (1970).

Breeding. Colony containing 100s of nests with eggs and young on island off Axim, Jun 1951 (Lamm & Horwood 1958). Nest building: Cape Coast, Jul (Gass 1954). 3 colonies in vicinity of Cape Coast 1977, no date (M. Macdonald).

682. PLOCEUS (= PLESIOSITAGRA) CUCULLATUS
(II.1213)   Black-headed Village Weaver   RB

Abundant resident (*P. c. cucullatus*) in villages and towns throughout the coastal and forest zones, also through the Volta Region to the northern savanna, but less abundant in north than in south.

Breeding. Nest building in any month, but peak is early part of wet season, Feb–Mar in south and later in north. Colonies with eggs and young: Legon, Mar–Apr and again Oct–Nov (Grimes 1972a); Mole, Jul–Aug (Greig-Smith 1977b).

683. PLOCEUS (= PLESIOSITAGRA) HEUGLINI
(II.1216)*   Heuglin's Masked Weaver   RB

Uncommon resident in woodland savanna in north, occurs Tamale (F. C. Holman *in* Bannerman 1949), Vea dam (F. Walsh), Mole (Greig-Smith 1976a), and collected Wenchi (Lowe 1937), Kete Kratchi (Count Zech) and Kumasi (Alexander 1902). Regular in suburbs of Accra, Legon and on inselbergs on the Accra Plains. Absent from coastal thicket zone west of Accra. Its distribution overlaps that of *P. velatus* both in the north and on the Accra Plains.

Breeding. Nests in association with the Red Weaver Ant *Oecophylla smaragdina* (Grimes 1973b). Males are polygamous, and usually in colonies containing 6–20 males. Nesting: Accra Plains, mainly Mar–Jul but also other months (Grimes 1973b). Eggs: Tamale, 24 Jul.

*Named *P. atrogularis* by MP&G.

684. PLOCEUS (= SITAGRA) LUTEOLUS
(II.1230)*   Little Weaver*   RB, Afm

Not uncommon resident (*P. l. luteolus*) of the drier woodland savanna in north. Regular Mole (Greig-Smith 1976a) and Bolgatanga (F. Walsh), but a partial migrant Tumu, early Oct to mid May (Sutton 1970). Occurs east of Lawra (W. P. Lowe *in* Bannerman 1949) and north of Tamale, although F. C. Holman initially identified it as *P. pelzelni* (Bannerman 1949, 1953).

Breeding. Active nests: Mole, Mar, Jul and Aug; C/2 Tumu, 19 Oct (Sutton 1970). Juveniles: Mole, Nov (Greig-Smith 1977b).

*Named *Sitagra luteola* by MP&G. Bannerman's English name is Slender-billed Weaver which is used by MP&G for *P. (= Sitagra) pelzelni.*

685. PLOCEUS MELANOCEPHALUS (= SITAGRA CAPITALIS)
(II.1220)   Black-headed Weaver   R?(B)

Status unknown, possibly resident. Only one record: at least 2 pairs in marsh at motel in Mole, one pair collected, wet season 1968 (Harvey & Harrison 1970). Record accepted by Greig-Smith (1976a), but not recorded there by Aberdeen students.

Breeding. Unrecorded. In Nigeria, mainly Jul–Oct, also May (Elgood 1982).

686. PLOCEUS NIGERRIMUS (=CINNAMOPTERYX CASTANEOFUSCUS)
(II.1245)*   Chestnut and Black Weaver   RB

Abundant common resident (*P. n. castaneofuscus*) in forest clearings near villages, in oil palm plantations, and in marshy habitats throughout forest zone; also edge of Accra Plains at Abokobi and near Dodowa and Odumasi Krobo (Grimes 1972a, L.G.G.).

Breeding. Colonial, often with *P. cucullatus* and at Cape Coast with *P. aurantius*. Nesting in main rains, but nest building in any month. Eggs: Jan–Jul. Juveniles: Tafo, Aug and Sep (M. Lockwood).

*Named *Melanopteryx castaneofuscus* by MP&G.

687. PLOCEUS NIGRICOLLIS (=HYPHANTURGUS BRACHYPTERUS)
(II.1223)   Black-necked Weaver* or (Swainson's) Spectacled Weaver   RB

Not uncommon resident (*P. n. brachypterus*) of undergrowth of secondary forest, forest clearings, coastal thicket zone, older residential areas of Accra and Legon and inselbergs on Accra Plains; also woodland savanna in north, but less common than in south. Occurs Cape Coast, Tarkwa, Takoradi, Anum, Kumsi, Tafo (C. M. Morrison, M. Lockwood). Collected Mampong in Ashanti, Wenchi and Ejura (Lowe 1937) — see also Bannerman (1949).

Breeding. Nesting mainly in wet season. Eggs: in oviduct Wenchi, 14 Jan (Lowe 1937); Mampong, 20 Mar (D. W. Lamm); C/2 Akropong in Akwapim, 2 Mar (C. M. Morrison). Nestlings: Nkwatia, Apr; Cape Coast, Feb (Macdonald 1979b); Akropong in Akwapim, 10 Aug (C. M. Morrison). Dependent young: Tafo, Sep (M. Lockwood); Mole, late Aug (Greig-Smith 1977b).

*The West African race *brachypterus* has bright olive green upperparts, the only black being confined to a mark through the eye, hence the more appropriate name in West Africa of Spectacled Weaver. The latter name, however, is used for *Hyphanturgus ocularis* by MP&G (II.1224).

688. PLOCEUS PELZELNI (=SITAGRA MONACHA)
(II.1232)*   Slender-billed Weaver   RB

Not uncommon local resident (*P. p. monachus*), confined to mangroves and swamps in coastal zone, particularly near estuaries. Regular Panbros (Grimes 1972a), Cape Coast (M. Macdonald), also Volta river near Ada and Densu (Sutton 1965b). The record north of Tamale by F. C. Holman (Bannerman 1949) refers to *P. luteola* not *P. pelzelni* (Bannerman 1953).

Breeding. Colonial, over water. Nest construction: Panbros, Jun (Grimes 1972a); Nakwa and Komenda, May and Jun (Macdonald 1979b). Eggs and nestlings: Panbros, Jul and Aug; Cape Coast, May (Macdonald 1979b).

*Bannerman's English name is Little Weaver which is used for *P. luteolus* by MP&G, who also use *Sitagra*.

689. PLOCEUS (=PHORMOPLECTES) PREUSSI
(II.1240)   Golden-backed Weaver   R(B)

Uncommon resident of middle and upper storey of mature and secondary forest. First recorded in Ghana south of Kumasi, a party of 5 on 27 Dec 1953 (Gass 1954) — overlooked by Hall & Moreau (1970). Occurs Kade (Sutton 1965b), Tafo and Atewa Forest Reserve (L.G.G., M. Lockwood), and Bia National Park (Macdonald & Taylor 1977). Also now known to occur Liberia and Ivory Coast (Thiollay 1985, Colston & Curry-Lindahl 1986).

Breeding. Unrecorded. Nesting in northeastern Congo, Dec and in breeding condition, Aug (MP&G).

690. PLOCEUS SUPERCILIOSUS (=PACHYPHANTES PACHYRHYNCHUS)

(II.1237)　Compact Weaver　　　　　　　　　　　　RB

Uncommon local resident in marshy grassland within the coast thicket zone and on Accra and Keta Plains, usually in groups of 5–15. Regular at Denu (Sutton 1965b), Cape Coast (M. Macdonald), western edge of Accra Plains and near mouth of the Volta River (Grimes 1972a). Collected "Fanti" by Aubinn, Accra by Shelley and Pong on the Accra Plains by Alexander (1902).

Breeding. Males are in full breeding dress from May. Nest building: Denu, 2 Jul (Sutton 1965b), sewage farm, Legon, 17 Jul (L.G.G.). Dependent young: Cape Coast, 22 Oct (Macdonald 1979b).

691. PLOCEUS (=CINNAMOPTERYX=MELANOPLOCEUS*) TRICOLOR

(II.1242)　Yellow-mantled Weaver　　　　　　　　RB

Not uncommon resident (*P. t. tricolor*), widespread in middle and upper storey of mature and secondary forest, and forest edge. Regular in Akwapim hills (C. M. Morrison), Tafo, Mpraeso (M. Lockwood, L.G.G.) and Amedzofe; occurs Hohoe, Bunsu, Subri River Forest Reserve (M. F. Hodges, Jr), Bia National Park (Taylor & Macdonald 1978b), and along the Ancobra and Tano rivers (M. Horwood), but rare Cape Coast (M. Macdonald). Collected Abokobi in last century (Shelley), Prahsu, Fumsu (Alexander 1902), Ejura and Mampong (Lowe 1937).

Breeding. Colonial; active colony high in canopy: Bunsu, Sep and Oct (L.G.G.); Kumasi, colony of c. 500 nests, Aug (F. C. Holman *in* Bannerman 1949). Eggs: Kumasi, mid Aug. Nestlings: Kumasi, Sep; Amedzofe, 31 Dec (L.G.G.); Tafo, Sep (M. Lockwood).

*In Bannerman (1949) the species is named *Cinnamopteryx tricolor,* but in Bannerman (1953) renamed *Melanoploceus tricolor,* this latter name being used by MP&G.

692. PLOCEUS VELATUS* (=PLESIOSITAGRA VITELLINUS)

(II.1218)*　Vitelline Masked Weaver　　　　　　　RB

Not uncommon local resident (*P. v. vitellinus*) of northern grassland savanna with scattered trees and shrubs, regular Tumu (Sutton 1970) and Mole (Greig-Smith 1976a). Also occurs eastern sector of Accra Plains, but no records on Keta Plains nor in coastal thicket zone west of Accra (M. Macdonald) — possibly overlooked. Males on Accra Plains do not appear to moult into a non-breeding dress. Not as common as *P. heuglini*.

Breeding. Not colonial on Accra Plains; each male builds 2–5 nests, often suspended low over water. Nest building: Accra Plains, Apr–Jul, but once in Dec 1972 after heavy rains in Nov (L.G.G.). Eggs: C/2 Accra Plains, Apr–Jul, 1 egg, Dec (L.G.G.); Tumu, Sep (Sutton 1970); Mole, Mar (Sutton 1965b).

*Named *P. vitellinus* by MP&G, who name *P. velatus* the Southern Masked Weaver; both are considered races of *P. velatus* by White.

693. QUELEA ERYTHROPS

(II.1263)　Red-headed Quelea　　　　　　　　　　AfM/B, R?B

An abundant intra-African migrant, mainly Jan–Aug, to coastal thicket zone (Macdonald 1979b), some forest clearings, e.g. Korforidua (M. Horwood), and Tafo where many 100s (in female dress) roost in Apr (M. Lockwood). Also Accra and Keta Plains (M. Horwood, Grimes 1977c), and in moist savanna woodland in north at Mole (Greig-Smith 1976a), in rice-cultivations at Tono dam (R. Passmore, D. Daramani), but not Tumu (Sutton 1970) nor Bolgatanga (F. Walsh). Collected along the Volta river on the Accra Plains (H. T. Ussher *in* Bannerman 1949), Accra Plains (Shelley & Buckley 1872), Kete Kratchi, Wenchi and Ejura (Lowe 1937). Previously occurred Kumasi, where it associated with *Ploceus nigerrimus* (F. C. Holman *in* Bannerman 1949). The majority leave Ghana after breeding and are thought to move to east Africa (Britton 1980, Cyrus 1986), but one male in worn dress was netted at Suhien, near Tafo, Nov (M. Lockwood).

Breeding. Colonial, many 100s of nests in Typha beds on Accra Plains, late May onwards, C/2 or 3 (Grimes 1977c); active nests Mole, early Sep. Female with brood patch Mole, Jul (Greig-Smith 1977b).

694. QUELEA QUELEA
(II.1262)   Red-billed Quelea (= Black-faced Dioch)   ?

Present status unknown. Large flocks once recorded, sometime in dry season Dec–Apr, at Binduri north of Gambaga (Alexander 1902). Recently recorded (*Q. q. quelea*) with *Quelea erythrops* at the Tono irrigation project in the far north (J. Stewart, D. Daramani).

Viduinae

The Indigobirds (Combassous) are taxonomically perhaps the most difficult group of African birds. The species and subspecies that follow are those defined by Payne (1973, 1976, 1982, 1985) who classifies them by the mimetic songs of the males and the distribution of their hosts. Some species differ from the species recognised in earlier standard works and the English names used are those of Payne (1982).

695. VIDUA (= HYPOCHERA) CHALYBEATA
(II.1340)*   Village Indigobird   R(B)

Resident (*V. c. neumanni*)*, thought to be widespread in north in open savanna with shrubs and scattered trees and probably not uncommon, its distribution overlapping its host *Lagonosticta senegala*. One was recently collected: Morago river in the northeast of Ghana (Payne 1982).

Breeding. Unrecorded. Its host *L. senegala* nests mainly May–Oct in Nigeria (Elgood 1982).

*The name used by White is *V. c. ultramarina* and that by MP&G is *Hypochera ultramarina orientalis*.

696. VIDUA LARVATICOLA
(Not in MP&G)   Baka Indigobird   R(B)

A new species (Payne 1982), resident in northern woodland savanna, probably not uncommon north of about 10°N, but abundance uncertain. Distribution overlaps its host *Estrilda larvata*. Thought to occur Tumu (Sutton 1970), Yegi and Yendi (Payne 1982: 77).

Breeding. Unrecorded. Its host species *E. larvata* nests Jul and Aug in Nigeria (Elgood 1982).

697. VIDUA MACROURA
(II.1344)   Pin-tailed Whydah   RB, Afm

Common widespread resident of open grassland with scattered shrubs, of abandoned and used farms, in coastal thicket zone east of Takoradi, Accra and Keta Plains, and throughout northern savanna zone. Also in forest clearings e.g. Tarkwa, Korforidua, Kumasi (M. Horwood) and Tafo (M. Lockwood), where flocks of 20–30, occasionally reaching 100, form in dry season Jan and Feb. In north, regular Mole, Bolgatanga, and Tumu. Seasonal Cape Coast and Nakwa, numbers decreasing Oct–Dec (Macdonald 1980a), with males in evidence at Denu after early May (Sutton 1965b).

Breeding. Host species at Cape Coast are *Estrilda troglodytes, E. melpoda* and *Lonchura cucullata* (Macdonald 1980a). Males in breeding dress: in south, late Feb to early Oct; in north: mainly May–Nov, but occasionally Dec (Sutton 1970, Shaw 1984). Eggs: Cape Coast, Mar–Sep (Macdonald 1980a).

698. VIDUA (= STEGANURA) INTERJECTA*
  (II.1346)*   Uelle Paradise Whydah*   R(B)
Resident, probably not uncommon in grassland with scattered trees in the drier northern sector of the Guinea Savanna. Occurs Mole where its host, the Red-winged Pytilia *Pytilia phoenicoptera,* is the common pytilia. Width of long rectrices in breeding males is in the range 30–40 mm (Payne 1985).
Breeding. Unrecorded. Its host *P. phoenicoptera* nests Nov–Feb in Nigeria (Elgood 1982).
*The name is that used by Payne (1985); White considers it a race of *Vidua orientalis* and Bannerman and MP&G a race of *Steganura orientalis.* The English name used by Payne (1985) is that used by Bannerman (1949) for *S. o. interjecta,* which was changed to Broad-tailed Paradise Whydah in Bannerman (1953).

699. VIDUA (= STEGANURA) TOGOENSIS*
  (II.1346)*   Togo Paradise Whydah*   R(B)
Probably not uncommon resident in southern areas of the northern woodland savanna, also south through the Volta Region to the Keta Plains. Collected Gambaga (Hartert 1899a), Kete Kratchi, and the type at Kete (= Keta?); also occurs Mole (Payne 1985) and Tumu (Lowe 1937). Width of long rectrices in breeding males is < 30 mm (Payne 1985).
Breeding. Unrecorded. Its host *P. hypogrammica* nests Jan in Nigeria (Serle 1957 *in* Elgood 1982).
*This name is used by Payne (1985); White considers it a race of *Vidua orientalis* and Bannerman and MP&G a race of *Steganura orientalis.* The English name is that used by Bannerman (1949: 396) for *S. o. togoensis* and was changed to Broad-tailed paradise Whydah in Bannerman (1953).

700. VIDUA RARICOLA
  (Not in MP&G)   Jambandu Indigobird
A new species (Payne 1982), resident and probably not uncommon in woodland savanna, distribution overlapping its host *Lagonosticta rara.* Occurs Mole (Harvey & Harrison 1970, R. B. Payne) and Yegi (Payne 1982).
Breeding. Its host *L. rara* nests Jul and Oct in Nigeria (Elgood 1982).

701. VIDUA WILSONI
  (Not in MP&G)   Wilson's Indigobird   RB, Afm
Not uncommon resident of coastal thicket zone, gardens and suburbs of Accra, and in northern savanna, distribution overlapping its host *Lagonosticta rufopicta.* Occurs Accra (Grimes 1972a), Cape Coast (Macdonald 1980a), Mole (R. B. Payne), Kete Kratchi, Larabanga (Payne 1982). Seasonal at Cape Coast, minimum numbers present late Oct to early Dec, and absent Nakwa, Oct–Dec (Macdonald 1980a).
Breeding. Nesting overlaps that of its host species *L. rufopicta.* Nesting: Cape Coast, Apr–Sep (Macdonald 1980a); Legon, May–Aug (L.G.G.); probably later inland because of the timing of the wet season. Egg in oviduct: Cape Coast, 10 Sep 1975 (Payne 1982). Juveniles: 12 collected Cape Coast, Sep and early Oct (Payne 1982: 56).

STURNIDAE

Sturninae

Three glossy starlings, *Lamprotornis chalcurus* (704), *L. chalybaeus* (705) and *L. chloropterus* (706), are very difficult to distinguish in the field, consequently their status and abundance in the following text is uncertain.

702. CINNYRICINCLUS LEUCOGASTER
(II.1114)   Violet-backed (Amethyst) Starling   AfM/(B)

Seasonally common (*C. l. leucogaster*) in savanna woodland in north, forest clearings and throughout coastal thicket zone to the Accra Plains. In dry season often in flocks of 50–60. There is a clear north/south migration, but data suggest that movements may be more complex. A passage migrant Mole, largest numbers during movement northwards at beginning of the rains, Jun, the return movement occurring Dec (Greig-Smith 1977a). Recorded Tumu, 28 Mar to 7 May only, a westerly movement occurring 28 Mar (Sutton 1970). Mainly a dry season visitor to Cape Coast, Oct to late Jan (Macdonald 1979a), but with 7 records early Apr to early Jul (Gass 1954). In Akwapim, Abokobi and elsewhere on Accra Plains sporadic in each month except Jul and Oct, although numbers are few in wet season, Apr–Jun (Grimes 1972a, L.G.G.).

Breeding. Male entering nest hole with green leaves: Botanical Gardens, Legon, 24 Apr (L.G.G.). In Nigeria, nesting Mar–Jun (Elgood 1982).

703. LAMPROTORNIS CAUDATUS
(II.1125)   Long-tailed Glossy Starling   RB, AfM/NB?

Uncommon local resident (*L. c. caudatus*), particularly in wooded suburbs of Tamale and Bolgatanga, but seasonal elsewhere in northern woodland savanna, usually in flocks of 5–20. Resident Tamale in Holman's day (Bannerman 1949), but seasonal, Feb–Oct, in 1950s (M. Horwood), and only occurs May–Sep Tumu (Sutton 1970), Gambaga and Pong Tamale. Not recorded Mole (Greig-Smith 1976a). Data suggest an influx into Ghana of non-breeding birds at the beginning of the wet season.

Breeding. Nesting in holes near Karaga, no date (Alexander 1902). Alexander was in the Gambaga district from late Nov to early May. No records since.

704. LAMPROTORNIS (= LAMPROCOLIUS) CHALCURUS
(II.1118)   Bronze-tailed Glossy Starling   R(B), AfM/NB?

Not uncommon (*L. c. chalcurus*) in northern savanna woodland, where it is possibly only a dry season migrant, also south through the Volta Region to the Accra and Keta Plains, where probably resident, flocks sometimes of 100 or more. Collected Bole, Jan (Lowe 1937), Kete Kratchi and Yendi (Bannerman 1949). Occurs Tamale, flocks of 50–80, Sep and Oct (M. Horwood), Accra Plains, but in fewer numbers than in Ussher's day (Ussher 1874, Grimes 1972a). Surprisingly this was the only glossy starling at Denu, Jan–Jul (Sutton 1965b). Probably occurs Mole (Greig-Smith 1976a), where there is an influx of glossy starlings in the dry season, Nov–Apr (Greig-Smith 1977a).

Breeding. Unrecorded. In Nigeria, eggs Jun; juveniles May (Elgood 1982).

705. LAMPROTORNIS (= LAMPROCOLIUS) CHALYBAEUS
    (II.1117)   Blue-eared Glossy Starling   AfM/NB
Uncommon non-breeding dry season migrant (*L. c. chalybaeus*) in the northern savanna (Greig-Smith 1977a). Recorded Gambaga, 30 Oct/1 Nov (R. B. Payne) and one collected Legon on Accra Plains, 15 Dec (Grimes 1978a), identified by C. W. Benson and housed in Zoology Department, University of Cambridge.

706. LAMPROTORNIS (= LAMPROCOLIUS) CHLOROPTERUS
    (II.1119)   Lesser Blue-eared (Swainson's) Glossy Starling   RB
Common widespread resident (*L. c. chloropterus*) in northern savanna woodland, often in flocks of 10–20 or more; also on the Accra Plains (Grimes 1972a). Collected Pong and on inselbergs on the Accra Plains, Tamale (Bannerman 1949) and Ejura, Jan (Lowe 1937). Occurs Mole, Dec and Jan (Sutton 1970, Macdonald 1978f), although omitted by Greig-Smith (1976a). Often in mixed flocks with *L. purpureus*. Holman (Bannerman 1948) thought it occurred Kumasi, but no records since.
    Breeding. Carrying nest material: Legon, Apr. Dependent juveniles (dark eyed): Legon, Jun (Grimes 1972a, L.G.G.).

707. LAMPROTORNIS (= LAMPROCOLIUS) CUPREOCAUDA
    (II.1123)   Copper-tailed Glossy Starling   R(B)
Not uncommon resident of middle and upper storey throughout the forest region. Collected Cape Coast, "Fanti", "Ashanti", in Wassaw district (near Tarkwa area), Prahsu, Fumsu and Kumasi (Bannerman 1949). Regular Cape Coast (M. Macdonald), occurs Akwapim hills, Tafo (M. Lockwood), Atewa Forest Reserve (N. Wood) and Bia National Park (Taylor & Macdonald 1978b). Ussher (1874) thought it occurred on the Accra Plains, but not recorded since.
    Breeding. Unrecorded anywhere in West Africa (MP&G).

708. LAMPROTORNIS (= LAMPROCOLIUS) PURPUREUS
    (II.1120)   Purple Glossy Starling   RB
Common resident (*L. p. purpureus*), widespread throughout the northern savanna and south through the Volta Region to the Accra and Keta Plains; the commonest glossy starling. Only occasional Winneba, but absent Cape Coast (M. Macdonald) and within forest clearings. In north, flocks of 200 or more regular in dry season, late Oct to Apr. On the Accra Plains a mixed starling roost of several 100s forms in the dry season in a neem plantation between Legon and Achimota. Collected at many localities in northern savanna and on Accra Plains (Bannerman 1949).
    Breeding. Eggs: female with well developed ovary Weija, 26 Feb (D. W. Lamm). Nest building under eaves, in drain pipes and holes in trees: Legon, Apr–Jul (Grimes 1972a). Nestlings: Mole, May (Greig-Smith 1977b).

709. LAMPROTORNIS (= LAMPROCOLIUS) SPLENDIDUS
    (II.1121)   Splendid Glossy Starling   RB
Not uncommon resident (*L. s. chrysonotis*) of middle and upper storey of mature and secondary forest. Regular Subri River Forest Reserve (M. F. Hodges, Jr). Located Tarkwa, flocks of 60 or more in Jun and Jul, but pairs in Sep (M. Horwood); also Mamfe and Akropong in Akwapim, near Ho and Tafo (M. Lockwood, L.G.G.).
    Breeding. Entering nest hole: Tafo, Feb (L.G.G.); Dayi River in Volta Region, 14 Apr (N. Wood).

710. ONYCHOGNATHUS FULGIDUS
(II.1129)   Chestnut-wing Starling   RB

Not uncommon resident (*O. f. hartlaubii*) of middle and upper storey of mature and secondary forest. Collected Kwissa, Prahsu (Alexander 1902). "Fanti", Aburi and in Akwapim (Bannerman 1949). Regular Agogo, Begoro (C. M. Morrison), Atewa Forest Reserve and Aduamoah near Mpraeso (L.G.G.), Subri River Forest Reserve (M. F. Hodges, Jr), Tafo (M. Lockwood) and occurs Bia National Park (Taylor & Macdonald 1978b).

Breeding. Copulation: near Mpraeso, 4 Mar (M. Horwood). Carrying nest material: Tafo, Jul. Same nest holes used in consecutive years Akropong, Oct–Nov (C. M. Morrison).

[ONYCHOGNATHUS MORIO
(II.1131)   Red-wing Starling

Listed for Tono dam by J. Stewart, but the record is not acceptable, since the normal habitat is isolated hill country with crags; in addition *Ptilostomus afer* (q.v.), which occurs at Tono (R. G. Passmore) and is more likely, does not appear on Stewart's list.]

711. POEOPTERA LUGUBRIS
(II.1133)   Narrow-tailed Starling   R(B)

Rare resident of middle and upper storey within forest zone, only a few records. Collected twice in "interior of Fanti" (Bannerman 1948), sporadic records Subri River Forest Reserve (M. F. Hodges, Jr), recorded Dixcove, 21 Nov (D. James).

Breeding. Unrecorded. In Nigeria, nesting Jan and exploring nest holes, Aug (Elgood 1982).

712. SPREO PULCHER
(II.1136)   Chestnut-bellied Starling   AfM?/(B)

Uncommon and local, possibly moves into Ghana from higher latitudes to breed at end of wet season. Occurs Bolgatanga, Aug and Nov (F. Walsh); regular in dry season at the Tono irrigation dam near Bolgatanga (J. Stewart, R. Passmore); one collected Bahare (= Baghari?) just north of Lawra, no date (Bannerman 1948).

Breeding. Unrecorded. In Nigeria, a biannual breeder, Feb-May and Sep–Nov (Wilkinson 1983). Two adults (pair) near an undoubted *Spreo* nest at Tono dam, 6 Feb 1987 (F. Walsh).

Buphaginae

713. BUPHAGUS AFRICANUS
(II.1137)   Yellow-billed Oxpecker   R(B)

Uncommon resident (*B. a. africanus*); groups of 10 or less within Mole Game Park (B. Woodell, F. Walsh, Greig-Smith 1976a). No other records.

Breeding. In Nigeria, Apr–Aug (Elgood 1982).

ORIOLIDAE

714. ORIOLUS AURATUS
(II.1103)   African Golden Oriole   AfM/(B)

Not uncommon (*O. a. auratus*), regular in woodland savanna in north, and in Volta Region, but sporadic on the Accra and Keta Plains and not recorded west of Accra. Everywhere seasonal, mainly as a dry season visitor. Occurs Mole, Oct–Apr

(Greig-Smith 1977a), but once 26 Aug (Harvey & Harrison 1970), N. W. Ashanti, Dec–May (Russell 1949a), and Ho, Oct–Jun (M. Horwood). Occasional Accra Plains, sporadic records Jan, Mar, Apr, Jun, Jul and Oct (Grimes 1972a, L.G.G.), and Denu, 29 Jul (Sutton 1965b).

Breeding. Unrecorded. In Nigeria, mainly Mar–Apr, which is when it is present in Ghana.

715. ORIOLUS BRACHYRHYNCHUS
(II.1105)   (Western) Black-headed Oriole   RB
Not uncommon resident (*O. b. brachyrhynchus*) in middle and upper storey, widespread in mature and secondary forest, forest edge and forest clearing. More often heard than seen, often with *Oriolus nigripennis*. Occurs Kimasi, Akropong in Akwapim, Begoro, Agogo, Worawora (C. M. Morrison), Hohoe and Amedzofe (Sutton 1965b), Tafo (M. Lockwood) and Bia National Park (Taylor & Macdonald 1978b). In Lowe's day, less common than *nigripennis* at Mampong in Ashanti (Lowe 1937).

Breeding. Female with well developed ovary Mpraeso, 23 Apr 1955 (D. W. Lamm). Juveniles Tafo, no date (M. Lockwood).

716. ORIOLUS NIGRIPENNIS
(II.1106)   Black-winged Oriole   RB
Not uncommon resident in middle and upper storey of forest zone, with much the same status and habitat as *O. brachyrhynchus,* but also in forest outliers to the north of the forests. Collected in many localities within forest belt (Bannerman 1939), but also Ejura, Feb (Lowe 1937) and occurs near Kintampo, 30 Jan 1978 (F. Walsh).

Breeding. Nesting in Ashanti, end of Feb (Lowe 1937).

[ORIOLUS ORIOLUS
(II.1102)   Golden Oriole
Because of the difficulty of distinguishing in the field *oriolus* from *auratus,* the single sighting of a female near Legon, 16 Jan 1966 (M. Edmunds *in* Grimes 1972a) is now not accepted.]

DICRURIDAE

717. DICRURUS ADSIMILIS
(II.1040)   Drongo (Glossy-backed Drongo)   RB
Common resident (*D. a. divaricatus = adsimilis*) throughout woodland savanna in north, and south to Volta Region; many collected in north and one collected near Takoradi in coastal zone (Hall & Moreau 1970). The forest race *D. a. atactus,* a possible hybrid between *divaricatus* and *coracinus* of Nigeria and elsewhere, is widespread in mature and secondary forest (Hall & Moreau 1970).

Breeding. Egg laying: Mampong in Ashanti, 21 Feb. Eggs: C/3 Pong Tamale, 18 Apr 1971 (F. Walsh). Nestlings: Legon, 21 Dec 1972; Shai Hills, 5 Jan 1974 (L.G.G.).

718. DICRURUS ATRIPENNIS
(II.1042)   Shining Drongo   R(B)
Rare resident of understorey of mature forest; few records, since not easily distinguished from *D. adsimilis atactus.* Collected Fumsu (Alexander 1902) and in "Fanti" (Bannerman 1939).

Breeding. Unrecorded. In Nigeria, female in breeding condition, Oct and Nov. Nesting, May (Elgood 1982).

719. DICRURUS LUDWIGII (= SHARPEI)
(II.1043)   Square-tailed Drongo   RB

Uncommon local resident (*D. l. sharpei*) in northern savanna, mainly confined to gallery forests with thick undergrowth, also in coastal zone. Collected Yegi and Wenchi (Lowe 1937), and Weija west of Accra (D. W. Lamm). Sporadic Mole (Greig-Smith 1976a); occurs Amedzofe (Sutton 1965b).

Breeding. Pair shot Wenchi were about to breed, 20 Jan (Lowe 1937). Fully developed egg in oviduct Weija, 10 Apr 1955 (D. W. Lamm).

CORVIDAE

720. CORVUS ALBUS
(II.1109)   Pied Crow   RB, Afm

Common resident, abundant in coastal districts and on Accra Plains, regular within forest clearings and along edges of major roads. Occurs locally, mainly in towns, through Volta Region to the northern savanna zone. A passage migrant Mole, present in considerable numbers at end of dry season with stragglers in wet season (Greig-Smith 1976a, 1977a). There is a possibility that it moves north to higher latitudes in the wet season to breed. Large roosts, known in 1930s, occur Achimota and within Accra; another at Legon was formed in 1970s after planted trees matured (Grimes 1972a, L.G.G.). Night flights (birds calling) occur over Legon, Oct (0100 hrs) and Jul (22.30 hrs).

Breeding. Nest building in south begins Dec and Jan, but most activity is in Apr and May. Electric pylons were used as nest sites in 1964, a year after they were constructed. At least 31 pylons were used along a 160 km stretch of coastal road in Jun 1969, 52 of them by Jun 1970. Eggs and young: Legon and Accra, Apr–Jul (Lamm 1958, Grimes 1972a); Tafo, May (M. Lockwood); Cape Coast, May–Jul (Macdonald 1979b).

721. PTILOSTOMUS AFER
(II.1112)   Piapiac (Black Magpie)   RB

Locally a common resident in woodland savanna in north, occurring Tono, near Bolgatanga, Bawku, Mole, Yendi and Tamale. Also through the Volta Region, occurring Ho and Adidome (M. Horwood), to the eastern sector of the Accra and Keta Plains, particularly where *Borassus* palms dominate. Usually associated with cattle. Collected Navrongo, Jan (Lowe 1937), and Gambaga (Bannerman 1939).

Breeding. Cooperative. Nest in *Borassus* palm, nestlings attended by 5 adults and 3 immatures near Kasu lagoon, 18 May 1974 (L.G.G.). Immatures with adults, a flock of c. 50, Shai Hills, 23 Jun 1973 (L.G.G.).

SUMMARY OF THE STATUS OF BIRD SPECIES OF GHANA

RB	Resident breeder
R(B)	Resident, but breeding not proved
PM	Palaearctic migrant
Afm	Migrates within Ghana
AfM/B	Migrates to and from Ghana to breed in Ghana
AfM/NB	Migrates to and from Ghana to spend non-breeding season in Ghana
V	Vagrant
?	Indicates a doubt over *the status immediately preceding the question mark*, but not of occurrence

NON-PASSERINES

PODICIPEDIDAE
1.	Podiceps ruficollis	Little Grebe	RB

PROCELLARIIDAE
2.	Procellaria gravis	Southern Greater Shearwater	V
3.	Procellaria puffinus	Manx Shearwater	V, PM

HYDROBATIDAE
4.	Hydrobates castro	Madeira Petrel	V
5.	Hydrobates leucorhoa	Leach's Petrel	V
6.	Hydrobates pelagicus	Storm Petrel	V
7.	Oceanites oceanicus	Wilson's Petrel	V

PHAETHONTIDAE
8.	Phaethon lepturus	White-tailed Tropic Bird	V

PELECANIDAE
9.	Pelecanus onocrotalus	White Pelican	AfM/NB, PM?
10.	Pelecanus rufescens	Pink-backed Pelican	R?(B)

SULIDAE
11.	Sula bassana	Cape Gannet	V
12.	Sula leucogaster	Brown Booby	V

PHALACROCORACIDAE
13.	Phalacrocorax africanus	Long-tailed Cormorant	RB
14.	Phalacrocorax carbo	African Cormorant	AfM?/NB

ANHINGIDAE
15.	Anhinga rufa	Darter	RB

ARDEIDAE
Botaurinae
16.	Botaurus stellaris	Bittern	V, PM
17.	Ixobrychus minutus	Little Bittern	RB, Afm/B, PM?
18.	Ixobrychus sturmii	Dwarf Bittern	RB, Afm?

Ardeinae
Tigriornithini
19.	Tigriornis leucolophus	White-crested Bittern	R(B)
	Nycticoracini		
20.	Nycticorax leuconotus	White-backed Night Heron	R(B)
21.	Nycticorax nycticorax	Night Heron	RB, PM?
	Ardeini		
22.	Ardea cinerea	Grey Heron	PM, RB
23.	Ardea goliath	Goliath Heron	R(B)
24.	Ardea melanocephala	Black-headed Heron	Afm/B
25.	Ardea purpurea	Purple Heron	PM, R?(B)
26.	Ardeola ibis	Cattle Egret	Afm/B, RB
27.	Ardeola ralloides	Squacco Heron	PM, RB
28.	Butorides striatus	Green-backed Heron	RB
29.	Egretta alba	Great White Heron	RB
30.	Egretta ardesiaca	Black Heron	RB, Afm/B?
31.	Egretta garzetta garzetta	Little Egret	RB, PM
32.	Egretta garzetta gularis	West African Reef-Heron	RB
33.	Egretta intermedia	Yellow-billed Egret	AfM/NB

SCOPIDAE
34.	Scopus umbretta	Hammerkop	R(B)

CICONIIDAE
Mycteriini
35.	Anastomus lamelligerus	Open-bill	AfM/NB
36.	Ibis ibis	Wood-Ibis	AfM/B

Ciconiini
37.	Ciconia abdimii	White-bellied or Abdim's Stork	AfM/NB
38.	Ciconia ciconia	White Stork	PM
39.	Ciconia episcopus	Woolly-necked Stork	Afm/(B)
40.	Ciconia nigra	Black Stork	V, PM

Leptoptilini
41.	Ephippiorhynchus senegalensis	Saddle-bill or Jabiru	AfM/B
42.	Leptoptilos crumeniferus	Marabou	AfM/B

THRESKIORNITHIDAE
Threskiornithinae
43.	Bostrychia hagedash	Hadada	R(B)
44.	Bostrychia olivacea	Green Ibis	R?(B)
45.	Bostrychia rara	Spotted-breasted Ibis	R(B)
46.	Plegadis falcinellus	Glossy Ibis	PM
47.	Threskiornis aethiopica	Sacred Ibis	Afm/(B)

Plataleinae
48.	Platalea alba	African Spoonbill	V

PHOENICOPTERIDAE
[Phoenicopterus minor   Lesser Flamingo]

ANATIDAE
Anserinae
Dendrocygnini
49.	Dendrocygna bicolor	Fulvous Tree-Duck	V, AfM?/B
50.	Dendrocygna viduata	White-faced Tree-Duck	RB, Afm

Anatinae
Tadornini
51.	Alopochen aegyptiaca	Egyptian Goose	V
52.	Tadorna tadorna	Shelduck	V, PM

Cairinini
53.	Nettapus auritus	Pigmy Goose	RB
54.	Plectropterus gambensis	Spur-winged Goose	R(B)
55.	Pteronetta hartlaubii	Hartlaub's Duck	RB
56.	Sarkidiornis melanota	Knob-billed Goose	R(B)

Anatini
57	Anas acuta	Pintail	PM
58.	Anas capensis	Cape Wigeon	V
59.	Anas clypeata	Shoveler	PM
60.	Anas crecca	Teal	PM
61.	Anas penelope	Wigeon	V, PM
62.	Anas querquedula	Garganey	PM

Aythyini
63.	Aythya ferina	Pochard	V, PM
64.	Aythya nyroca	White-eyed Pochard	PM

PANDIONIDAE
65.	Pandion haliaetus	Osprey	PM

ACCIPITRIDAE
Aegypinae
66.	Gypohierax angolensis	Palm-nut Vulture	RB
67.	Gyps bengalensis	White-backed Vulture	R(B)
68.	Gyps ruppellii	Rüppell's Griffon	.V
69.	Neophron monachus	Hooded Vulture	RB
70.	Neophron percnopterus	Egyptian Vulture	V
71.	Trigonoceps occipitalis	White-headed Vulture	RB

Accipitrinae
Circini
72.	Circaetus beaudouini	Beaudouin's Harrier-Eagle	V
73.	Circaetus cinerascens	Banded Harrier-Eagle	R(B)
74.	Circaetus cinereus	Brown Harrier-Eagle	R(B)
75.	Circaetus gallicus	Short-toed Eagle	PM
76.	Circus aeruginosus	Marsh Harrier	PM
77.	Circus macrourus	Pale Harrier	PM
78.	Circus pygargus	Montagu's Harrier	PM
79.	Dryotriorchis spectabilis	Serpent-Eagle	R(B)

80.	Polyboroides radiatus	Harrier-Hawk	RB
81.	Terathopius ecaudatus	Bateleur	RB

Accipitrini
82.	Accipiter badius	Shikra	RB, Afm/B
83.	Accipiter erythropus	Western Little Sparrow-Hawk	R(B)
84.	Accipiter melanoleucus	Great Sparrow-Hawk	R(B)
85.	Accipiter ovampensis	Ovampa Sparrow-Hawk	AfM/NB
86.	Accipiter tousselenii	West African Goshawk	RB
87.	Melierax gabar	Gabar Goshawk	R(B)
88.	Melierax metabates	Dark Chanting-Goshawk	R(B), AfM?/(B)
89.	Urotriorchis macrourus	Long-tailed Hawk	R(B)

Buteini
90.	Butastur rufipennis	Grasshopper Buzzard	AfM/NB
91.	Buteo auguralis	Red-necked Buzzard	AfM/B, Afm/B?
92.	Buteo buteo vulpinus	Steppe Buzzard	V, PM
93.	Buteo rufinus	Long-legged Buzzard	V, PM
94.	Kaupifalco monogrammicus	Lizzard Buzzard	RB, AfM/B

Aquilini
95.	Aquila rapax	Tawny Eagle	RB
96.	Aquila wahlbergi	Wahlberg's Eagle	R(B)
97.	Haliaeetus vocifer	Fish Eagle	RB
98.	Hieraaetus africanus	Cassin's Hawk-Eagle	RB
99.	Hieraaetus dubius	Ayres' Hawk-Eagle	RB
100.	Hieraaetus pennatus	Booted Eagle	PM
101.	Hieraaetus spilogaster	African Hawk-Eagle	R(B)
102.	Lophaetus occipitalis	Long-crested Hawk-Eagle	RB
103.	Polemaetus bellicosus	Martial Eagle	R(B)
104.	Stephanoaetus coronatus	Crowned Hawk-Eagle	RB

Milvini
105.	Aviceda cuculoides	Cuckoo Falcon	Afm/B
106.	Elanus caeruleus	Black-shouldered Kite	RB
107.	Elanus riocourii	Swallow-tailed Kite	AfM/NB
108.	Macheirhamphus alcinus	Bat-eating Buzzard	RB
109.	Milvus migrans	(Black) Kite	Afm/B, PM
110.	Pernis apivorus	Honey-Buzzard	PM

SAGITTARIIDAE
111.	Sagittarius serpentarius	Secretary Bird	AfM/NB

FALCONIDAE
112.	Falco alopex	Fox Kestrel	AfM/NB?
113.	Falco ardosiaceus	Grey Kestrel	RB, Afm/B
114.	Falco biarmicus	Lanner	RB, Afm
115.	Falco chicquera	Red-necked Falcon	R?(B), AfM/NB?
116.	Falco cuvieri	African Hobby	RB
117.	Falco naumanni	Lesser Kestrel	V, PM
118.	Falco peregrinus	Peregrine	PM, RB

119.	Falco subbuteo	Hobby	V, PM
120.	Falco tinnunculus	Kestrel	PM, R(B)
	[Falco vespertinus	Red-footed Falcon]	

PHASIANIDAE
Phasianinae

121.	Coturnix chinensis	Blue Quail	AfM/(B)
122.	Coturnix coturnix	Quail	PM
123.	Coturnix delegorguei	Harlequin Quail	V, AfM?/NB
124.	Francolinus ahantensis	Ahanta Francolin	RB
125.	Francolinus albogularis	White-throated Francolin	RB
126.	Francolinus bicalcaratus	Double-spurred Francolin	RB
127.	Francolinus lathami	Forest Francolin	RB
128.	Ptilopachus petrosus	Stone-Partridge	R(B)

Numidinae

129.	Agelastes meleagrides	White-breasted Guinea-Fowl	R(B)
130.	Guttera edouardi	Crested Guinea-Fowl	RB
131.	Numida meleagris	Guinea-Fowl	R(B)

TURNICIDAE

132.	Ortyxelos meiffrenii	Quail-Plover	AfM/B
133.	Turnix hottentotta	Black-rumped Button-Quail	V
134.	Turnix sylvatica	Button-Quail	R(B)

GRUIDAE
Balearicinae

135.	Balearica pavonina	Crowned Crane	AfM/NB

RALLIDAE
Rallinae

136.	Canirallus oculeus	Grey-throated Rail	R(B)
137.	Crex crex	Corn Crake	PM
138.	Crex egregia	African Crake	RB
139.	Gallinula angulata	Lesser Moorhen	AfM/B
140.	Gallinula chloropus	Moorhen	RB
141.	Himantornis haematopus	Nkulengu Rail	R(B)
142.	Limnocorax flavirostra	Black Crake	RB
143.	Porphyrio alleni	Allen's Gallinule	RB, Afm?
144.	Porphyrio porphyrio	Purple Gallinule	Afm?/B
145.	Porzana marginalis	Striped Crake	Afm?/B
	[Porzana porzana	Spotted Crake]	
146.	Sarothrura elegans	Buff-spotted Crake	?
147.	Sarothrura pulchra	White-spotted Crake	RB
	[Sarothrura rufa	Red-chested Crake]	

HELIORNITHIDAE

148.	Podica senegalensis	Finfoot	R(B)

OTIDIDAE

149.	Eupodotis melanogaster	Black-bellied Bustard	Afm/B

150.	Eupodotis senegalensis	Senegal Bustard	R(B)
151.	Neotis denhami	Denham's Bustard	AfM/NB?
152.	Otis arabs	Arabian Bustard	AfM/NB

JACANIDAE

153.	Actophilornis africana	Jacana	RB

ROSTRATULIDAE

154.	Rostratula benghalensis	Painted Snipe	Afm?/(B)?

HAEMATOPODIDAE

155.	Haematopus ostralegus	Oyster-catcher	PM

RECURVIROSTRIDAE

156.	Himantopus himantopus	Black-winged Stilt	RB, PM
157.	Recurvirostra avosetta	Avocet	V, PM

BURHINIDAE

158.	Burhinus capensis	Spotted Thicknee	AfM/NB?
159.	Burhinus senegalensis	Senegal Thicknee	R?/(B)
160.	Burhinus vermiculatus	Water Thicknee	R?(B)

GLAREOLIDAE
Cursorinae

161.	Cursorius chalcopterus	Violet-tipped Courser	AfM/(B)
162.	Cursorius temminckii	Temminck's Courser	R?B
163.	Pluvianus aegyptius	Egyptian Plover	R(B)

Glareolinae

164.	Glareola cinerea	Grey Pratincole	V
165.	Glareola nordmanni	Black-winged Pratincole	PM
166.	Glareola nuchalis	White-collared Pratincole	RB
167.	Glareola pratincola	Pratincole	Afm/B

CHARADRIIDAE

168.	Charadrius alexandrinus	Kentish Plover	PM
169.	Charadrius dubius	Little Ringed Plover	PM
170.	Charadrius forbesi	Forbes' Plover	RB, Afm/B
171.	Charadrius hiaticula	Ringed Plover	PM
172.	Charadrius marginatus	White-fronted Sand-Plover	RB
173.	Charadrius pecuarius	Kittlitz's Sand-Plover	RB
174.	Charadrius tricollaris	Three-banded Plover	V
175.	Pluvialis dominicus/ apricarius	Lesser Golden Plover/ Golden Plover	V
176.	Pluvialis squatarola	Grey Plover	PM
177.	Vanellus albiceps	White-headed Plover	AfM/(B)
178.	Vanellus lugubris	Senegal Plover	R(B), Afm
179.	Vanellus senegallus	Wattled Plover	RB
180.	Vanellus spinosus	Spur-winged Plover	R?(B)
181.	Vanellus superciliosus	Brown-chested Wattled Plover	V, AfM/NB
182.	Vanellus tectus	Black-headed Plover	AfM/(B)

SCOLOPACIDAE
Tringinae
Numeniini

183.	Limosa lapponica	Bar-tailed Godwit	PM
184.	Limosa limosa	Black-tailed Godwit	PM
185.	Numenius arquata	Curlew	PM
186.	Numenius phaeopus	Whimbrel	PM

Tringini

187.	Tringa erythropus	Spotted Redshank	PM
188.	Tringa flavipes	Lesser Yellowlegs	V
189.	Tringa glareola	Wood Sandpiper	PM
190.	Tringa hypoleucos	Common Sandpiper	PM
191.	Tringa nebularia	Greenshank	PM
192.	Tringa ochropus	Green Sandpiper	PM
193.	Tringa stagnatilis	Marsh Sandpiper	PM
194.	Tringa terek	Terek Sandpiper	V, PM
195.	Tringa totanus	Redshank	PM

Arenariinae

196.	Arenaria interpres	Turnstone	PM

Phalaropinae

197.	Phalaropus fulicarius	Grey Phalarope	V, PM

Gallinagoninae

198.	Gallinago gallinago	Common Snipe	PM
199.	Gallinago media	Great Snipe	PM
200.	Gallinago minima	Jack Snipe	PM
201.	Lymnodromus griseus	Short-billed Dowitcher	V

Calidrinae

202.	Calidris alba	Sanderling	PM
203.	Calidris alpina	Dunlin	V, PM
204.	Calidris canutus	Knot	PM
205.	Calidris ferruginea	Curlew Sandpiper	PM
206.	Calidris fuscicollis	White-rumped Sandpiper	V
207.	Calidris minuta	Little Stint	PM
208.	Calidris temminckii	Temminck's Stint	PM
209.	Tryngites subruficollis	Buff-breasted Sandpiper	V
210.	Philomachus pugnax	Ruff & Reeve	PM

STERCORARIIDAE

211.	Stercorarius parasiticus	Richardson's Skua	V
212.	Stercorarius pomarinus	Pomatorhine Skua	PM
213.	Stercorarius skua	Great Skua	V, PM?

LARIDAE
Larinae

214.	Larus cirrhocephalus	Grey-headed Gull	V, AfM/NB
215.	Larus fuscus	Lesser Black-backed Gull	PM
216.	Larus minutus	Little Gull	V

| 217. | Larus ridibundus | Black-headed Gull | PM |
| 218. | Larus sabini | Sabine's Gull | V |

Sterninae

219.	Anous stolidus	Noddy	V
220.	Anous tenuirostris	White-capped Noddy	V
221.	Sterna albifrons	Little Tern	RB, PM
222.	Sterna anaethetus	Bridled Tern	V
223.	Sterna balaenarum	Damara Tern	AfM/NB
224.	Sterna bengalensis	Lesser Crested Tern	V
225.	Sterna dougallii	Roseate Tern	PM
226.	Sterna fuscata	Sooty Tern	V
227.	Sterna hirundo	Common Tern	PM
228.	Sterna hybrida	Whiskered Tern	PM
229.	Sterna leucoptera	White-winged Black Tern	PM
230.	Sterna maxima	Royal Tern	AfM/NB
231.	Sterna nigra	Black Tern	PM
232.	Sterna nilotica	Gull-billed Tern	PM
233.	Sterna paradisaea	Arctic Tern	PM
234.	Sterna sandvicensis	Sandwich Tern	PM
235.	Sterna tschegrava	Caspian Tern	PM, AfM/NB?

RHYNCHOPIDAE

| 236. | Rhynchops flavirostris | Skimmer | R(B) |

PTEROCLIDIDAE

| 237. | Pterocles quadricinctus | Four-banded Sandgrouse | AfM/B |

COLUMBIDAE

238.	Columba guinea	Speckled Pigeon	RB
239.	Columba livia	Rock Pigeon	R(B)
240.	Columba malherbii	Gabon Bronze-naped Pigeon	R(B)
241.	Columba unicincta	Afep Pigeon	R(B)
242.	Oena capensis	Namaqua Dove	AfM/(B)
243.	Streptopelia decipiens	Mourning Dove	R(B)
244.	Streptopelia roseogrisea	Pink-headed (or Rose-grey) Dove	V
245.	Streptopelia semitorquata	Red-eyed Dove	RB
246.	Streptopelia senegalensis	Laughing Dove	RB
247.	Streptopelia turtur	Turtle Dove	PM
248.	Streptopelia vinacea	Vinaceous Dove	RB
249.	Treron australis	Green Pigeon	RB
250.	Treron waalia	Bruce's Green Pigeon	RB
251.	Turtur abyssinicus	Black-billed Blue-spotted Wood-Dove	RB
252.	Turtur afer	Blue-spotted Wood-Dove	RB, Afm?
253.	Turtur brehmeri	Blue-headed Dove	R(B)
254.	Turtur tympanistria	Tambourine Dove	R(B)

PSITTACIDAE

| 255. | Agapornis pullaria | Red-headed Lovebird | R(B) |
| 256. | Agapornis swinderniana | Black-collared Lovebird | R(B) |

257.	Poicephalus gulielmi	Red-headed Parrot	RB
258.	Poicephalus robustus	Brown-necked Parrot	R(B)
259.	Poicephalus senegalus	Yellow-bellied Parrot	RB
260.	Psittacula krameri	Rose-ringed Parrakeet	R(B)
261.	Psittacus erithacus	Grey Parrot	RB

MUSOPHAGIDAE

262.	Corytheola cristata	Great Blue Turaco	R(B)
263.	Crinifer piscator	Grey Plantain-eater	RB
264.	Musophaga violacea	Violet Turaco	R(B)
265.	Tauraco macrorhynchus	Black-tip Crested Turaco	R(B)
266.	Tauraco persa	Guinea Turaco	R(B)

CUCULIDAE
Cuculinae

267.	Cercococcyx mechowi	Dusky Long-tailed Cuckoo	R(B)
268.	Cercococcyx olivinus	Olive Long-tailed Cuckoo	R(B)
269.	Chrysococcyx caprius	Didric Cuckoo	RB, Afm/B
270.	Chrysococcyx cupreus	Emerald Cuckoo	R(B)
271.	Chrysococcyx flavigularis	Yellow-throated Green Cuckoo	?
272.	Chrysococcyx klaas	Klaas' Cuckoo	RB, Afm/B
273.	Clamator glandarius	Great Spotted Cuckoo	Afm/B, PM?
274.	Clamator jacobinus	Black and White Cuckoo	Afm/(B)
275.	Clamator levaillantii	Levaillant's Cuckoo	Afm/B, RB
276.	Cuculus canorus canorus	Cuckoo	PM
277.	Cuculus canorus gularis	African Cuckoo	Afm/B
278.	Cuculus clamosus	Black Cuckoo	R(B), AfM/NB?
279.	Cuculus solitarius	Red-chested Cuckoo	R(B)
280.	Pachycoccyx audeberti	Thick-billed Cuckoo	V?

Phaenicophaeninae

| 281. | Ceuthmochares aereus | Yellow-bill | RB |

Centropinae

282.	Centropus leucogaster	Black-throated Coucal	RB
283.	Centropus monachus	Blue-headed Coucal	R(B)
284.	Centropus senegalensis	Senegal Coucal	RB
285.	Centropus toulou	Black Coucal	Afm/B

TYTONIDAE

| 286. | Tyto alba | Barn Owl | RB |

STRIGIDAE
Buboninae

287.	Bubo africanus	Spotted Eagle-Owl	R(B)
288.	Bubo lacteus	Verreaux's Eagle-Owl	R(B)
289.	Bubo leucostictus	Akun Eagle-Owl	R(B)
290.	Bubo poensis	Fraser's Eagle-Owl	R(B)
291.	Bubo shelleyi	Banded Eagle-Owl	R(B)
292.	Ciccaba woodfordii	African Wood-Owl	RB
	[Glaucidium capense	Barred Owlet]	

293.	Glaucidium perlatum	Pearl-spotted Owlet	R(B)
294.	Glaucidium tephronotum	Red-chested Owlet	RB
295.	Lophostrix letti	Akun Scops Owl	R(B)
296.	Otus icterorhynchus	Sandy Scops Owl	R(B)
297.	Otus leucotis	White-faced Scops Owl	RB
298.	Otus scops	Scops Owl	RB, PM
299.	Scotopelia peli	Fishing Owl	R(B)
300.	Scotopelia ussheri	Rufous Fishing Owl	R(B)

CAPRIMULGIDAE
Caprimulginae

301.	Caprimulgus binotatus	Brown Nightjar	R?(B)
302.	Caprimulgus climacurus	Long-tailed Nightjar	RB, Afm/NB
303.	Caprimulgus europaeus	Nightjar	V, PM
	[Caprimulgus fossii	Gabon Nightjar]	
304.	Caprimulgus inornatus	Plain Nightjar	AfM?/(B), Afm
305.	Caprimulgus natalensis	White-tailed Nightjar	R(B)
306.	Caprimulgus pectoralis	Dusky Nightjar	?
307.	Caprimulgus ruficollis	Red-necked Nightjar	V, PM
	[Caprimulgus rufigena	Rufous-cheeked Nightjar]	
308.	Caprimulgus tristigma	Freckled Nightjar	R(B)
309.	Macrodipteryx longipennis	Standard-winged Nightjar	AfM/(B)
	[Macrodipteryx vexillarius	Pennant-winged Nightjar]	

APODIDAE
Apodinae
Chaeturini

310.	Chaetura cassini	Cassin's Spinetail	R(B)
311.	Chaetura melanopygia	Ituri Mottled-throated Spinetail	R(B)
312.	Chaetura sabini	Sabine's Spinetail	R(B)
313.	Chaetura ussheri	Mottled-throated Spinetail	RB, Afm

Apodini

314.	Apus aequatorialis	Mottled Swift	Afm/(B)
315.	Apus affinis	Little Swift	RB
316.	Apus apus	Common Swift	PM
317.	Apus batesi	Black Swift	R?(B)
318.	Apus caffer	White-rumped Swift	RB
319.	Apus melba	Alpine Swift	V, PM
320.	Apus pallidus	Mouse-coloured Swift	PM
321.	Cypsiurus parvus	Palm Swift	RB

COLIIDAE

322.	Colius striatus	Speckled Mousebird	R?(B)

TROGONIDAE

323.	Apaloderma narina	Narina's Trogon	R(B)

ALCEDINIDAE
Cerylinae

324.	Ceryle maxima	Giant Kingfisher	R(B)
325.	Ceryle rudis	Pied Kingfisher	RB

Alcedininae

326.	Alcedo cristata	Malachite Kingfisher	RB
327.	Alcedo leucogaster	White-bellied Kingfisher	R(B)
328.	Alcedo quadribrachys	Shining-blue Kingfisher	R(B)
329.	Ceyx lecontei	Dwarf Kingfisher	R(B)
330.	Ceyx picta	Pigmy Kingfisher	RB

Daceloninae

331.	Halcyon badia	Chocolate-backed Kingfisher	R(B)
332.	Halcyon chelicuti	Striped Kingfisher	RB, Afm
333.	Halcyon leucocephala	Grey-headed Kingfisher	Afm/B
334.	Halcyon malimbica	Blue-breasted Kingfisher	RB
335.	Halcyon senegalensis	Woodland Kingfisher	RB, Afm/B

MEROPIDAE

336.	Bombylonax breweri	Black-headed Bee-eater	R(B)
337.	Merops albicollis	White-throated Bee-eater	AfM/NB
338.	Merops apiaster	Bee-eater	PM
339.	Merops bulocki	Red-throated Bee-eater	RB
340.	Merops gularis	Black Bee-eater	RB
341.	Merops hirundineus	Swallow-tailed Bee-eater	RB
342.	Merops malimbicus	Rosy Bee-eater	AfM/NB
343.	Merops muelleri	Blue-headed Bee-eater	R(B)
344.	Merops nubicus	Carmine Bee-eater	Afm/(B)
	[Merops orientalis	Little Green Bee-eater]	
345.	Merops pusillus	Little Bee-eater	RB, Afm
346.	Merops superciliosus	Blue-cheeked Bee-eater	AfM/NB

CORACIIDAE

347.	Coracias abyssinica	Abyssinian Roller	AfM/NB
348.	Coracias cyanogaster	Blue-bellied Roller	R?(B), Afm
349.	Coracias garrulus	European Roller	PM
350.	Coracias naevia	Rufous-crowned Roller	Afm/(B)
351.	Eurystomus glaucurus	Broad-billed Roller	RB, Afm/B
352.	Eurystomus gularis	Blue-throated Roller	RB

UPUPIDAE

353.	Upupa epops	Hoopoe	AfM/(B), PM

PHOENICULIDAE

354.	Phoeniculus aterrimus	Black Wood-Hoopoe	R(B), Afm
355.	Phoeniculus bollei	White-headed Wood-Hoopoe	RB
356.	Phoeniculus castaneiceps	Forest Wood-Hoopoe	R(B)
357.	Phoeniculus purpureus	Green Wood-Hoopoe	RB, Afm

BUCEROTIDAE

358.	Bucorvus abyssinicus	Abyssinian Ground Hornbill	RB
359.	Bycanistes cylindricus	Brown-cheeked Hornbill	RB
360.	Bycanistes fistulator	Piping Hornbill	R(B)
361.	Bycanistes subcylindricus	Black-and-White-casqued Hornbill	R(B)
362.	Ceratogymna atrata	Black-casqued Hornbill	RB
363.	Ceratogymna elata	Yellow-casqued Hornbill	RB
364.	Tockus camurus	Red-billed Dwarf Hornbill	R(B)
365.	Tockus erythrorhynchus	Red-billed Hornbill	R(B)
366.	Tockus fasciatus	Pied Hornbill	RB
367.	Tockus hartlaubi	Black Dwarf Hornbill	RB
368.	Tockus nasutus	Grey Hornbill	RB, AfM/B
369.	Tropicranus albocristatus	White-crested Hornbill	RB

CAPITONIDAE

370.	Buccanodon duchaillui	Yellow-spotted Barbet	R(B)
371.	Gymnobucco calvus	Naked-faced Barbet	RB
372.	Gymnobucco peli	Bristle-nosed Barbet	R(B)
373.	Lybius bidentatus	Double-toothed Barbet	RB
374.	Lybius dubius	Bearded Barbet	RB
375.	Lybius hirsutus	Hairy-breasted Barbet	RB
376.	Lybius vieilloti	Vieillot's Barbet	RB
377.	Pogoniulus atro-flavus	Red-rumped Tinker-bird	R(B)
378.	Pogoniulus bilineatus	Lemon-rumped Tinker-bird	RB
379.	Pogoniulus chrysoconus	Yellow-fronted Tinker-bird	RB
380.	Pogoniulus scolopaceus	Speckled Tinker-bird	R(B)
381.	Pogoniulus subsulphureus	Yellow-throated Tinker-bird	RB
382.	Trachyphonus purpuratus	Yellow-billed Barbet	RB

INDICATORIDAE

383.	Indicator exilis	Least Honey-Guide	R(B)
384.	Indicator indicator	Black-throated Honey-Guide	RB
385.	Indicator maculatus	Spotted Honey-Guide	R(B)
386.	Indicator minor	Lesser Honey-Guide	R(B)
387.	Indicator willcocksi	Willcock's Honey-Guide	R(B)
	[Melichneutes robustus	Lyre-tailed Honey-Guide]	
388.	Melignomon eisentrauti	Serle's Honey-Guide	R(B)
389.	Prodotiscus insignis	Cassin's Honey-bird	RB
	[Prodotiscus regulus	Wahlberg's Honey-bird]	

PICIDAE
Jynginae

390.	Jynx torquilla	Wryneck	PM

Picuminae

391.	Verreauxia africana	Golden-brown Piculet	R(B)

Picinae

392.	Campethera abingoni	Golden-tailed Woodpecker	R(B)
393.	Campethera cailliautii	Green-backed Woodpecker	R(B)
394.	Campethera caroli	Brown-eared Woodpecker	R(B)
395.	Campethera maculosa	Golden-backed Woodpecker	R(B)
396.	Campethera nivosa	Buff-spotted Woodpecker	R(B)
397.	Campethera punctuligera	Fine-spotted Woodpecker	RB
398.	Dendropicos fuscescens	Cardinal Woodpecker	R(B)
399.	Dendropicos gabonensis	Melancholy Woodpecker	R(B)
400.	Dendropicos obsoletus	Brown-backed Woodpecker	RB
401.	Mesopicos goertae	Grey Woodpecker	RB
402.	Mesopicos pyrrhogaster	Fire-bellied Woodpecker	RB

PASSERINES

EURYLAIMIDAE

403.	Smithornis capensis	African Broadbill	R(B)
404.	Smithornis rufolateralis	Red-sided Broadbill	R(B)

PITTIDAE

405.	Pitta angolensis	African Pitta	R(B)

ALAUDIDAE

406.	Eremopterix leucotis	Chestnut-backed Sparrow-Lark	AfM/(B)
407.	Galerida cristata	Crested Lark	R(B)
408.	Galerida modesta	Sun Lark	RB
409.	Mirafra nigricans	Red-tailed Bush-Lark	AfM/(B)
410.	Mirafra rufocinnamomea	Flappet Lark	RB, Afm/B

HIRUNDINIDAE

411.	Delichon urbica	House Martin	PM
412.	Hirundo abyssinica	Striped Swallow	RB, Afm/B
413.	Hirundo aethiopica	Ethiopian Swallow	RB, Afm/B
414.	Hirundo daurica	Red-rumped Swallow	AfM?/(B)
415.	Hirundo fuligula	African Rock Martin	RB
416.	Hirundo griseopyga	Grey-rumped Swallow	R?B, Afm
417.	Hirundo leucosoma	Pied-winged Swallow	R?B, Afm/B
418.	Hirundo nigrita	White-throated Blue Swallow	RB, Afm/B
419.	Hirundo rustica	Swallow	PM, RB
420.	Hirundo semirufa	Rufous-chested Swallow	RB, Afm/B
421.	Hirundo senegalensis	Mosque Swallow	RB, Afm/B
422.	Hirundo smithii	Wire-tailed Swallow	RB
423.	Hirundo spilodera	Preuss's Cliff Swallow	RB, Afm
424.	Psalidoprocne nitens	Square-tailed Rough-wing Swallow	R(B)

425.	Psalidoprocne obscura	Fantee Rough-wing Swallow	R?B, Afm
426.	Riparia cincta	Banded Martin	AfM/NB?
427.	Riparia paludicola	African Sand Martin	R?(B), Afm?
428.	Riparia riparia	Sand Martin	PM

MOTACILLIDAE

429.	Anthus campestris	Tawny Pipit	PM
430.	Anthus cervinus	Red-throated Pipit	PM
431.	Anthus leucophrys	Plain-backed Pipit	RB, Afm
432.	Anthus novaeseelandiae	Richard's Pipit	V
433.	Anthus similis	Long-billed Pipit	R?(B)
434.	Anthus trivialis	Tree Pipit	PM
435.	Macronyx croceus	Yellow-throated Long-claw	RB
436.	Motacilla alba	African Pied Wagtail	RB
	[Motacilla clara	Mountain Wagtail]	
437.	Motacilla flava	Yellow Wagtails	PM

CAMPEPHAGIDAE

438.	Campephaga lobata	Wattled Cuckoo-Shrike	R(B)
439.	Campephaga phoenicea	Red-shouldered Cuckoo-Shrike	R(B), Afm
440.	Campephaga quiscalina	Purple-throated Cuckoo-Shrike	R(B)
441.	Coracina azurea	Blue Cuckoo-Shrike	RB
442.	Coracina pectoralis	White-breasted Cuckoo-Shrike	RB

PYCNONOTIDAE

443.	Andropadus ansorgei	Ansorge's Greenbul	R(B)
444.	Andropadus curvirostris	Cameroun Sombre Greenbul	RB
445.	Andropadus gracilirostris	Slender-billed Greenbul	RB
446.	Andropadus gracilis	Little Grey Greenbul	RB
447.	Andropadus latirostris	Yellow-whiskered Greenbul	R(B)
	[Andropadus montanus	Mountain Little Greenbul]	
448.	Andropadus virens	Little Greenbul	RB
449.	Baeopogon indicator	Honey-Guide Greenbul	RB
450.	Bleda canicapilla	Grey-headed Bristle-bill	R(B)
451.	Bleda eximia	Green-tailed Bristle-bill	R(B)
452.	Bleda syndactyla	Bristle-bill	R(B)
453.	Calyptocichla serina	Serine Greenbul	R(B)
454.	Chlorocichla flavicollis	Yellow-throated Leaf-love	R(B)
455.	Chlorocichla simplex	Simple Greenbul	RB
456.	Criniger barbatus	Bearded Greenbul	RB
457.	Criniger calurus	Thick-billed Red-tailed Greenbul	R(B)
458.	Criniger olivaceus	Yellow-throated Olive Greenbul	R(B)
459.	Ixonotus guttatus	Spotted Greenbul	R(B)

460.	Nicator chloris	Nicator	RB
461.	Phyllastrephus albigularis	White-throated Greenbul	R(B)
462.	Phyllastrephus baumanni	Baumann's Greenbul	R(B)
463.	Phyllastrephus icterinus	Icterine Greenbul	RB
464.	Phyllastrephus scandens	Leaf-love	RB
465.	Pycnonotus barbatus	White-vented Bulbul	RB
466.	Thescelocichla leucopleurus	White-tailed Greenbul	RB

LANIIDAE
Prionopinae

467.	Prionops caniceps	Red-billed Shrike	RB
468.	Prionops plumata	Straight-crested Helmet-Shrike	RB

Malaconotinae

469.	Dryoscopus gambensis	Puff-back	RB
470.	Dryoscopus sabini	Sabine's Puff-back	R(B)
471.	Laniarius barbarus	Gonolek	RB
472.	Laniarius ferrugineus	Tropical Boubou	R(B)
473.	Laniarius leucorhynchus	Sooty Boubou	R(B)
474.	Malaconotus blanchoti	Grey-headed Bush-Shrike	RB
475.	Malaconotus cruentus	Fiery-breasted Bush-Shrike	R(B)
476.	Malaconotus lagdeni	Lagden's Bush-Shrike	V
477.	Malaconotus multicolor	Many-coloured Bush-Shrike	R?(B)
478.	Malaconotus sulfureopectus	Sulphur-breasted Bush-Shrike	RB
479.	Nilaus afer	Northern Brubru	RB, Afm
480.	Tchagra australis	Brown-headed Bush-Shrike	RB
481.	Tchagra minuta	Black-cap Bush-Shrike	RB
482.	Tchagra senegala	Black-headed Bush-Shrike	RB

Laniinae

483.	Corvinella corvina	Yellow-billed Shrike	RB
484.	Lanius collaris	Fiscal	RB
485.	Lanius excubitor	Grey Shrike	V
486.	Lanius gubernator	Emin's Shrike	R?(B)
487.	Lanius senator	Woodchat Shrike	PM

MUSCICAPIDAE
Turdinae

488.	Alethe diademata	White-tailed Alethe	R(B)
489.	Alethe poliocephala	Brown-chested Alethe	RB
490.	Cercomela familiaris	Red-tailed Chat	RB
491.	Cercotrichas leucosticta	Northern-bearded Scrub-Robin	RB
492.	Cossypha albicapilla	White-crowned Robin-Chat	R(B)
493.	Cossypha cyanocampter	Blue-shouldered Robin-Chat	R(B)

494.	Cossypha niveicapilla	Snowy-headed Robin-Chat	R(B)
	[Cossypha polioptera	Grey-winged Robin-Chat]	
495.	Luscinia megarhynchos	Nightingale	PM
496.	Luscinia suecica	Bluethroat	PM
497.	Monticola saxatilis	Rock-Thrush	PM
498.	Monticola solitaria	Blue Rock-Thrush	PM
499.	Myrmecocichla albifrons	White-fronted Black Chat	RB
500.	Myrmecocichla cinnamomeiventris	White-crowned Cliff-Chat	RB
501.	Neocossyphus poensis	White-tailed Ant-Thrush	RB
502.	Oenanthe bottae	Heuglin's Red-breasted Wheatear	V
503.	Oenanthe oenanthe	Wheatear	PM
504.	Phoenicurus phoenicurus	Redstart	PM
505.	Saxicola rubetra	Whinchat	PM
	[Sheppardia cyornithopsis	Akalat]	
506.	Stiphrornis erythrothorax	Forest Robin	RB
507.	Stizorhina fraseri	Finsch's Rufous Flycatcher	RB
508.	Turdus pelios	Olive Thrush	RB
509.	Turdus princei	Grey Ground-Thrush	R(B)

Timaliinae

510.	Phyllanthus atripennis	Capuchin Babbler	R(B)
511.	Trichastoma cleaveri	Black-cap Illadopsis	R(B)
512.	Trichastoma fulvescens	Brown Illadopsis	R(B)
513.	Trichastoma puveli	Puvel's Illadopsis	R(B)
514.	Trichastoma rufescens	Rufous-winged Illadopsis	R(B)
515.	Trichastoma rufipennis	Pale-breasted Illadopsis	RB
516.	Turdoides plebejus	Brown Babbler	RB
517.	Turdoides reinwardii	Black-cap Babbler	RB

Picathartinae

518.	Picathartes gymnocephalus	Yellow-headed Rockfowl	RB

Sylviinae

519.	Acrocephalus arundinaceus	Great Reed Warbler	PM
520.	Acrocephalus rufescens	Rufous Swamp Warbler	RB
521.	Acrocephalus schoenobaenus	Sedge Warbler	PM
522.	Acrocephalus scirpaceus	Reed Warbler	PM
523.	Apalis flavida	Yellow-chested Apalis	RB
524.	Apalis nigriceps	Black-capped Apalis	R(B)
525.	Apalis sharpii	Sharpe's Apalis	RB
526.	Bathmocercus cerviniventris	Black-capped Warbler	R(B)
527.	Camaroptera brachyura	Grey-backed Camaroptera	RB
528.	Camaroptera chloronota	Olive-green Camaroptera	R(B)
529.	Camaroptera superciliaris	Yellow-browed Camaroptera	RB

530.	Cisticola aberrans	Rock-loving Cisticola	RB
531.	Cisticola brachyptera	Siffling Cisticola	RB
532.	Cisticola cantans	Singing Cisticola	RB
533.	Cisticola erythrops	Red-faced Cisticola	RB
534.	Cisticola eximia	Black-backed Cisticola	RB
535.	Cisticola galactotes	Winding Cisticola	RB
536.	Cisticola juncidis	Zitting Cisticola	RB
537.	Cisticola lateralis	Whistling Cisticola	RB
538.	Cisticola natalensis	Croaking Cisticola	RB
539.	Cisticola rufa	Rufous Cisticola	RB
540.	Cisticola ruficeps	Red-pate Cisticola	R(B)
541.	Eremomela badiceps	Brown-crowned Eremomela	RB
542.	Eremomela icteropygialis	Yellow-bellied Eremomela	AfM?/(B)
543.	Eremomela pusilla	Smaller Green-backed Eremomela	RB
544.	Hippolais icterina	Icterine Warbler	PM
545.	Hippolais pallida	Olivaceous Warbler	PM
546.	Hippolais polyglotta	Melodious Warbler	PM
547.	Hylia prasina	Green Hylia	RB
548.	Hypergerus atriceps	Oriole Warbler	RB
549.	Locustella luscinioides	Savi's Warbler	PM
550.	Macrosphenus concolor	Grey Longbill	RB
551.	Macrosphenus flavicans	Kemp's Longbill	R(B)
552.	Pholidornis rushiae	Tit-Hylia	RB
553.	Phylloscopus collybita	Chiffchaff	PM
554.	Phylloscopus sibilatrix	Wood Warbler	PM
555.	Phylloscopus trochilus	Willow Warbler	PM
556.	Prinia erythroptera	Red-wing Warbler	RB
557.	Prinia subflava	Tawny-flanked Prinia	RB
	[Schoenicola platyura	Fan-tailed Warbler]	
558.	Sphenoeacus mentalis	Moustache-Warbler	RB
559.	Sylvia atricapilla	Blackcap	PM
560.	Sylvia borin	Garden Warbler	PM
561.	Sylvia communis	Whitethroat	PM
562.	Sylvietta brachyura	Crombec	RB
563.	Sylvietta denti	Lemon-bellied Crombec	RB
564.	Sylvietta virens	Green Crombec	RB

Muscicapinae

565.	Artomyias ussheri	Ussher's Dusky Flycatcher	R(B)
566.	Bradornis pallidus	Pale Flycatcher	RB
567.	Ficedula albicollis	White-collared Flycatcher	PM
568.	Ficedula hypoleuca	Pied Flycatcher	PM
569.	Fraseria cinerascens	White-browed Forest Flycatcher	RB
570.	Fraseria ocreata	Forest Flycatcher	R(B)
571.	Melaenornis edolioides	Black Flycatcher	RB
572.	Muscicapa aquatica	Swamp Flycatcher	R(B)
573.	Muscicapa caerulescens	Ashy Flycatcher	R(B)
574.	Muscicapa cassini	Cassin's Grey Flycatcher	R(B)
575.	Muscicapa comitata	Dusky Blue Flycatcher	RB
576.	Muscicapa epulata	Little Grey Flycatcher	R(B)

577.	Muscicapa gambagae	Gambaga Dusky Flycatcher	R(B)
578.	Muscicapa griseigularis	Grey-throated Tit-Flycatcher	RB
579.	Muscicapa olivascens	Olivaceous Flycatcher	R(B)
580.	Muscicapa striata	Spotted Flycatcher	PM
581.	Muscicapa tessmanni	Tessman's Flycatcher	R(B)
582.	Myioparus plumbeus	Grey Tit-Flycatcher	RB

Platysteirinae

583.	Batis minima	Fernando Po Puff-back Flycatcher	R(B)
584.	Batis senegalensis	Senegal Puff-back Flycatcher	RB
585.	Bias musicus	Black and White Flycatcher	RB
586.	Megabyas flammulata	Shrike Flycatcher	RB
587.	Platysteira blissetti	Red-cheeked Wattle-eye	R(B)
588.	Platysteira castanea	Chestnut Wattle-eye	RB
589.	Platysteira concreta	Yellow-bellied Wattle-eye	R(B)
590.	Platysteira cyanea	Wattle-eye	RB

Monarchinae

591.	Erythrocercus mccalli	Chestnut-cap Flycatcher	RB
592.	Hyliota flavigaster	Yellow-bellied Flycatcher	R(B)
593.	Hyliota violacea	Violet-backed Flycatcher	R(B)
594.	Terpsiphone rufiventer	Red-bellied Paradise Flycatcher	RB
595.	Terpsiphone viridis	Paradise Flycatcher	RB, Afm
596.	Trochocercus longicauda	Blue Flycatcher	RB
597.	Trochocercus nigromitratus	Dusky Crested Flycatcher	R(B)
598.	Trochocercus nitens	Blue-headed Crested Flycatcher	R(B)

REMIZIDAE

| 599. | Remiz flavifrons | Yellow-fronted Penduline Tit | R(B) |
| 600. | Remiz parvulus | Yellow Penduline Tit | RB |

PARIDAE

| 601. | Parus funereus | Dusky Tit | RB |
| 602. | Parus leucomelas | Black Tit | RB |

CERTHIIDAE

| 603. | Salpornis spilonota | Spotted Creeper | RB |

NECTARINIIDAE

604.	Anthreptes collaris	Collared Sunbird	RB
605.	Anthreptes fraseri	Fraser's Scarlet-tufted Sunbird	R(B)
606.	Anthreptes gabonicus	Brown Sunbird	R(B)
607.	Anthreptes longuemarei	Violet-backed Sunbird	R(B)

608.	Anthreptes platura	Pygmy Sunbird	AfM/(B)
609.	Anthreptes rectirostris	Green Sunbird	RB
610.	Nectarinia adelberti	Buff-throated Sunbird	RB
611.	Nectarinia batesi	Bates' Sunbird	R(B)
612.	Nectarinia chloropygia	Olive-bellied Sunbird	RB
613.	Nectarinia coccinigaster	Splendid Sunbird	RB
614.	Nectarinia cuprea	Copper Sunbird	RB
615.	Nectarinia cyanolaema	Blue-throated Sunbird	R(B)
616.	Nectarinia fuliginosa	Carmelite Sunbird	R?(B)
617.	Nectarinia johannae	Madame Verreaux's Sunbird	R(B)
618.	Nectarinia minulla	Tiny Sunbird	R(B)
619.	Nectarinia olivacea	Olive Sunbird	RB
620.	Nectarinia pulchella	Beautiful Sunbird	RB, Afm
621.	Nectarinia reichenbachii	Reichenbach's Sunbird	?
622.	Nectarinia seimundi	Little Green Sunbird	R(B)
623.	Nectarinia senegalensis	Scarlet-chested Sunbird	RB
624.	Nectarinia superba	Superb Sunbird	RB
625.	Nectarinia venusta	Variable Sunbird	R(B)
626.	Nectarinia verticalis	Green-headed Sunbird	RB

ZOSTEROPIDAE

| 627. | Zosterops senegalensis | Yellow White-eye | RB |

EMBERIZIDAE

628.	Emberiza cabanisi	Cabanis' Bunting	RB, Afm
629.	Emberiza forbesi	Brown-rumped Bunting	R(B), Afm?
630.	Emberiza tahapisi	Cinnamon-breasted Rock-bunting	RB, Afm/B

FRINGILLIDAE

631.	Serinus gularis	Streaky-headed Seed-eater	R(B)
632.	Serinus leucopygius	White-rumped Seed-eater	R(B)
633.	Serinus mozambicus	Yellow-fronted Canary	RB

ESTRILDIDAE

634.	Amadina fasciata	Cut-throat	AfM?/(B)
635.	Amandava subflava	Zebra Waxbill	R?(B), Afm?
636.	Estrilda astrild	Waxbill	R?(B)
637.	Estrilda bengala	Red-cheeked Cordon-bleu	RB
638.	Estrilda caerulescens	Red-tailed Lavender Waxbill	R(B)
639.	Estrilda larvata	Black-faced Fire-Finch	R(B)
640.	Estrilda melpoda	Orange-cheeked Waxbill	RB, Afm
641.	Estrilda troglodytes	Black-rumped Waxbill	RB, Afm/B
642.	Hypargos nitidulus	Green-backed Twin-spot	R(B)
643.	Lagonosticta rara	Black-bellied Fire-Finch	R(B)
644.	Lagonosticta rubricata	African Fire-Finch	RB
645.	Lagonosticta rufopicta	Bar-breasted Fire-Finch	RB
646.	Lagonosticta senegala	Red-billed Fire-Finch	R(B)
647.	Lonchura bicolor	Black and White Mannikin	RB
648.	Lonchura cucullata	Bronze Mannikin	RB
649.	Lonchura fringilloides	Magpie Mannikin	RB

650.	Lonchura malabarica	Silver-bill	RB, Afm?
651.	Nesocharis capistrata	Grey-headed Olive-back	R(B)
652.	Nigrita bicolor	Chestnut-breasted Negro-Finch	RB
653.	Nigrita canicapilla	Grey-headed Negro-Finch	RB
654.	Nigrita fusconota	White-breasted Negro-Finch	RB
655.	Nigrita luteifrons	Pale-fronted Negro-Finch	?
656.	Ortygospiza atricollis	Quail-Finch	RB
657.	Parmoptila woodhousei	Flower-pecker Weaver-Finch	R(B)
658.	Pirenestes ostrinus	Black-bellied Seed-cracker	RB
659.	Pytelia hypogrammica	Yellow-winged Pytelia	R(B)
660.	Pytelia phoenicoptera	Red-winged Pytelia	R(B)
661.	Spermophaga haematina	Blue-bill	RB, Afm

PLOCEIDAE
Bubalornithinae

662.	Bubalornis albirostris	Buffalo-Weaver	RB

Passerinae

663.	Passer griseus	Grey-headed Sparrow	RB
664.	Petronia dentata	Bush Petronia	RB, Afm?
665.	Plocepasser superciliosus	Chestnut-crowned Sparrow-Weaver	RB, Afm
666.	Sporopipes frontalis	Speckled-fronted Weaver	R?B, Afm?/B

Ploceinae

667.	Amblyospiza albifrons	Grosbeak Weaver	Afm/B
668.	Anomalospiza imberbis	Parasitic Weaver	?
669.	Euplectes afer	Yellow-crowned Bishop	RB
670.	Euplectes ardens	Red-collared Widow-bird	?
671.	Euplectes hordeaceus	Black-winged Red Bishop	RB
672.	Euplectes macrourus	Yellow-mantled Widow-bird	RB, Afm
673.	Euplectes orix	Red Bishop	RB
674.	Malimbus cassini	Black-throated Malimbe	R?(B)
675.	Malimbus malimbicus	Crested Malimbe	R(B)
676.	Malimbus nitens	Gray's Malimbe	RB
677.	Malimbus rubriceps	Red-headed Weaver	RB
678.	Malimbus rubricollis	Red-headed Malimbe	RB
679.	Malimbus scutatus	Red-vented Malimbe	RB
680.	Ploceus albinucha	White-naped Weaver	RB
681.	Ploceus aurantius	Orange Weaver	RB
682.	Ploceus cucullatus	Black-headed Village Weaver	RB
683.	Ploceus heuglini	Heuglin's Masked Weaver	RB
684.	Ploceus luteolus	Little Weaver	RB, Afm
685.	Ploceus melanocephalus	Black-headed Weaver	R?(B)
686.	Ploceus nigerrimus	Chestnut and Black Weaver	RB
687.	Ploceus nigricollis	Black-necked Weaver	RB
688.	Ploceus pelzelni	Slender-billed Weaver	RB

689.	Ploceus preussi	Golden-backed Weaver	R(B)
690.	Ploceus superciliosus	Compact Weaver	RB
691.	Ploceus tricolor	Yellow-mantled Weaver	RB
692.	Ploceus velatus	Vitelline Masked Weaver	RB
693.	Quelea erythrops	Red-headed Quelea	AfM/B, R?B
694.	Quelea quelea	Red-billed Quelea	?

Viduinae

695.	Vidua chalybeata	Village Indigobird	R(B)
696.	Vidua larvaticola	Baka Indigobird	R(B)
697.	Vidua macroura	Pin-tailed Whydah	RB, Afm
698.	Vidua interjecta	Uelle Paradise Whydah	R(B)
699.	Vidua togoensis	Togo Paradise Whydah	R(B)
700.	Vidua raricola	Jambandu Indigobird	R(B)
701.	Vidua wilsoni	Wilson's Indigobird	RB, Afm

STURNIDAE
Sturninae

702.	Cinnyricinclus leucogaster	Violet-backed Starling	AfM/(B)
703.	Lamprotornis caudatus	Long-tailed Glossy Starling	RB, AfM/NB?
704.	Lamprotornis chalcurus	Bronze-tailed Glossy Starling	R(B), AfM/NB?
705.	Lamprotornis chalybaeus	Blue-eared Glossy Starling	AfM/NB
706.	Lamprotornis chloropterus	Lesser Blue-eared Glossy Starling	RB
707.	Lamprotornis cupreocauda	Copper-tailed Glossy Starling	R(B)
708.	Lamprotornis purpureus	Purple Glossy Starling	RB
709.	Lamprotornis splendidus	Splendid Glossy Starling	RB
710.	Onychognathus fulgidus [Onychognathus morio	Chestnut-wing Starling Red-wing Starling]	RB
711.	Poeoptera lugubris	Narrow-tailed Starling	R(B)
712.	Spreo pulcher	Chestnut-bellied Starling	AfM?/(B)

Buphaginae

713.	Buphagus africanus	Yellow-billed Oxpecker	R(B)

ORIOLIDAE

714.	Oriolus auratus	African Golden Oriole	AfM/(B)
715.	Oriolus brachyrhynchus	Black-headed Oriole	RB
716.	Oriolus nigripennis [Oriolus oriolus	Black-winged Oriole Golden Oriole]	RB

DICRURIDAE

717.	Dicrurus adsimilis	Drongo	RB
718.	Dicrurus atripennis	Shining Drongo	R(B)
719.	Dicrurus ludwigii	Square-tailed Drongo	RB

CORVIDAE

720.	Corvus alba	Pied Crow	RB, Afm
721.	Ptilostomus afer	Piapiac	RB

APPENDIX 1

Numbers and species ringed by M. Lockwood at Tafo, Ghana, and retrapped there in the same season as they were ringed and also in subsequent years

Species	Numbers of birds ringed						Retrapped in same year						Retrapped in subsequent years							
	1973	1974	1975	1976	1977	1978	1973	1974	1975	1976	1977	1978	1975	1976	1977	1978	1979	1980	1981	1982
Charadrius dubius	—	—	—	—	—	—	—	—	—	—	—	—	—	—	—	—	—	—	—	—
C. hiaticula	—	—	1	1	—	—	—	—	—	—	—	—	—	—	—	1	—	—	—	—
T. glareola	—	30	3	6	10	6	—	—	—	—	1	—	7	4	1	3	—	—	—	—
T. hypoleucos	—	51	14	23	25	16	—	6	4	5	—	3	—	—	—	—	—	—	1	—
T. ochropus	—	4	2	2	—	—	—	—	—	—	—	—	1	—	1	—	—	—	—	—
Gallinago gallinago	—	—	—	—	4	—	—	—	—	—	—	—	—	—	—	—	—	—	—	—
G. media	—	—	—	1	1	—	—	—	—	—	—	—	—	—	—	—	—	—	—	—
Hirundo rustica	83	456	464	635	3105	2190	2	21	10	19	26	21	3	8	15	11	—	—	—	—
Riparia riparia	—	1	1	—	7	18	—	—	—	—	—	—	—	—	—	—	—	—	—	1
Anthus cervinus	—	3	—	1	—	—	—	—	—	—	—	—	—	—	—	—	—	—	—	—
A. trivialis	—	2	20	2	1	—	—	—	—	—	—	—	—	—	—	—	—	—	—	—
Motacilla flava	6	106	277	172	253	18	—	—	14	8	4	—	7	7	6	—	—	—	—	—
Lanius senator	1	—	—	1	1	—	—	—	—	—	—	—	—	—	—	—	—	—	—	—
Luscinia megarhynchos	1	1	—	—	—	—	—	—	—	—	—	—	—	—	—	—	—	—	—	—
Saxicola rubetra	—	5	2	10	4	1	—	—	—	1	2	—	—	—	1	—	—	—	—	—
Acrocephalus arundinaceus	1	4	1	18	38	5	—	—	—	1	2	—	—	—	4	—	—	—	—	—
A. scirpaceus	1	1	—	14	19	3	1	—	—	—	—	—	—	—	—	1	—	—	—	—
Hippolais polyglotta	6	10	2	6	2	3	—	—	—	—	—	—	—	—	—	—	—	—	—	—
Phylloscopus trochilus	—	2	—	1	1	—	—	—	—	—	—	—	—	—	—	—	—	—	—	—
Sylvia borin	1	7	—	2	2	—	—	—	—	—	—	—	—	—	—	—	—	—	—	—
Muscicapa striata	—	—	1	—	—	—	—	—	—	—	—	—	—	—	—	—	—	—	1	—
Totals	102	683	791	897	3477	2262	3	27	28	34	35	24	18	19	28	16	—	—	2	1

APPENDIX 2

Swallows *Hirundo rustica* ringed at Tafo, Ghana (6°15'N, 00°22'W), and reported from abroad

Date ringed at Tofo	Date recovered	Country of recovery	Latitude	Longitude	Great circle distance (km) from Ghana	Compass direction (0°–360°) from Ghana	Interval between captures (days)
25.iii.77	15.x.80	Belgium	50°44'N	4°14'E	4971	4	1298
31.i.75	15.ix.75	France	47°53'N	1°52'W	4568	359	227
18.xii.75	8.viii.76	France	44°12'N	1°14'W	4157	359	234
24.ii.77	24.vi.78	France	45°14'N	4°57'E	4302	6	485
21.xi.77	24.vi.79	France	48°23'N	3°58'W	4633	357	580
24.xii.77	24.iv.78	France	45°16'N	0°04'E	4344	0·5	121
30.i.78	26.iv.81	France	43°18'N	0°25'W	4056	0	1182
11.xii.77	24.v.78	Germany	54°13'N	12°59'E	5404	10	164
4.iii.78	17.v.79	Germany	50°10'N	9°03'E	4898	8	439
26.ii.77	1.viii.77	Spain	41°56'N	0°30'W	3906	0	156
28.xi.77	9.viii.78	Spain	38°53'N	6°58'W	3627	351	254
25.x.75	10.v.76	Algeria	35°55'N	1°21'W	3238	359	198
4.xii.76	27.vi.78	Algeria	34°48'N	1°08'E	3042	2	570
4.i.76	8.v.76	Morocco	34°43'N	2°48'W	3113	356	125
9.xi.77	2.iv.79	Morocco	31°15'N	6°08'W	2783	349	509
12.xii.77	9.ix.78	Morocco	35°46'N	4°55'W	3252	353	271
30.i.78	17.ii.78	Morocco	33°04'N	7°37'W	3014	347	18
9.iii.78	31.iii.79	Morocco	31°42'N	4°57'W	2808	351	387

APPENDIX 3

Published recoveries of birds ringed outside Ghana and recovered within Ghana; data cover period ending November 1986. Co-ordinates in Gazetteer. Dates within brackets indicate date of letter containing information; ? indicates unknown dates.

	Species	Ringing Data Date	Country	Place	Recovery Data Date	Great Circle distance (km)	Compass direction (0°–360°) to Ghana	Interval between captures (days)	Locality in Ghana
3.	Procellaria puffinus	9.viii.65	UK	51°42'N, 05°18'W	9.x.65	5190	176	61	Half Assini
22.	Ardea cinerea	2.v.68	Yugoslavia	42°25'N, 20°24'E	19.i.69	4506	202	262	Anloga
		11.v.72	France	45°48'N, 00°54'W	17.v.73	4501	180	371	Apam
25.	Adrea purpurea	22.vi.65	Holland	52°12'N, 04°48'E	25.i.69	4964	186	1313	Near Atebubu
		5.vi.68	Holland	52°12'N, 04°48'E	27.iv.76	5120	185	2883	Near Akosombo
		7.vi.68	Holland	52°12'N, 04°48'E	15.iv.73	4985	185	1773	Near Warawana
		21.vi.68	Holland	52°12'N, 04°48'E	1.vii.70	4972	186	741	Bantama
		8.vi.71	France	43°16'N, 04°15'E	21.iv.73	5280	186	682	Near Shama
		9.vi.71	Holland	52°12'N, 04°48'E	24.x.72	4237	185	525	Tema
		11.vi.71	Holland	52°12'N, 04°48'E	10.i.72	5022	186	213	Near Kete Kratchi
		17.vi.76	Holland	52°12'N, 04°48'E	7.iv.80	5137	185	1390	Near Adawso
31.	Egretta garzetta	31.v.67	France	43°20'N, 04°26'E	1.vi.68	4173	185	366	Mepe
		26.vi.67	Ukraine	46°27'N, 31°35'E	2.v.68	5583	209	311	Elmina
38.	Ciconia ciconia	19.vi.66	Germany	53°16'N, 08°53'E	20.ii.67	5128	191	246	Near Branam
		19.vi.78	Germany	52°58'N, 09°13'E	10.x.80	5284	188	843	Near Keta
		8.vi.68	Spain	39°35'N, 06°02'W	?.iii.73	3304	181	~1727	Gambaga
		6.vi.69	Spain	40°09'N, 06°33'W	21.i.70	3485	181	229	East of Tamale
		28.v.74	Algeria	35°48'N, 05°48'E	11.xii.75	3009	193	562	Near Tamale
57.	Anas acuta	12.i.72	UK	54°30'N, 05°37'W	28.xii.72	5507	177	350	Half Assini
65.	Pandion haliaetus	5.viii.36	Sweden	59°01'N, 15°19'E	20.xi.36	6234	190	107	Takoradi
		5.vii.52	Sweden	59°03'N, 14°02'E	27.ix.54	6066	188	814	Sokpoe
		30.vi.57	Sweden	59°01'N, 16°28'E	3.xii.57	6061	190	156	Bator
		8.vii.60	Sweden	59°16'N, 18°32'E	15.x.60	5707	193	99	Nandom
		10.viii.65	Sweden	59°15'N, 15°12'E	27.i.71	5924	189	2027	Lake Volta
		30.vi.68	Sweden	57°06'N, 13°05'E	21.xii.73	5761	189	2000	Adawso
		29.vi.69	Sweden	58°34'N, 18°10'E	?.vi.70	5920	191	~351	Abotoasi
		13.vii.69	Sweden	60°06'N, 16°31'E	17.v.70	6069	189	308	Kpandu

65.	Pandion haliaetus (cont.)	1.vi.73	56°27'N, 15°11'E	Sweden	10.xi.73	5396	191	162	Saboba
		28.vi.73	59°18'N, 16°22'E	Sweden	5.v.75	6083	190	676	Senchi
		28.vi.73	59°18'N, 16°22'E	Sweden	23.xii.73	5953	190	178	Volta Lake
		10.vii.74	59°17'N, 17°02'E	Sweden	15.iv.76	6178	190	645	Nungua
		1.vii.75	58°05'N, 14°35'E	Sweden	25.i.77	5986	189	574	Ada
		23.vi.76	56°22'N, 14°31'E	Sweden	?.i.79	5732	190	~936	Akosombo
		3.vii.77	58°12'N, 12°18'E	Sweden	24.iv.78	5656	188	325	Salaga
		5.vii.77	58°30'N, 13°10'E	Sweden	21.iv.78	5912	188	290	Adawso
		28.vi.78	56°35'N, 13°24'E	Sweden	27.x.81	5710	189	1217	Volta Lake
		30.vi.78	58°29'N, 13°09'E	Sweden	?	5728	189	?	Yegi
		20.vi.80	59°20'N, 18°15'E	Sweden	19.i.83	6106	191	943	Volta Lake
		6.viii.71	65°20'N, 18°15'E	Lapland	1.vi.72	6729	201	300	Mpraeso
92.	Buteo buteo vulpinus	1.iv.67	37°06'N, 11°00'E	Tunisia	23.ix.69	3606	197	905	Keta lagoon
109.	Milvus migrans	23.vi.63	49°55'N, 08°24'E	Germany	29.i.80	4674	190	6064	Kpandae
		26.vi.78	49°48'N, 08°28'E	Germany	19.xii.78	4422	191	176	Near Bolgatanga
		13.vi.72	46°00'N, 01°20'W	France	1.v.73	4280	180	322	Ayerade
		11.vi.69	46°24'N, 06°54'E	Switzerland	24.ii.74	4356	188	1719	Near Poasi
		24.vi.71	46°54'N, 07°00'E	Switzerland	28.iii.72	4200	190	277	Near Nabuggo
		16.vi.73	46°12'N, 06°12'E	Switzerland	14.xii.73	4228	189	181	Near Masaka
		14.vi.72	37°02'N, 03°27'W	Spain	?.xi.73	3362	174	505	~Agbenohoe
		22.vi.77	39°54'N, 06°39'W	Spain	7.xii.77	3292	171	168	Bolgatanga
		25.vi.77	41°19'N, 05°05'W	Spain	15.i.79	3569	174	569	Tamale
110.	Pernis apivorus	4.viii.64	56°03'N, 13°04'E	Sweden	15.v.66	5589	190	649	Sekudumasi
		30.vii.35	59°23'N, 14°20'E	Sweden	Winter 36/37	6020	189	?	Nteso, Kwahu
		7.vii.39	59°30'N, 14°19'E	Sweden	?	5974	188	?	20 miles N of Kumasi
		12.viii.47	59°28'N, 14°21'E	Sweden	11.iv.55	6011	188	2799	Asakraka, Kwahu
		15.viii.65	58°07'N, 13°34'E	Sweden	17.i.67	5972	189	520	Asuboi
		5.viii.68	64°24'N, 20°28'E	Sweden	?.xii.68	6606	191	~132	Japekrom
		31.vii.68	58°03'N, 11°34'E	Sweden	10.iv.70	5745	187	618	Abotoasi
		15.vii.37	50°43'N, 07°00'E	Germany	4.xi.55	4963	189	6687	Near Lake Bosumtwi
		24.vii.76	51°56'N, 07°51'E	Germany	5.vi.80	5044	190	1412	Anyinesu
		28.vii.70	52°18'N, 05°36'E	Holland	9.v.73	5036	189	1015	Kotuo

Moreau (1972: 210) mentions that Finnish birds have been recovered in Ghana but these data have not been traced.

120.	Falco tinnunculus	14.vii.79	51°17'N, 05°46'E	Holland	6.vi.80	4921	189	327	Near Feteyana
		17.iv.67	37°06'N, 11°00'E	Tunisia	22.ii.70	3598	197	1010	Near Abo

Moreau (1972: 216) mentions a Czech bird recovered in Ghana but the data has not been traced.

171.	Charadrius hiaticula	17.viii.70	62°30'N, 06°02'E	Norway	10.x.71	6352	183	419	Korle lagoon
		13.ix.72	62°57'N, 08°25'E	Norway	17.i.73	6371	184	126	Keta
		13.viii.58	56°07'N, 16°14'E	Sweden	5.xi.61	5729	191	1180	Afiadenyigba

Appendix 3 (continued)

Species	Ringing Data Date	Ringing Data Country	Ringing Data Place	Recovery Data Date	Recovery Data Great Circle distance (km)	Recovery Data Compass direction (0°–360°) to Ghana	Recovery Data Interval between captures (days)	Locality in Ghana
171. Charadrius hiaticula (cont.)	27.viii.60	Sweden	56°07'N, 16°14'E	14.iv.66	5812	191	2056	Ada
	12.ix.60	Sweden	56°07'N, 16°14'E	3.xi.61	5800	191	417	Atiava
	6.vii.62	Sweden	56°02'N, 15°30'E	13.i.66	5776	190	1287	Dzelukope
	19.viii.62	Sweden	56°02'N, 15°30'E	28.x.62	5813	190	70	Accra
	6.viii.74	Sweden	56°07'N, 16°14'E	22.xii.75	5740	190	473	Adina
	20.viii.81	Sweden	57°11'N, 11°32'E	1.xii.81	5898	188	103	Mankesim
	24.viii.69	Germany	52°57'N, 08°25'E	27.xii.69	5437	188	125	Near Accra
	8.vii.77	UK	53°06'N, 00°21'E	12.xii.82	5253	179	1921	Genui
	17.v.82	UK	54°05'N, 02°49'W	15.xii.82	5394	179	212	Teshie
	21.viii.76	Poland	54°12'N, 18°34'E	(9.i.79)	3662	208	~871	Big Ada
176. Pluvialis squatarola	12.x.72	UK	52°39'N, 00°13'W	21.ix.77	5215	179	1866	Anloga
	9.x.76	UK	51°21'N, 00°54'E	(3.xii.76)	5156	183	~55	Half Assini
	10.ix.61	Sweden	60°18'N, 17°25'E	2.xii.61	6255	189	83	Keta
186. Numenius phaeopus	15.vii.76	UK	60°15'N, 01°28'W	28.ii.77	6046	178	228	Near Keta
	14.viii.81	UK	60°21'N, 00°58'W	28.x.81	6147	181	101	Half Assini
189. Tringa glareola	27.vii.60	Sweden	56°07'N, 16°14'E	14.iv.66	5887	193	2087	Near Ada
	6.vii.62	Sweden	56°07'N, 16°14'E	17.i.66	5880	193	1291	Dzelukope
	2.viii.62	Sweden	55°38'N, 12°34'E	28.i.73	5486	193	3832	Near Abudom
	20.vii.68	Sweden	59°07'N, 15°14'E	30.i.70	6029	189	559	Ehi
	3.viii.68	Sweden	59°13'N, 15°14'E	24.xii.68	5812	191	143	Ada
	9.viii.72	Sweden	59°13'N, 15°14'E	22.ii.73	6055	189	197	Afiadenyigba
	10.viii.73	Poland	54°13'N, 18°34'E	1.viii.75	5618	193	721	Anloga
	23.viii.77	Germany	51°39'N, 09°56'E	18.x.79	5143	190	787	Near Keta
190. Tringa hypoleucos	5.vii.66	Finland	60°07'N, 24°42'E	25.xii.66	6348	194	173	Alakple
	14.viii.66	Finland	61°29'N, 21°21'E	4.vii.68	6427	191	690	Near Ada
	23.viii.69	Sweden	55°38'N, 12°34'E	20.iii.74	5514	191	652	Near Golokwati
	8.viii.78	Sweden	56°07'N, 16°14'E	11.i.79	5752	191	156	Agorta
	11.viii.86	Sweden	56°07'N, 16°14'E	15.xi.86	5759	200	96	Asutsuare
191. Tringa nebularia	19.viii.72	Germany	52°00'N, 07°42'E	6.i.74	5281	189	505	Near Elmina
	26.viii.72	Germany	52°00'N, 07°42'E	28.i.73	5164	187	155	Near Keta lagoon
	13.viii.69	Holland	52°12'N, 06°12'E	4.i.71	5146	185	510	Near Adina

No.	Species	Date ringed	Country	Coordinates	Date recovered				Location
191.	Tringa nebularia (cont.)								
195.	Tringa totanus	16.viii.82	Sweden	59°07'N, 15°14'E	15.viii.84	6050	189	729	Klamadoboi
		19.vii.66	Sweden	56°07'N, 16°14'E	19.x.66	5925	192	92	Half Assini
196.	Arenaria interpres	28.vii.71	Sweden	67°16'N, 16°33'E	30.i.73	7012	187	551	Near Accra
		21.vi.64	Finland	59°56'N, 24°27'E	c.27.ii.67	6427	194	~981	Winneba
		4.viii.74	UK	52°53'N, 00°30'E	5.i.78	5259	180	1250	Anloga
		9.ix.75	UK	52°53'N, 00°09'E	5.xii.75	5338	182	87	Takoradi
		15.xii.79	Namibia	22°41'S, 14°31'E	29.x.80	3705	332	319	Kumasi
202.	Calidris alba	22.vii.53	Sweden	56°07'N, 16°14'E	23.xi.54	5748	191	489	Keta lagoon
		6.viii.67	UK	52°23'N, 03°11'E	13.ix.67	5319	177	38	Accra
		12.viii.68	UK	52°53'N, 00°30'E	c.5.xi.68	5224	179	~85	Keta
		31.viii.69	UK	52°53'N, 00°31'E	(6.xi.75)	5331	183	~2290	Beyin
		31.vii.77	UK	53°21'N, 03°19'W	c.13.ix.78	5345	178	~409	Apam
205.	Calidris ferruginea	17.ix.57	Sweden	56°07'N, 16°14'E	15.v.62	5748	191	1701	Keta
211.	Stercorarius parasiticus	26.vi.68	Finland	60°56'N, 21°08'E	25.xii.68	6381	192	182	Prampram
		6.vii.70	UK	58°57'N, 02°42'W	7.i.72	5982	178	550	Near Apam
		18.vii.73	UK	59°32'N, 01°32'W	(22.vi.77)	6072	180	~1435	Takoradi
215.	Larus fuscus	28.vii.34	Sweden	57°12'N, 18°02'E	7.i.35	5936	191	189	Keta
		23.vii.35	Sweden	57°12'N, 12°03'E	20.i.36	5837	187	181	Keta
221.	Sterna albifrons	22.vii.48	Sweden	55°36'N, 14°16'E	?.xii.49	5691	189	~511	Keta
		8.vi.65	Sweden	56°10'N, 16°01'E	(3.iii.66)	5742	191	~268	Anyako
225.	Sterna dougallii	20.iv.49	Indonesia	07°30'S, 110°00'E	4.xii.52	11988	260	1320	Keta

At least 182 British ringed birds have been recovered along the Ghana coastline

No.	Species	Date ringed	Country	Coordinates	Date recovered				Location
226.	Sterna fuscata	13.vii.60	USA	24°38'N, 82°52'W	3.xi.61	9072	114	478	Ada
		17.vii.60	USA	24°38'N, 82°52'W	31.x.61	9004	114	471	Near Accra
		8.vii.63	USA	24°38'N, 82°52'W	6.iv.64	9072	114	273	Ada
		24.vi.64	USA	24°38'N, 82°52'W	4.vi.66	8761	114	710	Half Assini
		8.vi.67	USA	24°38'N, 82°52'W	26.i.68	8882	114	232	Takoradi
		9.vi.67	USA	24°38'N, 82°52'W	30.xii.67	8835	114	204	Asanta
		10.vi.67	USA	24°38'N, 82°52'W	20.iv.68	8835	114	315	Asanta

At least 293 ringed birds from western Europe have been recovered along the Ghana coastline; the following were ringed in Poland:

No.	Species	Date ringed	Country	Coordinates	Date recovered				Location
227.	Sterna hirundo	20.vi.57	Poland	54°01'N, 21°34'E	20.v.59	5663	196	699	Anyako
		15.vii.65	Poland	54°13'N, 18°34'E	2.x.65	5691	194	79	Near Accra
		8.vi.75	Poland	51°20'N, 17°13'E	29.ix.75	5414	195	113	Cape Coast
		15.vi.80	Poland	51°19'N, 17°04'E	12.iii.81	5381	195	270	Off Shore
		27.vi.80	Poland	53°31'N, 14°12'E	(10.vii.81)	5465	190	~378	Keta
228.	Sterna hybrida	12.vi.59	France	46°48'N, 01°12'E	24.xii.61	4557	180	925	Anloga
		19.vii.67	France	46°00'N, 05°00'E	c.20.i.68	4474	185	~185	Keta
		6.vi.70	France	47°30'N, 01°54'E	11.ii.72	4624	181	615	Keta
		25.vi.65	Spain	39°18'N, 00°20'W	4.x.65	3695	179	101	Near Osudoku

Appendix 3 (continued)

	Species	Ringing Data Date	Country	Place	Recovery Data Date	Great Circle distance (km)	Compass direction (0°–360°) to Ghana	Interval between captures (days)	Locality in Ghana
228.	Sterna hybrida (cont.)	?.vi.65	Spain	39°18'N, 00°20'W	28.xi.66	3638	181	~516	Nkawkaw
230.	Sterna maxima	6.vii.60	Morocco	c.30°00'N, 10°00'W	28.i.61	2917	164	206	Shama
231.	Sterna nigra	26.vi.65	Holland	52°12'N, 04°48'E	30.vi.67	5158	184	735	Keta
		26.vi.65	Holland	52°12'N, 04°48'E	15.viii.67	5158	184	781	Keta
		25.x.73	Mauritania	19°24'N, 16°30'W	15.vi.74	2167	137	173	Tabo
		19.xi.73	Mauritania	19°24'N, 16°30'W	15.ii.74	2415	128	88	Near Keta
		8.ii.68	Ivory Coast	05°12'N, 03°42'W	19.i.71	540	80	1076	Near Denu
		24.ii.68	Ivory Coast	05°12'N, 03°42'W	24.xi.68	378	85	274	Sakumo lagoon
		18.vii.81	Sweden	58°30'N, 14°30'E	27.iii.82	6012	189	252	Near Keta
233.	Sterna paradisaea	At least 18 British ringed birds and some Finnish birds have been recovered along the coast of Ghana							
234.	Sterna sandvicensis	At least 548 ringed birds from Western Europe have been recovered along the coast of Ghana, of which 84% are British ringed birds							
235.	Sterna tschegrava	29.vi.53	Finland	60°15'N, 26°25'E	16.xii.54	6421	210	535	Keta lagoon
		20.vi.58	Finland	60°00'N, 24°36'E	15.i.59	6223	209	209	Volta Lake
		20.vi.58	Finland	60°00'N, 24°36'E	6.v.59	6345	208	320	Keta lagoon
		5.vii.59	Finland	65°24'N, 24°48'E	5.xi.59	6883	209	123	Near Bekwai
		27.vi.60	Finland	60°00'N, 24°36'E	1.xi.61	6056	210	492	N of Bimbila
		4.vii.61	Finland	65°24'N, 24°48'E	5.v.66	6893	207	1765	Keta
		23.vi.69	Finland	60°38'N, 20°57'E	20.vi.71	6330	203	727	Keta
		26.vi.69	Finland	59°54'N, 23°42'E	16.x.69	6283	208	112	Volta Lake
		23.vi.70	Finland	60°36'N, 21°00'E	12.xi.70	6306	204	142	Keta
		26.vi.70	Finland	59°55'N, 24°02'E	9.viii.72	6332	207	774	Keta
		16.vii.70	Finland	65°24'N, 24°48'E	30.xi.70	6883	207	137	Keta
		22.vi.71	Finland	60°40'N, 20°56'E	15.iii.73	6332	203	631	Keta
		19.vi.73	Finland	60°40'N, 20°55'E	18.ii.74	6331	203	244	Keta
		11.vii.73	Finland	59°52'N, 22°41'E	17.i.75	6189	207	555	Volta Lake
		24.vi.79	Finland	60°15'N, 26°25'E	15.i.80	6428	210	205	Keta
		4.vii.79	Finland	65°22'N, 24°50'E	28.vii.80	6956	208	389	Labadi, Accra
		3.vii.58	Sweden	60°13'N, 18°28'E	?.ii.63	6200	190	~1688	Dzozde
		23.vi.65	Sweden	57°25'N, 16°29'E	(2.viii.67)	5893	190	~770	Keta
		23.vi.65	Sweden	58°31'N, 17°05'E	4.xii.70	6020	190	1990	Keta
		12.vi.66	Sweden	58°28'N, 18°01'E	15.v.67	6011	191	337	Afiadenyigba

235.	Sterna tschegrava (cont.)	18.vi.66	60°16'N	18°21'E	Sweden	25.xi.66	6228	190	160	Keta
		16.vii.69	55°25'N	16°29'E	Sweden	c.22.iv.70	5675	192	~280	Yegi
		19.vi.70	60°23'N	17°34'E	Sweden	13.xi.70	6225	190	147	Keta
		23.vi.70	58°28'N	18°01'E	Sweden	16.vi.73	6029	191	1089	Afife
		23.vi.70	58°28'N	18°01'E	Sweden	17.vi.73	6029	191	1090	Afife
		10.vi.72	60°16'N	18°21'E	Sweden	(7.iii.74)	6228	190	~635	Keta
		23.vi.72	57°25'N	16°29'E	Sweden	13.vii.74	5891	191	750	Anyako
		9.vi.73	57°25'N	16°29'E	Sweden	18.xi.73	5893	190	162	Anyako
		10.vi.73	57°25'N	16°29'E	Sweden	29.ix.77	5891	191	1572	Keta
		22.vi.73	58°20'N	17°07'E	Sweden	4.iii.74	6002	190	255	Keta
		8.vi.75	58°20'N	17°07'E	Sweden	16.x.83	5950	193	3052	Biaso
		5.vi.76	60°16'N	18°21'E	Sweden	21.x.76	6226	190	138	Anyako
		12.vii.76	58°20'N	17°07'E	Sweden	(26.iv.82)	6000	191	~2144	Anyako
		3.vii.80	58°08'N	17°02'E	Sweden	(1.vii.82)	5997	190	~728	Anloga
319.	Apus melba	5.vii.71	47°24'N	08°12'E	Switzerland	22.i.72	4484	189	201	Near Pampawie
419.	Hirundo rustica	26.vi.63	52°49'N	01°56'E	UK	(28.i.64)	5052	180	~216	Sunyani
		27.ix.66	53°14'N	02°17'W	UK	18.iv.67	5026	178	203	Prang
		27.vi.69	54°34'N	03°36'W	UK	20.x.69	5349	178	115	Onwi
		27.vi.77	52°51'N	02°50'W	UK	25.x.77	5120	179	120	Okaekurum
		1.ix.80	53°30'N	01°22'W	UK	28.i.81	5285	178	149	Anyako
		28.viii.61	51°14'N	05°07'E	Belgium	30.xi.62	5163	185	428	Mankrong
		14.ix.62	50°59'N	02°52'E	Belgium	1.xii.62	4990	183	78	Near Tafo
		1.x.68	50°56'N	04°02'E	Belgium	9.ii.69	5093	184	131	Kromain
		12.vii.76	51°02'N	04°00'E	Belgium	20.ii.77	4980	184	253	Tafo
		21.viii.76	50°51'N	03°18'E	Belgium	26.ii.77	4970	183	189	Tafo
		13.ix.76	50°44'N	04°14'E	Belgium	21.ii.78	4964	184	526	Tafo
		30.ix.77	50°44'N	04°14'E	Belgium	30.i.78	4901	184	123	Tafo
		15.viii.77	50°44'N	04°14'E	Belgium	7.iii.78	4901	184	204	Tafo
		7.ix.77	50°44'N	04°14'E	Belgium	7.iii.78	4901	184	181	Tafo
		19.ix.77	50°44'N	04°14'E	Belgium	8.xii.77	4901	184	80	Tafo
		27.vii.43	52°15'N	10°30'E	Germany	16.i.48	5323	190	1634	Domenasi
		27.viii.77	48°54'N	08°12'E	Germany	17.x.77	4897	190	51	Near Agona
		5.viii.61	51°18'N	05°27'E	Holland	25.xii.62	5133	186	233	Accra
		26.vii.62	51°18'N	03°36'E	Holland	1.xi.62	4873	186	98	Krukrom
		27.vii.69	52°30'N	06°00'E	Holland	10.i.70	5158	188	167	Near Lake Bosumtwi
		18.viii.72	51°30'N	05°54'E	Holland	15.xii.72	5070	187	119	Aboabo
		5.vi.73	49°42'N	06°06'E	Luxembourg	26.x.73	4859	186	143	Near Dzodze
		18.viii.67	47°24'N	06°36'E	France	2.xii.72	4671	188	106	Near Nsawam
		5.vi.72	46°36'N	03°18'E	France	8.xii.72	4566	184	186	Near Prampram

Appendix 3 (continued)

	Species	Ringing Data			Recovery Data				Locality in Ghana
		Date	Country	Place	Date	Great Circle distance (km)	Compass direction (0°–360°) to Ghana	Interval between captures (days)	
419.	Hirundo rustica (cont.)	29.vi.72	France	46°18'N, 03°00'E	15.i.73	4444	185	200	Near Lake Bosumtwi
		13.ix.68	France	49°29'N, 02°59'E	27.iii.69	4838	182	195	Near Keta
		19.vii.73	France	47°18'N, 01°33'W	17.xi.73	4569	179	121	Tafo
		6.ix.73	France	47°34'N, 06°38'E	14.i.74	4632	189	130	Tafo
		13.vi.76	France	45°53'N, 02°24'E	20.ii.77	4996	185	253	Tafo
		7.ix.76	France	47°54'N, 01°54'E	21.x.76	4479	186	44	Npuasu
		29.viii.77	France	48°55'N, 08°09'E	24.xii.77	4749	188	117	Tafo
		5.ix.77	France	45°52'N, 01°04'W	23.ii.78	4342	179	171	Tafo
		8.viii.77	Spain	38°53'N, 06°46'W	25.i.78	3628	171	170	Tafo
		6.vii.75	Ireland	53°20'N, 06°10'W	19.ix.75	5389	176	75	Cape Coast (R. B. Payne)
437.	Motacilla flava	10.viii.52	Baltic	c.57°00'N, 16°30'E	14.xi.52	5780	193	96	Dorma Ahenkro
		10.viii.52	Sweden	56°07'N, 16°14'E	14.xi.52	5683	193	96	Sunyani
		17.viii.65	Sweden	56°07'N, 16°14'E	13.xii.67	5765	195	848	Babianiha
		24.viii.60	Sweden	55°14'N, 12°30'E	29.xi.60	5577	188	97	Duffor
		25.vi.71	Sweden	65°28'N, 22°02'E	27.x.72	6832	190	490	Agbakofe
		7.ix.75	Sweden	55°16'N, 12°36'E	9.iii.76	5111	190	184	Nsuta
		17.viii.76	Germany	49°15'N, 09°10'E	15.ii.77	4864	189	182	Tafo
519.	Acrocephalus arundinaceus	7.viii.76	Austria	47°46'N, 16°48'E	20.ii.77	4421	184	252	Tafo
521.	A. schoenobaenus	27.viii.73	UK	53°49'N, 01°14'W	26.iv.74	4481	182	273	Lawra
522.	A. scirpaceus	15.vii.81	UK	52°39'N, 00°42'W	27.ix.81	4955	180	74	Kete Kratchi
		3.viii.66	Sweden	57°31'N, 14°11'E	30.ix.66	5781	189	58	Effiduasi
		12.viii.76	Holland	52°36'N, 05°54'E	1.xi.77	5085	189	173	Near Wamfie
		10.viii.69	UK	51°24'N, 01°15'W	7.xii.69	5058	179	119	Asrema
544.	Hippolais icterina	28.vi.74	France	49°12'N, 02°36'E	5.v.76	4639	182	676	Near Kadjebi
555.	Phylloscopus trochilus	3.v.65	Belgium	50°54'N, 04°30'E	30.iv.66	4847	187	336	Near Nkoranza
		5.viii.72	UK	50°17'N, 03°39'W	17.xii.77	4737	179	1960	Dwenem
580.	Muscicapa striata	27.vi.52	UK	54°16'N, 02°42'W	31.x.52	5444	179	126	Tarkwa

APPENDIX 4
Species totals and numbers of migrants analysed by eco-taxonomic groups

	Total number of species in each family in Ghana	Extra-African migrant species	African species	Marine	Lowland forest	Lowland savanna stenotopic	Lowland savanna eurytopic	Total Intra-African migrants
			African species (migrant totals in brackets)*					
A: AQUATIC FAMILIES								
Podicipedidae	1		1				1	
Procellariidae	2	2						
Hydrobatidae	4	3	1	1				
Phaethontidae	1		1	1				
Pelecanidae	2		2				2(1)	1
Sulidae	2		2	2(1)				1
Phalacrocoracidae	2		2				2	
Anhingidae	1		1				1	
Ardeidae Botaurinae	3	1	2			2(2)		2
Ardeinae	15	1	14		1	8(2)	5(2)	4
Scopidae	1		1				1	
Ciconiidae	8	2	6			3(2)	3(4)	6
Threskiornithidae								
Threskiornithinae	5	1	4		2	1(1)	1	1
Plataleinae	1		1				1	
Anatidae Anserinae	2		2			2(2)		2
Anatinae	14	8	6		1	2	3	
Pandionidae	1	1						
Gruidae	1		1				1(1)	1
Rallidae	12	1	11		4	4(4)	3	4
Heliornithidae	1		1			1		
Jacanidae	1		1			1		
Rostratulidae	1		1			1(1)		1
Haematopididae	1	1						
Recurvirostridae	2	1	1			1		
Glareolidae Glareolinae	4	1	3			3(1)		1
Charadriidae	15	5	10			5(4)	5(1)	5
Scolopacidae Tringinae	13	13						
Arenariinae	1	1						
Phalaropinae	1	1						
Gallinagoninae	4	4						
Calidrinae	9	9						
Stercorariidae	3	3						
Laridae Larinae	5	4	1			1(1)		1
Sterninae	17	9	8	8(3)				3
Rhynchopidae	1		1			1		
Alcedinidae Cerylinae	2		2				2	
Alcedininae	5		5		2	1	2	
Totals	**164**	**72**	**92**	**12(4)**	**10**	**37(20)**	**33(9)**	**33**

*The numbers in brackets are included in the total for each habitat in columns 4–7, e.g. 8(3) means 8 species occur in the Marine habitat, of which 3 are migrants.

Appendix 4 (cont.)

	Total number of species in each family in Ghana	Extra-African migrant species	African species	Marine	Lowland forest	Lowland savanna stenotopic	Lowland savanna eurytopic	Total Intra-African migrants
			African species (migrant totals in brackets)*					
B: PREDATORS								
Accipitridae Aegypinae	6		6		1	2	3	
Accipitrinae	39	8	31		11	2	18(9)	9
Sagittariidae	1		1				1(1)	1
Falconiidae	9	3	6			1	5(4)	4
Tytonidae	1		1				1	
Strigidae	14		14		6	2	6	
Totals	**70**	**11**	**59**		**18**	**7**	**34(14)**	**14**
C: GROUND BIRDS								
Phasianidae Phasianinae	8	1	7		2	1	4(2?)	2
Numidinae	3		3		2		1	
Turnicidae	3		3				3(1)	1
Otididae	4		4				4(3)	3
Burhinidae	3		3				3(2)	2
Glareolidae Cursorinae	3		3				3(1)	1
Pteroclididae	1		1				1(1)	1
Totals	**25**	**1**	**24**		**4**	**1**	**19(10)**	10
D: OTHER NON-PASSERINE FAMILIES								
Columbidae	17	1	16		4	1	11(1)	1
Psittacidae	7		7		2	1	4	
Musophagidae	5		5		2		3	
Cuculidae								
Cuculinae	14	1	13		4		9(6)	6
Phaenicophaeninae	1		1		1			
Centropinae	4		4		1	1(1)	2	1
Caprimulgidae	9	1	8		1	1	6(3)	3
Apodidae	12	3	9		4		5(1)	1
Coliidae	1		1				1	
Trogonidae	1		1		1			
Alcedinidae								
Daceloninae	5		5		1	1	3(3)	3
Meropidae	11	1	10		3(1)	1(1)	6(3)	5
Coraciidae	6	1	5		1		4(3)	4
Upupidae	1		1				1(1)	1
Phoeniculidae	4		4		2		2(1)	1
Bucerotidae	12		12		9		3(1)	1
Capitonidae	13		13		8		5	
Indicatoridae	7		7		4		3	
Picidae								
Jynginae	1	1						
Picuminae	1		1		1			
Picinae	11		11		3		8	
Totals	**143**	**9**	**134**		**52(1)**	**6(2)**	**76(24)**	**27**

Appendix 4 (cont.)

	Total number of species in each family in Ghana	Extra-African migrant species	African species	Marine	Lowland forest	Lowland savanna stenotopic	Lowland savanna eurytopic	Total Intra-African migrants
					African species (migrant totals in brackets)*			
E: PASSERINES								
Eurylaemidae	2		2		2			
Pittidae	1		1		1(1)			1
Alaudidae	5		5				5(2)	2
Hirundinidae	18	2	16		3	1	12(5)	5
Motacillidae	9	5	4				4	
Campephagidae	5		5		3		2	
Pycnonotidae	24		24		22	1	1	
Laniidae Prionopinae	2		2		1		1	
Malaconotinae	14		14		3		11(1)	1
Laniinae	5	1	4				4	
Muscicapidae Turdinae	22	7	15		8	3	4(1)	1
Timaliinae	8		8		6		2	
Picathartinae	1		1		1			
Sylviinae	46	13	33		14	4	15	
Muscicapinae	18	3	15		9	3	3	
Platysteirinae	8		8		5	1	2	
Monarchinae	8		8		4		4(1)	1
Remizidae	2		2				2	
Paridae	2		2		1		1	
Certhidae	1		1				1	
Nectariniidae	23		23		12	2	9(4)	4
Zosteropidae	1		1				1	
Emberizidae	3		3				3(1)	1
Fringillidae	3		3				3	
Estrildidae	28		28		9	4	15(3)	3
Ploceidae								
Bubalornithinae	1		1				1	
Passerinae	4		4				4	
Ploceinae	28		28		9	1	18(1)	1
Viduinae	7		7				7	
Sturnidae Sturninae	11		11		4		7(1)	1
Buphaginae	1		1				1	
Oriolidae	3		3		2		1	
Dicruridae	3		3		2		1	
Corvidae	2		2				2	
Totals	**319**	**31**	**288**		**121(1)**	**20**	**147(20)**	**21**

APPENDIX 5

Species collected by Pel (LP) and Nagtglas (LN) in the Rijksmuseum van Natuurlijke Historie, Leiden, Holland; by Lamm (S) in the Smithsonian Institution, Washington, DC, USA; those in the Zoology Department, University of Ghana, Legon, Ghana (U); by Payne (see footnote * at end) in the Zoology Department, University of Michigan, Ann Arbor, USA (M); and at the Game Reserve at Mole. Ghana (GR).

NON-PASSERINES

PODICIPEDIDAE
Podiceps ruficollis	U

PROCELLARIIDAE
Procellaria gravis	LP

SULIDAE
Sula leucogaster	LP

PHALACROCORACIDAE
Phalacrocorax africanus	LP, LN, U

ARDEIDAE
Botaurus stellaris	GR
Ixobrychus minutus	GR
Ixobrychus sturmii	LP
Tigriornis leucolophus	LP, S
Nycticorax leuconotus	LP
Nycticorax nycticorax	LP
Ardea cinerea	LP, U
Ardea melanocephala	LP
Ardea purpurea	LP
Butorides striatus	LP, LN, U, GR, S
Ardeola ralloides	LN, U
Ardeola ibis	LP, U
Egretta alba	LP
Egretta garzetta garzetta	LP, U
Egretta garzetta gularis	LP, LN, U

SCOPIDAE
Scopus umbretta	U, GR

CICONIIDAE
Ciconia ciconia	GR
Ciconia nigra	LP

THRESKIORNITHIDAE
Bostrychia hagedash	GR, S
Threskiornis aethiopica	LP

ANATIDAE
Dendrocygna viduata	LP, U, GR
Plectropterus gambensis	GR
Sarkidiornis melanota	U

PANDIONIDAE
Pandion haliaetus	LP

ACCIPITRIDAE
Gypohierax angolensis	LP, U, GR, S
Neophron monachus	LP
Circaetus beaudouini	U
Circus macrourus	LP, U
Dryotriorchis spectabilis	U

Polyboroides radiatus	LP
Terathopius ecaudatus	U, GR
Accipiter badius	U, GR
Accipiter erythropus	LP
Accipiter melanoleucus	LP, U
Accipiter toussenelii	LP, U, S
Melierax metabates	S
Urotriorchis macrourus	LP, LN
Butastur rufipennis	GR, S
Buteo auguralis	U, GR
Kaupifalco monogrammicus	U, GR
Aquila wahlbergi	U
Lophaetus occipitalis	U
Elanus caeruleus	LP, GR
Milvus migrans	LP, U, GR
Pernis apivorus	LP

FALCONIDAE

Falco ardosiaceus	U
Falco biarmicus	U
Falco cuvieri	LN, U
Falco tinnunculus	GR

PHASIANIDAE

Francolinus ahantensis	LP
Francolinus albogularis	U, GR
Francolinus bicalcaratus	LN, U, GR, S
Francolinus lathami	LP, U
Ptilopachus petrosus	U, GR, S
Agelastes meleagrides	LP
Guttera edouardi	LP
Numida meleagris	GR

TURNICIDAE

Turnix sylvatica	S

RALLIDAE

Canirallus oculeus	LP, LN, S
Crex egregia	S
Gallinula angulata	S
Gallinula chloropus	GR
Himantornis haematopus	LP
Limnocorax flavirostra	LP, U, S
Porphyrio alleni	LP, S
Porzana marginalis	S
Sarothrura pulchra	LP, LN

HELIORNITHIDAE

Podica senegalensis	LP, U

OTIDIDAE

Eupodotis melanogaster	U
Eupodotis senegalensis	S
Neotis denhami	U

JACANIDAE

Actophilornis africana	LP, LN, U, GR

ROSTRATULIDAE

Rostratula benghalensis	S

RECURVIROSTRIDAE

Himantopus himantopus	LP, U

BURHINIDAE

Burhinus capensis	GR
Burhinus senegalensis	U, S

GLAREOLIDAE

Cursorius chalcopterus	GR
Cursorius temminckii	LP, S
Pluvianus aegyptius	U, GR
Glareola pratincola	LP, U

CHARADRIIDAE

Charadrius dubius	LP, LN
Charadrius forbesi	GR
Charadrius hiaticula	LP
Charadrius pecuarius	LP, S
Pluvialis squatarola	LP, LN, U
Vanellus lugubris	LP, LN
Vanellus senegallus	LN, U, S

SCOLOPACIDAE

Numenius arquata	U
Numenius phaeopus	LN, U
Tringa glareola	U, GR
Tringa hypoleucos	LP, GR
Tringa nebularia	LP, LN, U
Tringa stagnatilis	LP, U
Tringa totanus	LP
Arenaria interpres	LN
Gallinago media	GR, S
Calidris ferruginea	LP, S
Calidris minuta	LP

LARIDAE

Sterna albifrons	GR**
Sterna fuscata	LP, S, U
Sterna hirundo	LP, U, GR**, S
Sterna maxima	LP
Sterna nigra	LP, GR**
Sterna paradisaea	LP
Sterna sandvicensis	U, GR**

RHYNCHOPIDAE

Rhynchops flavirostris	U

PTEROCLIDIDAE

Pterocles quadricinctus	GR

COLUMBIDAE

Oena capensis	GR
Streptopelia semitorquata	LP, LN, GR
Streptopelia turtur	GR
Streptopelia vinacea	GR, S
Treron australis	LP, LN, U, GR
Treron waalia	GR
Turtur abyssinicus	GR
Turtur afer	LP, LN, M, S
Turtur brehmeri	LP, LN
Turtur tympanistria	LP, LN, M

PSITTACIDAE

Agapornis pullaria	LN, GR
Poicephalus gulielmi	LN
Poicephalus senegalus	LN, U, GR
Psittacus erithacus	S

MUSOPHAGIDAE

Corytheola cristata	LP, LN, U, GR, S
Crinifer piscator	LN, U, GR
Musophaga violacea	LP, LN, U, GR
Tauraco macrorhynchus	LP, LN, S
Tauraco persa	LP, U

CUCULIDAE

Chrysococcyx caprius	LP, LN, M
Chrysococcyx cupreus	LP, LN, S
Chrysococcyx klaas	LN, GR, S
Clamator levaillantii	U, GR, S
Cuculus canorus gularis	LN
Cuculus clamosus	LP, LN
Pachycoccyx audeberti	U
Ceuthmochares aereus	LP, LN, S
Centropus leucogaster	LP, LN, U, S
Centropus monachus	LP, LN
Centropus senegalensis	LP, LN, U, GR

TYTONIDAE

Tyto alba	U, GR, S

STRIGIDAE

Bubo africanus	U, GR
Bubo leucostictus	LP, U
Bubo poensis	LP, U, S
Ciccaba woodfordii	U
Otus leucotis	U
Scotopelia peli	LP

CAPRIMULGIDAE

Caprimulgus binotatus	LP
Caprimulgus climacurus	LP, U, GR
Caprimulgus natalensis	S
Macrodipteryx longipennis	U, S

APODIDAE

Cypsiurus parvus	LN

TROGONIDAE

Apaloderma narina	LN, S

ALCEDINIDAE

Ceryle maxima	LP, U, GR, S
Ceryle rudis	LP, LN, U
Alcedo cristata	LN, U, S
Alcedo leucogaster	LN
Alcedo quadribrachys	LP, GR, S
Ceyx picta	LN, GR
Halcyon badia	S
Halcyon chelicuti	U, GR, S
Halcyon malimbica	LP, GR
Halcyon senegalensis	LN, GR, S

MEROPIDAE

Merops albicollis	LP, LN, U, S
Merops bulocki	GR
Merops gularis	LP, LN, S
Merops hirundineus	S
Merops nubicus	GR
Merops pusillus	LP, LN, M, GR, S

CORACIIDAE

Coracias abyssinica	U, GR

Coracias cyanogaster	S
Coracias naevia	GR
Eurystomus glaucurus	LP, LN, U, GR
Eurystomus gularis	LP, LN, S

UPUPIDAE
Upupa epops senegalensis	GR

PHOENICULIDAE
Phoeniculus aterrimus	GR
Phoeniculus bollei	S
Phoeniculus castaneiceps	S
Phoeniculus purpureus	GR

BUCEROTIDAE
Bucorvus abyssinicus	LP
Bycanistes cylindricus	LP, LN
Bycanistes fistulator	LP, LN, U
Ceratogymna atrata	LP, LN, U
Ceratogymna elata	LP, LN, U
Tockus camurus	LN, S
Tockus fasciatus	LP, U, S
Tockus hartlaubi	LN, S
Tockus nasutus	U, GR
Tropicranus albocristatus	S

CAPITONIDAE
Buccanodon duchaillui	LN, S
Gymnobucco calvus	LP, LN, S
Gymnobucco peli	S
Lybius bidentatus	LN, S
Lybius dubius	GR
Lybius hirsutus	LP, LN, S
Lybius vieilloti	LP, LN, U, GR
Pogoniulus atro-flavus	LN
Pogoniulus bilineatus	LN, S
Pogoniulus chrysoconus	GR
Pogoniulus scolopaceus	LP, LN, U, S
Pogoniulus subsulphureus	LN, S
Trachyphonus purpuratus	LN

INDICATORIDAE
Indicator indicator	GR, S
Indicator maculatus	LP
Indicator minor	S

PICIDAE
Jynx torquilla	GR
Campethera nivosa	LP, LN
Campethera punctuligera	GR, S
Dendropicos fuscescens	GR
Dendropicos gabonensis	S
Dendropicos obsoletus	GR
Mesopicos goertae	GR, S
Mesopicos pyrrhogaster	S

PASSERINES

EURYLAIMIDAE
Smithornis rufolateralis	LN, S

PITTIDAE
Pitta angolensis	LP, U

ALAUDIDAE
Galerida modesta	S
Mirafra rufocinnamomea	GR, S

HIRUNDINIDAE
Hirundo abyssinica	LP, GR
Hirundo fuligula	S
Hirundo nigrita	LP, S
Hirundo rustica lucida	GR
Hirundo semirufa	LN, M, GR, S
Psalidoprocne nitens	LN
Psalidoprocne obscura	LP, GR
Riparia paludicola	GR

MOTACILLIDAE
Anthus leucophrys	U, S
Anthus trivialis	S
Macronyx croceus	LP, LN, U, S
Motacilla flava	S

CAMPEPHAGIDAE
Campephaga phoenicea	LN, GR, S
Campephaga quiscalina	LN, S
Coracina azurea	LN, S
Coracina pectoralis	GR

PYCNONOTIDAE
Andropadus curvirostris	S
Andropadus gracilirostris	LP, LN
Andropadus gracilis	LP, LN, S
Andropadus latirostris	LP, U
Andropadus virens	M, S
Baeopogon indicator	LP
Bleda canicapilla	LN, U
Bleda eximia	LP, LN
Calyptocichla serina	LN
Chlorocichla simplex	LP, LN, S
Criniger barbatus	LP
Criniger calurus	LP, LN
Nicator chloris	LP, S
Phyllastrephus albigularis	S
Phyllastrephus icterinus	LP
Pycnonotus barbatus	LP, U, GR
Thescelocichla leucopleurus	LP, LN, S

LANIIDAE
Prionops caniceps	LP, S
Prionops plumata	U, GR
Dryoscopus gambensis	LN, GR, S
Dryoscopus sabini	LP, LN, S
Laniarius barbarus	LP, LN, U, GR, S
Laniarius ferrugineus	LN, U, S
Laniarius leucorhynchus	LP
Malaconotus blanchoti	S
Malaconotus cruentus	LP
Malaconotus multicolor	LN
Malaconotus sulfureopectus	LN, M, GR, S
Nilaus afer	GR, S
Tchagra australis	M
Tchagra minuta	GR, S
Tchagra senegala	LP, LN, U, M, GR
Corvinella corvina	U, S
Lanius collaris	LP, LN, M, S

MUSCICAPIDAE

Alethe diademata	LP, LN, S
Alethe poliocephala	LP, LN
Cercomela familiaris	GR
Cossypha albicapilla	GR, S
Cossypha cyanocampter	LP
Cossypha niveicapilla	LP, LN, M, GR
Myrmecocichla albifrons	S, GR
Neocossyphus poensis	LP, LN, U
Phoenicurus phoenicurus	S
Saxicola rubetra	U, S
Stiphrornis erythrothorax	LP, LN, S, U
Stizorhina fraseri	LN, S
Turdus pelios	U, GR
Phyllanthus atripennis	LP
Trichastoma fulvescens	LN
Trichastoma rufescens	S
Trichastoma rufipennis	S
Turdoides plebejus	U, GR, S
Turdoides reinwardii	U, S
Camaroptera brachyura	U, GR, M, S
Camaroptera chloronota	S
Cisticola aberrans	S
Cisticola brachyptera	M, S
Cisticola cantans	S
Cisticola erythrops	M, S
Cisticola galactotes	LP
Cisticola juncidis	S
Cisticola lateralis	GR, S
Cisticola natalensis	U, S
Cisticola rufa	GR, S
Cisticola ruficeps	S
Eremomela badiceps	LN, S
Eremomela pusilla	GR, S
Hylia prasina	LP, S
Hypergerus atriceps	LP, LN, S
Macrosphenus concolor	LN, S
Phylloscopus sibilatrix	S
Prinia erythroptera	M, GR, S
Prinia subflava	LN, GR
Sphenoeacus mentalis	GR, S
Sylvia borin	GR
Sylvietta brachyura	GR
Artomyias ussheri	S
Bradornis pallidus	GR, S
Ficedula hypoleuca	M, GR
Fraseria cinerascens	LP
Melaenornis edolioides	LN, GR
Muscicapa comitata	LN, S
Muscicapa striata	S
Myioparus plumbeus	GR
Batis senegalensis	GR, S
Bias musicus	LN, S
Megabyas flammulata	S
Platysteira blissetti	S
Platysteira castanea	S
Platysteira concreta	LP (Guinea Coast)
Platysteira cyanae	LN, GR, S
Erythrocercus mccalli	S
Hyliota flavigaster	S
Terpsiphone rufiventer	LP, LN, U, S
Terpsiphone viridis	GR, S
Trochocercus longicauda	GR
Trochocercus nitens	LN

PARIDAE
Parus funereus	LN
Parus leucomelas	GR, S

NECTARINIIDAE
Anthreptes collaris	LN, U, S
Anthreptes fraseri	S
Anthreptes longuemarei	GR
Anthreptes platura	S
Anthreptes rectirostris	LN
Nectarinia adelberti	LN, S
Nectarinia chloropygia	LN, S
Nectarinia coccinigaster	LP, LN, M, S
Nectarinia cuprea	LP, LN, GR, S
Nectarinia cyanolaema	LN
Nectarinia minulla	U
Nectarinia olivacea	U, S
Nectarinia pulchella	GR
Nectarinia senegalensis	GR, S
Nectarinia superba	LN, S
Nectarinia verticalis	LN, U, M, S

ZOSTEROPIDAE
Zosterops senegalensis	GR

EMBERIZIDAE
Emberiza cabanisi	GR, S
Emberiza forbesi	S
Emberiza tahapisi	GR

FRINGILLIDAE
Serinus mozambicus	GR, S

ESTRILDIDAE
Estrilda bengala	GR
Estrilda caerulescens	GR, S
Estrilda melpoda	GR, S
Estrilda troglodytes	S, M
Hypargos nitidulus	LN
Lagonosticta larvata	GR
Lagonosticta rara	GR
Lagonosticta rubricata	M, S
Lagonosticta rufopicta	GR, S
Lagonosticta senegala	GR
Lonchura bicolor	LN, S
Lonchura cucullata	LN, U, M, S
Lonchura fringilloides	S
Lonchura malabarica	S
Nigrita bicolor	LN, S
Nigrita canicapilla	LN, S
Nigrita fusconota	LN
Ortygospiza atricollis	S
Pirenestes ostrinus	S
Pytelia phoenicoptera	GR, S
Spermophaga haematina	LP, LN, M

PLOCEIDAE
Passer griseus	U, M, GR
Petronia dentata	GR, S
Plocepasser superciliosus	GR
Amblyospiza albifrons	LP, LN
Euplectes afer	LN, GR, S
Euplectes ardens	U
Euplectes hordeaceus	LP, LN, GR
Euplectes macrourus	LP, LN, U, M, GR, S

Euplectes orix	LN, U, GR, S
Malimbus malimbicus	LP, LN, S
Malimbus nitens	LP, LN, S
Malimbus rubricollis	LN
Malimbus scutatus	LP, S
Ploceus cucullatus	LP, LN, M, GR, S
Ploceus luteolus	M, GR
Ploceus nigerrimus	LP, M, S
Ploceus nigricollis	M, GR, S
Ploceus superciliosus	LN, S
Ploceus tricolor	LN
Quelea erythrops	GR, S
Vidua macroura	M, GR, S
Vidua interjecta	GR
Vidua raricola	M
Vidua wilsoni	M

STURNIDAE

Cinnyricinclus leucogaster	LP, LN, GR
Lamprotornis caudatus	GR
Lamprotornis chalcurus	S
Lamprotornis chloropterus	S
Lamprotornis cupreocauda	LN, U
Lamprotornis purpureus	U, GR, S
Lamprotornis splendidus	LN, S
Onychognathus fulgidus	LN

ORIOLIDAE

Oriolus auratus	U, GR
Oriolus brachyrhynchus	LP, S
Oriolus nigripennis	LP, LN, S

DICRURIDAE

Dicrurus adsimilis	U, GR, S
Dicrurus atripennis	LN
Dicrurus ludwigii	S

CORVIDAE

Corvus alba	LP, U
Ptilostomus afer	U, S

The number of species in collections at

	Leiden		Smithsonian	University of		Game Park
Pel	Nagtglas		Institution	Legon	Michigan	Mole
154	141		198	114	31	153

Total number of species collected is 414

*Collected by R. B. Payne in the vicinity of the University of Cape Coast, many of which are preserved as skeletons.
**The terns were collected in coastal waters not at Mole.

APPENDIX 6

Honours theses resulting from the 5 expeditions to Ghana by members of the Zoology Department, University of Aberdeen, Scotland

Brenchley, A. 1979. The moult ecology and biometrics of nine tropical granivorous passerines.

Davidson, N. C. 1975. Some behavioural aspects of *Phoeniculus purpureus* Müller in northern Ghana, and the evolution and systematics of the Phoeniculidae.

Greig-Smith, P. W. 1975. A study of behaviour in the Woodland Kingfisher *Halcyon senegalensis* in northern Ghana.

Fisher, P. 1978. The feeding ecology of some West African granivorous birds with special reference to interspecific differences.

Harris, R. 1979. The wet season feeding ecology and daily activity of the Red-throated Bee-eater, *Merops bulocki* in northern Ghana. July/August 1978.

Shaw, P. 1979. The territorial and mating systems of the Pin-tailed Whydah, *Vidua macroura* (Pallas).

These and the reports, listed below, are retained within the University of Aberdeen.

Aberdeen University Ghana Expeditions to Mole National Park:—

Report 1 1974 Editor A. G. Marshall
Report 2 1975 Editor A. G. Marshall
Report 3 1976 Editors J. A. H. Benzie, A. G. Marshall
Report 4 1977 Editor M. L. Gorman
Report 5 1978 Editor A. Anderson

APPENDIX 7

The weights (gm) of some Ghanaian birds. All data were obtained during the wet season except, for those preceded by (D) (Dry season). Abbreviations used are: M = male, F = female, I = immature, J = juvenile. Data without one of these symbols refer to adult weights. The data are taken from the following references:

(a) Greig-Smith, P. & Davidson, N. C. 1977b
(b) Fry, C. H. 1970
(c) Karr, J. R. 1976
(d) Walsh, J. F. & Grimes, L. G. 1981
(e) Grimes, L. G. 1978a
(f) Grimes, L. G. 1980
(g) Lockwood, G. *et al.* 1980

ARDEIDAE
Butorides striatus	(a)	193

PHASIANIDAE
Francolinus bicalcaratus	(b)	400, 409, 505
Ptilopachus petrosus	(b)	143

RALLIDAE
Porphyrio alleni	(a)	140

JACANIDAE
Actophilornis africana	(b)	147

COLUMBIDAE
Streptopelia semitorquata	(b)	M 224
Streptopelia senegalensis	(a)	98
	(b)	90
Streptopelia vinacea	(b)	F 103
Treron australis	(a)	239
Treron waalia	(a)	268
Turtur abyssinicus	(a)	59.0 ± 3.9 (n = 10)
	(D)	55.0, 57.0
	(b)	59.7 (n = 9)
Turtur afer	(a)	66.5 ± 5.7 (n = 8)
	(D)	62.0, 62.5

PSITTACIDAE
Agapornis pullaria	(b)	29.5

CUCULIDAE
Chrysococcyx caprius	(a)	M 26.2, 28.6
Chrysococcyx klaas	(a)	M 23.0, 23.0
	(b)	F 26.0
Clamator levaillantii	(a)	122
Centropus senegalensis	(e) (D)	M 159.4

STRIGIDAE
Glaucidium perlatum	(a)	J 61.0

CAPRIMULGIDAE
Caprimulgus climacurus	(a)	M 43.5; F 36.3, 39.0; 38.5
	(b)	M 36.0, F 37.0

APODIDAE
Chaetura melanopygia	(g)	52

ALCEDINIDAE

Ceryle maxima	(a)	282
	(D)	305
Alcedo cristata	(a)	11·0, 11·5, 11·7, 12·5
	(D)	13·5
	(b)	12·9 (n = 9)
Alcedo quadribrachys	(a)	35·6 ± 2·3 (n = 7)
	(D)	36·5, 37·0
Ceyx picta	(a)	11·4 ± 1·1 (n = 13); J 10·6 ± 0·6 (n = 10);
	(D)	11·4 ± 0·7 (n = 5)
	(b)	10·7 (n = 11)
Halcyon chelicuti	(a)	32·5, 35·0
Halcyon leucocephala	(a) (D)	44·0
Halcyon malimbica	(a)	90·8 ± 8·0 (n = 11)
	(D)	103
Halcyon senegalensis	(a)	54·0, 55·4
	(b)	64·0

MEROPIDAE

Merops albicollis	(e) (D)	22·3, 22·1, 20·6, 20·5
Merops bulocki	(a)	22·6 ± 1·5 (n = 52)
	(D)	19·9, 21·6, 23·0, 23·5
	(b)	22·6 (n = 42)
Merops hirundineus	(a)	21·8 ± 1·5 (n = 9); J 19·5, 20·5
Merops pusillus	(a)	11·6, 13·2
	(b)	13·0

PHOENICULIDAE

Phoeniculus aterrimus	(a)	M 22·8
	(b)	IF 18·0
Phoeniculus purpureus	(a)	M 76·0, 90, 96, 99; F 56·0, 63·5; J 59·5
	(b)	61·0

CAPITONIDAE

Lybius dubius	(a)	M 92·0 ± 8·5 (n = 8); F 87·6 ± 6·9 (n = 5);
		94, 95, 99
	(D)	M 85, 85
Lybius vieilloti	(b)	36·0
Pogoniulus chrysoconus	(a)	9·6, 9·8

INDICATORIDAE

Indicator indicator	(a)	54·0, 50·5, J 37·0
	(e) (D)	F 44·1
Indicator minor	(a)	26·5, 32·0

PICIDAE

Campethera abingoni	(a) (D)	55·0
Campethera nivosa	(c)	38·5
Campethera punctuligera	(a)	M 67; F 71
	(b)	F 74·0
Mesopicos goertae	(a)	M 50·0, 52·0; F 45·5; 49·0, 52·5
	(b)	M 40·5

ALAUDIDAE

Mirafra rufocinnamomea	(b)	23·0

HIRUNDINIDAE

Hirundo rustica lucida	(b)	12·5
Hirundo semirufa	(b)	13·0, 15·0
Psalidoprocne obscura	(a)	10·0
	(c)	10·0

CAMPEPHAGIDAE

Camephaga phoenicea	(a)	28·1; F 25·5, 27·5, 29·0, 30·0; IM 27·5
	(D)	F 35·5
	(b)	30·0, 30·0, 30·0

PYCNONOTIDAE

Andropadus curvirostris	(c)	20·5, 22·5
Andropadus virens	(c)	21·5, 22·5, 23·5
	(e)	25·2
Chlorocichla flavicollis	(a)	45·5, 55·0
Chlorocichla simplex	(c)	46·5
	(e) (D)	M 50·0; F 42·5, 43·1; 42·7
Phyllastrephus baumanni	(c)	27·5, 30·5
Pycnonotus barbatus	(a)	35·9 ± 1·9 (n = 44)
	(D)	40·5
	(b)	35·6 (35)
	(c)	35·0, 35·5
	(e) (D)	37·6

LANIIDAE

Prionops plumata	(a)	43·0 ± 3·0 (n = 12); J 39·8 ± 2·0 (n = 6)
	(b)	42·0, 45·0, 48·0
Dryoscopus gambensis	(a)	M 31·1, 36·0, 39·0; F 31·0, 34·4;
	(D)	F 35·5
	(b)	M 37·5 (n = 4); F 34·0, 36·0
	(e)	36·4
Laniarius barbarus	(a)	47·1 ± 3·4 (n = 11)
	(D)	46·0
	(c)	43·0, 46·5
	(e) (D)	48·1; F 44·9
Laniarius ferrugineus	(c)	61·5
Malaconotus sulfureopectus	(a)	M 31·0, 34·0; F 28·0, 29·5; 29·6, 30·0
	(b)	30·0, 31·0
	(c)	M 29·5; 31·5
	(e)	29·8, 25·5
Nilaus afer	(a)	17·3, 18·9; M 19·9
	(b)	10·5, 16·0, 20·0, 21·0
Tchagra minuta	(a)	M 30·0; F 32·2
	(b)	33
Tchagra senegala	(a)	62·0
	(b)	48·0 (n = 4)
Corvinella corvina	(a)	J 66·5
	(f)	65·4 (n = 11)

MUSCICAPIDAE

Cercomela familiaris	(a)	15·1, 15·6
	(b)	16·0
Cossypha albicapilla	(a)	59·2 ± 4·1 (n = 9)
	(D)	53·0, 65·0
	(b)	57·0, 58·5, 60·0
Cossypha niveicapilla	(a)	33·8 ± 3·1 (n = 14)
	(D)	31·5, 39·5
	(b)	32·0, 32·0, 37·0, 49·0, 53·0
Luscinia megarhynchos	(e) (D)	22·5
Myrmecocichla albifrons	(b) .	M 20·5; F 18·5
Turdus pelios	(a)	64·9 ± 3·2 (n = 11)
	(D)	68·8 ± 2·6 (n = 5)
	(b)	67·2 (n = 4)
	(e) (D)	60·1, 65·8, 60·7, 58·7, 57·9, 59·8
Trichastoma fulvescens	(c)	26·5, 30·5
Turdoides plebejus	(a)	61·0, 66·5, 67·0, 71·0
	(b)	60·0, 64·5, 69·0
	(e)	M 63·2
Turdoides reinwardii	(a)	78·0, 79·0, 86, 91
	(D)	75·0, 83
	(e) (D)	M 82·5; F 69·1, 73·3, 76·5, 75·5, 75·7
Acrocephalus arundinaceus	(d) (D)	27·0
Acrocephalus rufescens	(e) (D)	17·9, 19·6; M 23·2

Acrocephalus schoenobaenus	(d) (D)	10·5, 12·8, 10·5, 10·5, 10·8
Acrocephalus scirpaceus	(d) (D)	8·6, 10·0
Apalis flavida	(c)	8·0, 9·0, 10·0
Camaroptera brachyura	(a)	10·5 ± 1·0 (n = 16); J 8·5, 10·5
	(b)	10·9 (n = 7)
	(c)	11·0
Camaroptera chloronota	(b)	8·0, 10·0
	(c)	12·3
Cisticola cantans	(b)	13·0
Cisticola erythrops	(a)	12·7, 13·0, 13·0, 13·2, 15·6; F 12·1, 13·0, 14·1; J 12·7
	(b)	13·0, 14·0, 15·0
	(c)	13·7
Cisticola galactotes	(a)	M 17·5, 19·2; F 18·5; 16·6, 17·1, 17·1
	(b)	16·2 (n = 4)
Cisticola lateralis	(a)	17·0, 18·0, 18·3, 19·0, 19·6
	(b)	16·4 (n = 9)
Cisticola natalensis	(b)	20·0, 24·0
Cisticola rufa	(b)	7·6 (n = 8)
Cisticola ruficeps	(a)	9·8
	(b)	10·0, 10·0, 11·0
Eremomela pusilla	(a)	6·1 ± 0·2 (n = 26)
	(D)	6·1 ± 0·2 (n = 5)
	(b)	6·5 (n = 12)
Hypergerus atriceps	(a)	28·9 ± 2·2 (n = 7)
Locustella luscinioides	(d) (D)	15·0
Macrosphenus flavicans	(c)	14·5
Phylloscopus trochilus	(a) (D)	7·4, 7·9
Prinia erythroptera	(a)	5·6, 8·3, 14·5
	(b)	12·5 (n = 9)
Prinia subflava	(a)	7·5, 7·5, 7·6, 7·7, 8·3
	(b)	7·5 (n = 9)
	(e) (D)	9·4
Sphenoeacus mentalis	(a)	33·5 ± 1·8 (n = 9)
	(b)	30·0, 32·5, 35·0
Sylvia borin	(e) (D)	15·5, 19·6
Sylvietta brachyura	(a)	8·0 ± 0·4 (n = 6)
	(b)	7·0, 8·5
Sylvietta virens	(e) (D)	7·9
	(c)	7·6, 8·3
Bradornis pallidus	(a)	19·7, 20·3, 22·5, 23·5; J 18·5, 22·0
	(b)	20·7 (n = 14)
Ficedula hypoleuca	(a) (D)	F 11·6, 11·8
Melaenornis edolioides	(a)	30·8 ± 1·7 (n = 9)
	(b)	28·0, 32·0
	(c)	59·5
Muscicapa aquatica	(d)	10·2, 11·0
Myioparus plumbeus	(a)	11·5, 12·0, 12·3, 13·0
	(b)	14·0
Batis senegalensis	(a)	9·4 ± 0·6 (n = 6); F 9·3 ± 1·1 (n = 8); 9·0; (D) M 9·3; F 9·0, 9·0
	(b)	M 9·0, 9·0, 9·0; F 9·1 (n = 5)
Platysteira blissetti	(c)	M 12·0
Platysteira cyanea	(a)	M 14·3 ± 0·6 (n = 4); F 13·0 ± 0·9 (n = 8); J 11·7
	(D)	M 15·0
	(b)	M 13·0, 13·5, 14·0; F 13·5, 15·0
	(e) (D)	F 12·7; (D) I 11·5
Hyliota flavigaster	(a)	F 12·2; J 11·4
	(b)	11·5
Terpsiphone rufiventer	(e) (D)	14·5
Terpsiphone viridis	(a)	M 11·3, 15·0, 16·0; F 14·5, 14·7, 14·9, 15·6; 12·3, 14·5; J 13·0
	(D)	14·4 ± 1·5 (n = 7)
	(b)	14·5, 15·3, 16·0

Trochocercus longicauda   (a)   8·2, 8·5, 8·8, 9·3, 9·5; F 6·7
                             (D)   6·3
                             (b)   8·4 (n = 5)

PARIDAE
Parus leucomelas   (a)   16·1 ± 1·2 (n = 10)
                             (b)   15·6 (n = 7)

CERTHIIDAE
Salpornis spilonota   (b)   25·0

NECTARINIIDAE
Nectarinia chloropygia   (c)   F 5·0
Nectarinia cuprea   (a)   M 7·2 ± 0·3 (n = 5); F 6·1 ± 0·5 (n = 5);
                             (D)   F 6·6
                             (b)   M 7·2 (n = 8); F 6·6 (n = 4)
                             (c)   F 8·3
Nectarinia pulchella   (a)   M 7·1 ± 1·1 (n = 12); F 6·6 ± 0·5 (n = 7)
                             (b)   M 7·2 (n = 6); F 7·1 (n = 6)
Nectarinia senegalensis   (a)   M 10·3 ± 0·6 (n = 16); F 8·4 ± 0·9 (n = 7); J
                                      9·4, 10·1, 10·2
                             (b)   M 10·2 (n = 7); F 8·9 (n = 11); I 7·5, 10·0,
                                      10·1
Nectarinia verticalis   (a)   M 13·2
                             (D)   M 11·8
                             (c)   M 13·7; F 13·5

ZOSTEROPIDAE
Zosterops senegalensis   (a)   8·1, 8·7
                             (b)   8·0, 9·0

EMBERIZIDAE
Emberiza cabanisi   (a)   M 24·0; F 24·1, 25·5
                             (b)   22·0, 22·5
Emberiza forbesi   (a)   14·5, 14·9, 16·0, 16·0
Emberiza tahapisi   (a) (D) 12·8

FRINGILLIDAE
Serinus mozambicus   (a)   M 10·8 ± 1·7 (n = 40); F 10·4 ± 1·0
                                      (n = 31); 10·5 ± 0·6 (n = 7); J 9·6
                             (b)   10·2 (n = 45)

ESTRILDIDAE
Estrilda bengala   (a)   M 9·3 ± 0·7 (n = 14); F 9·6 ± 0·6 (n = 14)
                             (b)   M 9·0 (n = 29); F 9·5 (n = 32)
Estrilda caerulescens   (a)   8·4 ± 0·7 (n = 10)
                             (b)   7·2 (n = 5)
Estrilda larvata   (a)   M 9·0, 9·5, 9·7, 10·5; F 8·8, 9·3; 10·6
                             (b)   8·7 (n = 9)
Estrilda melpoda   (a)   7·6 ± 0·7 (n = 43)
                             (b)   7·4 (n = 22)
Estrilda troglodytes   (c)   8·5
Lagonosticta rara   (a)   M 9·7; F 9·2, 10·4; 10·3, 11·3
                             (D)   F 9·1
                             (b)   9·6 (n = 4)
Lagonosticta rubricata   (c)   10·2
Lagonosticta rufopicta   (a)   9·1 ± 1·1 (n = 11)
                             (D)   8·3, 9·0
                             (b)   9·0 (n = 16)
                             (c)   10·8, 11·5
Lagonosticta senegala   (a)   M 7·9 ± 0·5 (n = 5); F 7·8 ± 0·9 (n = 4);
                             (D)   M 7·8
                             (b)   8·5 (n = 15)
                             (c)   F 9·8

Lonchura cucullata   (a)   8·0, 8·7, 8·9, 9·0
                                  (D) 8·9, 9·7
                            (b)   9·3 (n = 54)
Nesocharis capistrata   (a)   10·4, 10·5
Nigrita bicolor   (c)   10·5
Nigrita canicapilla   (c)   15·0
Pytelia hypogrammica   (a)   M 14·3
Pytelia phoenicoptera   (a)   13·9, 14·0, 14·9
                                  (D) 13·7, 16·1
                            (b)   14·1 (n = 6)
Spermophaga haematina   (c)   M 22·5, 24·5

PLOCEIDAE
Passer griseus   (a)   25·0
                            (b)   24·5, 24·0
                            (c)   26·5, 29·5
Petronia dentata   (a) (D) 15·5, 16·7
Amblyospiza albifrons   (c)   F 31·5
Euplectes afer   (a)   M 14·7 ± 2·7 (n = 81); F/IM 13·9 ± 1·0
                                       (n = 44); 15·1 ± 0·9 (n = 7)
                            (b)   M 14·9 (n = 16); F 14·2 (n = 41)
Euplectes hordeaceus   (a)   M 21·4, 22·2
                            (b)   M 21·0, 22·0
Euplectes macrourus   (a)   M 21·3; F/IM 17·4 ± 1·0 (n = 6); J 14·9
                            (b)   22·1 (n = 7); F 19·7 (n = 8)
Euplectes orix   (a)   M 17·0 ± 1·0 (n = 30); F/IM 15·5 ± 2·2
                                       (n = 20)
                            (b)   M 16·0 (n = 10); F/I 14·6 (n = 22)
Malimbus rubriceps   (a)   M 22·0
Ploceus cucullatus   (a)   F 29·5, 30·5, 31·0, 32·3, 32·7
                            (b)   F 35·7 ± 4·3 (n = 15)
                            (c)   M 32·5
Ploceus heuglini   (a)   23·0, 26·4
Ploceus luteolus   (a)   M 13·0; F 11·2, 12·5, 12·8, 13·5; 12·5, 12·9
                            (b)   M 13·0, 14·0, 15·0; 12·7 (n = 4)
Ploceus melanocephalus   (b)   M 22·0; F 17·0
Ploceus nigricollis   (a)   M 24·6 ± 0·9 (n = 7); F 23·7 ± 3·2 (n = 8);
                                       23·2; J 23·5, 23·9
                            (b)   F 22·0
                            (c)   23·5, 26·4, 27·5
                            (e) (D) 23·7
Ploceus superciliosus   (a)   32·0, 35·3, 36·0
                            (b)   32·5 (n = 10)
Quelea erythrops   (a)   M 17·7, 21·7; F/I M 16·0 ± 2·5 (n = 8)
                            (b)   M 19·0, 20·0; F 14·0, 15·9, 16·0
Vidua chalybeata   (a)   M 11·7, 12·4, 12·5; F 10·7, 11·8;
                                  (D) F 12·5
                            (b)   M 9·0
Vidua macroura   (a)   M 12·8; F 12·7 ± 0·9 (n = 6)
                            (b)   M 13·3 (n = 5); F 12·6 (n = 6); I 12·1
                                       (n = 4)

STURNIDAE
Lamprocolius chalybaeus   (e) (D) 83·0
Lamprocolius chalcurus   (e) (D) F 80·5
Lamprotornis purpureus   (b)   91·0
                            (e)   98·2

DICRURIDAE
Dicrurus adsimilis   (a)   34·5
                            (b)   34·0, 40·1, 40·5
Dicrurus ludwigii   (a)   24·5, 27·0, 28·5

APPENDIX 8
Species and subspecies named from skins collected in Ghana.
(Data from White 1961–1965)

THRESKIORNITHIDAE
Bostrychia rara (Rothschild, Hartert & Kleinschmidt), 1897.

ACCIPITRIDAE
Dryotriorchis spectabilis spectabilis (Schlegel), 1863.
Accipiter melanoleucus temminckii (Hartlaub), 1855.
Accipiter erythropus erythropus (Hartlaub), 1855.
Accipiter toussenelii macroscelides (Hartlaub), 1855.
Urotriorchis macrourus (Hartlaub), 1855.

PHASIANIDAE
Francolinus albogularis buckleyi (O.-Grant), 1892.
Francolinus ahantensis ahantensis Temminck, 1851.
Agelastes meleagrides Bonaparte, 1850.

RALLIDAE
Canirallus oculeus oculeus (Hartlaub) 1855.
Himantornis haematopus haematopus Hartlaub, 1855.

PSITTACIDAE
Agapornis pullaria pullaria (Linnaeus), 1758.
Poicephalus gulielmi fantiensis Neumann, 1908.
Poicephalus senegalus versteri (Finsch), 1863.
Psittacus erithacus erithacus Linnaeus, 1758.

MUSOPHAGIDAE
Musophaga violacea Isert, 1789.
Tauraco persa persa (Linnaeus), 1758

CUCULIDAE
Chrysococcyx flavigularis Shelley, 1879
Centropus leucogaster leucogaster (Leach), 1814.

STRIGIDAE
Bubo leucostictus Hartlaub, 1855.
Bubo shelleyi Sharpe & Ussher, 1872.
Ciccaba woodfordi nuchalis (Sharpe), 1870.
Glaucidium tephronotum tephronotum Sharpe, 1875.
Otus icterorhynchus icterorhynchus (Shelley), 1873.
Scotopelia peli (Bonaparte), 1851.
Scotopelia ussheri Sharpe, 1871.

CAPRIMULGIDAE
Caprimulgus binotatus Bonaparte, 1851.
Caprimulgus natalensis accrae (Shelley), 1875.
Caprimulgus tristigma sharpei (Alexander), 1901.

APODIDAE
Chaetura ussheri ussheri Sharpe, 1870.

TROGONIDAE
Apaloderma narina constantia (Sharpe & Ussher), 1872.

PHOENICULIDAE
Phoeniculus bollei bollei (Hartlaub), 1858.
Phoeniculus castaneiceps castaneiceps (Sharpe), 1871.

BUCEROTIDAE
Bycanistes cylindricus cylindricus (Temminck), 1831.
Bycanistes subcylindricus subcylindricus (Sclater), 1870.

Ceratogymna atrata (Temminck), 1835.
Tockus camurus pulchrirostris (Schlegel), 1863.
Tockus fasciatus semifasciatus (Hartlaub), 1855.
Tockus hartlaubi hartlaubi Gould, 1861.
Tropicranus albocristatus macrourus (Bonaparte), 1851.

CAPITONIDAE
Lybius hirsutus hirsutus (Swainson), 1821.
Gymnobucco calvus calvus (Lafresnaye), 1841.
Gymnobucco peli peli Hartlaub, 1857.
Pogoniulus scolopaceus scolopaceus (Bonaparte), 1851.
Pogoniulus bilineatus sharpei (O.-Grant), 1907.
Pogoniulus subsulphureus chrysopygus (Shelley), 1889.
Trachyphonus purpuratus goffinii (Schlegel), 1863.

INDICATORIDAE
Indicator minor ussheri (Sharpe), 1902.
Indicator willcocksi willcocksi Alexander, 1901.

PICIDAE
Dendropicos gabonensis lugubris (Hartlaub), 1857.

EURYLAIMIDAE
Smithornis rufolateralis rufolateralis Gray, 1864.

ALAUDIDAE
Mirafra rufocinnamomea buckleyi (Shelley), 1873.

HIRUNDINIDAE
Hirundo abyssinica puella (Temminck & Schlegel), 1847.
Hirundo semirufa gordoni (Jardine), 1851.
Hirundo senegalensis saturatior Bannerman, 1923.
Psalidoprocne obscura (Hartlaub), 1855.

CAMPEPHAGIDAE
Campephaga quiscalina quiscalina Finsch, 1869.
Campephaga lobata lobata (Temminck), 1824.

PYCNONOTIDAE
Andropadus virens erythropterus (Hartlaub), 1858.
Bleda eximia eximia (Hartlaub), 1855.
Criniger calurus verreauxi (Sharpe), 1871.
Phyllastrephus albigularis albigularis (Sharpe), 1881.
Pycnonotus barbatus inornatus (Fraser), 1843.

LANIIDAE
Prionops caniceps caniceps (Bonaparte), 1851.
Laniarius ferrugineus major (Hartlaub), 1848.
Laniarius leucorhynchus (Hartlaub), 1848.
Malaconotus lagdeni (Sharpe), 1884.
Malaconotus multicolor multicolor (Gray), 1845.
Tchagra australis ussheri (Sharpe), 1882.
Tchagra minuta minuta (Hartlaub), 1858.
Corvinella corvina togoensis Neumann, 1900.
Lanius collaris smithii (Fraser), 1843.
Lanius senator badius (Hartlaub), 1854.

MUSCICAPIDAE
Alethe poliocephala cantanonota (Sharpe), 1871.
Cercotrichas leucosticta leucosticta (Sharpe), 1883.
Stiphrornis erythrothorax erythrothorax Hartlaub, 1855.
Cossypha albicapilla giffardi (Hartert), 1899.
Cossypha cyanocampter cyanocampter (Bonaparte), 1850.
Stizorhina fraseri finschi (Sharpe), 1870.
Turdus princei princei (Sharpe), 1873.

Phyllanthus atripennis haynesi (Sharpe), 1871.
Trichastoma cleaveri cleaveri (Shelley), 1874.
Trichastoma fulvescens gularis (Sharpe), 1870.
Trichastoma fulvescens moloneyanus (Sharpe), 1892.
Turdoides reinwardii stictilaema (Alexander), 1901.
Apalis nigriceps nigriceps (Shelley), 1873.
Apalis sharpii sharpii Shelley, 1884.
Bathmocercus cerviniventris cerviniventris (Sharpe), 1877.
Cisticola brachyptera brachyptera (Sharpe), 1870.
Cisticola cantans swanzii (Sharpe), 1870.
Cisticola eximia winneba Lynes, 1931.
Cisticola galactotes amphilecta (Reichenow), 1875.
Cisticola juncidis uropygialis (Fraser), 1843.
Cisticola natalensis strangei (Fraser), 1843.
Cisticola ruficeps guinea Lynes, 1930.
Eremomela badiceps fantiensis Macdonald, 1940.
Hylia prasina superciliaris (Hartlaub), 1855.
Pholidornis rushiae ussheri (Reichenow), 1905.
Hypergerus articeps (Lesson), 1831.
Prinia erythroptera erythroptera (Jardine), 1849.
Sphenoeacus mentalis mentalis (Fraser), 1843.
Sylvietta virens flaviventris (Sharpe), 1877.
Artomyias ussheri Sharpe, 1871.
Bradornis pallidus modestus (Shelley), 1873.
Fraseria cinerascens Hartlaub, 1857.
Muscicapa caerulescens nigrorum (Collin & Hartert), 1927.
Muscicapa gambagae (Alexander), 1901.
Platysteira blissetti blissetti (Sharpe), 1872.
Platysteira concreta concreta (Hartlaub), 1855.
Hyliota violacea nehrkorni Hartlaub, 1892.
Trochocercus nitens reichenowi (Sharpe), 1904.

REMIZIDAE
Remiz flavifrons waldroni (Bannerman), 1935.

PARIDAE
Parus leucomelas guineensis (Shelley), 1900.

NECTARINIIDAE
Anthreptes rectirostris rectirostris (Shaw), 1811.
Nectarinia superba ashantiensis (Bannerman), 1922.

FRINGILLIDAE
Serinus gularis canicapilla (Dubus), 1855.

ESTRILDIDAE
Estrilda larvata togoensis Neumann, 1907.
Hypargos nitidulus schlegeli (Sharpe), 1870.
Lagonosticta rubricata polionota (Shelley), 1873.
Lagonosticta rufopicta rufopicta (Fraser), 1843.
Nigrita bicolor bicolor (Hartlaub), 1844.
Nigrita canicapilla emiliae (Sharpe), 1870.
Nigrita fusconota uropygialis (Sharpe), 1869.
Parmoptila woodhousei rubrifrons (Sharpe & Ussher), 1872.
Pytelia hypogrammica Sharpe, 1870.
Spermophaga haematina haematina (Vieillot), 1805.

PLOCEIDAE
Euplectes orix franciscanus (Isert), 1789.
Malimbus malimbicus nigrifrons (Hartlaub), 1855.
Malimbus rubricollis bartletti (Sharpe), 1890.
Ploceus pelzelni monachus (Sharpe), 1890.

ORIOLIDAE
Oriolus auratus auratus Vieillot, 1817.

DICRURIDAE
Dicrurus adsimilis atactus (Oberholser), 1899.

APPENDIX 9

Gazetteer

Abetifi	06°41'N, 00°45'W	Babianika	07°20'N, 02°20'W
Abo	06°06'N, 00°48'E	Baghari (Bahare)	10°45'N, 02°52'W
Aboabo	06°12'N, 00°30'W	Bamboi	08°09'N, 02°02'W
Abokobi	05°44'N, 00°12'W	Banda	08°10'N, 02°22'W
Abossey	05°19'N, 00°09'W	Bantama	07°42'N, 00°42'W
Abotoasi	07°14'N,00°11'E	Bator	06°02'N, 00°15'E
Aboyoase	07°15'N, 00°09'E	Bawku	11°05'N, 00°11'W
Abudom	07°38'N, 01°43'W	Bebianiha	06°27'N, 02°18'W
Aburi	05°53'N, 00°11'W	Begoro	06°24'N, 00°21'W
Accra	05°30'N, 00°15'W	Bekwai	06°28'N, 01°34'W
Achimota	05°38'N, 00°16'W	Berekum	07°26'N, 02°35'W
Ada	05°46'N, 00°39'E	Beyin	05°00'N, 02°38'W
Adawso	05°56'N, 00°13'W	Bia N.P.	06°38'N, 03°08'W
Adina	06°06'N, 01°00'E	Biaso	07°04'N, 02°26'W
Aduamoah	06°43'N, 00°47'W	Bimbila	08°52'N, 00°05'E
Afegame	07°10'N, 00°37'E	Bibiani	06°27'N, 02°20'W
Afiadenyigba	06°12'N, 00°31'E	Binduri	10°59'N, 00°16'W
Afife	06°02'N, 00°33'E	Bokonkade	
Afram River	06°18'N, 00°00'E	(= Dogonkade)	
Agbakofe	06°01'N, 00°26'E	Bole	09°03'N, 02°23'W
Agbenohoe	07°00'N, 00°25'E	Bolgatanga	10°48'N, 00°53'W
Agogo	06°48'N, 01°06'W	Bongo Hills	10°54'N, 00°49'W
Agona	05°30'N, 00°42'W	Bopa	06°08'N, 02°35'W
Agorta	06°00'N, 00°27'E	Bosumtwi Lake	06°39'N, 01°30'W
Akosombo	06°17'N, 00°03'E	Branan	08°00'N, 02°00'W
Ahanta F. R.	05°23'N, 02°28'W	Bronikron F.R.	05°23'N, 02°28'W
Akim-Oda	05°55'N, 00°58'W	Buipe	08°48'N, 01°34'W
Akropong Akwapim	05°58'N, 00°06'W	Bulinga	09°55'N, 02°14'W
Akuse	06°07'N, 00°06'E	Butri (Boutry)	04°50'N, 01°56'W
Akutuase	05°15'N, 01°30'W		
Akwatia	06°02'N, 00°49'W	Cape Coast	05°06'N, 01°15'W
Alakple	05°55'N, 01°00'E	Cape Three Points	04°44'N, 02°05'W
Amanfro	05°33'N, 00°22'W	Christiansborg	05°32'N, 00°10'W
Amansuri Lake	05°00'N, 02°35'W		
Amedzofe	06°52'N, 00°28'E	Daboase	05°09'N, 01°40'W
Anamobu	05°10'N, 01°10'W	Dabocrom	04°55'N, 01°50'W
Anhwian	05°45'N, 00°15'E	Daboya	09°33'N, 01°31'W
Ankaful	05°07'N, 01°22'W	Dafo	06°59'N, 00°30'E
Ankasa G P R	05°10'N, 02°39'W	Damongo	09°05'N, 01°50'W
Anloga	05°45'N, 00°55'E	Dawhenya	05°53'N, 00°18'E
Antubia	06°20'N, 02°50'W	Dayi River	06°45'N, 00°20'E
Anyako	06°00'N, 00°34'E	Denu	06°06'N, 01°11'E
Anyinesu	07°14'N, 01°35'W	Dixcove	04°48'N, 01°56'W
Apam	05°18'N, 00°42'W	Djebobo Mountain	08°17'N, 00°37'E
Asakraka	06°27'N, 01°29'W	Dodi	06°32'N, 00°06'E
Asankrangwa	05°48'N, 02°25'W	Dodowa	05°54'N, 00°08'W
Asanta	04°50'N, 02°14'W	Dogonkade	
Asrema	05°55'N, 00°11'W	(Donkokade)	08°40'N, 00°30'W
Asuansi-Krua	05°20'N, 01°16'W	Domenasi	05°20'N, 01°05'W
Asuboi	05°34'N, 00°15'W	Dompoasi	06°18'N, 01°32'W
Asukawkaw River	c. 07°40'N, 00°17'E	Dorma Ahenkro	07°16'N, 02°52'W
Asutsuare	06°03'N, 00°16'E	Du	10°31'N, 00°59'W
Atebubu	07°45'N, 00°59'W	Duffor	06°00'N, 01°00'E
Ateihu	05°35'N, 01°45'W	Dunkwa	05°59'N, 01°45'W
Atewa F. R.	06°17'N, 00°34'W	Dwenem	07°41'N, 02°47'W
Atiavi	05°33'N, 00°30'E	Dzelukope	05°32'N, 00°35'E
Axim	04°53'N, 02°14'W	Dzodze	06°08'N, 01°00'E
Ayerade	07°30'N, 01°40'W		

Effiduasi	06°31′N, 01°14′E	Makongo	08°18′N, 00°38′W
Efutu-Jukwa	05°14′N, 01°20′W	Mampong Akwapim	05°54′N, 00°08′W
Ehi	06°05′N, 01°00′E	Mampong Ashanti	07°04′N, 01°24′W
Ejinase	05°15′N, 01°30′W	Mankesim	05°17′N, 01°03′W
Ejura	07°23′N, 01°15′W	Mankrong	05°10′N, 01°13′W
Elmina	05°06′N, 01°27′W	Masaka (= Masarka)	08°38′N, 00°32′W
Esen Apam F.R.	05°38′N, 00°47′W	Mepe	06°02′N, 00°17′E
Esiama	04°55′N, 02°21′W	Mole G. R.	09°22′N, 02°00′W
		Morago River	10°40′N, 00°14′W
Feteyana	07°35′N, 02°47′W	Mpraeso	06°37′N, 00°45′W
Fumso	06°06′N, 01°25′W		
		Nabuggo	09°44′N, 00°50′W
Gambaga	10°31′N, 00°22′W	Nakpanduri	10°39′N, 00°20′W
Genui	05°49′N, 00°51′E	Nakwa	05°15′N, 01°02′W
Goaso	06°49′N, 02°32′W	Nalerigu	10°32′N, 00°22′W
Golokwati	07°01′N, 00°25′E	Nandom	10°30′N, 02°27′W
		Nangodi	10°55′N, 00°36′W
Half Assini	05°03′N, 02°53′W	Nasia River Lagoon	10°08′N, 00°47′W
Hamale	11°00′N, 02°42′W	Navrongo	10°55′N, 01°03′W
Hemang	05°11′N, 01°34′W	Nchirra	07°54′N, 02°00′W
Ho	06°37′N, 00°28′E	Nkawkaw	06°35′N, 00°45′W
Hohoe	07°10′N, 00°28′E	Nkoranza	07°36′N, 01°42′W
		Nkwatia	06°42′N, 00°44′W
Iture	05°06′N, 01°20′W	Npuasu	07°48′N, 02°48′W
		Nsawam	05°49′N, 00°20′W
		Nsuta	07°01′N, 01°14′W
Japekrom	07°21′N, 02°28′W	Nteso	06°23′N, 00°23′W
Jasikan	07°28′N, 00°33′E	Nungua	05°41′N, 00°07′W
Jirapa	10°30′N, 02°42′W	Nyanyanu	05°29′N, 00°24′W
Juaso	06°41′N, 01°07′W		
Jukwa	05°15′N, 01°20′W	Obuasi	06°15′N, 01°36′W
		Oda (Akim-Oda)	05°55′N, 00°58′W
Kadjebi	07°32′N, 00°28′E	Odumasi F. R.	06°11′N, 00°03′W
Kade	06°05′N, 00°50′W	Odumasi Krobo	06°08′N, 00°00′
Kakum F. R.	05°20′N, 01°22′W	Okaekurum	06°49′N, 01°19′W
Karaga	09°55′N, 00°25′W	Onwi	06°31′N, 01°27′W
Karamenga	10°32′N, 00°48′W	Opintin F. R.	c.05°43′N, 00°27′W
Kasu (Ke) Lagoon	06°00′N, 00°30′E	Osudoku	06°04′N, 00°12′E
Kedzie (Keji)	05°55′N, 01°01′E		
Keta	05°54′N, 01°00′E	Pampawie	07°36′N, 00°31′E
Kete Kratchi	07°48′N, 00°04′W	Patenga (Batenga)	09°47′N, 00°18′W
Kibi	06°10′N, 00°34′W	Pepiasi	06°40′N, 00°45′W
Kikam-Bobrana	04°55′N, 02°30′W	Poasi	07°36′N, 00°30′E
Kintampo	08°06′N, 01°40′W	Pong Tamale	09°42′N, 00°50′W
Klamadoboi	06°04′N, 00°06′E	Pra Suhien F. R.	05°19′N, 01°24′W
Kombunga	09°25′N, 00°41′W	Prahsu	05°56′N, 01°20′W
Komenda	05°05′N, 01°29′W	Prampram	05°42′N, 00°08′E
Korforidua	06°07′N, 00°15′W	Prang	08°00′N, 00°53′W
Kotuo	07°30′N, 02°36′W	Pwalagu (= Pualagu)	10°35′N, 00°52′W
Kpandae	08°28′N, 00°01′W		
Kpandu	06°59′N, 00°15′E	Sa	10°14′N, 01°06′W
Kpong	06°13′N, 00°04′E	Saboba	09°26′N, 00°09′E
Krobo Hill	06°05′N, 00°00′	Sakumo Lagoon	
Kromain	05°23′N, 00°57′W	(Salt Pans)	05°31′N, 00°17′W
Krukrom	05°20′N, 00°09′W	Salaga	08°34′N, 00°42′W
Kumasi	06°45′N, 01°35′W	Saltpond	05°12′N, 01°04′W
Kumbungu	09°33′N, 00°56′W	Sang	09°24′N, 00°17′W
Kwahu Tafo	06°42′N, 00°41′W	Sekondi	04°59′N, 01°43′W
Kwabenya	05°41′N, 00°12′W	Sefwi Wiaswso	06°41′N, 02°29′W
		Sekwi	09°40′N, 00°18′W
Larabanga	09°12′N, 01°48′W	Sekyere Hemang	05°12′N, 01°34′W
Lawra	10°40′N, 02°50′W	Sekondumasi	07°11′N, 01°22′W
Legon	05°39′N, 00°11′W	Senchi	06°07′N, 00°03′E
Lovi	09°22′N, 02°00′W	Shama	05°02′N, 01°35′W
Lungbunga	09°40′N, 01°12′W	Shai hills	c.05°53′N, 00°03′E

Sissili valley	10°16′N, 01°15′W
Sogakofe	06°01′N, 00°35′E
Sokpoe	05°36′N, 00°21′E
Subri River F.R.	05°16′N, 01°38′W
Sugari	10°12′N, 00°20′W
Sugu	09°50′N, 00°58′W
Suhien — see Pra Suhien F.R.	
Suhuma F.R.	c.06°04′N, 02°29′W
Suhum–Tafo road	06°11′N, 00°28′W
Sunyani	07°20′N, 02°18′W
Srogboe	05°48′N, 00°50′E
Tabo	05°06′N, 02°54′W
Tafo	06°15′N, 00°22′W
Takoradi	04°55′N, 01°45′W
Tamale	09°20′N, 00°49′W
Tarkwa	05°18′N, 01°58′W
Tema	05°30′N, 00°00′
Teshie	05°35′N, 00°06′W
Tono dam	c.11°00′N, 01°00′W
Tsito	06°31′N, 00°31′E
Tuluwe	08°42′N, 00°55′W
Tumu	10°55′N, 01°59′W

Vakpo	06°50′N, 00°18′E
Vea dam	10°55′N, 00°51′W
Volta Lake	c.07°18′N, 00°09′E
Wa	10°05′N, 02°30′W
Walewale	10°20′N, 00°46′W
Wamfie	07°24′N, 02°42′W
Warawana	07°30′N, 00°24′E
Wassaw (Wásá)	area near Tarkwa
Waya	06°27′N, 00°37′E
Weija	05°34′N, 00°20′W
Wenchi	07°45′N, 02°03′W
Winneba	05°22′N, 00°38′W
Wiawso	06°12′N, 02°29′W
Worawora	07°30′N, 00°20′E
Worobong F.R.	06°27′N, 00°24′W
Yapei	09°20′N, 01°11′W
Yendi	09°25′N, 00°01′W
Yeji (Yegi)	08°13′N, 00°39′W
Zongoiri Rapids	10°36′N, 00°25′W
Zuarungu	10°44′N, 00°50′W

REFERENCES

Alexander, B. 1901a. Remarks on his collection of birds made in the Gold Coast. *Bull. Brit. Orn. Cl.* 12: 10–12.

————— 1901b. A new species of nightjar from the hinterland of the Gold Coast. *Bull. Brit. Orn. Cl.* 12: 29.

————— 1902. On the birds of the Gold Coast Colony and its hinterland. *Ibis* Ser. 8(2): 278–333, 355–377.

Baker, H. G. 1962. 'The Ecological Study of Vegetation in Ghana'. Chapter 9, in *Agriculture and Land Use in Ghana* (Ed. J. B. Wills). Oxford University Press.

Bannerman, D. A. 1912a. On a collection of birds made by W. P. Lowe on the west coast of Africa and outlying islands; with field notes by the collector. *Ibis* Ser. 9(6): 219–268.

————— 1912b. On two new species of birds from West Africa. *Bull. Brit. Orn. Cl.* 29: 23–24.

————— 1922. New races of Ethiopian sun-birds. *Bull. Brit. Orn. Cl.* 43: 7–9.

————— 1923. Remarks on the distribution of the Senegal Swallow (*Hirundo senegalensis*) with description of a new race from the Gold Coast (*H. s. saturatior*). *Bull. Brit. Orn. Cl.* 43: 85–86.

————— 1930–1951. *Birds of Tropical West Africa,* 8 vols. Oliver & Boyd.

————— 1934. Remarks on a collection of birds recently made in Ashanti, Gold Coast by W. P. Lowe. *Bull. Brit. Orn. Cl.* 54: 122–123.

————— 1935a. Exhibition of, and remarks on, several species obtained by W. P. Lowe in Ashanti, together with a note on *Bycanistes subcylindricus* and *B. subquadratus* with text figures of the heads of these two forms. *Bull. Brit. Orn. Cl.* 55: 126–130.

————— 1935b. Description of a new race of the Yellow-fronted Penduline Tit (*Anthroscopus flavifrons waldroni*).*Bull. Brit. Orn. Cl.* 55: 131.

————— 1935c. Extension of range of *Andropadus curvirostris leoninus. Bull. Brit. Orn. Cl.* 55: 131–132.

————— 1935d. Exhibition of, and remarks on, young and eggs of the Ahanta Francolin (*Francolinus ahantensis ahantensis*). *Bull. Brit. Orn. Cl.* 55: 132–134.

————— 1935e. Exhibition of, and remarks on, a Wattled Cuckoo-Shrike (*Lobotus lobotus*) and a Rufous-winged Akalat (*Illadopsis rufescens*), with further observations upon Mr Willoughby Lowe's collection from Ashanti. *Bull. Brit. Orn. Cl.* 55: 154–155.

————— 1939. A new race of the Penduline Tit (*Anthoscopus parvulus aureus*) from the Gold Coast. *Bull. Brit. Orn. Cl.* 55: 41–42.

————— 1953. *The Birds of West and Equatorial Africa,* 2 vols. Oliver & Boyd.

Barry, R. C. & Chorley, R. J. 1982. *Atmosphere, Weather & Climate,* 4th Edition. Methuen.

Barus, U., Sixl, W. & Majumdar, G. 1978. Helminths of the ploceid *Textor cuculatus* from Ghana. *Angewandte Parasit.* 19: 111–114.

Beattie A. G. & Wills, J. B. 1962. 'Introduction'. Chapter 1, in *Agriculture and Land Use in Ghana* (Ed. J. B. Wills). Oxford University Press.

Bigger, M. 1976. Oscillations of tropical insect populations. *Nature* 259: 207–209.

Blake, E. 1975. First recorded occurrence of the European Shelduck in the Southern hemisphere. *Ostrich* 46: 258.

Boateng, E. A. 1959. *A Geography of Ghana.* Cambridge University Press.

Booth, A. H. 1959. On the mammalian fauna of the Accra Plains. *West African Sc. Ass. J.* 5: 26–36.

Bosman, W. 1705. *A New and Accurate Description of the North and South coast of Guinea.* London.

Bouet, G. 1955/1961. Oiseaux de L'Afrique Tropicale, Parts 1 & 2. *Faune Tropicale* 16 & 17. O.R.S.T.O.M. Paris.

Bourdillon, B. H. 1944. Terns on Lagos Beach, Nigeria. *Ibis* 86: 405–407.

Bowen, W., Gardiner, N., Harris, B. J. & Thomas, J. D. 1962. Communal nesting of *Phalacrocorax africanus, Bulbulcis ibis* and *Anhinga rufa* in southern Ghana. *Ibis* 104: 246–247.

Brash, H. T. 1962. 'Geomorphology'. Chapter 5, in *Agriculture and Land Use in Ghana* (Ed. J. B. Wills). Oxford University Press.

Britton, P. L. (Ed.). 1980. *Birds of East Africa.* East African Nat. Hist. Soc. Nairobi.

Broekhuysen, G. J., Liversidge, R. & Rand, R. W. 1961. The Southern African Gannet *Morus capensis* 1. Distribution and movements. *Ostrich* 32: 1–19.

Brosset, A. 1971a. Recherches sur la biologie des *Pycnonotidés* du Gabon. *Biologia Gabonica* 7: 423–460.

———— 1971b. Premières observations sur la reproduction de six oiseaux Africains. *Alauda* 39: 112–126.

———— 1981a. Évolution divergente des comportements chez deux bulbuls sympatriques (Pycnonotidae). *Alauda* 49: 94–111.

———— 1981b. La périodicité de la reproduction chez un Bulbul de forêt equatoriale africaine *Andropadus latirostris* ses incidences démographiques. *Rev. Ecol. (Terre et Vie)* 35: 109–129.

———— 1982. The social life of the African Forest Yellow-whiskered Greenbul *Andropadus latirostris*. *Z. Tierpsychol.* 60: 239–255.

Brown, A. P. 1964. Palaearctic migrants in West Africa. *Nigerian Field* 29: 174–177.

Brown, L. 1970. *African Birds of Prey*. Collins.

Browne, P. W. P. 1980. Birds observed near Lome, Togo in 1976 and 1977. *Malimbus* 2: 51–55.

Burton, R. & Cameron, V. L. 1883. *To the Gold Coast for Gold*. London.

Button, J. A. 1964. The identification of *Andropadus* Bulbuls. *Bull. Nig. Orn. Soc.* 1: 11.

Cansdale, G. S. 1948. Gulls on the Gold Coast. *The Field* 191: 134.

Chapin, J. P. 1953. The Birds of the Belgian Congo. 3. *Bull. Amer. Mus. Nat. Hist.* 75A.

———— 1962. Sibling species of small African Honey-Guides. *Ibis* 104: 40–44.

Cheke, R. A. 1982. More bird records from the Republic of Togo. *Malimbus* 4(2): 55–63.

———— 1986. The supposed occurrence of the White-necked Picathartes *Picathartes gymnocephalus* in Togo. *Bull. Brit. Orn. Cl.* 106: 152.

Cheke, R. A. & Walsh, F. 1980. Bird records from the Republic of Togo. *Malimbus* 2: 112–120.

Clancey, P. A. 1976. The Shelduck *Tadorna tadorna* in South Africa. *Ostrich* 47: 145.

Claridge, W. W. 1964. *A History of the Gold Coast and Ashanti*, 2 Vols, 2nd Edition. Cass: London.

Cockburn, T. A. 1946. Some birds of the Gold Coast, with observations on their virus and parasitic infections. *Ibis* 88: 387–394.

Cockburn, T. A. & Findlay, G. M. 1945. The Wood-Ibis colony at Daboya, Gold Coast. *Ibis* 87: 95–97.

Collins, W. B. 1955. Sounds in the forest. *Nigerian Field* 20: 84–88.

Collar, N. J. & Stuart, S. N. 1975. *Threatened Birds of Africa and Related Islands*. ICPB/IUCN, Cambridge.

Colston, P. A. 1981. A newly described species of *Melignomon* (Indicatoridae) from Liberia, West Africa. *Bull. Brit. Orn. Cl.* 101: 289–291.

Colston, P. A. & Curry-Lindahl, K. 1986. *The Birds of Mount Nimba, Liberia*. British Museum (Natural History).

Craig, A. 1983. The timing of breeding and wing-moult of four African Sturnidae. *Ibis* 125: 346–352.

Cyrus, D. P. 1986. Seasonal and spatial distribution of Red headed Quelea (*Quelea erythrops*) in South Africa. *Ostrich* 57(3): 162–169.

Dahm, A. G. 1969. A Corn-crake, *Crex crex* L., trapped in Kumasi, Ghana. *Bull. Brit. Orn. Cl.* 89: 76–78.

Dalziel, J. M. 1922. *Bird Life around Accra*. Gov. Printer, Accra.

Davidson, N. C. 1976. The evolution and systematics of the Phoeniculidae. *Bull. Nig. Orn. Soc.* 12: 2–17.

———— 1978a. Weight, prenuptial moult and feeding of Bishop Birds in northern Guinea savanna in Ghana. *Bull. Nig. Orn. Soc.* 14(46): 54–65.

———— 1978b. Additions to local avifauna: Bia National Park, Ghana. *Bull. Nig. Orn. Soc.* 14(46): 88.

Davidson, N. C., Greig-Smith, P. W. & Fisher, P. 1978. Weight changes of some savanna finches in Ghana. *Bull. Nig. Orn. Soc.* 14(46): 73–79.

De Roo, A., Huselmans, J. & Verheyen, W. 1971. Contribution à l'Ornithologie de la République du Togo. *Rev. Zool. Bot. Afr.* 83: 84–94.

Dekeyser, P. L. 1951. Mission A. Villiers au Togo et au Dahomey (1950). III Oiseaux. *Études Dahomeennes* 5: 47–84.

Dekeyser, P. L. & Derivot, J. H. 1966/1967. *Les Oiseaux de L'Ouest Africain,* 2 vols. I.F.A.N. University of Dakar, Senegal.

Demey, R. 1986. Two new species for Ivory Coast. *Malimbus* 8(1): 44.

Dingle, H. & Khamala, C. P. M. 1972. Seasonal changes in insect abundance and biomass in an east African grassland with reference to breeding and migration of birds. *Ardea* 60: 216–221.

Douaud, J. 1956. Les oiseaux des monts du Togo (Afrique Occidentale). *Alauda* 24: 219–227.

Dunn, E. K. 1981. Roseates on a life-line. *Birds* 8(6): 42–45.

Dunn, E. K. & Mead, C. J. 1982. Relationship between sardine fisheries and recovery rates of ringed terns in West Africa. *Seabird Report* No. 6 (1977–81): 98–104.

Earlé, R. A. 1981. Factors governing avian breeding in acacia savanna, Pietermaritzburg, parts 1, 2 & 3. *Ostrich* 52: 65–73, 74–83, 235–243.

Eccles, S. D. 1985. Reichenbach's Sunbird *Nectarinia reichenbachii* new to Ivory Coast. *Malimbus* 7(2): 140.

Elgood, J. H. 1982. *The Birds of Nigeria*. British Ornithologists' Union, Check-list No. 4.

Elgood, J. H., Fry, C. H. & Dowsett, R. J. 1973. African migrants in Nigeria. *Ibis* 115: 1–45, 375–411.

Erard, C. & Vielliard, J. 1977. *Sarothrura rufa* (Vieillot) au Togo. *L'Oiseau et R.F.O.* 47: 309–310.

Field, G. D. 1974. Nearctic waders in Sierra Leone — Lesser Golden Plover and Buff-breasted Sandpiper. *Bull. Brit. Orn. Cl.* 94: 76–78.

Field, G. D. & Owen, D. F. 1969. Little Gull in Sierra Leone. *Bull. Brit. Orn. Cl.* 89: 94.

Finsch, O. 1869. Ueber eine Vögelsammlung aus Westafrica. *J. Orn.* 17: 334–337.

Fogden, M. P. L. 1972. The seasonality and population dynamics of equatorial forest birds in Sarawak. *Ibis* 114: 307–343.

Foggie, A. & Piasecki, B. 1962. 'Timber, fuel and minor forest produce'. In *Agriculture and Land Use in Ghana* (Ed. J. B. Wills). Oxford University Press.

Fraser, L. 1843a. On eight new species of birds from western Africa. *Proc. Zool. Soc. Lond.* Part II: 16–17.

———— 1843b. On a new *Rhinolophus* and four new species of birds from western Africa. *Proc. Zool. Soc. Lond.* Part II: 25–27.

———— 1843c. On *Cricetomys Gambianus* and various species of birds from western Africa. *Proc. Zool. Soc. Lond.* Part II: 51–53.

Friedmann, H. 1955. *The Honey-Guides*. Smithsonian Institution, Washington, D.C. USA.

Fry, C. H. 1970. Migration, moult and weights of birds in northern Guinea savanna in Nigeria and Ghana. *Ostrich* Suppl. 8: 239–263.

———— 1982. Spanish Black Kites in West Africa. *Malimbus* 4(1): 49.

Gass, M. D. I. 1954. Gold Coast bird notes. *Nigerian Field* 19: 23–30, 76–83.

————1957. Some migrant birds of Ghana. *Nigerian Field* 22: 166–168.

———— 1963. The Bee-eaters of Ghana. *Nigerian Field* 28: 31–34.

Genelly, R. E. 1968. Birds of the Mole Game Reserve. *Nigerian Field* 34: 171–182.

Gibbs, D. G. & Leston, D. 1970. Insect phenology in a forest cocoa-farm locality in West Africa. *J. Appl. Ecol.* 7: 519–548.

Gijzen, A. 1938. 's Rijks Museum van Natuurliske Historie 1820–1915. W. L. & J. Brusse.

Gillon, Y. & Gillon, D. 1967. Recherches écologiques dans la savanna de Lampto (Cote d'Ivoire): cycle annuel des effectifs et des biomasses d'arthropodes de la strate herbacée. *Terre et Vie* 21: 262–277.

Good, A. I. 1952–1953. Birds of French Cameroun. *Inst. Franc. Afr. Noire. Sér. Sci. Nat.* 2: 1–203, 3: 1–269.

Goodwin, D. 1982. *Estrildid Finches of the World*. British Museum (Natural History).

Gordon, C. A. 1849. Notes on the habits of some birds, collected on the coast of western Africa. *Jardine's Contribution to Ornithology for 1849*: 1–13. Edinburgh.

Gore, M. E. J. 1981. *Birds of The Gambia*. British Ornithologists' Union, Check-list No. 3.

Gray, G. R. 1864. On a new species of *Smithornis*. *Proc. Zool. Soc. Lond.* 1864: 143.

Greig-Smith, P. W. 1976a. The composition and habitat preferences of the avifauna of the Mole National Park, Ghana. *Bull. Nig. Orn. Soc.* 12(42): 49–66.

Greig-Smith, P. W. 1976b. Observations on the social behaviour of Helmet Shrikes. *Bull. Nig. Orn. Soc.* 12(41): 25–30.

——————— 1977a. Bird migration at Mole National Park, Ghana. *Bull. Nig. Orn. Soc.* 13(43): 3–14.

——————— 1977b. Breeding dates of birds in Mole National Park, Ghana. *Bull. Nig. Orn. Soc.* 13(44): 89–93.

——————— 1978a. Observations on the Striped Kingfisher *Halcyon chelicuti*. *Bull. Nig. Orn. Soc.* 14(45): 14–23.

——————— 1978b. Migration of savanna birds revealed by local records. *Bull. Nig. Orn. Soc.* 14(46): 89.

——————— 1978c. Behaviour of woodland kingfishers in Ghana. *Ostrich* 49: 67–75.

——————— 1978d. The formation, structure, and function of mixed-species insectivorous bird flocks in West African savanna woodland. *Ibis* 120: 284–297.

——————— 1979. Selection of feeding areas by Senegal Kingfishers (*Halcyon senegalensis*). *Z. Tierpsychol* 49: 197–209.

——————— 1980. Ranging behaviour of birds in savanna and riverine forest habitats in Ghana. *Ibis* 122: 109–116.

Greig-Smith, P. W. & Davidson, N. C. 1977a. Weight changes of some Guinea Savanna birds in Ghana. *Bull. Nig. Orn. Soc.* 13(44): 94–97.

———————, ——————— 1977b. Weights of West African savanna birds. *Bull. Brit. Orn. Cl.* 97: 96–99.

Grimes, L. G. 1963. Some observations on *Picathartes gymnocephalus* in Ghana. *Nigerian Field* 28: 55–63.

——————— 1964. Some notes on the breeding of *Picathartes gymnocephalus* in Ghana. *Ibis* 106: 258–260.

——————— 1965. Antiphonal singing in *Laniarius barbarus barbarus* and the auditory reaction time. *Ibis* 107: 101–104.

——————— 1966. Antiphonal singing and call notes of *Laniarius barbarus barbarus*. *Ibis* 108: 122–126.

——————— 1967. Breeding of the Black Heron in Ghana. *Bull. Brit. Orn. Cl.* 87: 1–2.

——————— 1969a. Moon watching — a means of migration study. *Bull. Nig. Orn. Soc.* 6(22): 56–57.

——————— 1969b. The Spotted Redshank *Tringa erythropus* in Ghana. *Ibis* 111: 246–251.

——————— 1971. The distribution of the Red-eyed Turtle Dove. *Bull. Nig. Orn. Soc.* 8(31/32): 61.

——————— 1972a. *The Birds of the Accra Plains*. Stencilled publication.

——————— 1972b. The successive use of the same nest by the Laughing Dove *Streptopelia senegalensis* and its subsequent use by the Kurrichaine Thrush *Turdus libonyanus*. *Bull. Nig. Orn. Soc.* 9(35): 57.

——————— 1973a. Birds, bats and aircraft. *Universitas* 2: 154–166.

——————— 1973b. The breeding of the Heuglin's Masked Weaver and its nesting association with the Red Weaver Ant. *Ostrich* 44: 170–175.

——————— 1974a. The potential bird and bat hazards to aircraft in the vicinity of the international airport at Accra, Ghana. *Ghana J. Sci.* 13: 10–19.

——————— 1974b. Radar tracks of Palaearctic waders departing from the coast of Ghana in spring. *Ibis* 116: 165–171.

——————— 1974c. Dialects and geographical variation in the song of the Splendid Sunbird *Nectarinia coccinigaster*. *Ibis* 116: 314–329.

——————— 1974d. Weather conditions in temperate latitudes and the occurrence of Alpine and Mottled Swifts at Accra. *Bull. Nig. Orn. Soc.* 10(37): 38–39.

——————— 1974e. The syllabic notation of the Red-eyed Turtle Dove *Streptopelia semitorquata* on the Accra Plains. *Bull. Nig. Orn. Soc.* 10(37): 40–43.

——————— 1974f. Tern numbers at Accra during Autumn. *Bull. Nig. Orn. Soc.* 10(38): 50.

——————— 1974g. Duetting in *Hypergerus atriceps* and its taxonomic relationship to *Eminia lepida*. *Bull. Brit. Orn. Cl.* 94: 89–96.

——————— 1975a. The dawn song of the Grey-backed Eremomela *Eremomela pusilla*. *Bull. Brit. Orn. Cl.* 95: 92–93.

Grimes, L. G. 1975b. Notes on the breeding of the Kakelaar at Legon, Ghana. *Bull. Nig. Orn. Soc.* 11: 65–67.

———— 1976. The occurrence of cooperative breeding behaviour in African Birds. *Ostrich* 47: 1–15.

———— 1977a. Bird and bat movements observed by radar near Accra, Ghana. *Nigerian Field* 42: 17–21.

———— 1977b. A radar study of tern movements along the coast of Ghana. *Ibis* 119: 28–36.

———— 1977c. Nesting of the Red-headed Quelea *Quelea erythrops* on the Accra Plains, Ghana. *Ibis* 119: 216–220.

———— 1978a. Weights of Ghanaian birds and distribution data for two species. *Bull. Nig. Orn. Soc.* 14(46): 84–85.

———— 1978b. Occurrence of the Javan Little Tern *Sterna albifrons sinensis* in West Africa. *Bull. Brit. Orn. Cl.* 98: 114.

———— 1979a. Sexual dimorphism in the Yellow-billed Shrike *Corvinella corvina* and in other African shrikes (subfamily Laniinae). *Bull. Brit. Orn. Cl.* 99: 33–36.

———— 1979b. The Yellow-billed Shrike *Corvinella corvina*; an abnormal host of the Yellow-billed Cuckoo *Cuculus gularis*. *Bull. Brit. Orn. Cl.* 99: 36–38.

———— 1980. Observations of group behaviour and breeding biology of the Yellow-billed Shrike *Corvinella corvina*. *Ibis* 122: 166–192.

Grimes, L. G. & Darko, K. 1968. Some recent breeding records of *Picarthartes gymnocephalus* in Ghana and notes on its distribution in West Africa. *Ibis* 110: 93–99.

Grimes, L. G. & Gardiner, N. 1963. Looking for *Picathartes gymnocephalus* in Ghana. *Nigerian Field* 28: 55–63.

Grimes, L. G. & Vanderstichelen, G. 1979. Initial departure directions of waders. *Bull. Nig. Orn. Soc.* 10(38): 62–63.

Hall, B. P. & Moreau, R. E. 1970. *An Atlas of Speciation in African Passerine Birds.* British Museum (Natural History).

Hall, J. B. & Jeník, J. 1968. Contribution towards the classification of savanna in Ghana. *Bull. Inst. Fond. Afr. Noire* 30 (Ser. A): 84–99.

Hall, J. B. & Swaine, M. D. 1976. Classification and ecology of closed forest in Ghana. *J. Ecol.* 64: 913–951.

————, ———— 1981. *Distribution and Ecology of Vascular Plants in a Tropical Rain Forest: forest vegetation in Ghana.* Junk: The Hague.

Hancock, N. J. (Ed.) 1968. Oxford expedition to Ghana 1968. *Bull. Oxf. Univ. Explor. Cl.* 17: 117–128.

Hare, F. K. 1982. 'Wind and Storms'. In *Encyclopaedia Britannica* 19: 862–875.

Hartert, E. 1899a. List of a collection of birds made at Gambaga, in the Gold Coast hinterland, by Captain W. Giffard. *Novit. Zool.* 6: 403–422.

———— 1899b. Three new birds collected near Gambaga, Gold Coast hinterland. *Bull. Brit. Orn. Cl.* 10: 5.

Hartlaub, G. 1848. Description de cinq nouvelles espèces d'oiseaux de l'Afrique occidentale. *Rev. Zool.* 1848: 108–110.

———— 1850. Ornithology of the coasts and islands of western Africa. *Jardine's Contribution to Ornithology in 1850*: 129–140.

———— 1853. Versuch einer synoptischen Ornithologie Westafrica's. *J. Orn.* 1: 385–400.

———— 1854. Versuch einer synoptischen Ornithologie Westafrica's. *J. Orn.* 2: 1–32, 97–128, 193–218, 289–308.

———— 1855a. Beschreibung einiger neuen, von Herrn H.S. Pel, holländischen Residenten an der Goldküste, daselbst gesammelten Vögelarten. *J. Orn.* 3: 353–360.

———— 1855b. Systematisches Verzeichniss der von Herrn H.S. Pel auf der Goldküste zwischen Cap Tres Puntas und Accrah gesammelten Vögel. *J. Orn.* 3: 360–361.

———— 1857. *System der Ornithologie West Africa's.* Bremen.

———— 1858. On new species of birds from western Africa, in the collection of the British Museum. *Proc. Zool. Soc. Lond.* 26: 291–293.

———— 1892. On a new species of flycatcher of the genus *Hyliota*. *Ibis* Ser. 6(4): 373–374.

Harvey, W. G. & Harrison, I. D. 1970. The birds of the Mole Game Reserve. *Bull. Nig. Orn. Soc.* 7(27): 43–52, 7(28): 63–75.

Hepburn, I. 1986. Operation Roseate. *Birds* 11(2): 38–41.

Hodasi, J. K. M. 1976. The helminth parasites of the helmet guinea-fowl (*Numida meleagris galeata* Pallas) in Ghana. *Bull. Anim. Hlth. Prod. Afr.* 24: 81–87.

Holman, F. C. 1947. Birds of the Gold Coast.*Ibis* 89: 623–650.

Holthuis, L. B. 1868. Biografische Notities Betreffende verzamelaars voor het Rijksmuseum van Natuurlijke Historie te Leiden. 1. Hendrik Severinus Pel (1818–1876). *Zoologische Bijdragen* No 10.

Honeywell, R. A. 1971. Some interesting observations from Ghana. *Bull. Nig. Orn. Soc.* 8(30): 30–32.

Hopkins, B. 1974. *Forest and Savanna,* 2nd edition. Heinemann.

Horwood, M. J. 1964. Notes on some West African Bee-eaters. *Bull. Nig. Orn. Soc.* 1(1): 2–5.

Isert, P. E. 1788. *Reise Nach Guinea und den Caribaischen Inseln in Columbien.* Copenhagen: J. F. Morthorst.

Jardine, W. 1852. *Contribution to Ornithology for 1851*: 141. Edinburgh.

Jeffrey, S. M. 1970. Yellow-legged Owlet from western Ghana. *Bull. Nig. Orn. Soc.* 7(28): 61–62.

Jeník, J. & Hall, J. B. 1966. The ecological effects of the harmattan wind in the Djebobo Massif (Togo Mountains, Ghana). *J. Ecol.* 54: 767–779.

Karr, J. R. 1976. Weights of African birds. *Bull. Brit. Orn. Cl.* 96: 92–96.

Keith, S., Benson, C. W. & Stuart Irwin, M. P. 1970. The genus *Sarothrura* (Aves, Rallidae). *Bull. Amer. Mus. Nat. Hist.* 143: 1–84.

Lamm, D. W. 1956. A nesting study of the Pied Crow at Accra, Ghana. *Ostrich* 29: 59–70.

————— 1959. Feeding rates for the Grey-headed Sparrow *Passer griseus* at Accra, Ghana. *Ostrich* 30: 161.

Lamm, D. W. & Horwood, M. 1958. Species recently added to the list of Ghana birds. *Ibis* 100: 175–178.

Lane, D. A. 1962. 'The forest vegetation'. Chapter 10, in *Agriculture and Land Use in Ghana* (Ed. by J. B. Wills). Oxford University Press.

Langham, N. P. E. 1971. Seasonal movements of British terns in the Atlantic Ocean. *Bird Study* 18: 155–175.

Laubmann, A. 1926. Ueber eine neue Rasse von *Alcedo (Ispidella) leucogaster. Anz. Ornith. Ges. Bay. München* 10: 89–91.

Lawson, G. W. & Jeník, J. 1967. Observation on microclimate and vegetation interrelationships on the Accra Plains (Ghana). *J. Ecol.* 55: 773–785.

Lawson, G. W., Jeník, J. & Armstrong-Mensah, K. O. 1968. A study of a vegetation catena in Guinea Savanna at Mole Game Reserve (Ghana). *J. Ecol.* 56: 505–522.

Lawson, W. J. 1984. The West African mainland forest dwelling population of *Batis*; a new species. *Bull. Brit. Orn. Cl.* 104: 144–146.

Lockwood, G., Lockwood, M. P. & Macdonald, M. A. 1980. Chapin's Spinetail Swift *Telacanthura melanopygia* in Ghana. *Bull. Brit. Orn. Cl.* 100: 162–164.

Louette, M. 1981a. A new species of Honeyguide from West Africa (Aves, Indicatoridae). *Rev. Zool. Afr.* 95: 131–135.

————— 1981b. *The Birds of Cameroun: an annotated check-list.* Brussels.

Lowe, W. P. 1937. Report on the Lowe-Waldron Expedition to the Ashanti Forest and Northern Territories of the Gold Coast. *Ibis* Ser. 14(1): 345–368, 635–662, 830–864.

Lynes, H. 1930. Review of the genus *Cisticola. Ibis* Ser. 12(6). Suppl.

————— 1932. Account of his 1930–31 tour with Mr J. Vincent across Central Africa with descriptions of new *Cisticola. Bull. Brit. Orn. Cl.* 52: 4–13.

Lynes, H. & Sclater, W. L. 1934. Lynes-Vincent tour in Central and West Africa in 1930–31. *Ibis* Ser. 13(4): 1–51.

Macdonald, J. D. 1940. Notes on African birds. *Ibis* Ser. 14(4): 340–342.

Macdonald, M. A. 1976. Field identification of theYellow-billed Egret. *Bull. Nig. Orn. Soc.* 12(42): 73–75.

————— 1977a. Notes on Ciconiiformes at Cape Coast, Ghana. *Bull. Nig. Orn. Soc.* 13(44): 139–144.

Macdonald, M. A. 1977b. Probable double-brooding by Black Kite in Ghana. *Bull. Nig. Orn. Soc.* 13(44): 147.

———— 1977c. Short-billed Dowitcher in Ghana. *Bull. Nig. Orn. Soc.* 13(44): 148.

———— 1978a. Seasonal changes in numbers of waders at Cape Coast, Ghana. *Bull. Nig. Orn. Soc.* 14(45): 28–35.

———— 1978b. Lesser Golden Plover in Ghana. *Bull. Nig. Orn. Soc.* 14(45): 47–48.

———— 1978c. Records of Palaearctic migrants in Ghana. *Bull. Nig. Orn. Soc.* 14(46): 66–70.

———— 1978d. Further evidence for migration of birds of northern Guinea savanna. *Bull. Nig. Orn. Soc.* 14(46): 80–81.

———— 1978e. The Yellow-billed Egret in West Africa. *Rev. Zool. Afr.* 92: 191–200.

———— 1978f. Additions to local avifaunas: Mole Game Reserve, Ghana. *Bull. Nig. Orn. Soc.* 14(46): 88.

———— 1979a. Evidence for migration and other movements of African birds in Ghana. *Rev. Zool. Afr.* 93: 413–424.

———— 1979b. Breeding data for birds in Ghana. *Malimbus* 1(1): 36–42.

———— 1980a. Observations on Wilson's Widowfinch and the Pintailed Whydah in southern Ghana, with notes on their hosts. *Ostrich* 51(1): 21–24.

———— 1980b. The ecology of the Fiscal Shrike in Ghana, and a comparison with studies from southern Africa. *Ostrich* 51(2): 65–74.

———— 1980c. Observations on the Dierderik Cuckoo in southern Ghana. *Ostrich* 51(2): 75–79.

———— 1980d. Breeding of the Black Kite in southern Ghana. *Ostrich* 51(2): 118–120.

———— 1980e. Further notes on uncommon forest birds in Ghana. *Bull. Brit. Orn. Cl.* 100: 170–172.

Macdonald, M. A. & Taylor, I. A. 1976. First occurrences of the Cape Wigeon *Anas capensis* in Ghana. *Bull. Nig. Orn. Soc.* 12(41): 44.

————, ———— 1977. Notes on some uncommon forest birds in Ghana. *Bull. Brit. Orn. Cl.* 97: 116–120.

Mackworth-Praed, C. W. & Grant, C. H. B. 1970–1973. *African Handbook of Birds.* Series 3: *Birds of West Central and Western Africa,* 2 vols. Longmans.

Maclean, G. L. 1976. Factors governing breeding of African birds in non-arid habitats. *Proc. 16th Int. Orn. Congr.:* 258–271.

Maze, R. L. 1971. A preliminary study of the Guinea savanna avifauna at the Mole Game Reserve in Ghana. *Ghana J. Sci.* 10(1): 38–48.

McArdle, T. D. 1958. The Bare-headed Rockfowl *Picathartes gymnocephalus. Nigerian Field* 28: 55–63.

McCrae, A. W. R. & Walsh, J. F. 1974. Association between nesting birds and polistine wasps in north Ghana. *Ibis* 116: 215–217.

Mees, G. F. 1977. The subspecies of *Chlidonias hybridus* (Pallas), their breeding distribution and migrations (Aves, Laridae, Sterninae). *Zool. Verhandelingen.* No. 157.

———— 1986. A list of birds recorded from Bangka Island, Indonesia. *Zool. Verhandelingen.* No. 232.

Meises, W. von 1961. *Pipus heteroclitus* (A. Lichtenstein), der erste Sandregenpfeifer von Ghana. *Die Vogelwarte* 21(2): 144–146.

Miles, A. C. 1955. Recollections of the Gold Coast forty years ago. *Nigerian Field* 20: 105–111.

Millet-Horsin. 1923. Contribution a l'étude de la Faune ornithologique du Bas-Togo. *Bull. Comite d'Études Hist. et Sci. de l'Afr. Occid. Fr.* (Jan–Mai 1923): 47–73.

Moorhouse, I. D. 1968. Notes on some Palaearctic migrants in Ghana. *Bull. Nig. Orn. Soc.* 5(17): 13–15.

Moreau, R. E. 1966. *The Bird Faunas of Africa and its Islands.* Academic Press.

———— 1972. *The Palaearctic-African Bird Migration Systems.* Academic Press.

Morony, J. J., Bock, W. J. & Farrand, J. 1975. *Reference List of the Birds of the World.* New York.

Morrison, C. M. 1947. Field notes on some Gold Coast birds. *Nigerian Field* 12: 59–64.

———— 1952. Field notes on Gold Coast birds. *Nigerian Field* 17: 25–37.

Owen, D. F. 1969. The migration of the Yellow Wagtail from the equator. *Ardea* 57: 77–85.

Payne, R. B. 1973. Behaviour, mimetic song and song dialects, and relationships of the parasitic indigobirds (Vidua) of Africa. *Ornith. Mono.* No 11, American Ornithologists' Union.

———— 1976. Some mimicry and species relationships among the West African pale-winged indigobirds. *Auk* 93: 25–38.

———— 1978. Microgeographic variation in songs of the Splendid Sunbird *Nectarinia coccinigaster*: population dynamics, habitats and song dialects. *Behaviour* 65: 282–308.

———— 1982. Species limits in the indigobirds (Ploceidae, *Vidua*) of West Africa: mouth mimicry, song mimicry and description of new species. *Misc. Pub. Mus. Zool. Univ. Michigan* No. 162.

———— 1985. The species of Parasitic Finches in West Africa. *Malimbus* 7(2): 103–113.

Pettet, A. 1977. Seasonal changes in nectar-feeding by birds at Zaria, Nigeria. *Ibis* 119: 291–308.

Pitman, C. R. S. & Took, J. M. E. 1973. The eggs of the African Marsh Grass-Warbler *Cisticola galactotes* (Temminck). *Arnoldia* 6(24): 1–12.

Raethel, H. S. 1965. White-breasted Guinea-fowl *Agelastes meleagrides* Bp. at West Berlin Zoo. *Int. Zoo Yearbook* 5: 165–166.

Reichenow, A. 1872. Briefliche Reiseberichte aus West Africa (1). *J. Orn.* 20: 390–392.

———— 1874. Zur Vogelfauna Westafrika's. *J. Orn.* 22: 353–388.

———— 1875. Zur Vogelfauna Westafrika's. *J. Orn.* 23: 1–50.

———— 1891. Ueber eine Vogelsammlung aus Togoland. *J. Orn.* 39: 369–394.

———— 1892. Zur Vogelfauna von Togoland. *J. Orn.* 40: 233–236.

———— 1897. Zur Vogelfauna von Togoland. *J. Orn.* 45: 1–57.

———— 1902. Die Vögel des deutschen Schutzgebietes Togo. *J. Orn.* 50: 9–43.

Reichenow, A. & Lühder, W. 1873. Briefliche Reiseberichte aus West Africa (2). *J. Orn.* 21: 209–218.

Reynolds, J. F. 1968. Notes on the birds observed in the vicinity of Tabora, Tanzania, with special reference to breeding data. *J. E. Afr. Nat. Hist. Soc. & Nat. Mus.* 27: 117–139.

Robertson, W. B. 1969. Transatlantic migration of juvenile Sooty Terns. *Nature* 223: 632–634.

Robins, C. R. 1966. Observations on the seabirds of Annobon and other parts of the Gulf of Guinea. *Stud. Trop. Oceanogr. Miami* 4: 128–133.

Robson, N. F. & Robson, J. H. 1979. Sight record of Buffbreasted Sandpiper in Southern Africa. *Ostrich* 50: 116–117.

Rose Innes, R. & Mabey, G. L. 1964. Studies on browse plants in Ghana. *The Empire Journal of Experimental Agriculture* 32: 114–124.

Roux, F. & Jarry, G. 1984. Numbers, composition and distribution of populations of Anatidae wintering in West Africa. *Wildfowl* 35: 48–60.

Russell, A. C. 1949a. Collecting for a zoo. *Nigerian Field* 14: 10–19.

———— 1949b. Birds of Cape Coast reservoir. *Nigerian Field* 14: 146–150.

Ryan, P. G. 1981. The Whiterumped Sandpiper in Southern Africa. *Ostrich* 52: 225.

Sclater, W. L. 1924. Some observations on the genus *Pedilorhynchus*. *Bull. Brit. Orn. Cl.* 45: 44–46.

Serle, W. 1956. Notes on *Anomalophrys superciliosus* (Reichenow) in West Africa with special reference to its nidification. *Bull. Brit. Orn. Cl.* 76: 101–104.

———— 1957. A contribution to the ornithology of the Eastern Region of Nigeria. *Ibis* 99: 371–418, 628–685.

Serle, W., Morel, G. J. & Hartwig, W. 1977. *Birds of West Africa*. Collins.

Seth-Smith, D. W. 1931. Notes from the Gold Coast. *Ibis* Ser. 13(1): 90.

Sharland, R. E. 1955. Birds seen at sea. *Nigerian Field* 20: 168–171.

———— 1963. Bird ringing in Nigeria and Ghana in 1962. *Nigerian Field* 28: 129–131.

———— 1964. Bird ringing in Nigeria and Ghana in 1963. *Nigerian Field* 29: 177–180.

Sharland, R. E. & Harris, B. J. 1959. Bird ringing in Nigeria and Ghana during 1958. *Nigerian Field* 24: 72–75.

————, ———— 1961. Bird ringing in Nigeria and Ghana during 1960. *Nigerian Field* 26: 65–68.

Sharpe, R. B. 1869a. On a collection of birds from the Fantee country in Western Africa. *Ibis* Ser. 2(5): 186–195.

Sharpe, R. B. 1869b. On two more collections of birds from the Fantee country. *Ibis* Ser. 2(5): 381–388.

———— 1870a. On a fourth collection of birds from the Fantee country. *Ibis* Ser. 2(6): 52–59.

———— 1870b. On additional collections of birds from the Fantee country. *Ibis* Ser. 2(6): 470–488.

———— 1871a. Description of two new species of African birds. *Ibis* Ser. 3(1): 100–102.

———— 1871b. On seven new or lately described species of African birds. *Ibis* Ser. 3(1): 414–417.

———— 1872a. On recent collections of birds from the Fantee country in western Africa. *Ibis* Ser. 3(2): 66–74.

———— 1872b. Description of some new species of birds in the National collection. *Ann. Mag. Nat. Hist.* Ser. 4(10): 450–451.

———— 1873a. On the Cuculidae of the Ethiopian Region. *Proc. Zool. Soc. Lond.* 1873: 578–624.

———— 1873b. On three new species of birds. *Proc. Zool. Soc. Lond.* 1873: 625–626.

———— 1877. On new species of warblers in the collection of the British Museum. *Proc. Zool. Soc. Lond.* 1877: 22–24.

———— 1882. On a new species of *Muscicapa* from western Africa. *Proc. Zool. Soc. Lond.* 1882: 590–591.

———— 1884. Description of a new species of *Laniarius* from Ashantee. *Proc. Zool. Soc. Lond.* 1884: 54–55.

———— 1892. Descriptions of some new species of Timeliine birds from West Africa. *Proc. Zool. Soc. Lond.* 1892: 227–228.

———— 1899. On birds collected by Colonel H. P. Northcott in the Gold Coast hinterland. *Bull. Brit. Orn. Cl.* 10: 6–7.

Sharpe, R. B. & Ussher, H. T. 1872. On three new species of birds from the Fantee country. *Ibis* Ser. 3(2): 181–183.

Shaw, P. 1984. The social behaviour of the Pin-tailed Whydah *Vidua macroura* in northern Ghana. *Ibis* 126: 463–473.

Shelley, G. E. 1873. Description of six new species of West African birds. *Ibis* Ser. 3(3): 138–143.

———— 1874a. Description of a new Timaliine bird from West Africa. *Ibis* Ser. 3(4): 89–90.

———— 1874b. Note on *Dryotriorchis*, a new genus of Harrier Eagle from West Africa. *Ibis* Ser. 3(4): 90–91.

———— 1875. A few stray notes on African birds. *Ibis* Ser. 3(5): 379–383.

———— 1879. Description of two new species of African birds. *Proc. Zool. Soc. Lond.* 1879: 679–680.

———— 1884. On two new species of birds from Africa. *Ibis* Ser. 5(2): 45–49.

Shelley, G. E. & Buckley, T. E. 1872. Two months' bird-collecting on the Gold Coat. *Ibis* Ser. 3(2): 281–293.

Sinclair, A. R. E. 1978. Factors affecting the food supply and breeding season of resident birds and movements of Palaearctic migrants in a tropical African savanna. *Ibis* 120: 480–497.

Sinclair, J. C. 1974. *Larus minutus* in Angola. *Bull. Brit. Orn. Cl.* 94: 57.

Skorupa, J. P., Kalina, J., Butynski, T. M., Tabor, G. & Kellogg, E. 1985. Notes on the breeding biology of Cassin's Hawk Eagle *Hieraaetus africanus*. *Ibis* 127: 120–122.

Snow, D. W. 1976. *Agapornis swinderniana* in Ghana. *Bull. Brit. Orn. Cl.* 96: 106.

———— (Ed.) 1978. *An Atlas of Speciation in African Non-Passerine Birds*. British Museum (Natural History).

———— 1979. Atlas of speciation in African non-passerine birds — *Addenda* and *Corrigenda*. *Bull. Brit. Orn. Cl.* 99: 66–68.

Snow, D. W. & Louette, M. 1981. Atlas of speciation in African non-passerine birds — *Addenda* and *Corrigenda* 2. *Bull. Brit. Orn. Cl.* 101: 336–339.

Sutton, R. W. W. 1965a. Notes on Ghanaian birds seen in 1964. *Ibis* 107: 251–253.

———— 1965b. Notes on birds seen in Ghana in 1964. *Bull. Nig. Orn. Soc.* 2(7/8): 55–62, 102–107.

Sutton, R. W. W. 1970. Bird records from Ghana in 1967 and 1968/1969. Parts 1 & 2. *Bull. Nig. Orn. Soc.* 7(27/28): 53–56, 76–92.

Swaine, M. D., Hall, J. B. & Lock, J. M. 1976. The forest-savanna boundary in west-central Ghana. *Ghana J. Sci.* 16(1): 35–52.

Taylor, C. J. 1960. *Synecology and Silviculture in Ghana.* Nelson.

Taylor, I. R. & Macdonald, M. A. 1978a. The status of some northern Guinea savanna birds in Mole National Park, Ghana. *Bull. Nig. Orn. Soc.* 14(45): 4–8.

——————, ——————— 1978b. The birds of the Bia National Park, Ghana. *Bull. Nig. Orn. Soc.* 14(45): 36–41.

——————, ——————— 1979a. A population of *Anthus similis* on the Togo range in eastern Ghana. *Bull. Brit. Orn. Cl.* 99: 29–30.

——————, ——————— 1979b. Migration of savanna birds revealed by local records. *Malimbus* 1: 70.

Thiollay, J.-M. 1970. Recherches écologiques dans la savane de Lamto (Côte d'Ivoire): le peuplement avien. Essai d'étude quantitative. *Terre et Vie* 24: 108–144.

——————— 1971. L'avifaune de la Région de Lamto. *Ann. Univ. Abidjan* Ser. E, Ecologie 4: 5–132.

——————— 1976. Les Rapaces d'une zone de contact savane-forêt en Côte-d'Ivoire: modalitès et succès de la reproduction. *Alauda* 44: 275–300.

——————— 1977. Distribution saisonnière des rapaces diurnes en Afrique Occidentale. *L'Oiseau et R.F.O.* 47: 253–294.

——————— 1978. Les migration de rapaces en Afrique occidentale: adaptions écologiques aux fluctuations saisonieres de production des ecosystemes. *Terre et Vie* 32: 89–133.

——————— 1985. The birds of the Ivory Coast. *Malimbus* 7: 1–59.

Thomas, G. 1978. Roseate future? *Birds* 7(2): 30–31.

Thomas, J. D. 1966. Some preliminary observations on the fauna and flora of a small man made lake in the West African savanna. *Bull. Inst. Fr. Afr. Noire* 28, Ser A, 1966: 542–562.

Thompson, H. N. 1910. *Report on Forests: Gold Coast.* HMSO London.

Trewartha, G. T. 1962. *The Earth's Problem Climates.* Methuen.

Ukoli, F. M. A. 1967. Some dilepidid and hymenolepidid cestodes from birds in Ghana. *J. W. Afr. Sci. Ass.* 12: 65–93.

——————— 1968a. Four species of the family Cyclocoelidae Kossack, 1911 (Trematoda) from birds in Ghana. *Nig. J. Sci.* 2: 73–84.

——————— 1968b. *Eurycephalus* sp. and two other echinostomes from birds in Ghana. *Ghana J. Sci.* 8: 52–62.

Urban, E. K., Fry, C. H. & Keith, S. 1986. *The Birds of Africa*, Vol. 2. Academic Press.

Ussher, H. T. 1874. Notes on the ornithology of the Gold Coast. *Ibis* Ser. 3(4): 43–75.

Walker, H. O. 1962. 'Weather and Climate'. Chapter 2, in *Agriculture and Land Use in Ghana* (Ed. J. B. Wills). Oxford University Press.

Walsh, J. F. 1977. Nesting of the Jabiru Stork *Ephippiorhynchus senegalensis* in West Africa. *Bull. Brit. Orn. Cl.* 97: 136.

——————— 1981. Rotating behaviour of the incubating Yellow-bellied Fruit Pigeon *Treron waalia. Bull. Brit. Orn. Cl.* 101: 311.

——————— 1987. Inland records of Western Reef Heron *Egretta gularis. Malimbus* 9: 58.

Walsh, J. F. & Grimes, L. G. 1981. Observations on some Palaearctic birds in Ghana. *Bull. Brit. Orn. Cl.* 101: 327–334.

Walsh, J. F. & Walsh, B. 1976. Nesting association between the Red-headed Weaver *Malimbus rubriceps* and raptorial birds. *Ibis* 118: 106–108.

White, C. M. N. 1960, 1962. *A Check-list of the Ethiopian Muscicapidae (Sylviinae).* Occ. Pap. Nat. Mus. Southern Rhodesia. 1960. 24B: 399–430; 1962, 26B: 653–694, 695–738.

——————— 1961, 1962, 1963. *A Revised Check-list of African Passerine Birds.* 1965. *A revised Check-list of African Non-Passerine Birds.* Government of Zambia: Lusaka.

Wilkinson, R. 1983. Biannual breeding and moult-breeding overlap of the Chestnut-bellied Starling *Spreo pulcher. Ibis* 125: 353–361.

Wink, M. 1976. Palaearktische Zugvogel in Ghana (Westafrika). *Bonn. Zool. Beitr.* 27: 67–86.

——————— 1979. *Hypochera lorenzi* in Ghana. *Malimbus* 1(1): 68.

Wink, M. 1981. On the diets of warblers, weavers and other Ghanaian birds. *Malimbus* 3: 114–115.

Wink, M. & Bennett, G. F. 1976. Blood parasites of some birds from Ghana. *J. Wildlife Dis.* 12: 587–590.

Winterbottom, J. M. 1933. Bird population studies: a preliminary analysis of the Gold Coast avifauna. *J. Anim. Ecol.* 2: 82–97.

Wood, G. A. R. 1975. *Cocoa,* 3rd Edition. Longmans.

Wood, N. 1977. A feeding technique of Allen's Gallinule *Porphyrio alleni. Ostrich* 48: 120–121.

Woodell, S. R. J. & Newton, L. E. 1975. A Standard-winged Nightjar breeding in the forest zone of Ghana. *Nigerian Field* 40: 169–171.

Yanney-Ewusie, J. 1968. Preliminary studies of the phenology of some woody species of Ghana. *Ghana J. Sci.* 8(3/4): 126–151.

Yates, J. M. St. J. 1937. Ringed birds recovered on the west coast. *Nigerian Field* 6: 70.

INDEX OF ENGLISH NAMES

INDEX OF GENERA